Watering

A good quality **hose** is a sound investment. The extra expense is worthwhile if the hose kinks less and lasts longer. Look for a hose that has no visible veining and features a long brass nozzle and brass screw-ends. Even if you have a sprinkler system, you'll need a garden hose for supplying water to freshly planted trees and shrubs.

A **watering wand** attaches to the end of your hose. Its long handle makes it easy to water hard-to-reach corners of beds as well as containers and hanging baskets. The wand head showers plants like raindrops instead of blasting them with a hard stream of water.

A **watering can** always comes in handy. Choose one with a large head to disperse water gently. A rounded handle makes the can easier to grip when it's full.

Timers are great for regulated watering. Use timers to turn on garden hoses, soaker hoses, or drip systems. Automatic irrigation systems with underground piping can also be controlled by specialized timers. Because watering early in the day is better than later, rely on timers to get the watering done while you're still asleep. They're also useful for keeping your landscape healthy while you're out of town.

Soaker hoses have tiny holes that allow water to seep into the soil and deliver moisture directly to roots. Snake these special hoses around the roots of plants beneath a layer of mulch.

Drip irrigation kits are another way to supplement Mother Nature. Like soaker hoses, small plastic tubing lies on top of the ground beneath a bed of mulch. Tiny emitters release water where needed.

Automatic irrigation systems, also called **underground sprinklers,** rely on a series of pipes buried in trenches to carry water throughout the landscape. Pop-up heads, like this one, or heads attached to risers spray water when turned on manually or by a timer.

Weeding

A **weed hound** helps dig out weeds from a standing position.

Use a **warren hoe** to chop out weeds by their roots. The pointed blade of the warren hoe makes it easy to cut away and remove established root systems.

Pruning

Bypass hand pruners are essential. Buy a good pair with blades you can sharpen. Bypass pruners work like scissors, with both blades moving. They make cleaner cuts than anvil pruners, which feature one fixed edge and one moving cutting blade.

Bypass loppers should find a home in your toolshed. With longer handles for leverage and bigger blades than hand pruners, loppers are necessary for cutting branches that are thicker than a pencil. Using hand pruners on a large stem can hurt both your hand and the plant. Clean cuts are essential to good plant health. Torn, jagged edges invite insects and diseases. Loppers guarantee a good cut.

A **pruning saw** is needed for removing large branches that are too big for loppers to grasp. The small, serrated blade is strong enough to cut into green wood but light enough for easy handling.

Hedge trimmers have long blades and handles. They are designed for cutting along the surfaces of shrubs to trim, maintain, and shape them.

A **pole pruner** easily removes overhead branches and fronds. Wear eye protection when you're working above your head.

Safety

Work boots are essential. You need work boots with sturdy soles to press down on shovels. The tough exteriors offer foot protection and provide ankle support.

Leather gloves are necessary for landscaping projects; cotton garden gloves won't do. Good leather gloves protect your hands against thorns, sharp branches, and tools. Look for gloves with laces that tighten at the wrist to keep out dirt. (Rubber gloves might be required for handling chemicals.)

Eye protection is a must. You need to wear safety goggles whenever debris or chemicals might become airborne, such as when you're digging, tilling, or spraying.

Face masks prevent you from breathing airborne particles into your mouth and nose. If you need eye protection, you also need a face mask. When spraying chemicals, you might need a special **respirator** that provides more protection.

A **straw hat** protects your face from the sun. Open-weave material breathes to keep you from overheating. Use a sun hat and sunscreen when you're working outdoors.

Landscaping 1-2-3. *(For Zones 7, 8, 9, and 10)*

Meredith® Book Development Team
Project Editor: John P. Holms
Art Director: John Eric Seid
Writer and Illustrator: Jo Kellum, ASLA
Contributing Writers: Elizabeth Conner, Julie Martens, Jennie McIlwain, Lisa Wolfe Williams
Photographer: Doug Hetherington
Designer: Ann DuChaine—Ann DuChaine Creative
Contributing Designer: Tim Abramowitz
Copy Chief: Catherine Hamrick
Copy and Production Editor: Terri Fredrickson
Contributing Copy Editors: Lorraine Ferrell, Sherry Rindells
Contributing Proofreaders: Janet Anderson, Maria Duryee, Dan Degen, Margaret Smith
Indexer: Donald Glassman
Managers, Book Production: Pam Kvitne, Marjorie J. Schenkelberg
Electronic Production Coordinator: Paula Forest
Editorial Assistants: Renee E. McAtee, Karen Schirm

Meredith® Books
Editor in Chief: James D. Blume
Design Director: Matt Strelecki
Managing Editor: Gregory H. Kayko
Executive Editor, Home Depot Books: Benjamin W. Allen

Director, Retail Sales and Marketing: Terry Unsworth
Director, Sales, Special Markets: Rita McMullen
Director, Sales, Premiums: Michael A. Peterson
Director, Sales, Retail: Tom Wierzbicki
Director, Book Marketing: Brad Elmitt
Director, Operations: George A. Susral
Director, Production: Douglas M. Johnston

Vice President, General Manager: Jamie L. Martin

Meredith Publishing Group
President, Publishing Group: Stephen M. Lacy
Vice President, Finance and Administration: Max Runciman

Meredith Corporation
Chairman and Chief Executive Officer: William T. Kerr

Chairman of the Executive Committee: E. T. Meredith III

The Home Depot®
Senior Vice President, Marketing and Communications: Dick Hammill
Project Director: Hugh Miskel
Marketing Manager: Nathan Ehrlich
Wisdom of the Aisles: Countless Home Depot store associates

Contact us by any of these methods:
1 Leave a voice message at (800) 678-2093
2 Write to **Meredith Books, Home Depot Books, 1716 Locust Street, Des Moines, IA 50309-3023**
3 Send e-mail to **hi123@mdp.com**. Visit The Home Depot website at **homedepot.com**

Landscaping 1-2-3

Selection & Design

Trees

Shrubs

Groundcovers & Vines

STEP-BY-STEP

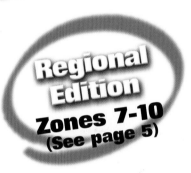

Regional Edition
Zones 7-10
(See page 5)

Meredith® BOOKS

Landscaping 1-2-3

for Zones 7, 8, 9, and 10

Chapter 1
design 10

Chapter 2
selection 20

King Sago
(Cycas revoluta)
Page 201

Chapter 3
how-to 44

Hybrid Clematis
(Clematis hybrida)
Page 180

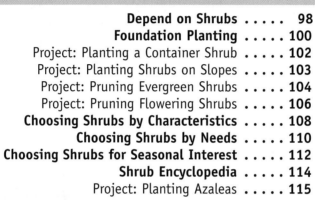

Landscaping 1-2-3®

How to Use this Book

Learn Landscaping from the Experts

L andscaping 1-2-3® from the landscaping experts at The Home Depot® is specifically tailored for Climate Zones 7, 8, 9, and 10. Inside you'll find everything you need to help you plan, design, select, install, and care for a landscape that will make your yard a showcase. First, you will become familiar with some basic landscaping terminology. Then you'll learn how to find your climate zone. Pages 6 and 7 explain how the book is arranged and lay out the steps to creating a great landscape. Pages 8 and 9 introduce you to features in this book that will make putting your plans to work quick and easy.

The Language of Landscaping

Knowing a few basic landscaping terms will help you understand what the pros are talking about when they're making a plan.

• **Evergreen** An evergreen keeps fresh-looking leaves all year, even in winter. Evergreens shed leaves and grow new ones but never lose their leaves completely.

• **Deciduous** A deciduous plant sheds its leaves and goes through a yearly period of dormancy. Deciduous plants are often noted for fall colors.

• **Perennial** Most perennials, with the exception of some evergreens, go into dormancy during the winter months and reappear in spring.

• **Tree** A tree is a woody plant that has one or more main trunks. It grows at least to the height of an adult person. Trees can be evergreen or deciduous. Some palms are listed

as trees, according to their use in the landscape.

• **Shrub** Shrubs are evergreen or deciduous. They vary in height and width but are generally lower and have a wider spread than trees. Some palms are listed as shrubs,

Trees, shrubs, groundcover, and vines as well as flowering accents are all part of this beautiful and effective backyard landscape.

according to the way they are used in the landscape.

• **Groundcover** This is not a true horticultural term. There are differing opinions on what is or is not a groundcover. Groundcovers here are evergreen or deciduous plants that spread to cover large areas of ground or to act as the low, front layer of a planting bed. Vines growing prostrate, spreading shrubs, low compact shrubs, ornamental grasses, clumping plants, flat spreading plants, or even perennials might be considered groundcovers.

• **Vine** Vines are climbers. Some have tendrils to grasp any nearby support. Others twist and twine over anything in their path. Still others attach themselves with tiny aerial rootlets to cover hard surfaces. Though some trailing plants are included as groundcovers, plants listed as vines are those used primarily to grow vertically on fences, posts, arbors, trellises, and walls.

Find Your Climate Zone

The first step to landscaping success is understanding climate zones and their effect on plant selection and care. Plants that are right for your climate zone, soil type, and watering needs will make themselves at home in your yard and are less likely to be troubled by insects and disease. *All the plant selection guides, projects, and landscaping information in this book are specific to Zones 7, 8, 9, and 10.*

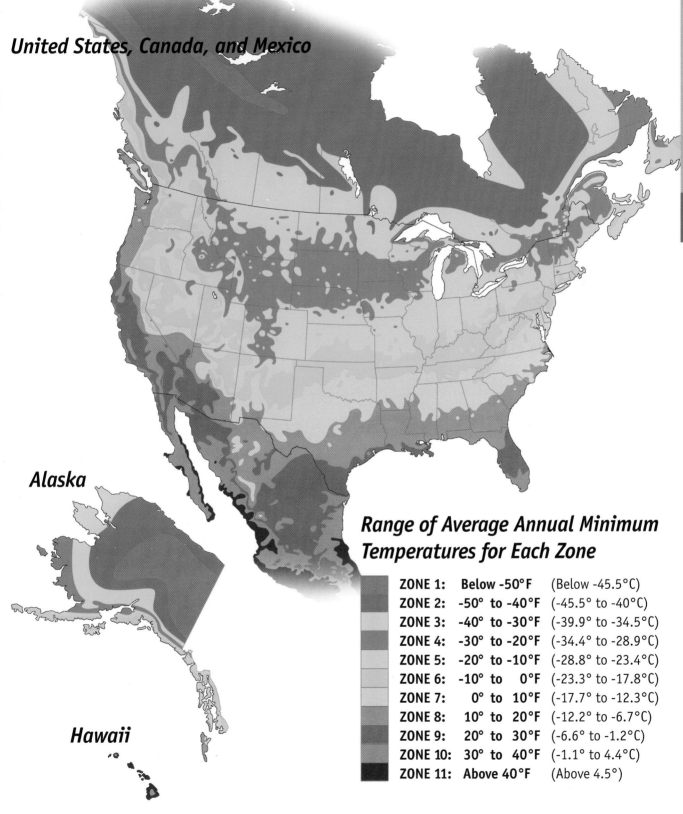

United States, Canada, and Mexico

Alaska

Hawaii

Range of Average Annual Minimum Temperatures for Each Zone

ZONE 1:	Below -50°F	(Below -45.5°C)
ZONE 2:	-50° to -40°F	(-45.5° to -40°C)
ZONE 3:	-40° to -30°F	(-39.9° to -34.5°C)
ZONE 4:	-30° to -20°F	(-34.4° to -28.9°C)
ZONE 5:	-20° to -10°F	(-28.8° to -23.4°C)
ZONE 6:	-10° to 0°F	(-23.3° to -17.8°C)
ZONE 7:	0° to 10°F	(-17.7° to -12.3°C)
ZONE 8:	10° to 20°F	(-12.2° to -6.7°C)
ZONE 9:	20° to 30°F	(-6.6° to -1.2°C)
ZONE 10:	30° to 40°F	(-1.1° to 4.4°C)
ZONE 11:	Above 40°F	(Above 4.5°)

Planning and Executing Your Landscape

This book is organized the way you should organize your landscaping plans.

Chapter One–*Design* gives you basic design concepts.

Chapter Two–*Selection* helps you choose the right plant for your yard. All the selection guides are specific to Zones 7, 8, 9, and 10.

Chapter Three–*How-To* shows you how to install and care for plants.

Chapters Four, Five, and Six–*Trees, Shrubs, Groundcovers, and Vines* guide you through the specifics of selection, care, and feeding.

Chapter Seven–*Hottest Climates* deals with landscaping in arid and humid areas of Zones 9 and 10.

The path to a great landscape is easy to take if you've done your homework and have a solid plan.

Four Steps to a Great Landscape

1) Plan Before You Plant

Make landscaping decisions in an orderly manner to create an orderly landscape. Like building a house, planning comes first, then the foundation, walls, and roof.

2) Layout Bedlines

Lay out shapes for lawn areas and planting beds first. Work around existing plants you'd like to keep within new planting beds. Fill new

beds by starting with trees. Then add shrubs. Complete the design with groundcovers and vines. The goal is an attractive, balanced composition that makes the most of outdoor areas while defining and complementing your home.

Because plants mature at different rates, be patient as your landscape takes shape. Balance rapid and slow growers in the design mix so you can have plants to enjoy as you move through the growing phases.

3) Place Trees and Shrubs

Trees and shrubs are the foundation, forming the structure of the landscape. Make decisions about these big plants first. They are also the walls of outdoor rooms, shaping the space within your yard and providing protection and privacy.

4) Add Groundcover and Vines

Groundcovers define the landscape by filling in planting beds that frame lawns. They give planting areas a lush, rich look, adding layers of greenery and flowers. Vines emphasize overhead structures, such as trellises and arbors, drawing the eye down and into the landscape.

Ideally, grass should be added when the rest of the work is done. However, you might want to incorporate some of your present lawn into a new landscape design. The key is to not let the current shape of grassy areas dictate where planting areas should go. Changing the size and shape of an old lawn can give you a refreshing new look.

Finishing Touches

Seasonal flowers are accessories, giving the finished landscape interest and accent. However, they can be in the way while you're working. Grow them in pots instead of beds while the yard is a work-in-progress. You should be focused on the basics—layout and structure—not tiptoeing around plants that have been placed out of order in the landscape.

The Bottom Line

Unless you've done your homework and your plan is well thought out, all the flowers in the world won't make your landscape a success. That's why you should go step-by-step through the entire landscaping process, starting with design in Chapter One. Before you begin, check pages 8 and 9 for special features that will help you along the way.

Placement of trees and shrubs adds privacy around a hot tub area. Seasonals add impact and color.

Wisdom of the Aisles

Call Before You Dig

Cutting through a cable or gas line is potentially dangerous and can be hazardous to your pocketbook as well. Utility and cable companies are happy to mark the locations of underground lines for you at no charge. Pick up the phone before you pick up a shovel to avoid cutting lines and cutting off your service.

If You Want to Hire a Pro

If design and planning have you stumped, consult an expert. Associates at home and garden centers often offer informal design advice as part of their service. If you want to consult a professional gardener, you have several options. **Landscape architects** are professionals licensed to prepare plans and guide planting, grading, and landscape construction. **Garden designers** might not be licensed, but they are often very qualified and can offer advice on planning and preparing your landscape. **Design/build contractors** will often provide free design services as long as they're hired to do the work as well.

Always ask for references, visit sites in progress, and see completed jobs before you negotiate a contract. Show the designer yardscapes you like. Don't be satisfied until you get what you want. Set a budget and stick to it. Never pay the entire fee up-front. Expect a licensed architect to charge a higher fee.

How to Pick the Right Plants

1) Selection Guides

Plant selection guides that range from the general to the specific make shopping decisions easier. First you'll find comprehensive lists of plants that grow within Zones 7, 8, 9, and 10. (See Chapter Two: "Selection," page 20.) Then throughout the book there are lists designed to help you narrow your choices into groups of plants that will work in your landscape and stay healthy. These lists will also spark your imagination and offer plant choices you might not otherwise have considered.

Use these dedicated selection guides to determine the right plant for the right job. Establishing privacy or blocking poor views might be a top priority. Selection guides, such as the one shown above, list plants suitable for screening and filtering. There are lists for sun or shade, for different soil conditions, and for particular site conditions (slopes, small spaces, or salt spray). You'll find selection guides that group plants by similar characteristics or solve similar landscaping problems. Each plant listed in a selection guide refers you to the page where the plant is described in detail.

2) Plant Descriptions

These entries, as shown below, tell you about outstanding features, growth rate, mature size, light requirements, and form. You'll see from the photos what each plant looks like. There's also a description of how to grow each plant and its purpose in the landscape. Each description contains both botanical and common names. The "More Choices" entry will refer you to specific selection guides for proper use of the featured plant.

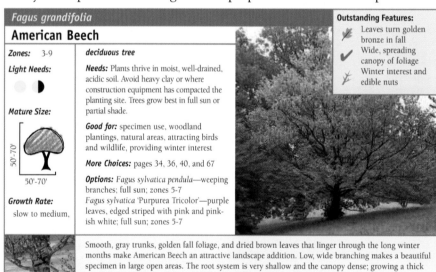

Fagus grandifolia
American Beech

Zones: 3-9

Light Needs:

Mature Size:
50'-70'
50'-70'

Growth Rate: slow to medium,

deciduous tree

Needs: Plants thrive in moist, well-drained, acidic soil. Avoid heavy clay or where construction equipment has compacted the planting site. Trees grow best in full sun or partial shade.

Good for: specimen use, woodland plantings, natural areas, attracting birds and wildlife, providing winter interest

More Choices: pages 34, 36, 40, and 67

Options: *Fagus sylvatica pendula*—weeping branches; full sun; zones 5-7
Fagus sylvatica 'Purpurea Tricolor'—purple leaves, edged striped with pink and pinkish white; full sun; zones 5-7

Outstanding Features:
- Leaves turn golden bronze in fall
- Wide, spreading canopy of foliage
- Winter interest and edible nuts

Smooth, gray trunks, golden fall foliage, and dried brown leaves that linger through the long winter months make American Beech an attractive landscape addition. Low, wide branching makes a beautiful specimen in large open areas. The root system is very shallow and the canopy dense; growing a thick stand of grass can be a challenge. Mulch instead for improved tree health and less work for you. Nuts are edible and enjoyed by several species of birds and squirrels.

Understanding Rates of Growth

How fast a plant will grow depends on site conditions, how quickly it settles into its new home, and length of the growing season. With so many variables, it isn't possible to predict the number of inches or feet you can expect a plant to grow per year, but they can be generally classified as rapid, medium, and slow growers.

The Name Game

Common vs. Botanical
Cross-Referencing by Common and Botanical Names Makes Plants Easy to Identify.

Common names for plants vary greatly from region to region. The same plant can even have several different common names. This creates the potential for confusion. Plant experts have agreed to use botanical (Latin) names to maintain consistency and make sure everyone is talking about the same thing.

Selection Guides **are alphabetized by common names.** Because most people recognize plants by their common names, the Selection Guides reflect the most common usage.

Plant Descriptions **are alphabetized by botanical names.** Latin is the language for accurate plant identification. It's a good idea to know the botanical name even if you're not sure how to say it. Don't worry about how the words are pronounced. Knowing a little Latin will help you get the right plant.

Multiple Indexes Selection Guides and *Plant Descriptions* are cross-referenced throughout the book. Beginning on page 214 you'll find a general index for easy access to projects and landscaping information. There's also an index of botanical and common names to make plants easy to find no matter what they're called.

Note: Availability of specific plants varies by area and local conditions (see page 21). Check with your garden center for plants that will thrive in your particular area.

Special Features for Quick Reference

✔ *Information about hardiness and climate will help you eliminate plants that won't live where you do and help you pick the right ones for your planting zone.*

In the Zone

New plants may need daily watering for the first few weeks, especially during hot weather. In cooler seasons, you can water every other day for the first week. After that, cut back to once a week for 2 to 3 months, then reduce to once a month, until shrubs have weathered a full growing season. Water faithfully unless Nature supplies at least ½ inch of water during the week. Once established, properly sited plants will need supplemental water only during hot, dry spells.

✔ *Every project includes a list of tools and materials you'll need to get the job done right.*

Step-by-Step Projects

(Planting Bare-Root Roses step-by-step project page, shown as example)

TOOL TIP

Round-point shovels are great for digging holes and scooping out soil. Shovels with fiberglass handles usually last longer than wooden-handled shovels.

✔ *Having the right tool and knowing how to use it can make a world of difference.*

Design Tip

The front yard is more heavily influenced by architecture than the backyard. Your house and front yard landscape are seen together from the street. On the other hand, the backyard is usually seen when looking from the house, not at it. If the architecture makes a formal style appropriate, use a traditional approach to design in front. If you also like informally styled outdoor spaces, grow a more free-form landscape in the back.

✔ *Hints from a landscape architect will make your yard look its best.*

Homer's Hindsight

When I landscaped our first home, I picked out plants by purchasing whatever caught my eye at the garden center. The yard looked all right at first. After a while, it was a mess! And it was a lot of work trying to keep that many different kinds of plants healthy and neat. Landscaping is easier with a strategy.

✔ *Homer helps you avoid mistakes before you make them.*

✔ *Solid shopping tips from the pros.*

BUYER'S GUIDE

If you want a larger tree than those in stock, ask a garden associate about ordering a B&B tree for you. Some stores stock balled-and-burlapped trees only upon request. Inquire about the approximate measurements of the rootball and dig the proper-sized hole before the tree arrives. Ask if delivery is available for a fee when you order your tree. If so, find out where the tree will be left. Don't be surprised if the delivery driver takes it no farther than the curb. You'll need a sturdy wheelbarrow waiting to get the tree to the hole. You may want to hire a professional or get a friend to help with a big tree; B&B trees are heavy.

Wisdom of the Aisles

Most trees and shrubs require no fertilizer at all during their first year in your landscape. That's because they've been heavily fertilized during nursery production to make them look their best on the shelves. If you add fertilizer at planting and then apply more fertilizer later in the growing season, you've probably given your new plants a double-dose of chemicals they don't need. Wait until the second year of growth.

✔ *Great advice you can't get anywhere else— tried-and-true wisdom of the aisles from the experts at Home Depot.*

✔ *Good ideas go along with step-by-step instructions to make projects even easier.*

Good idea! **Putting the Best Face on Things.** Before backfilling, turn your shrub so that its best side is facing the direction from which it will be viewed. Once the dirt's in the hole, it's harder to adjust the shrub's direction.

Chapter 1
design

A successful landscape design defines the function of outdoor spaces. Lush foliage around the pond on the left creates a sense of privacy and tranquillity for this backyard getaway, while dramatic use of color and form define the public spaces above and below.

Four Elements of Design

T **his is where you unlock the secrets of landscape design.** Start with the four building blocks that form the basis of outdoor composition.

1) Color is the first element—easy to identify, but challenging to use correctly. So many colors are appealing that it can be hard to limit your choices.

Flower beds are obvious sources of color. Trees, shrubs, groundcovers, and vines are bloomers as well. Leaf color, seasonal variations, and the hues of bark and branches also have impact. Both flowers and foliage need to work with other features— paving, outdoor furniture and fabrics, and the colors of your home.

Color evokes an emotional response. Bright colors give a garden a cheerful, pleasing look. Just one

noticeable color contrasting with green leaves gives a landscape a sophisticated appearance. Too many colors in too many places compete for attention and overwhelm the design. Carefully placed color directs your guests right to your front door.

2) Texture is a subtle but important element of good design. The more you know about texture and how it works, the more professional your landscape will be.

You might think of texture as something you touch—the roughness of sandpaper or the smoothness of silk—but it's also

something you see. Coarsely textured plants have big leaves, large flowers, or rough, peeling bark. They are characterized as bold or architectural. Finely textured plants have tiny leaves and twigs, or flowers with many small petals. Many species of plants fall somewhere in between. Leaf texture matters in landscape design because flowering time is usually brief.

Textures blend or contrast. If you're using a lot of different colors in your landscape, minimize the difference in textures. Conversely, if you have a shady yard with few hues, a variety of textures adds interest. Place a large-leaf, coarsely textured plant, such as fatsia, behind a tiny-leaf, finely textured plant, such as a fern. The contrast in textures will be eye-catching.

3) *Line* impacts landscape design.

The horizontal outlines of walkways, patios, driveways, and bedlines carve fluid shapes and create spaces. They separate planting areas from the lawn, creating areas for trees, shrubs, groundcovers, and vines. Bedlines should complement existing landscaping—the shape of your house on the land, paved areas, trees, and fences.

Vertical lines are also important. If everything is the same height, your landscape will appear flat and dull. Trees are the most obvious example. Upright, spiky foliage, such as iris leaves, also adds a vertical accent to the landscape. Fencing and posts will contribute vertical lines to your yard. Too many vertical lines, however, will make a yard small and crowded. The goal is to frame and balance open spaces with vertical lines.

4) *Form* defines the physical presence

of a plant and the space it takes up in your yard. Knowing the mature shape of a plant is critical when plant shopping. If you want a plant that will stay low and neat, don't buy one that is naturally large and arching. You won't be able to prune it into a compact shape, and the plant won't be attractive when confined to an unnatural form.

The shape of a young plant is not necessarily the same as it will be when it matures. Study the form symbols with the plant descriptions in this book or on plant tags. Ask before you buy. You may hear the terms regular or irregular. Regular forms are symmetrical—neatly rounded, compact, pyramidal, or oval. Irregular forms are uneven, resist pruning and are described as airy, natural, loose, arching, spreading, or sculptural. What you buy depends on your design. Choose regular shrubs for a neatly clipped hedge or formal garden. If you're seeking an airy backdrop for a cottage garden or a woodland scene, irregular forms are best. A single plant with uneven form can serve as living sculpture.

Vertical lines create drama in a landscape design. The height of the palm draws attention to the corner of this garden and helps define the landscape's boundaries.

Choosing Colors That Work with Your Home

If your home is a neutral color, such as tan, buff, gray, beige, brown, or white, just about any flower or foliage color will look good beside it. Houses featuring unusual colors, such as lavender-painted siding or pink-tinted stucco, should depend heavily on dark greens and whites. But keep things fun by repeating the house color in nearby plants. Matching the color or using flower hues a little darker will emphasize the scheme.

Bold color schemes present other challenges. Hot pink flowers and yellow, golden, or bluish foliage won't work well with a red brick house. Plant lots of dark green instead, and stick to white, dark purple, or pale pink flowers. Yellow can work if separated from the brick by a layer of dark green leaves. Oranges and reds will clash; use them elsewhere in your yard, away from the house.

design 1

Professional Principles of Design

Now that you've gone through the elements of design, the next step is learning how to apply them in your landscape. The methods professionals use to manage design elements are known as the principles of design. Here's what they are and how they can help you create a beautiful and functional landscape. If you need help planning your landscape, work with a professional designer to give your yard style.

A walkway leading to the front door winds through a landscape unified by color. Roses repeat the pink blossoms of Anthony Waterer Spirea, (Spiraea bumalda 'Anthony Waterer').

1) Unity is the glue that holds a landscape together, and repetition is the means to achieve it. Without unity, a yard is a hodgepodge of plants. Trees, shrubs, groundcovers, and vines are lovely individually, but they must work together to make your design cohesive.

At first, examples of unity can be hard to spot. But if you look closely at yards you admire in your neighborhood or study attractive landscapes in books and magazines, you will notice that no matter how much styles vary, well-executed landscapes all share a certain elusive quality: the plants in well-designed landscapes seem to belong where they are placed. The secret is unity, and here's how to get it.

Repetition gives your landscape a unified look. Even cottage gardens, which contain a multitude of flowers, are held together by repetition of one or more elements: color, texture, line, or form. For example, in a cottage garden, the flowers might be united by a color theme of mostly pinks or shades of

yellow. Or perhaps there are many bright colors tied together with generous helpings of white. Landscapes that feature multitudes of flowers need a good solid background for structure. Evergreen trees and shrubs, walls, or picket fences are common choices of unifying materials.

You don't have to have a cottage garden to need unity in your landscape. Start by selecting the trees and shrubs that form the

Design Tip

Planting the same kind of plant in more than one place is a surefire way to add unity to your landscape through repetition. But you can also repeat a characteristic common to different kinds of plants. For example, wispy ornamental grasses have fine texture. So do delicate ferns, some grass-like clumping groundcovers, and shrubs with tiny leaves. Plant them together to create a mass of fine texture, which makes an excellent background for showing off a coarse-textured, large-leaved plant as an accent. Or, set plants with similar textures in different places throughout your yard. This makes it easier to deal with different conditions. In the example above, you can plant ferns in the shade and ornamental grasses in the sun, repeating the fine textures of both plants and unifying your landscape. Texture isn't the only element you can repeat. Using similar colors, lines, or forms will also add unity.

backbone of your composition. Limit yourself to a core group of plants that grow well in your area. Using 8-2-2 (8 kinds of shrubs, 2 kinds of trees, and 2 kinds of groundcovers) is a proven combination. You can vary this, but

The repetition of form provides unity in this landscape. Plants with mounded forms shape the scene.

don't be tempted to introduce too many different plants at this early stage. Think of these core plants as wardrobe basics; you can mix and match them for different looks. Using the same kind of plant in more than one place in your yard is an example of repetition and a good way to achieve unity.

When you're ready to add more plants to your basic landscape, keep the value of repetition in mind. Set showier plants together in groups, known as masses, so they'll have an attractive impact on the composition. (Scattering plants tends to dilute their effect.) Adding masses of the same species of plant in more than one place will create a cohesive and unified look.

2) Accent is the second principle of landscape design. This is the fun stuff: eye-catching plants with brightly colored flowers, unusual forms, or noticeable leaves. A showy plant isn't necessarily an accent. Like real estate, it's all about location, location, location.

A plant must stand out from its

surroundings to serve as an accent. Too many varieties of showy plants too close together will compete for attention. Contrast is the key. A plant becomes distinctive when its color, texture, line, or form contrasts with its setting.

Create contrast by placing an eye-catching plant in a mass of similar plants. Your accent plant will be showcased, making its special qualities noticeable. You can choose a single accent plant, known as a specimen, to stand alone, or set a few of the same kind of accent plants together for a bigger impact. Groups of three work well in many settings.

Lacy burgundy foliage of a Japanese Maple contrasts with the bright green coarse-textured leaves of hostas to create an accent.

Homer's Hindsight

When I landscaped our first home, I picked out plants by purchasing whatever caught my eye at the garden center. The yard looked all right at first, but after a while, it was a mess! And it was a lot of work trying to keep that many different kinds of plants healthy and neat. I'm doing things differently at our second house. I have a pretty good idea of what characteristics a plant should have and where it will go in my yard before I buy it. I still purchase some plants from time to time just because they're pretty, but it's a lot easier to work them into the landscape now that I have a strategy.

Creating Focal Points

Position colorful plants where they'll draw attention to what you want your visitors to see. Your landscape should focus first on the house and then on your front door. If it's hard to tell which house is yours, add an address plate near a bright, eye-catching planting so the mailbox isn't the only indication of your house number. This way, you'll focus attention on your home, not your mailbox. Use attractive plantings at property entrances and in parking areas. This makes guests feel welcome. Lead them to the door with landscaping—putting the brightest colors there denotes a destination.

Growing in Style

The exterior of your home should fit your personal style, just as the interior does. The appearance of your home—its architectural style—has a big role in setting the scene. Bungalows, colonial mansions, rustic log homes, and adobe houses all have their own distinctive look. Though you could choose the same plants for any of these houses, the way you arrange the plants to create a setting is the essence of style. Setting a style for your landscape is the result of a combination of influences. Understanding them will make it easier for you to create a landscape in the style that's right for you.

1) Formal style will

complement many traditional types of architecture, with such features as an even number of windows symmetrically placed, balanced wings, or formal columns. This style also works well in small city gardens. Formality is achieved by arranging plants, walkways, benches, and other outdoor features along an invisible line, known as an axis. Plants on one side of the axis match, or mirror, those on the opposite, creating symmetry. Arrange plants in groups that are evenly divisible by two. Pairs of plants establish instant symmetry as do two matching shrubs on each side of a walkway. Plants set in rows, or in recognizable geometric patterns, such as squares, diamonds, rectangles, and circles, also lend a formal style to a landscape. (Repeat shapes found on your house, such as windows or trim.) The more symmetry, the more formal your design. Formal landscaping shows the designer's hand in nature. Your choice of plant material also affects formality. Plants that can be clipped into smooth hedges, round balls, or neat cones add a formal touch.

Regional Styles

Let where you live influence the style of your landscape. Including native plants will make your landscape look appropriate for its location, and the plants will be more likely to survive. Using other indigenous materials will also give your landscape a local flavor. Local plants and materials look best when paired with architectural styles that are typical of the region. Paving materials, such as brick, stone, tile, or pebbles, may be produced in your region, as well as the kind of wood and finish you choose for fences, gates, benches, rails, and arbors. A Cape Cod will look wonderful with a weathered picket fence covered with climbing roses framing the entry. Such a design reflects the English heritage of the Northeast.

  If your house features a look borrowed from elsewhere, such as a Charleston-style townhouse in San Antonio, design the landscape to match the architecture first and the region second. In this example, a formal city garden with neat, crisscrossing paths, a free-standing fountain, and low beds edged with neat rows of plants would make an appropriate landscape. The owner should include native plants whenever their natural forms are appropriate to the landscape style. Use Texas mountain laurels instead of large azaleas that will struggle in San Antonio's alkaline soils.

From the mirror-image layout of planting beds and graveled pathways to a pair of pineapple finials, the concept of symmetry is present everywhere in this formal landscape design.

2) *Informal style* is the natural arrangement of elements. It complements a wide range of architectural styles. Informal landscapes are asymmetrical—their components don't match up like a mirror. Instead of dividing the landscape with an axis, arrange planting beds in broad, sweeping curves. This will soften the hard lines of any house and make it seem nestled into the landscape.

Though they don't feature mirror images, asymmetrical landscapes must be balanced. If you have a large shade tree at one end of a planting bed, balance it with three large shrubs at the far end. This approach sets a scene that looks balanced instead of lopsided.

Plants with natural and irregular forms are informal. Those that arch, spread, twist, or seem fluffy or airy give landscapes a casual style.

3) *Combining styles*

should be done carefully. As long as you don't have formal features competing with informal ones, you can combine styles successfully. Use one style to set the dominant tone of your landscape, then create little accent areas of the opposite style. A landscape full of curving bedlines without a central axis is informal, but you can add a few formal touches. For example, a pair of ornamental trees framing a view adds a formal tone, but won't be out of place in an informal setting.

Asymmetrical composition gives this landscape an informal air. Plants were chosen to please the eye with no thought of creating matching patterns.

Combining styles can also add contrast. A formally clipped hedge surrounding a bed of plants with delicate flowers and foliage on lanky stems will create an appealing scene showing off both kinds of plants to their best advantage.

How much work do you want to do? Maintenance
considerations affect choice of style. If you enjoy pruning, try a formal landscape with lots of plants clipped into neat shapes. If you want to spend more time admiring your

landscape than working in it, an informal style might suit your needs. To reduce maintenance chores, avoid mixing many different kinds of plants closely together. You'll find it difficult to meet their individual needs unless you enjoy puttering with plants. Consider growing conditions when choosing plants. The right plant in the right place is still the first rule of landscaping.

The front yard is more heavily influenced by architecture than the backyard. Your house and front yard landscape are seen together from the street. On the other hand, the backyard is usually seen when looking from the house, not at it. If the architecture makes a formal style appropriate, use a traditional approach to design in front; if you also like informally styled outdoor spaces, grow a more free-form landscape in the back.

A pair of pots adds a formal touch to an informally designed landscape, drawing attention to the bench. A pair of matching shrubs or small trees could do the same.

Assessing Your Yard

G **reat landscapes start at home, not at the store.** The first things you need to decide are what you have that's worth keeping, what you need to get rid of, and what problems need to be solved before you can start making improvements.

1) Create a Base and Site Map

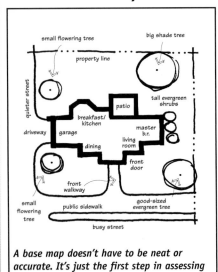

A base map doesn't have to be neat or accurate. It's just the first step in assessing your property.

To assess your yard, you'll need to take an objective look at your property. It helps to have a sketch on which you can take notes. Make a photocopy of your original survey if you have one. If you can't find your survey, make a rough sketch showing the shape of your lot with the house and any paving on it. Don't worry about making the drawing neat and pretty or getting accurate dimensions. The purpose of this sketch is to make it easier to take notes about different areas. Mark approximate locations of trees, water features, and existing bedlines to indicate the locations and shapes of planting beds and lawn areas. The result is a rough base map.

With your base map in hand, walk your property and look at the exterior spaces from different angles, including from across the street. Note the parking areas and walkways. Go inside the house and look out windows; views from the inside are part of landscaping, too.

You're looking for assets and liabilities. Assets are things that you want to keep. Attractive planting areas, healthy shrubs, big shade trees, small accent trees, good stands of lawn, and pretty vines are assets. Mark good views looking into your property and looking outward. Nicely paved areas, welcoming walkways, and interesting architectural features on your home are also worth noting. Anything you like is an asset.

Now it's time to be blunt. List all the liabilities you see. Scribble notes and arrows all over your sketch. Use a different color ink to contrast with the notes you made about assets.

Liabilities include unattractive or unhealthy plants, trees or shrubs that block good views or make interior rooms dark and gloomy, plants that are messy or require constant maintenance, scraggly lawn areas, or deteriorating paving, walls, or fences. Include poor views seen

while looking at your home, out the windows, or from within your yard looking out toward adjacent properties. Note areas that don't have enough privacy, shade, or seating to be comfortable.

Other common liabilities include traffic noises, glare, inadequate parking, and noticeable utility areas. Look for unattractive aspects of your

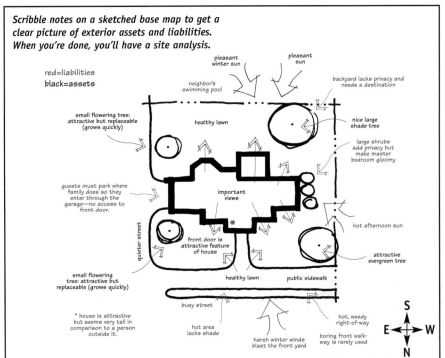

Scribble notes on a sketched base map to get a clear picture of exterior assets and liabilities. When you're done, you'll have a site analysis.

house. Blank, windowless walls, old closed-in garages with driveways leading nowhere, and tall foundations will make your list. Drainage problems should be noted, too: Spots that stay wet or are difficult to keep moist are important factors in plant selection.

Good landscaping overcomes liabilities and makes the most of the assets of your home. It could be painful to be objective now, but it's easier to fix problems if you know what they are.

2) *Inventory Your Needs*

Landscape architects and garden designers visit with their clients before beginning work. They learn about a family's likes and dislikes, their budget, and their priorities before they begin. You'll need to do the same thing. Though it seems as though all the answers would be obvious (after all, you're your own client), a little research goes a long way toward setting obtainable landscaping goals.

List your needs and your goals. Some things might be obvious, such as providing additional parking or adding more shade. Others will take more thought—making your walkway more inviting or adding privacy to make your patio more usable or more intimate.

Follow these observations with notations about the cause of the current condition. For example, if your walkway is uncomfortable, it may be too narrow. Adding borders of bricks, pavers, or stones can widen the paving to make it more inviting. Or, crumbling, uneven paving might need replacing.

3) *Set a Budget* Decide how

much you'd like to spend and then research the costs of plants, materials, delivery, and labor if you're hiring help. Most people find that landscaping costs more than they think, so budgets have to be flexible. Compared with the cost of your house, landscaping is a reasonable investment. If you're building a new home, set aside 10 percent of the cost for landscaping. If that's impossible, find a percentage you can live with and stick to it. You'll be glad you didn't spend all your money on the interior when it comes time to dress up the exterior—after all, that's the area most people will see.

Smart Design—Inside and Out

You're missing a design bet if you don't plan your landscape to work from both the inside and outside of your home. Windows are picture frames that invite you into a living world. Creating great views from favorite interior spaces such as bedrooms, family rooms, kitchens, and living rooms will give you hours of enjoyment when you can't be outside.

Landscape Assessment Quiz

How well do you know your property?

Answer these questions before you head for the garden center. Prepare a packet with all the notes you've gathered, including the snapshots of your home and yard, and bring it along. Accurate information will help you get you what you want.

1) What's your exposure?

Knowing the direction your house faces (the exposure) will help you design your landscape and select the right plant. Some plants will thrive on southern exposure but freeze on the northern side of your house. Others grow in eastern sun but wilt in hot, western sun. Use a compass to find north or track where the sun rises (east) and sets (west). If you're facing west, north is to your right.

2) How's your sun and shade?

Knowing how the amount of sun or shade affects plants is essential to their survival. (See pages 30-31.) Observe at various times of the day (10 a.m., noon, 3 p.m., and 5 p.m.) to see how the sun affects your property. Buildings, walls, evergreen trees, and shrubs also might provide shade most of the year. Trees, shrubs, and vines will allow winter sunlight to filter through during dormancy but will cast shade during the summer. Does the project area receive morning sun or afternoon sun? Refer to your notes and combine that with information about exposure: East-facing areas receive morning light unless shaded, and west-facing spots generally receive afternoon sun.

3) What's your soil like? Dig a few

sample holes in your project area and examine the soil. (See pages 36 and 38 for information on soil and percolation tests.) Some basic questions are: What color is the soil a few inches beneath the surface? Is the soil moist or dry? The ideal soil will roll into a ball yet crumble easily, will be dark in color and will hold water and nutrients. For a detailed analysis, visit your county extension service and arrange for a soil test.

Paying attention to the public spaces of your yard will make your home welcoming and attractive. Though the entire front yard is important, landscaping around the front door is critical.

Prioritizing Your Plans

Plan your design and then break it down into manageable projects. Completing work on specific areas is more satisfying than scattering your efforts. Improving your landscape in phases stretches your budget, too. Before you choose which project area to work on first, prioritize your needs. First, look at your public and private spaces.

1) **Public Spaces** The

exterior area around your house can be broadly classified in two categories—public and private. Public spaces are the parts of your yard that you present to guests and the public, including passersby and workers who access your property. For many people, these public areas are a top priority. Completing this portion of a landscape makes a home look its best from the street and beautifies the neighborhood. Making public areas the first priority is a practical decision, too. A well-designed landscape welcomes people, gives them a place to park, and provides clear access to the house. Good landscaping adds value

to your home by enhancing curb appeal. If you're making improvements in the landscaping to enhance sales value, public spaces will be your priority.

On most lots, the front yard is the public space, and many people begin their landscape efforts there. That's fine if public space is your top priority. In fact, most builders will spend the entire landscape allowance on the front yard because that's what helps sell the house. But don't automatically concentrate on the front yard if you'd really rather begin by working on more private family areas. Prioritize your efforts to meet your family's needs, or you might never get around to sprucing up the area you'd use the most.

Vine-covered trellises are a good way to filter outside views and create private spaces while maintaining an open and airy feeling.

2) **Private Spaces** Family

entries, entertainment areas, and spots to sit, read, talk, or snooze in the fresh air are quiet private spaces. Active private areas include children's play areas and places for growing vegetables or favorite flowers. Utility areas are also

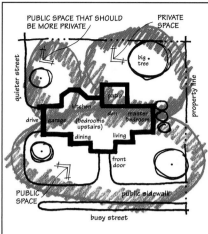

Before beginning work, you'll want to sketch the public and private areas of your landscape to help set priorities.

Brick steps, pots of flowers, and a pretty garden gate mark the entry to somewhere special. Lush plantings and walls make this backyard patio private and comfortable.

private—there's no need for neighbors to share a view of garbage cans, dog runs, and storage spots.

Most backyards and some side yards are private spaces. If you don't enjoy being in your backyard, or feel you're on display when you sit there, make some changes. A lack of destination, poor views, no privacy, drainage problems, too little or too much shade, and unattractive plants are common backyard problems. If some of these descriptions sound like your backyard, working on it may be more important than on the public spaces. Let family members

have a say. The landscape is part of your home and should meet everyone's needs —including pets.

Focus Your Work

Dividing your landscaping goals into phases makes achieving them more likely. It's much more satisfying to complete a project area within your yard than it is to get bogged down trying to do all the work at once. Doing the job in phases is also a good way to stretch a budget. Set priorities to concentrate your efforts.

Design Tip

Multiple Priorities Planning phases for landscaping public and private spaces isn't an either/or proposition. You can devise a plan that includes major work on a private space, such as the backyard, as well as minor improvements for the front. Those changes can make it immediately more presentable and create the groundwork for a bigger overhaul later on.

Combined Spaces

Lots don't always divide neatly in half, with the front as public space and the back as private space. You can also carve out private spaces within the front yard, increasing the area's usefulness. Low hedges, walls, or fences distinguish a private space from a public one. Barriers about waist-high seem friendly and unchallenging, giving you the best of both worlds—you can have a public conversation and still offer privacy with outdoor seating behind the hedge.

You might need to separate a private area to make the public space more appealing. If everyone is entering your house through a messy garage strewn with toys and tools, rethink your landscape. Block views of doors that you don't want people to use. A vine-covered trellis or artfully arranged trees and shrubs keep family entries from becoming visible targets for guests. Make the public area welcoming by including a wide, inviting, well-lit walkway close to where people get out of their cars or approach from public sidewalks. (You might create separate guest parking.) Keep the landscape fresh and tidy around the door you'd like guests to use. If it looks like no one ever goes there, no one ever will.

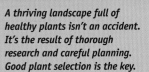

A thriving landscape full of healthy plants isn't an accident. It's the result of thorough research and careful planning. Good plant selection is the key.

The Right Plant in the Right Place

If there's a common equation for good results in the landscaping trade it would be something like this: right + right + right = success. But, you don't need chalk and a blackboard to figure out that the *right* plant in the *right* place with the *right* care will guarantee landscaping success.

Hen and chicks (Sempervivum tectorum), a tough groundcover, grows in full sun in hot climates, but prefers some shade in desert areas.

Proper plant selection is critical. A lovely plant in the wrong place won't thrive or serve its intended purpose, and will require constant attention. A poorly chosen plant might grow too large for the space and require excessive pruning. Choosing the wrong location for a plant means that conditions are unfavorable for growth, resulting in more work on your part. Finally, there's an artistic issue. The wrong plant in the wrong place just won't work well within your landscape design.

Follow these steps to choose the right plant for the right place:

1) Determine Your Needs Chapter One is a road map for figuring out what you want; if you skipped it, go back and work through the exercises so you'll understand the roles each plant plays within your landscape design. You may need some plants to supply privacy, others to dress up the front of your house, and still others to add interest to a backyard patio. Before plant shopping, pick a specific project area within your yard and list the purposes new plants should serve to make that area work.

Make existing elements on your site work for you. Selecting plants that thrive in rocky soil and full sun turns this barren stone outcropping into a garden.

selection 2

Reduce yard work. Proper plant selection in the beginning will help keep maintenance requirements at a manageable level later on. That's because plants that thrive in their setting are less susceptible to insects and disease problems than those that struggle to survive. Plants that are right for their location require less coaxing to grow. Plants that are correctly sited have room to mature. Their natural forms fit their chosen sites and don't need a lot of pruning.

2) Define Existing Conditions

You need to know what conditions exist within your project area and which plants will thrive there. Refer to notes you made during your site analysis (see page 16), but repeat the exercise focusing on your project area. Note whether the area is hilly or flat; wet, moist, or dry; and sunny or shady in mornings and afternoons. Learn which direction your area faces and whether it's protected from harsh winds or exposed to them. Check to see whether the soil is hard and compacted or rich and soft. Look for any special conditions, such as salt spray from ocean breezes, confined root space, or city conditions such as car exhaust.

BUYER'S GUIDE

Don't overlook a good plant just because it isn't in full bloom at the store. You're better off buying a vigorous plant that's shaped properly according to its species than you would be if you made flowers the top shopping criteria. Your purchases are for the long run.

3) Study Your Options

Use the selection guides that follow to help you get started in the decisionmaking process. These lists of plants are a good first step toward choosing the right plants for the right places in your yard. They'll help you match your needs, your desires, and the conditions of your yard with a variety of suitable plants. To get a complete picture of your options, you'll need to look up descriptions of plants on the pages listed. It's also important to supplement your research with observations about what grows in your area. Seek the advice of local experts, too. Talented gardeners and associates at garden centers are valuable sources of information when it comes to choosing plants for your region.

Examine the selection guides and eliminate any plant that doesn't include your climate zone within its growing range (see page 5 to determine your climate zone). But keep in mind that not every plant with a zone number that matches yours will grow where you live. That's because climate zones are based on the minimal temperatures at which plants will thrive. This

Japanese painted fern (Athyrium nipponicum 'Pictum') is an attractive groundcover that thrives in moist, shady spots.

information is valuable, but it's not the final word in plant selection. Other climate factors such as annual rainfall and humidity also play a role in choosing plants. Local soil conditions and soil pH affect which plants you'll find for sale in your area, too. Availability is also dependent in part upon local growers who supply plants to stores.

Plants for Zone 7

Locate where you live on the map found on page 5 to determine your climate zone. The plants in the following lists will thrive in **Zone 7.** These lists categorize plants by height. Follow the page numbers listed to the encyclopedia entries. These will give you complete information on the plants you're considering. Availability varies by area and conditions (see page 21). Check with your garden center.

Trees for Zone 7

◆ Small Trees (30 feet or under)

Common Name	Zones	Page
Crepe Myrtle	7-9	82
Lagerstroemia indica		
Flowering Dogwood	5-9	76
Cornus florida		
Hollywood Juniper	4-9	195
Juniperus chinensis 'Torulosa'		
Japanese Flowering Crabapple	4-8	85
Malus floribunda		
Japanese Maple	5-8	71
Acer palmatum		
Kousa Dogwood	5-8	76
Cornus kousa		
Lilac Chaste Tree	6-10	199
Vitex agnus-castus		
Lusterleaf Holly	7-9	80
Ilex latifolia		
Possum Haw	3-9	79
Ilex decidua		
Purple-Leaf Plum	4-8	88
Prunus cerasifera 'Atropurpurea'		
Redbud	3-9	75
Cercis canadensis		
Saucer Magnolia	5-9	84
Magnolia x soulangiana		
Savannah Holly	5-9	80
Ilex opaca 'Savannah'		
Star Magnolia	4-9	84
Magnolia stellata		
Sweet Bay Magnolia	5-9	85
Magnolia virginiana		
Washington Hawthorn	3-9	77
Crataegus phaenopyrum		
Wax Myrtle	7-9	86
Myrica cerifera		
Yaupon Holly	7-10	81
Ilex vomitoria		
Yoshino Cherry	5-8	88
Prunus x yedoensis		

◆ Medium Trees (30 to 60 feet)

Common Name	Zones	Page
American Arborvitae	3-9	95
Thuja occidentalis		
Arizona Cypress	7-9	194
Cupressus arizonica		
Bradford Pear	4-8	89
Pyrus calleryana 'Bradford'		
Chinese Elm	5-9	97
Ulmus parvifolia		
Chinese Pistache	6-9	87
Pistacia chinensis		
Eastern Red Cedar	3-9	81
Juniperus virginiana		
Green Ash	3-9	78
Fraxinus pennsylvanica		
Japanese Pagoda Tree	6-8	94
Sophora japonica		
Japanese Zelkova	5-9	97
Zelkova serrata		
Laurel Oak	7-10	197
Quercus laurifolia		
Leyland Cypress	6-9	77
X Cupressocyparis leylandii		
Red Maple	3-9	70
Acer rubrum		
Weeping Willow	4-9	94
Salix babylonica		
Yellowwood	6-8	75
Cladrastis lutea		

◆ Large Trees (60 feet or more)

Common Name	Zones	Page
American Beech	3-9	78
Fagus grandifolia		
Bald Cypress	4-10	95
Taxodium distichum		
Bristlecone Fir	7-8	70
Abies bracteata		
Bur Oak	2-8	91
Quercus macrocarpa		
California Incense Cedar	5-8	73
Calocedrus decurrens		
Canadian Hemlock	3-7	96
Tsuga canadensis		
Dawn Redwood	4-8	86
Metasequoia glyptostroboides		
Deodar Cedar	6-9	74
Cedrus deodara		
Fruitless American Sweetgum	5-9	83
Liquidambar styraciflua 'Rotundiloba'		
Ginkgo	3-9	79
Ginkgo biloba		
Littleleaf Linden	3-7	96
Tilia cordata		
Pecan	5-9	74
Carya illinoinensis		
Pin Oak	4-8	92
Quercus palustris		
River Birch	4-9	73
Betula nigra		
Scarlet Oak	4-9	91
Quercus coccinea		
Shumard Oak	5-9	93
Quercus shumardii		
Silver Maple	3-9	72
Acer saccharinum		
Southern Magnolia	6-10	83
Magnolia grandiflora		
Sugar Maple	4-8	72
Acer saccharum		
White Oak	4-9	90
Quercus alba		
White Pine	3-8	87
Pinus strobus		
Willow Oak	4-8	92
Quercus phellos		

Shrubs for Zone 7

◆ Small Shrubs (3 feet or under)

Common Name	Zones	Page
Dwarf Alberta Spruce	3-8	136
Picea glauca 'Conica'		
Dwarf Leucothoe	3-8	134
Leucothoe axillaris		
Gumpo Azalea	6-9	116
Azalea hybrida		
Heller Japanese Holly	5-8	128
Ilex crenata 'Helleri'		
Iceberg Rose	4-9	142
Rosa 'Iceberg'		
Korean Boxwood	5-9	119
Buxus microphylla koreana		
Limemound Spirea	4-9	147
Spiraea japonica Limemound		
Margo Koster Rose	5-8	142
Rosa 'Margo Koster'		
Old Gold Juniper	4-10	131
Juniperus chinensis 'Old Gold'		
Otto Luyken Laurel	6-8	137
Prunus laurocerasus 'Otto Luyken'		

Common Name	Zones	Page
Parson's Juniper	3-9	132
Juniperus chinensis 'Parsonii'		
Rockspray Cotoneaster	6-9	122
Cotoneaster horizontalis		
The Fairy Rose	4-9	144
Rosa 'The Fairy'		

◆ Medium Shrubs (3 to 6 feet)

Common Name	Zones	Page
American Beautyberry	7-10	120
Callicarpa americana		
Annabelle Hydrangea	3-9	126
Hydrangea arborescens 'Annabelle'		
Anthony Waterer Spirea	3-9	145
Spiraea japonica 'Anthony Waterer'		
Baby's Breath Spirea	4-8	147
Spiraea thunbergii		
Betty Prior Rose	4-9	139
Rosa 'Betty Prior'		
Bridalwreath Spirea	5-8	146
Spiraea prunifolia		
Butterfly Bush	5-9	119
Buddleia davidii		
Carefree Beauty Rose	4-8	139
Rosa Carefree Beauty		
Carolina Azalea	4-9	115
Azalea carolinianum		
Compact Japanese Holly	5-8	129
Ilex crenata 'Compacta'		
Country Dancer Rose	4-9	140
Rosa 'County Dancer'		
Dwarf Burning Bush	3-8	123
Euonymus alatus 'Compacta'		
Dwarf Yaupon Holly	7-10	130
Ilex vomitoria 'Nana'		
Fru Dagmar Hastrup Rose	2-9	140
Rosa 'Fru Dagmar Hastrup'		
Glen Dale Azaleas	6-9	116
Azalea Glen Dale Hybrids		
Glossy Abelia	7-9	114
Abelia x grandiflora		
Golden Arborvitae	6-10	148
Thuja orientalis 'Aurea Nana'		
Graham Thomas Rose	5-9	141
Rosa Graham Thomas		
Inkberry	3-10	129
Ilex glabra 'Compacta'		
Japanese Aucuba	7-10	114
Aucuba japonica		
Kurume Azalea	6-9	118
Azalea obtusum		
Nikko Blue Hydrangea	6-9	126
Hydrangea macrophylla 'Nikko Blue'		
Oakleaf Hydrangea	5-9	127
Hydrangea quercifolia		
Pink Meidiland Rose	5-8	143
Rosa Pink Meidiland		
Rosa Rubrifolia	4-9	143
Rosa rubrifolia		

Nikko Blue Hydrangea (Hydrangea macrophylla 'Nikko Blue') Page 126

Common Name	Zones	Page
Sea Green Juniper *Juniperus chinensis 'Sea Green'*	4-8	132
Shibori Spirea *Spiraea japonica 'Shibori'*	4-8	145
Showy Jasmine *Jasminum floridum*	7-9	131
Therese Bugnet Rose *Rosa 'Therese Bugnet'*	3-9	144

◆ Large Shrubs (6 feet or more)

Common Name	Zones	Page
Border Forsythia *Forsythia x intermedia*	6-9	125
Catawba Rhododendron *Rhododendron catawbiense*	4-8	138
Cherry Laurel *Prunus caroliniana*	6-9	137
Chinese Variegated Privet *Ligustrum sinense 'Variegatum'*	7-10	135
Cleyera *Cleyera japonica*	7-10	121
Doublefile Viburnum *Viburnum plicatum tomentosum*	4-8	149
Dwarf Burford Holly *Ilex cornuta 'Bufordii Nana'*	6-9	128
European Cranberrybush *Viburnum opulus 'Roseum'*	3-8	149
Golden Eunonymus *Euonymus japonicus 'Aureus'*	7-9	124
Miss Kim Lilac *Syringa patula 'Miss Kim'*	3-7	148
Mountain Laurel *Kalmia latifolia*	4-9	133
Nandina *Nandina domestica*	6-9	135
Nellie R. Stevens Holly *Ilex x 'Nellie R. Stevens'*	6-9	130
Pampas Grass *Cortaderia selloana*	7-10	121
PeeGee Hydrangea *Hydrangea paniculata 'Grandiflora'*	3-8	127
Pyracantha *Pyracantha coccinea*	6-8	138
Redtip Photinia *Photinia x fraseri*	6-9	136
Rose of Sharon *Hibiscus syriacus*	5-9	125
Sasanqua Camellia *Camellia sasanqua*	7-9	120
Thorny Elaeagnus *Elaeagnus pungens*	7-9	122
Vanhoutte Spirea *Spiraea x vanhouttei*	3-8	146
Waxleaf Ligustrum *Ligustrum lucidum*	7-10	134

Groundcover for Zone 7

Common Name	Zones	Page

◆ Low Groundcovers (12" or less)

Common Name	Zones	Page
Ajuga *Ajuga reptans*	4-9	156
Bar Harbor Juniper *Juniperus horizontalis 'Bar Harbor'*	3-9	165
Bath's Pink *Dianthus gratianopolitanus 'Bath's Pink'*	4-9	160
Bloody Cranesbill *Geranium sanguineum*	3-8	162
Blue Chip Juniper *Juniperus horizontalis 'Blue Chip'*	3-9	165
Blue Rug Juniper *Juniperus horizontalis 'Wiltonii '*	3-9	166
Creeping Thyme *Thymus leucotrichus*	5-9	173
English Ivy *Hedera helix*	5-9	162
Evergreen Candytuft *Iberis sempervirens*	4-8	164

Aaron's Beard
(Hypericum calycinum)
Page 164

Common Name	Zones	Page
Goldmoss *Sedum acre*	4-9	171
Hardy Ice Plant *Delosperma nubigenum*	6-9	207
Hens and Chicks *Sempervivum tectorum*	4-10	209
Lady's Mantle *Alchemilla mollis*	4-7	157
Lily-of-the-Valley *Convallaria majalis*	2-9	159
Littleleaf Periwinkle *Vinca minor*	4-8	173
Maidenhair Fern *Adiantum pedatum*	3-8	156
Memorial Rose *Rosa wichuraiana*	4-9	170
Mondo Grass *Ophiopogon japonicus*	7-9	168
Moneywort *Lysimachia nummularia*	3-8	167
Moss Phlox *Phlox subulata*	2-9	169
Pachysandra *Pachysandra terminalis*	4-9	168
Pink Panda Strawberry *Fragaria 'Pink Panda'*	3-9	161
Prostrate Rosemary *Rosmarinus officinalis 'Irene'*	7-10	171
Snow-on-the-Mountain *Aegopodium podagraria 'Variegatum'*	3-9	156
Spotted Dead Nettle *Lamium maculatum*	3-9	167
Sweet Woodruff *Asperula odorata*	4-8	158
Variegated Algerian Ivy *Hedera canariensis 'Variegata'*	7-10	208

◆ Tall Groundcovers (12" or more)

Common Name	Zones	Page
Aaron's Beard *Hypericum calycinum*	5-9	164
Alba Meidiland Rose *Rosa Alba Meidiland*	4-8	170
Andorra Compact Juniper *Juniperus horizontalis 'Plumosa Compacta'*	3-9	166
Arum *Arum italicum*	6-10	157
Asiatic Jasmine *Trachelospermum asiaticum*	7-10	173
Autumn Fern *Dryopteris erythrosora*	6-9	160
Bearberry Cotoneaster *Cotoneaster dammeri*	5-9	159
Blanket Flower *Gaillardia x grandiflora*	2-9	161
Blue Pacific Shore Juniper *Juniperus conferta 'Blue Pacific'*	5-9	165
Catmint *Nepeta x faassenii*	4-8	168
Coral Bells *Heuchera sanguinea*	3-8	163
Dwarf Coyote Brush *Baccharis pilularis*	7-10	207
Dwarf Japanese Garden Juniper *Juniperus procumbens 'Nana'*	4-9	166
Fleabane *Erigeron hybrid*	2-10	160

Common Name	Zones	Page
Flower Carpet Rose *Rosa 'Flower Carpet'*	4-10	171
Fountain Grass *Pennisetum alopecuroides*	5-9	169
Germander *Teucrium prostratum*	4-9	172
Hosta *Hosta species*	3-8	163
Japanese Blood Grass *Imperata cylindrica 'Red Baron'*	5-9	164
Japanese Painted Fern *Athyrium nipponicum 'Pictum'*	4-9	158
Japanese Primrose *Primula japonica*	5-8	170
Lamb's Ear *Stachys byzantina*	4-8	172
Lenten Rose *Helleborus orientalis*	4-8	163
Liriope *Liriope muscari*	7-10	167
Purple-Leaf Wintercreeper *Euonymus fortunei 'Coloratus'*	4-8	161
Rock Rose *Helianthemum nummularium*	5-8	162
Silver Brocade Artemisia *Artemisia stelleriana 'Silver Brocade'*	3-9	157
Stonecrop *Sedum spectabile*	3-10	172
Variegated Japanese Sedge *Carex morrowii 'Variegata'*	6-9	158

Vines for Zone 7

Common Name	Zones	Page
American Bittersweet *Celastrus scandens*	3-8	179
Armand Clematis *Clematis armandii*	7-9	179
Blaze Climbing Rose *Rosa 'Blaze'*	5-10	184
Boston Ivy *Parthenocissus tricuspidata*	4-8	183
Carolina Yellow Jessamine *Gelsemium sempervirens*	7-9	181
Chinese Wisteria *Wisteria sinensis*	5-9	185
Chocolate Vine *Akebia quinata*	5-9	178
Climbing Cecil Brunner Rose *Rosa 'Climbing Cecil Brunner'*	6-10	185
Climbing Hydrangea *Hydrangea petiolaris*	4-7	182
Climbing Iceberg Rose *Rosa 'Climbing Iceberg'*	4-10	184
Climbing Peace Rose *Rosa 'Climbing Peace'*	5-9	184
Cross-Vine *Bignonia capreolata*	6-9	178
Hall's Honeysuckle *Lonicera japonica 'Halliana'*	4-10	211
Hybrid Clematis *Clematis hybrid*	3-9	180
Joseph's Coat Climbing Rose *Rosa 'Joseph's Coat'*	4-10	185
Passion Flower *Passiflora incarnata*	7-10	213
Porcelain Vine *Ampelopsis brevipedunculata*	4-8	178
Silver Lace Vine *Polygonum aubertii*	4-9	183
Sweet Autumn Clematis *Clematis paniculata*	4-9	181
Trumpet Honeysuckle *Lonicera sempervirens*	4-9	182
Trumpet Vine *Campsis radicans*	4-9	179
Virginia Creeper *Parthenocissus quinquefolia*	4-9	182

Plants for Zone 8

Locate your home on the map on page 5 to determine your climate zone. **The plants in the following lists are good for Zone 8.** Availability varies by area and conditions (see page 21). Check with your garden center. Plants on these lists are categorized by height. Turn to the pages listed for more information on growth rate and for ranges of height and spread.

Trees for Zone 8

Common Name	Zones	Page
◆ Small Trees (30 feet or under)		
Crepe Myrtle	7-9	82
Lagerstroemia indica		
Desert Willow	8-10	194
Chilopsis linearis		
Flowering Dogwood	5-9	76
Cornus florida		
Hollywood Juniper	4-9	195
Juniperus chinensis 'Torulosa'		
Japanese Flowering Crabapple	4-8	85
Malus floribunda		
Japanese Maple	5-8	71
Acer palmatum		
Kousa Dogwood	5-8	76
Cornus kousa		
Lilac Chaste Tree	6-10	199
Vitex agnus-castus		
Loquat	8-10	195
Eriobotrya japonica		
Lusterleaf Holly	7-9	80
Ilex latifolia		
Mediterranean Fan Palm	8-10	193
Chamaerops humilis		
Olive	8-10	195
Olea europaea		
Paloverde	8-10	193
Cercidium texanum		
Pindo Palm	8-10	192
Butia capitata		
Possum Haw	3-9	79
Ilex decidua		
Purple-Leaf Plum	4-8	88
Prunus cerasifera 'Atropurpurea'		
Redbud	3-9	75
Cercis canadensis		
Saucer Magnolia	5-9	84
Magnolia x soulangiana		
Savannah Holly	5-9	80
Ilex opaca 'Savannah'		
Star Magnolia	4-9	84
Magnolia stellata		
Sweet Bay Magnolia	5-9	85
Magnolia virginiana		
Washington Hawthorn	3-9	77
Crataegus phaenopyrum		
Wax Myrtle	7-9	86
Myrica cerifera		
Windmill Palm	8-10	199
Trachycarpus fortunei		
Yaupon Holly	7-10	81
Ilex vomitoria		
Yoshino Cherry	5-8	88
Prunus x yedoensis		
◆ Medium Trees (30 to 60 feet)		
American Arborvitae	3-9	95
Thuja occidentalis		
Arizona Cypress	7-9	194
Cupressus arizonica		
Bradford Pear	4-8	89
Pyrus calleryana 'Bradford'		
Chinese Elm	5-9	97
Ulmus parvifolia		
Chinese Pistache	6-9	87
Pistacia chinensis		
Eastern Red Cedar	3-9	81
Juniperus virginiana		
Green Ash	3-9	78
Fraxinus pennsylvanica		
Japanese Pagoda Tree	6-8	94
Sophora japonica		

Common Name	Zones	Page
Japanese Zelkova	5-9	97
Zelkova serrata		
Laurel Oak	7-10	197
Quercus laurifolia		
Leyland Cypress	6-9	77
X Cupressocyparis leylandii		
Red Maple	3-9	70
Acer rubrum		
Sabal Palm	8-10	198
Sabal palmetto		
Weeping Willow	4-9	94
Salix babylonica		
Yellowwood	6-8	75
Cladrastis lutea		
◆ Large Trees (60 feet or more)		
American Beech	3-9	78
Fagus grandifolia		
Bald Cypress	4-10	95
Taxodium distichum		
Bristlecone Fir	7-8	70
Abies bracteata		
Bur Oak	2-8	91
Quercus macrocarpa		
California Incense Cedar	5-8	73
Calocedrus decurrens		
Dawn Redwood	4-8	86
Metasequoia glyptostroboides		
Deodar Cedar	6-9	74
Cedrus deodara		
Fruitless American Sweetgum	5-9	83
Liquidambar styraciflua 'Rotundiloba'		
Ginkgo	3-9	79
Ginkgo biloba		
Pecan	5-9	74
Carya illinoinensis		
Pin Oak	4-8	92
Quercus palustris		
River Birch	4-9	73
Betula nigra		
Scarlet Oak	4-9	91
Quercus coccinea		
Shumard Oak	5-9	93
Quercus shumardii		
Silver Maple	3-9	72
Acer saccharinum		
Southern Live Oak	8-10	93
Quercus virginiana		
Southern Magnolia	6-10	83
Magnolia grandiflora		
Sugar Maple	4-8	72
Acer saccharum		
White Oak	4-9	90
Quercus alba		
White Pine	3-8	87
Pinus strobus		
Willow Oak	4-8	92
Quercus phellos		

Shrubs for Zone 8

Common Name	Zones	Page
◆ Small Shrubs (3 feet or under)		
Dwarf Alberta Spruce	3-8	136
Picea glauca 'Conica'		
Dwarf Leucothoe	5-9	134
Leucothoe axillaris		
Gumpo Azalea	6-9	116
Azalea hybrida		
Heller Japanese Holly	5-8	128
Ilex crenata 'Helleri'		

Common Name	Zones	Page
Iceberg Rose	4-9	142
Rosa 'Iceberg'		
Korean Boxwood	5-9	119
Buxus microphylla koreana		
Limemound Spirea	4-9	147
Spiraea japonica Limemound		
Margo Koster Rose	5-8	142
Rosa 'Margo Koster'		
Old Gold Juniper	4-10	131
Juniperus chinensis 'Old Gold'		
Otto Luyken Laurel	6-8	137
Prunus laurocerasus 'Otto Luyken'		
Parson's Juniper	3-9	132
Juniperus chinensis 'Parsonii'		
Rockspray Cotoneaster	6-9	122
Cotoneaster horizontalis		
The Fairy Rose	4-9	144
Rosa 'The Fairy'		
White Rock Rose	8-10	200
Cistus x hybridus		
◆ Medium Shrubs (3 to 6 feet)		
American Beautyberry	7-10	120
Callicarpa americana		
Annabelle Hydrangea	3-9	126
Hydrangea arborescens 'Annabelle'		
Anthony Waterer Spirea	3-9	145
Spiraea japonica 'Anthony Waterer'		
Baby's Breath Spirea	4-8	147
Spiraea thunbergii		
Betty Prior Rose	4-9	139
Rosa 'Betty Prior'		
Bridalwreath Spirea	5-8	146
Spiraea prunifolia		
Butterfly Bush	5-9	119
Buddleia davidii		
Carefree Beauty Rose	4-8	139
Rosa Carefree Beauty		
Carolina Azalea	4-9	115
Azalea carolinianum		
Compact Japanese Holly	5-8	129
Ilex creneta 'Compacta'		
Country Dancer Rose	4-9	140
Rosa 'Country Dancer'		
Dwarf Burning Bush	3-8	123
Euonymus alatus 'Compacta'		
Dwarf Yaupon Holly	7-10	130
Ilex vomitoria 'Nana'		
Fru Dagmar Hastrup Rose	2-9	140
Rosa 'Fru Dagmar Hastrup'		
Glen Dale Azaleas	6-9	116
Azalea Glen Dale Hybrids		
Glossy Abelia	7-9	114
Abelia x grandiflora		
Golden Arborvitae	6-10	148
Thuja orientalis 'Aurea Nana'		
Graham Thomas Rose	5-9	141
Rosa Graham Thomas		
Gruss an Aachen Rose	5-9	141
Rosa 'Gruss an Aachen'		
Indian Hawthorn	8-10	204
Rhaphiolepis indica		
Inkberry	3-10	129
Ilex glabra 'Compacta'		
Japanese Aucuba	7-10	114
Aucuba japonica		
Japanese Fatsia	8-10	124
Fatsia japonica		
King Sago	8-10	201
Cycas revoluta		
Kurume Azalea	6-9	118
Azalea obtusum		
Nikko Blue Hydrangea	6-9	126
Hydrangea macrophylla 'Nikko Blue'		
Oakleaf Hydrangea	5-9	127
Hydrangea quercifolia		
Pink Meidiland Rose	5-8	143
Rosa Pink Meidiland		
Rosa Rubrifolia	4-9	143
Rosa rubrifolia		

Common Name	Zones	Page
Sea Green Juniper	4-8	132
Juniperus chinensis 'Sea Green'		
Shibori Spirea	4-8	145
Spiraea japonica 'Shibori'		
Showy Jasmine	7-9	131
Jasmnum floridum		
Texas Silverado Sage	8-9	202
Leucophyllum frutescens 'Silverado'		
Therese Bugnet Rose	3-9	144
Rosa 'Therese Bugnet'		
Variegated Pittosporum	8-10	204
Pittosporum tobira 'Variegata'		

◆ Large Shrubs (6 feet or more)

Common Name	Zones	Page
Border Forsythia	6-9	125
Forsythia x intermedia		
Catawba Rhododendron	4-8	138
Rhododendron catawbiense		
Cherry Laurel	6-9	137
Prunus caroliniana		
Chinese Variegated Privet	7-10	135
Ligustrum sinense 'Variegatum'		
Cleyera	7-10	121
Cleyera japonica		
Doublefile Viburnum	4-8	149
Viburnum plicatum tomentosum		
Dwarf Burford Holly	6-9	128
Ilex cornuta 'Bufordii Nana'		
European Cranberrybush	3-8	149
Viburnum opulus 'Roseum'		
Gardenia	8-10	201
Gardenia jasminoides		
Golden Eunonymus	7-9	124
Euonymus japonicus 'Aureus'		
Mountain Laurel	4-9	133
Kalmia latifolia		
Nandina	6-9	135
Nandina domestica		
Nellie R. Stevens Holly	6-9	130
Ilex x 'Nellie R. Stevens'		
Oleander	8-10	203
Nerium oleander		
Pampas Grass	7-10	121
Cortaderia selloana		
PeeGee Hydrangea	3-8	127
Hydrangea paniculata 'Grandiflora'		
Pyracantha	6-8	138
Pyracantha coccinea		
Redtip Photinia	6-9	136
Photinia x fraseri		
Rose of Sharon	5-9	125
Hibiscus syriacus		
Sasanqua Camellia	7-9	120
Camellia sasanqua		
Southern Indian Azalea	8-10	117
Azalea indica		
Sweet Viburnum	8-10	205
Viburnum odoratissimum		
Thorny Elaeagnus	7-9	122
Elaeagnus pungens		
Vanhoutte Spirea	3-8	146
Spiraea x vanhouttei		
Waxleaf Ligustrum	7-10	134
Ligustrum lucidum		

Groundcover for Zone 8

Common Name	Zones	Page
◆ Low Groundcovers (12" or less)		
Ajuga	4-9	156
Ajuga reptans		
Artillery Fern	8-10	169
Pilea serpyllacea 'Rotundifolia'		
Bar Harbor Juniper	3-9	165
Juniperus horizontalis 'Bar Harbor'		
Bath's Pink	4-9	160
Dianthus gratianopolitanus 'Bath's Pink'		
Bloody Cranesbill	3-8	162
Geranium sanguineum		
Blue Chip Juniper	3-9	165
Juniperus horizontalis 'Blue Chip'		

Common Name	Zones	Page
Blue Rug Juniper	3-9	166
Juniperus horizontalis 'Wiltonii'		
Creeping Thyme	5-9	173
Thymus leucotrichus		
English Ivy	5-9	162
Hedera helix		
Evergreen Candytuft	4-8	164
Iberis sempervirens		
Goldmoss	4-9	171
Sedum acre		
Hardy Ice Plant	6-9	207
Delosperma nubigenum		
Hens and Chicks	4-10	209
Sempervivum tectorum		
Lily-of-the-Valley	2-9	159
Convallaria majalis		
Littleleaf Periwinkle	4-8	173
Vinca minor		
Maidenhair Fern	3-8	156
Adiantum pedatum		
Memorial Rose	4-9	170
Rosa wichuraiana		
Mondo Grass	7-9	168
Ophiopogon japonicus		
Moneywort	3-8	167
Lysimachia nummularia		
Moss Phlox	3-9	169
Phlox subulata		
Moss Verbena	8-10	209
Verbena pulchella		
Pachysandra	4-9	168
Pachysandra terminalis		
Pink Panda Strawberry	3-9	161
Fragaria 'Pink Panda'		
Prostrate Rosemary	7-10	171
Rosmarinus officinalis 'Irene'		
Snow-on-the-Mountain	3-9	156
Aegopodium podagraria 'Variegatum'		
Spotted Dead Nettle	3-9	167
Lamium maculatum		
Sweet Woodruff	4-8	158
Asperula odorata		
Variegated Algerian Ivy	7-10	208
Hedera canariensis 'Variegata'		

Common Name	Zones	Page
◆ Tall Groundcovers (12" or more)		
Aaron's Beard	5-9	164
Hypericum calycinum		
Alba Meidiland Rose	4-8	170
Rosa Alba Meidiland		
Andorra Compact Juniper	3-9	166
Juniperus horizontalis 'Plumosa Compacta'		
Arum	6-10	157
Arum italicum		
Asiatic Jasmine	7-10	173
Trachelospermum asiaticum		
Autumn Fern	6-9	160
Dryopteris erythrosora		
Bearberry Cotoneaster	5-9	159
Cotoneaster dammeri		
Blanket Flower	2-9	161
Gaillardia x grandiflora		
Blue Pacific Shore Juniper	5-9	165
Juniperus conferta 'Blue Pacific'		
Cast-Iron Plant	8-10	206
Aspidistra elatior		
Catmint	4-8	168
Nepeta x faassenii		
Coral Bells	3-8	163
Heuchera sanguinea		
Dwarf Coyote Brush	7-10	207
Baccharis pilularis		
Dwarf Japanese Garden Juniper	4-9	166
Juniperus procumbens 'Nana'		
Fleabane	2-10	160
Erigeron hybrid		
Flower Carpet Rose	4-10	171
Rosa 'Flower Carpet'		
Fountain Grass	5-9	169
Pennisetum alopecuroides		
Germander	4-9	172
Teucrium prostratum		
Holly Fern	8-10	159
Cyrtomium falcatum		
Hosta	3-8	163
Hosta species		
Japanese Blood Grass	5-9	164
Imperata cylindrica 'Red Baron'		

Common Name	Zones	Page
Japanese Painted Fern	4-9	158
Athyrium nipponicum 'Pictum'		
Japanese Primrose	5-8	170
Primula japonica		
Lamb's Ear	4-8	172
Stachys byzantina		
Lenten Rose	4-8	163
Helleborus orientalis		
Liriope	7-10	167
Liriope muscari		
Purple-Leaf Wintercreeper	4-8	161
Euonymus fortunei 'Coloratus'		
Silver Brocade Artemisia	3-9	157
Artemisia stelleriana 'Silver Brocade'		
Rock Rose	5-8	162
Helianthemum nummularium		
Stonecrop	3-10	172
Sedum spectabile		
Variegated Japanese Sedge	6-9	158
Carex morrowii 'Variegata'		

Vines for Zone 8

Common Name	Zones	Page
American Bittersweet	3-8	179
Celastrus scandens		
Armand Clematis	7-9	179
Clematis armandii		
Blaze Climbing Rose	5-10	184
Rosa 'Blaze'		
Boston Ivy	4-8	183
Parthenocissus tricuspidata		
Carolina Yellow Jessamine	7-9	181
Gelsemium sempervirens		
Chinese Wisteria	5-9	185
Wisteria sinensis		
Chocolate Vine	5-9	178
Akebia quinata		
Climbing Cecil Brunner Rose	6-10	185
Rosa 'Climbing Cecil Brunner'		
Climbing Iceberg Rose	4-10	184
Rosa 'Climbing Iceberg'		
Climbing Peace Rose	5-9	184
Rosa 'Climbing Peace'		
Creeping Fig	8-10	211
Ficus pumila		
Cross-Vine	6-9	178
Bignonia capreolata		
Fatshedera	8-10	181
X Fatshedera lizei		
Hall's Honeysuckle	4-10	211
Lonicera japonica 'Halliana'		
Hybrid Clematis	3-9	180
Clematis hybrid		
Joseph's Coat Climbing Rose	4-10	185
Rosa 'Joseph's Coat'		
Lady Bank's Climbing Rose	8-10	183
Rosa banksiae		
Passion Flower	7-10	213
Passiflora incarnata		
Porcelain Vine	4-8	178
Ampelopsis brevipedunculata		
Silver Lace Vine	4-9	183
Polygonum aubertii		
Star Jasmine	8-10	213
Trachelospermum jasminoides		
Sweet Autumn Clematis	4-9	181
Clematis paniculata		
Trumpet Honeysuckle	4-9	182
Lonicera sempervirens		
Trumpet Vine	4-9	179
Campsis radicans		
Virginia Creeper	4-9	182
Parthenocissus quinquefolia		

Plants for Zone 9 and 10

If you live in Zones 9 or 10, check out the plants on these lists.
Availability varies by area and conditions (see page 21). Check with your garden center. These lists are organized by plant height. Turn to the pages listed for more information about how fast plants grow and for ranges of height and spread.

Trees for Zones 9 and 10

Common Name	Zones	Page
◆ Small Trees (30 feet or under)		
Bailey Acacia	10	192
Acacia baileyana		
Crepe Myrtle	7-9	82
Lagerstroemia indica		
Crimson Bottlebrush	9-10	193
Callistemon citrinus		
Desert Willow	8-10	194
Chilopsis linearis		
Flowering Dogwood	5-9	76
Cornus florida		
Hollywood Juniper	4-9	195
Juniperus chinensis 'Torulosa'		
Lilac Chaste Tree	6-10	199
Vitex agnus-castus		
Loquat	8-10	195
Eriobotrya japonica		
Lusterleaf Holly	7-9	80
Ilex latifolia		
Mediterranean Fan Palm	8-10	193
Chamaerops humilis		
Mesquite	10	197
Prosopis glandulosa		
Mexican Bird-of-Paradise	10	192
Caesalpinia mexicana		
Olive	8-10	195
Olea europaea		
Paloverde	8-10	193
Cercidium texanum		
Pindo Palm	8-10	192
Butia capitata		
Possum Haw	3-9	79
Ilex decidua		
Redbud	3-9	75
Cercis canadensis		
Saucer Magnolia	5-9	84
Magnolia x soulangiana		
Savannah Holly	5-9	80
Ilex opaca 'Savannah'		
Sea Grape	10	194
Coccoloba uvifera		
Star Magnolia	4-9	84
Magnolia stellata		

Common Name	Zones	Page
Sweet Bay Magnolia	5-9	85
Magnolia virginiana		
Washington Hawthorn	3-9	77
Crataegus phaenopyrum		
Wax Myrtle	7-9	86
Myrica cerifera		
White Bird-of-Paradise	9-10	198
Strelitzia nicolai		
Windmill Palm	8-10	199
Trachycarpus fortunei		
Yaupon Holly	7-10	81
Ilex vomitoria		
◆ Medium Trees (30 to 60 feet)		
American Arborvitae	3-9	95
Thuja occidentalis		
Arizona Cypress	7-9	194
Cupressus arizonica		
Canary Island Date Palm	9-10	196
Phoenix canariensis		
Chinese Elm	5-9	97
Ulmus parvifolia		
Chinese Pistache	6-9	87
Pistacia chinensis		
Coast Live Oak	9	90
Quercus agrifolia		
Eastern Red Cedar	3-9	81
Juniperus virginiana		
Green Ash	3-9	78
Fraxinus pennsylvanica		
Japanese Zelkova	5-9	97
Zelkova serrata		
Laurel Oak	7-10	197
Quercus laurifolia		
Queen Palm	10	198
Syagrus romanzoffianum		
Red Maple	3-9	70
Acer rubrum		
Sabal Palm	8-10	198
Sabal palmetto		
Senegal Date Palm	9-10	196
Phoenix reclinata		
Weeping Willow	4-9	94
Salix babylonica		
◆ Large Trees (60 feet or more)		
American Beech	3-9	78
Fagus grandifolia		
Bald Cypress	4-10	95
Taxodium distichum		
Date Palm	9-10	196
Phoenix dactylifera		
Deodar Cedar	6-9	74
Cedrus deodara		
Fruitless American Sweetgum	5-9	83
Liquidambar styraciflua 'Rotundiloba'		
Ginkgo	3-9	79
Ginkgo biloba		
Mexican Washington Palm	9-10	199
Washingtonia robusta		
Pecan	5-9	74
Carya illinoinensis		
River Birch	4-9	73
Betula nigra		
Royal Palm	10	197
Roystonea elata		
Scarlet Oak	4-9	91
Quercus coccinea		
Shumard Oak	5-9	93
Quercus shumardii		
Silver Maple	3-9	72
Acer saccharinum		
Southern Live Oak	8-10	93
Quercus virginiana		
Southern Magnolia	6-10	83
Magnolia grandiflora		
White Oak	4-9	90
Quercus alba		

Shrubs for Zones 9 and 10

Common Name	Zones	Page
◆ Small Shrubs (3 feet or under)		
African Iris	9-10	203
Moraea iridioides		
Bouvardia	9-10	200
Bouvardia longiflora 'Albatross'		
Bunny Ears Cactus	10	203
Opuntia microdasys		
Dwarf Leucothoe	5-9	134
Leucothoe axillaris		
Gumpo Azalea	6-9	116
Azalea hybrida		
Iceberg Rose	4-9	142
Rosa 'Iceberg'		
Korean Boxwood	5-9	119
Buxus microphylla koreana		
Limemound Spirea	4-9	147
Spiraea japonica Limemound		
Old Gold Juniper	4-10	131
Juniperus chinensis 'Old Gold'		
Parson's Juniper	3-9	132
Juniperus chinensis 'Parsonii'		
Pink Ruffles Azalea	9-10	118
Azalea Rutherford Hybrids 'Pink Ruffles'		
Rockspray Cotoneaster	6-9	122
Cotoneaster horizontalis		
The Fairy Rose	4-9	144
Rosa 'The Fairy'		
White Rock Rose	8-10	200
Cistus x hybridus		
◆ Medium Shrubs (3 to 6 feet)		
American Beautyberry	7-10	120
Callicarpa americana		
Annabelle Hydrangea	3-9	126
Hydrangea arborescens 'Annabelle'		
Anthony Waterer Spirea	3-9	145
Spiraea japonica 'Anthony Waterer'		
Betty Prior Rose	4-9	139
Rosa 'Betty Prior'		
Bird-of-Paradise	9-10	205
Strelitzia reginae		
Butterfly Bush	5-9	119
Buddleia davidii		
Cape Honeysuckle	10	205
Tecomaria capensis		
Carolina Azalea	4-9	115
Azalea carolinianum		
Country Dancer Rose	4-9	140
Rosa 'Country Dancer'		
Downy Jasmine	9-10	202
Jasminum multiflorum		
Dwarf Yaupon Holly	7-10	130
Ilex vomitoria 'Nana'		
Escallonia	9-10	123
Escallonia x exoniensis 'Frades'		
Fru Dagmar Hastrup Rose	2-9	140
Rosa 'Fru Dagmar Hastrup		
Glen Dale Azaleas	6-9	116
Azalea Glen Dale Hybrids		
Glossy Abelia	7-9	114
Abelia x grandiflora		
Golden Arborvitae	6-10	148
Thuja orientalis 'Aurea Nana'		
Graham Thomas Rose	5-9	141
Rosa Graham Thomas		
Gruss an Aachen Rose	5-9	141
Rosa 'Gruss an Aachen'		
Indian Hawthorn	8-10	204
Rhaphiolepis indica		

Redbud
(*Cercis canadensis*)
Cultivar—Alba
Page 75

Common Name	Zones	Page
Inkberry	3-10	129
Ilex glabra 'Compacta'		
Japanese Aucuba	7-10	114
Aucuba japonica		
Japanese Fatsia	8-10	124
Fatsia japonica		
King Sago	8-10	201
Cycas revoluta		
Kurume Azalea	6-9	118
Azalea obtusum		
Nikko Blue Hydrangea	6-9	126
Hydrangea macrophylla 'Nikko Blue'		
Oakleaf Hydrangea	5-9	127
Hydrangea quercifolia		
Rosa Rubrifolia	4-9	143
Rosa rubrifolia		
Texas Silverado Sage	8-9	202
Leucophyllum frutescens 'Silverado'		
Therese Bugnet Rose	3-9	144
Rosa 'Therese Bugnet'		
Variegated Pittosporum	8-10	204
Pittosporum tobira 'Variegata'		

◆ Large Shrubs (6 feet or more)

Common Name	Zones	Page
Border Forsythia	6-9	125
Forsythia x intermedia		
Cherry Laurel	6-9	137
Prunus caroliniana		
Chinese Hibiscus	9-10	201
Hibiscus rosa-sinensis		
Chinese Variegated Privet	7-10	135
Ligustrum sinense 'Variegatum'		
Cleyera	7-10	121
Cleyera japonica		
Dwarf Burford Holly	6-9	128
Ilex cornuta 'Bufordii Nana'		
Gardenia	8-10	201
Gardenia jasminoides		
Golden Eunonymus	7-9	124
Euonymus japonicus 'Aureus'		
Ixora	10	202
Ixora coccinea		
Mountain Laurel	4-9	133
Kalmia latifolia		
Nandina	6-9	135
Nandina domestica		
Nellie R. Stevens Holly	6-9	130
Ilex x 'Nellie R. Stevens'		
New Zealand Tea Tree	9-10	133
Leptospermum scoparium		
Oleander	8-10	203
Nerium oleander		
Pampas Grass	7-10	122
Cortaderia selloana		
Pygmy Date Palm	9-10	204
Phoenix roebelenii		
Redtip Photinia	6-9	136
Photinia x fraseri		
Rose of Sharon	5-9	125
Hibiscus syriacus		
Sasanqua Camellia	7-9	120
Camellia sasanqua		
Showy Jasmine	7-9	131
Jasminum floridum		
Southern Indian Azalea	8-10	117
Azalea indica		
Sweet Viburnum	8-10	205
Viburnum odoratissimum		
Thorny Elaeagnus	7-9	122
Elaeagnus pungens		
Variegated Croton	10	200
Codiaeum variegatum var. pictum		
Waxleaf Ligustrum	7-10	134
Ligustrum lucidum		

Fleabane
(Erigeron hybrid)
Cultivar—'Darkest of all'
Page 160

Groundcovers for Zones 9 and 10

◆ Low Groundcovers (12" or less)

Common Name	Zones	Page
Ajuga	4-9	156
Ajuga reptans		
Artillery Fern	8-10	169
Pilea serpyllacea 'Rotundifolia'		
Bar Harbor Juniper	3-9	165
Juniperus horizontalis 'Bar Harbor'		
Bath's Pink	4-9	160
Dianthus gratianopolitanus 'Bath's Pink'		
Blue Chip Juniper	3-9	165
Juniperus horizontalis 'Blue Chip'		
Blue Rug Juniper	3-9	166
Juniperus horizontalis 'Wiltonii '		
Creeping Thyme	5-9	173
Thymus leucotrichus		
English Ivy	5-9	162
Hedera helix		
Freeway Daisy	10	209
Osteospermum fruticosum		
Goldmoss	4-9	171
Sedum acre		
Hardy Ice Plant	6-9	207
Delosperma nubigenum		
Hens and Chicks	4-10	209
Sempervivum tectorum		
Lily-of-the-Valley	2-9	159
Convallaria majalis		
Memorial Rose	4-9	170
Rosa wichuraiana		
Mondo Grass	7-9	168
Ophiopogon japonicus		
Moss Phlox	2-9	169
Phlox subulata		
Moss Verbena	8-10	209
Verbena pulchella		
Pachysandra	4-9	168
Pachysandra terminalis		
Pink Panda Strawberry	3-9	161
Fragaria 'Pink Panda'		
Prostrate Rosemary	7-10	171
Rosmarinus officinalis 'Irene'		
Spotted Dead Nettle	3-9	167
Lamium maculatum		
Snow-on-the-Mountain	3-9	156
Aegopodium podagraria 'Variegatum'		
Variegated Algerian Ivy	7-10	208
Hedera canariensis 'Variegata'		

◆ Tall Groundcovers (12" or more)

Common Name	Zones	Page
Aaron's Beard	5-9	164
Hypericum calycinum		
Andorra Compact Juniper	3-9	166
Juniperus horizontalis 'Plumosa Compacta'		
Arum	6-10	157
Arum italicum		
Asiatic Jasmine	7-10	173
Trachelospermum asiaticum		
Autumn Fern	6-9	160
Dryopteris erythrosora		
Barrel Cactus	9-10	208
Echinocactus spp.		
Bearberry Cotoneaster	5-9	159
Cotoneaster dammeri		
Blanket Flower	2-9	161
Gaillardia x grandiflora		
Blue Pacific Shore Juniper	5-9	165
Juniperus conferta 'Blue Pacific'		
Cast-Iron Plant	8-10	206
Aspidistra elatior		
Mexican Heather	9-10	207
Cuphea hyssopifola		
Dwarf Coyote Brush	7-10	207
Baccharis pilularis		
Dwarf Japanese Garden Juniper	4-9	166
Juniperus procumbens 'Nana'		
Dwarf Lily of the Nile	9-10	206
Agapanthus africanus 'Peter Pan'		
Fleabane	2-10	160
Erigeron hybrid		
Flower Carpet Rose	4-10	171
Rosa 'Flower Carpet'		
Fountain Grass	5-9	169
Pennisetum alopecuroides		

Common Name	Zones	Page
Germander	4-9	172
Teucrium prostratum		
Gold Mound Lantana	9-10	208
Lantana camara 'Gold Mound'		
Holly Fern	8-10	159
Cyrtomium falcatum		
Japanese Ardisia	9-10	206
Ardisia japonica		
Japanese Blood Grass	5-9	164
Imperata cylindrica 'Red Baron'		
Japanese Painted Fern	4-9	158
Athyrium nipponicum 'Pictum'		
Liriope	7-10	167
Liriope muscari		
Mexican Heather	9-10	207
Cuphea hyssopifola		
Silver Brocade Artemisia	3-9	157
Artemisia stelleriana 'Silver Brocade'		
Stonecrop	3-10	172
Sedum spectabile		
Variegated Japanese Sedge	6-9	158
Carex morrowii 'Variegata'		

Vines for Zones 9 and 10

Common Name	Zones	Page
Allamanda	10	210
Allamanda cathartica		
Armand Clematis	7-9	179
Clematis armandii		
Blaze Climbing Rose	5-10	184
Rosa 'Blaze'		
Bougainvillea	9-10	211
Bougainvillea		
Butterfly Vine	9-10	212
Mascagnia macroptera		
Carolina Yellow Jessamine	7-9	181
Gelsemium sempervirens		
Chinese Wisteria	5-9	185
Wisteria sinensis		
Chocolate Vine	5-9	178
Akebia quinata		
Climbing Cecil Brunner Rose	6-10	185
Rosa 'Climbing Cecil Brunner'		
Climbing Iceberg Rose	4-10	184
Rosa 'Climbing Iceberg'		
Climbing Peace Rose	5-9	184
Rosa 'Climbing Peace'		
Creeping Fig	8-10	211
Ficus pumila		
Cross-Vine	6-9	178
Bignonia capreolata		
Evergreen Wisteria	9-10	212
Millettia reticulata		
Fatshedera	8-10	181
X Fatshedera lizei		
Hall's Honeysuckle	4-10	211
Lonicera japonica 'Halliana'		
Hybrid Clematis	3-9	180
Clematis hybrid		
Joseph's Coat Climbing Rose	4-10	185
Rosa 'Joseph's Coat'		
Lady Bank's Climbing Rose	8-10	183
Rosa banksiae		
Madagascar Jasmine	10	213
Stephanotis floribunda		
Mandevilla	10	212
Mandevilla x amabilis		
Passion Flower	7-10	213
Passiflora incarnata		
Silver Lace Vine	4-9	183
Polygonum aubertii		
Star Jasmine	8-10	213
Trachelospermum jasminoides		
Sweet Autumn Clematis	4-9	181
Clematis paniculata		
Trumpet Honeysuckle	4-9	182
Lonicera sempervirens		
Trumpet Vine	4-9	179
Campsis radicans		
Virginia Creeper	4-9	182
Parthenocissus quinquefolia		

Screening and Privacy

The results of your assessment revealed some views that should be blocked, such as unappealing garbage cans or air-conditioners within your own yard. Other scenes might be off your property—a neighbor's messy garage, ugly signs, or unkempt alleyways that will spoil your time outdoors. The beauty of landscaping is that you don't look at anything you don't want to. You can make unwanted views disappear behind plants, fences, arbors, or walls.

Evergreens make dense barriers that block views to the outside and guarantee privacy.

1) Define Privacy Needs

In addition to pinpointing unpleasant views, your site analysis reveals areas that may be unusable because they lack privacy. Blocking views to add or enhance privacy is important. However, it's rarely necessary to block every view from every angle. Doing so turns your home into a fortress. Instead, look at your yard notes on public and private spaces. Are the private spaces truly private? Do you need to make changes to increase privacy and make these spaces more usable? Would some public areas be better as private spaces?

2) Concentrate Efforts

When you've answered these questions, you'll know where to add privacy. Walk those areas. Identify the directions from which people can see into private areas. (Don't forget to look up; a neighboring multistory home or building may pose a problem.) These directions are angles of view. Identifying them will help you place plants to block views and enhance privacy without walling in your entire yard.

3) Filter Views

Now that you know which views to block, it's time to add screening. This term describes plants or objects positioned to block views. There are several screening options: fences, arbors, walls, and plants.

Evergreen plants are often used as screens because they retain their foliage year-round. Some are so dense they form screens like living walls.

Deciduous plants can also be used

This custom fence along the property line offers privacy, while the combination of low shrubs and flowering trees integrate the fence into the design.

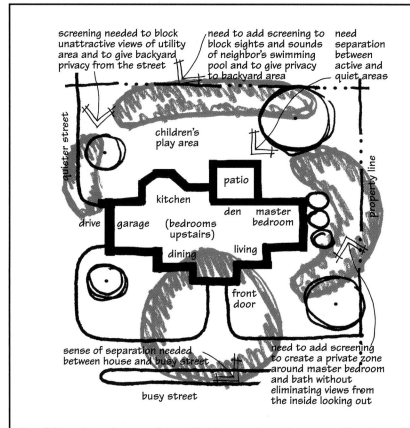

screening needed to block unattractive views of utility area and to give backyard privacy from the street

need to add screening to block sights and sounds of neighbor's swimming pool and to give privacy to backyard area

need separation between active and quiet areas

quieter street

children's play area

patio

kitchen

den master bedroom

drive garage (bedrooms upstairs)

living

dining

property line

front door

sense of separation needed between house and busy street

busy street

need to add screening to create a private zone around master bedroom and bath without eliminating views from the inside looking out

You might want to make a second sketch that focuses only on where you need to add screening to provide privacy, to block views looking outward, to conceal unattractive areas on your property, or to provide a sense of separation between areas of your yard. Use your earlier sketches and notes as references.

Strong climbers such as Climbing Hydrangea (H. petiolaris, Page 182) add texture to fences.

Use plants and the terrain of your yard to carve out private spaces. Here, an intimate patio nestled against a slope is surrounded by trees and shrubs. Shrubs planted between the house and paving make the spot comfortable.

for screening, though you'll rarely find such notations in their descriptions. Look for plants with a rapid growth rate or ones described as good choices for informal hedges.

Rapid-growing deciduous plants are good choices when you need to establish a sense of separation. This means that you add screening to distinguish between your public and private space. Instead of blocking views completely, you may enhance some spots in your yard by filtering the views that look inward or out toward another area. A filtered view is not blocked completely. There is enough screening to establish some distinction between areas. Adding a filtered screen to your yard creates an illusion of privacy without sacrificing breezes or views you enjoy. Though you can see out through the filtered screen and others can see in through it, the presence of something between areas creates a sense of separation necessary for a feeling of privacy.

Design Tip

During warm months when you're out in your yard, deciduous trees, shrubs, and vines block unwanted views with their foliage. These views will become visible again in fall, winter, and early spring when plants are bare. The structure of the plant (its trunk and branches) still filters views after leaves have fallen, which may provide a sense of adequate separation. If not, combine fast-growing deciduous plants with slower-growing evergreens. Deciduous plants are good choices for screening along the southern exposure. When leaves fall, they'll let in winter sunlight.

A single row of Hollywood Juniper (Juniperus chinensis 'Torulosa') separates two driveways.

Plant Selection   **29**

Though you may be eager to plant flowers, screening should be a top priority. Adding privacy and blocking poor views will improve the way you feel about your yard. And the sooner you get plants in the ground, the sooner they can start growing to add the screening your landscape needs.

Plants for Privacy

Availability varies by area and conditions (see page 21). Check with your garden center.

Properly balanced screening keeps the neighbors at a distance without making the backyard feel like a fortress.

Evergreen shrubs for screening

Common Name	Zones	Page	Growth
Cape Honeysuckle *Tecomaria capensis*	10	205	R
Catawba Rhododendron *Rhododendron catawbiense*	4-8	138	S
Cherry Laurel *Prunus caroliniana*	6-9	137	R
Chinese Hibiscus *Hibiscus rosa-sinensis*	9-10	201	R
Chinese Variegated Privet *Ligustrum sinense 'Variegatum'*	7-10	135	R
Escallonia *Escallonia x exoniensis 'Frades'*	9-10	123	R
Glossy Abelia *Abelia x grandiflora*	7-9	114	M
Inkberry *Ilex glabra 'Compacta'*	3-10	129	M
Ixora *Ixora coccinea*	10	202	M
Nandina *Nandina domestica*	6-9	135	M
Nellie R. Stevens Holly *Ilex x 'Nellie R. Stevens'*	6-9	130	M
New Zealand Tea Tree *Leptospermum scoparium*	9-10	133	M
Oleander *Nerium oleander*	8-10	203	M
Redtip Photinia *Photinia x fraseri*	6-9	136	R
Sasanqua Camellia *Camellia sasanqua*	7-9	120	M
Sweet Viburnum *Viburnum odoratissimum*	8-10	205	M
Texas Silverado Sage *Leucophyllum frutescens 'Silverado'*	8-10	202	S
Thorny Elaeagnus *Elaeagnus pungens*	7-9	122	R
Waxleaf Ligustrum *Ligustrum lucidum*	7-10	134	R

Evergreen trees for screening

Common Name	Zones	Page	Growth
American Arborvitae *Thuja occidentalis*	3-9	95	S
Arizona Cypress *Cupressus arizonica*	7-9	194	R
Bristlecone Fir *Abies bracteata*	7-8	70	S
Canadian Hemlock *Tsuga canadensis*	3-7	96	M
Deodar Cedar *Cedrus deodara*	6-9	74	M
Eastern Red Cedar *Juniperus virginiana*	3-9	81	M
Hollywood Juniper *Juniperus chinensis 'Torulosa'*	4-9	195	M
Leyland Cypress *X Cupressocyparis leylandii*	6-9	77	R
Lusterleaf Holly *Ilex latifolia*	7-9	80	S
Savannah Holly *Ilex opaca 'Savannah'*	5-9	80	S
Sweet Bay Magnolia *Magnolia virginiana*	5-9	85	M
Wax Myrtle *Myrica cerifera*	7-9	86	R
White Pine *Pinus strobus*	3-8	87	R
Yaupon Holly *Ilex vomitoria*	7-20	81	R

Evergreen vines for screening

Common Name	Zones	Page	Growth
Allamanda *Allamanda cathartica*	10	210	R
Armand Clematis *Clematis armandii*	7-9	179	R
Bougainvillea *Bougainvillea*	9-10	211	R
Carolina Yellow Jessamine *Gelsemium sempervirens*	7-9	181	R
Chocolate Vine *Akebia quinata*	5-9	178	M
Cross-Vine *Bignonia capreolata*	6-9	178	R
Evergreen Wisteria *Millettia reticulata*	9-10	212	R
Lady Bank's Climb. Rose *Rosa banksiae*	8-10	183	R
Madagascar Jasmine *Stephanotis floribunda*	10	213	M
Star Jasmine *Trachelospermum jasminoides*	8-10	213	M

Rate of Growth:
R: Rapid
M: Medium
S: Slow
Botanical name in italics

Rapid-growing deciduous trees for filtered views

Common Name	Zones	Page
Bald Cypress	4-10	95
Taxodium distichum		
Bradford Pear	4-8	89
Pyrus calleryana 'Bradfora'		
Chinese Elm	5-9	97
Ulmus parvifolia		
Crepe Myrtle	7-9	82
Lagerstroemia indica		
Desert Willow	8-10	194
Chilopsis linearis		
Green Ash	3-9	78
Fraxinus pennsylvanica		
Japanese Pagoda Tree	6-8	94
Sophora japonica		
Japanese Zelkova	5-9	97
Zelkova serrata		
Laurel Oak	7-10	197
Quercus laurifolia		
Lilac Chaste Tree	6-10	199
Vitex agnus-castus		
Mesquite	10	197
Prosopis glandulosa		
Pin Oak	4-8	92
Quercus palustris		
Purple-Leaf Plum	4-8	88
Prunus cerasifera 'Atropurpurea'		
Red Maple	3-9	70
Acer rubrum		
Redbud	3-9	75
Cercis canadensis		
River Birch	4-9	73
Betula nigra		
Saucer Magnolia	5-9	84
Magnolia x soulangiana		
Scarlet Oak	4-9	91
Quercus coccinea		
Shumard Oak	5-9	93
Quercus shumardii		
Silver Maple	3-9	72
Acer saccharinum		
Willow Oak	4-8	92
Quercus phellos		

Deciduous shrubs for screening

Common Name	Zones	Page	Growth
Baby's Breath Spirea	4-8	147	R
Spiraea thunbergii			
Border Forsythia	6-9	125	R
Forsythia x intermedia			
Bridalwreath Spirea	5-8	146	R
Spiraea prunifolia			
Dwarf Burning Bush	3-8	123	S
Euonymus alatus 'Compacta'			
Miss Kim Lilac	3-7	148	S
Syringa patula 'Miss Kim'			
PeeGee Hydrangea	3-8	127	R
Hydrangea paniculata 'Grandiflora'			
Rose of Sharon	5-9	125	R
Hibiscus syriacus			
Vanhoutte Spirea	3-8	146	R
Spiraea x vanhouttei			

Rapid-growing deciduous vines for screening

Common Name	Zones	Page
Chinese Wisteria	5-9	185
Wisteria sinensis		
Climbing Cecil Brunner Rose	6-10	185
Rosa 'Climbing Cecil Brunner'		
Passion Flower	7-20	213
Passiflora incarnata		
Silver Lace Vine	4-9	183
Polygonum aubertii		
Trumpet Vine	4-9	179
Campsis radicans		

Fast-growing Chinese Wisteria (Wisteria sinensis, page 185) blocks overhead views from a building nearby.

Combining Plants and Materials

Choose a variety of evergreen or deciduous plants to screen for privacy or to block unpleasant views.

Plant a combination of the two to enjoy the advantages of both. This works particularly well when rapid-growing deciduous trees are planted among slower-growing evergreen shrubs. The trees quickly establish a sense of separation, while the shrubs slowly fill in to block views completely from a lower angle. Such combinations add privacy to low decks, patios, and other outdoor seating areas. The shrubs eventually block views from eye-level while you're seated, making the area seem comfortably private. The trees filter higher views that need not be obscured completely. Open space between the top of the shrubs and the bottom of the tree canopies will be filtered by tree trunks but won't be closed in. This permits sunlight and breezes to enter without walling off the seating area.

You can also combine evergreen and deciduous plants with fences, walls, trellises, or arbors to enhance privacy and block unattractive sights. These structures have the advantage of immediate impact. Use them where you can't wait for plants to grow. (First compare the cost of construction to the expense of adding big plants.) Use vines, shrubs, and trees to give the hard surfaces of these structures a softer look. Leaves, stems, branches, and trunks will also make the screen denser and block unwanted views more completely.

Open areas require plants that can thrive in direct sun for most of the day. Morning rays are less intense than midday or afternoon sun.

Sun and Shade

Understanding sun and shade requirements for your plants is important. The symbols for sun and shade on plant tags tell you how much sunlight a plant needs to thrive. To find the right plants for your yard, learn to interpret the tags. If you find a tag with all three symbols, the plant can grow successfully in any light condition.

Full sun

A tag with a circle or sun shape that isn't blackened indicates a plant that will tolerate a full day of hot, direct sun. The hottest climates are a possible exception; protection from the sun might be necessary during the hottest part of the day. The intensity and heat of the sun diminishes as you move into northern zones. Plants that have only the full-sun symbol on their tags will not grow as well in partially shaded spots; flowers and foliage may be reduced.

Part shade

A circle half shaded and half open indicates that partial shade is the optimum condition. Morning sunlight followed by afternoon shade is best for these plants. The term partial shade also describes areas where the sun is filtered by overhead canopies, allowing some rays to penetrate during the day. Plant tags describe this condition as dappled or filtered shade. Both terms mean the same thing and are different types of partial shade.

Full sun/part shade

Though plant tags don't differentiate between morning and afternoon sun, you can still decide what a plant needs by looking for combinations of symbols. Tags with both full-sun and partial-shade symbols indicate a plant can grow in conditions ranging from sunny all day long to sunny for just part of the day. Choose plants with both of these symbols to grow in areas of your yard that are sunny all day or

Choosing plants that thrive in shade turns dim corners into lovely and useful areas of your landscape.

sunny in the afternoons. In hotter climates, intense midday and afternoon sun can be deadly to plants requiring some shade. If the plant tag has a full-sun symbol, the plant should tolerate a half day of hot afternoon sun. Remember, the partial-shade symbol tells you the plant can thrive with less than a full day of sun.

If you have dappled shade areas that receive some direct sunlight during a portion of the day, look for plants that include both the full-sun circle and the partial-shade symbol on their tags.

Stop, Look, and Listen

Plants can't talk, but they will tell you when something is wrong. Look for signs that plants aren't seeing the right kind of light. After allowing a few months for them to establish, the only solution is to move your plants where the light better suits them.

Too much sun: Leaves wilt (even shortly after watering) and quickly become brown and crispy as though they've been fried.

Too much shade: Growth is tall, weak, and spindly; stems lean toward the light; foliage and flowers are sparse.

Part shade/deep shade

Plants that need some sunlight filtered through other plant canopies but should stay deeply shaded most of the day, have both the deep-shade symbol and the partial-shade symbol. These plants thrive in conditions that range from almost no light to a half-day's sun. Morning sun is usually best for plants with these symbols, though the weaker rays of an afternoon winter sun are likely to be okay.

Deep shade If you need plants

where there is little or no direct sunlight, look for plants with a solid dark circle on their tags. These plants thrive with low light levels, though nothing grows in the dark. In hotter climates, it's important that plants tagged for deep shade do not receive any midday or afternoon sun, especially during the hottest months of the year. Too much sun is fatal for deep shade-loving plants.

Plants for Full Sun

You can take the guesswork out of buying plants. This section groups plants into selection guides by light requirements. Check out the lists on the following pages for plants that thrive in full sun, partial shade, and deep shade. You'll see plants on more than one list; they grow in varying amounts of sunlight. Look for plants that include your zone within their growing range. (If you don't know what planting zone you live in, see page 5.) Then, turn to the pages listed for photos and a complete description of plants you'd like to know more about. Availability varies by area and conditions (see page 21). Check with your garden center.

Trees for full sun

Common Name	Zones	Page
American Beech	3-9	78
Fagus grandifolia		
Arizona Cypres	7-9	194
Cupressus arizonica		
Bailey Acacia	10	192
Aciacia baileyana		
Bald Cypress	4-10	95
Taxodium distichum		
Bradford Pear	4-8	89
Pyrus calleryana 'Bradford'		
Bur Oak	2-8	91
Quercus macrocarpa		
California Incense Cedar	5-8	73
Calocedrus decurrens		
Candian Hemlock	3-7	96
Tsuga canadensis		
Canary Island Date Palm	9-10	196
Pheonix canariensis		
Chinese Elm	5-9	97
Ulmus parvifolia		
Chinese Pistache	6-9	87
Pistacia chinensis		
Coast Live Oak	9	90
Quercus agrifolia		
Crepe Myrtle	7-9	82
Lagerstroemia indica		
Crimson Bottlebrush	9-10	193
Callistemon citrinus		
Date Palm	9-10	196
Phoenix dactylifera		
Dawn Redwood	4-8	86
Metasequoia glyptostroboides		
Deodar Cedar	6-9	74
Cedrus deodara		
Desert Willow	8-10	194
Chilopsis linearis		
Eastern Red Cedar	3-9	81
Juniperus virginiana		
Fruitless American Sweetgum	5-9	83
Liquidambar styraciflua 'Rotundiloba'		
Ginkgo	3-9	79
Ginkgo biloba		
Hollywood Juniper	4-9	195
Juniperus chinensis 'Torulosa'		
Japanese Flowering Crabapple	4-8	85
Malus floribunda		
Japanese Pagoda Tree	6-8	94
Sophora japonica		
Kousa Dogwood	5-8	76
Cornus kousa		
Laurel Oak	7-10	197
Quercus laurifolia		
Leyland Cypress	6-9	77
X Cupressocyparis leylandii		
Lilac Chaste Tree	6-10	199
Vitex agnus-castus		
Littleleaf Linden	3-7	96
Tilia cordata		
Loquat	8-10	195
Eriobotrya japonica		
Lusterleaf Holly	7-9	80
Ilex latifolia		
Mediterranean Fan Palm	8-10	193
Chamaerops humilis		
Mesquite	10	197
Prosopis glandulosa		
Mexican Bird-of-Paradise	10	192
Caesalpinia mexicana		

Common Name	Zones	Page
Mexican Washington Palm	9-10	199
Washingtonia robusta		
Olive	8-10	195
Olea europaea		
Paloverde	8-10	193
Cercidium texanum		
Pecan	5-9	74
Carya illinoinensis		
Pin Oak	4-8	92
Quercus palustris		
Pindo Palm	8-10	192
Butia capitata		
Possum Haw	3-9	79
Ilex decidua		
Purple-Leaf Plum	4-8	88
Prunus cerasifera 'Atropurpurea'		
Queen Palm	10	198
Syagrus romanzoffianum		
Redbud	3-9	75
Cercis canadensis		
River Birch	4-9	73
Betula nigra		
Royal Palm	10	197
Roystonea elata		
Sabal Palm	8-10	198
Sabal palmetto		
Saucer Magnolia	5-9	84
Magnolia x soulangiana		
Savannah Holly	5-9	80
Ilex opaca 'Savannah'		
Scarlet Oak	4-9	91
Quercus coccinea		
Sea Grape	10	194
Coccoloba uvifera		
Senegal Date Palm	9-10	196
Phoenix reclinata		
Shumard Oak	5-9	93
Quercus shumardii		
Silver Maple	3-9	72
Acer saccharinum		
Southern Magnolia	6-10	83
Magnolia grandiflora		
Sugar Maple	4-8	72
Acer saccharum		
Sweet Bay Magnolia	5-9	85
Magnolia virginiana		
Washington Hawthorn	3-9	77
Crataegus phaenopyrum		
Wax Myrtle	7-9	86
Myrica cerifera		
Weeping Willow	4-9	94
Salix babylonica		
White Bird-of-Paradise	9-10	198
Strelitzia nicolai		
White Oak	4-9	90
Qurecus alba		
White Pine	3-8	87
Pinus strobus		
Willow Oak	4-8	92
Quercus phellos		
Windmill Palm	8-10	199
Trachycarpus fortunei		
Yaupon Holly	7-10	81
Ilex vomitoria		
Yellowwood	6-8	75
Cladrastis lutea		
Yoshino Cherry	5-8	88
Prunus x yedoensis		

Shrubs for full sun

Common Name	Zones	Page
African Iris	9-10	203
Moraea iridioides		
American Beautyberry	7-10	120
Callicarpa americana		
Annabelle Hydrangea	3-9	126
Hydrangea arborescens 'Annabelle'		
Anthony Waterer Spirea	3-9	145
Spiraea japonica 'Anthony Waterer'		
Baby's Breath Spirea	4-8	147
Spiraea thunbergii		
Betty Prior Rose	4-9	139
Rosa 'Betty Prior'		
Bird-of-Paradise	9-10	205
Strelitzia reginae		
Border Forsythia	6-9	125
Forsythia x intermedia		
Bridal Wreath Spirea	5-8	146
Spiraea prunifolia		
Bunny Ears Cactus	10	203
Opuntia microdasys		
Butterfly Bush	5-9	119
Buddleia davidii		
Carefree Beauty Rose	4-8	139
Rosa Carefree Beauty		
Catawba Rhododendron	4-8	138
Rhododendron catawbiense		
Cherry Laurel	6-9	137
Prunus caroliniana		
Chinese Hibiscus	9-10	201
Hibiscus rosa-sinensis		
Chinese Variegated Privet	7-10	135
Ligustrum sinense 'Variegatum'		
Cleyera	7-10	121
Cleyera japonica		
Compact Japanese Holly	5-8	129
Ilex creneta 'Compacta'		
Country Dancer Rose	4-9	140
Rosa 'Country Dancer'		
Doublefile Viburnum	4-8	149
Viburnum plicatum tomentosum		
Downy Jasmine	9-10	202
Jasminum multiflorum		
Dwarf Alberta Spruce	3-8	136
Picea glauca 'Conica'		
Dwarf Burford Holly	6-9	128
Ilex cornuta 'Burfordii Nana'		
Dwarf Burning Bush	3-8	123
Euonymus alatus 'Compacta'		
Dwarf Yaupon Holly	7-10	130
Ilex vomitoria 'Nana'		
European Cranberrybush	3-8	149
Viburnum opulus 'Roseum'		
Fru Dagmar Hastrup Rose	2-9	140
Rosa 'Fru Dagmar Hastrup'		
Gardenia	8-10	201
Gardenia jasminoides		
Glossy Abelia	7-9	114
Abelia x grandiflora		
Golden Arborvitae	6-10	148
Thuja orientalis 'Aurea Nana'		
Golden Euonymus	7-9	124
Euonymus japonicus 'Aureus'		
Graham Thomas Rose	5-9	141
Rosa Graham Thomas		

Common Name	Zones	Page
Gruss an Aachen Rose *Rosa 'Gruss an Aachen'*	5-9	141
Heller Japanese Holly *Ilex creneta 'Helleri'*	5-8	128
Iceberg Rose *Rosa 'Iceberg'*	4-9	142
Indian Hawthorn *Rhaphiolepis indica*	8-10	204
Inkberry *Ilex glabra 'Compacta'*	3-10	129
Ixora *Ixxora coccinea*	10	202
Japanese Aucuba *Aucuba japonica*	7-10	114
King Sago *Cycas revoluta*	8-10	201
Kurume Azalea *Azalea obtusum*	6-9	118
Limemound Spirea *Spiraea japonica Limemound*	4-9	147
Margo Koster Rose *Rosa 'Margo Koster'*	5-8	142
Miss Kim Lilac *Syringa patula 'Miss Kim'*	3-7	148
Mountain Laurel *Kalmia latifolia*	4-9	133
Nandina *Nandina domestica*	6-9	135
Nellie R. Stevens Holly *Ilex x 'Nellie R. Steven's'*	6-9	130
New Zealand Tea Tree *Leptospermum scoparium*	9-10	133
Nikko Blue Hydrangea *Hydrangea macrophylla 'Nikko Blue'*	6-9	126
Old Gold Juniper *Juniperus chinesnsis 'Old Gold'*	4-10	131
Oleander *Nerium oleander*	8-10	203
Pampas Grass *Cortaderia selloana*	7-10	121
Parson's Juniper *Juniperus chinensis 'Parsonii'*	3-9	132
PeeGee Hydrangea *Hydrangea paniculata 'Grandiflora'*	3-8	127
Pink Meidiland Rose *Rosa Pink Meidiland*	5-8	143
Pink Ruffles Azalea *Azalea Rutherford Hybrids 'Pink Ruffles'*	9-10	118
Pygmy Date Palm *Phoenix roebelenii*	9-10	204
Pyracantha *Pyracantha coccinea*	6-8	138
Redtip Photinia *Photinia x fraseri*	6-9	136
Rockspray Cotoneaster *Cotoneaster horizontalis*	6-9	122
Rosa Rubrifolia *Rosa rubrifolia*	4-9	143
Rose of Sharon *Hibiscus syriacus*	5-9	125
Sea Green Juniper *Juniperus chinensis 'Sea Green'*	4-8	132
Shibori Spirea *Spiraea japonica 'Shibori'*	4-8	145
Showy Jasmine *Jasminum floridum*	7-9	131
Sweet Viburnum *Viburnum odoratissimum*	8-10	205
Texas Silverado Sage *Leucophyllum frutescens 'Silverado'*	8-10	202
The Fairy Rose *Rosa 'The Fairy'*	4-9	144
Therese Bugnet Rose *Rosa 'Therese Bugnet'*	3-9	144
Thorny Elaeagnus *Elaeagnus pungens*	7-9	122
Vanhoutte Spirea *Spiraea x vanhouttei*	3-8	146
Variegated Croton *Codiaeum variegatum var. pictum*	10	200
Variegated Pittosporum *Pittosporum tobira 'Variegata'*	8-10	204
Waxleaf Ligustrum *Ligustrum lucidum*	7-10	134
White Rock Rose *Cistus x hybridus*	8-10	200

Groundcovers for full sun

Common Name	Zones	Page
Alba Meidiland Rose *Rosa Alba Meidiland*	4-8	170
Andorra Compact Juniper *Juniperus horizontalis 'Plumosa Compacta'*	3-9	166
Arum *Arum italicum*	6-10	157
Asiatic Jasmine *Trachelospermum asiaticum*	7-10	173
Artillery Fern *Pilea serpyllacea 'Rotundifolia'*	8-10	169
Bar Harbor Juniper *Juniperus horizontalis 'Bar Harbor'*	3-9	165
Barrel Cactus *Echinocactus spp.*	9-10	208
Bath's Pink *Dianthus gratianopolitanus 'Bath's Pink'*	4-9	160
Bearberry Cotoneaster *Cotoneaster dammeri*	5-9	159
Blanket Flower *Gaillardia x grandiflora*	2-9	161
Bloody Cranesbill *Geranium sanguineum*	3-8	162
Blue Chip Juniper *Juniperus horzontalis 'Blue Chip'*	3-9	165
Blue Pacific Shore Juniper *Juniperus conferta 'Blue Pacific'*	5-9	165
Blue Rug Juniper *Juniperus horizontalis 'Wiltonii'*	3-9	166
Catmint *Nepeta x faassenii*	4-8	168
Coral Bells *Heuchera sanguinea*	3-8	163
Creeping Thyme *Thymus leucotrichus*	5-9	173
Dwarf Coyote Brush *Baccharis pilularis*	7-10	207
Dwarf Japanese Garden Juniper *Juniperus procumbens 'Nana'*	4-9	166
Dwarf Lily of the Nile *Agapanthus africanus 'Peter Pan'*	9-10	206
English Ivy *Hedera helix*	5-9	162
Evergreen Candytuft *Iberis sempervirens*	4-8	164
Fleabane *Erigeron hybrid*	2-10	160
Flower Carpet Rose *Rose 'Flower Carpet'*	4-10	171
Fountain Grass *Pennisetum alopecuroides*	5-9	169
Freeway Daisy *Osteospermum fruticosum*	10	209
Germander *Teucrium prostratum*	4-9	172
Gold Mound Lantana *Lantana camara 'Gold Mound'*	9-10	208
Goldmoss *Sedum acre*	4-9	171
Hardy Ice Plant *Delosperma nubigenum*	6-9	207
Hens and Chicks *Sempervivum tectorum*	4-10	209
Japanese Blood Grass *Imperata cylindrica 'Red Baron'*	5-9	164
Lamb's Ear *Stachys byzantina*	4-8	172
Littleleaf Periwinkle *Vinca minro*	4-8	173
Memorial Rose *Rosa wichuraiana*	4-9	170
Mexican Heather *Cuphea hyssopifola*	9-10	207
Mondo Grass *Ophiopogon japonicus*	7-9	168
MossPhlox *Phlox subulata*	2-9	169
Moss Verbena *Verbena pulchella*	8-10	209
Pink Panda Strawberry *Fragaria 'Pink Panda'*	3-9	161

Common Name	Zones	Page
Prostrate Rosemary *Rosmarinus officinalis 'Irene'*	7-10	171
Purple-Leaf Wintercreeper *Euonymus fortunei 'Coloratus'*	4-8	161
Rock Rose *Helianthemum nummularium*	5-8	162
Silver Brocade Artemisia *Artemesia stelleriana 'Silver Brocade'*	3-9	157
Stonecrop *Sedum spectabile*	3-10	172
Sweet Woodruff *Asperula odorata*	4-8	158
Variegated Japanese Sedge *Carex morrowii 'Variegata'*	6-9	158

Vines for full sun

Common Name	Zones	Page
Allamanda *Allamanda cathartica*	10	210
American Bittersweet *Celastrus scandens*	3-8	179
Armand Clematis *Clematis armandii*	7-9	179
Blaze Climbing Rose *Rosa 'Blaze'*	5-10	184
Boston Ivy *Parthenocissus tricuspidata*	4-8	183
Bougainvillea *Bougainvillea*	9-10	211
Butterfly Vine *Mascagnia macroptera*	9-10	212
Carolina Yellow Jessamine *Gelsemium sempervirens*	7-9	181
Chinese Wisteria *Wisteria sinensis*	5-9	185
Chocolate Vine *Akebia quinata*	5-9	178
Climbing Cecil Brunner Rose *Rosa 'Climbing Cecil Brunner'*	6-10	185
Climbing Hydrangea *Hydrangea petiolaris*	4-7	182
Climbing Iceberg Rose *Rosa 'Climbing Iceberg'*	4-10	184
Climbing Peace Rose *Rosa 'Climbing Peace'*	5-9	184
Creeping Fig *Ficus pumila*	8-10	211
Cross-Vine *Bignonia capreolata*	6-9	178
Evergreen Wisteria *Millettia reticulata*	9-10	212
Hall's Honeysuckle *Lonicera japonica 'Halliana'*	4-10	211
Hybrid Clematis *Clematis hybrid*	3-9	180
Joseph's Coat Climbing Rose *Rosa 'Joseph's Coat'*	4-10	185
Lady Bank's Climbing Rose *Rosa banksiae*	8-10	183
Madagascar Jasmine *Stephanotis floribunda*	10	213
Mandevilla *Mandevilla splendens 'Red Riding Hood'*	10	212
Passion Flower *Passiflora incarnata*	7-10	213
Porcelain Vine *Ampelopsis brevipedunculata*	4-8	178
Silver Lace Vine *Polygonum aubertii*	4-9	183
Star Jasmine *Trachelospermum jasminoides*	8-10	213
Sweet Autumn Clematis *Clematis paniculata*	4-9	181
Trumpet Honeysuckle *Lonicera sempervirens*	4-9	182
Trumpet Vine *Campsis radicans*	4-9	179
Virginia Creeper *Parthenocissus quinquefolia*	4-9	182

Plants for Shade

Need help finding plants to grow in shaded areas? These lists are guides to help you find trees, shrubs, groundcovers, and vines for partial or deep shade. If you see plants on more than one list, they grow in varying degrees of shade. Look for plants that include your zone within their growing range and skip plants that don't. (If you don't know what planting zone you live in, see page 5.) Then turn to the pages listed for photos and a complete description of plants you'd like to know more about. Availability varies by area and conditions (see page 21). Check with your garden center.

Trees for shade

Common Name	Zones	Page	Shade
American Beech *Fagus grandifolia*	3-9	78	P - D
Bristlecone Fir *Abies bracteata*	7-8	70	P - D
California Incense Cedar *Calocedrus decurrens*	5-8	73	P - D
Canadian Hemlock *Tsuga canadensis*	3-7	96	P - D
Coast Live Oak *Quercus agrifolia*	9	90	P - D
Flowering Dogwood *Cornus florida*	5-9	76	P - D
Hollywood Juniper *Juniperus chinensis 'Torulosa'*	4-9	195	P - D
Japanese Maple *Acer palmatum*	5-8	71	P - D
Kousa Dogwood *Cornus kousa*	5-8	76	P - D
Laurel Oak *Quercus laurifolia*	7-10	197	P - D
Lilac Chaste Tree *Vitex agnus-castus*	6-10	199	P - D
Loquat *Eriobotrya japonica*	8-10	195	P - D
Lusterleaf Holly *Ilex latifolia*	7-9	80	P - D
Mediterranean Fan Palm *Chamaerops humilis*	8-10	193	P - D
Pin Oak *Quercus palustris*	4-8	92	P - D
Possum Haw *Ilex decidua*	3-9	79	P - D
Redbud *Cercis canadensis*	3-9	75	P - D
River Birch *Betula nigra*	4-9	73	P - D
Sabal Palm *Sabal palmetto*	8-10	198	P - D
Saucer Magnolia *Magnolia x soulangiana*	5-9	84	P - D
Savannah Holly *Ilex opaca 'Savannah'*	5-9	80	P - D
Silver Maple *Acer saccharinum*	3-9	72	P - D
Southern Magnolia *Magnolia grandiflora*	6-10	83	P
Star Magnolia *Magnolia stellata*	4-9	84	P

Common Name	Zones	Page	Shade
Sugar Maple *Acer saccharum*	4-8	72	P - D
Sweet Bay Magnolia *Magnolia virginiana*	5-9	85	P - D
Washington Hawthorn *Crataegus phaenopyrum*	3-9	77	P - D
Wax Myrtle *Myrica cerifera*	7-9	86	P - D
White Bird-of-Paradise *Strelitzia nicolai*	9-10	198	P - D
Windmill Palm *Trachycarpus fortunei*	8-10	199	P - D
Yaupon Holly *Ilex vomitoria*	7-10	81	P - D
Yellowwood *Cladrastis lutea*	6-8	75	P - D

Shrubs for shade

Common Name	Zones	Page	Shade
African Iris *Moraea iridioides*	9-10	203	P - D
American Beautyberry *Callicarpa americana*	7-10	120	P - D
Annabelle Hydrangea *Hydrangea arborescens 'Annabelle'*	3-9	126	P - D
Anthony Waterer Spirea *Spiraea japonica 'Anthony Waterer'*	3-9	145	P - D
Baby's Breath Spirea *Spiraea thunbergii*	4-8	147	P - D
Bird-of-Paradise *Strelitzia reginae*	9-10	205	P - D
Bouvardia *Bouvardia longiflora 'Albatross'*	9-10	200	P
Bridalwreath Spirea *Spiraea prunifolia*	5-8	146	P - D
Catawba Rhododendron *Rhododendron catawbiense*	4-8	138	P - D
Cherry Laurel *Prunus caroliniana*	6-9	137	P - D
Chinese Hibiscus *Hibiscus rosa-sinensis*	9-10	201	P - D1
Chinese Variegated Privet *Ligustrum sinense 'Variegatum'*	7-10	135	P - D

Level of Shade:
P: Partial   D: Deep
Botanical name in italics

Common Name	Zones	Page	Shade
Cleyera *Cleyera japonica*	7-10	121	P - D
Compact Japanese Holly *Ilex creneta 'Compacta'*	5-8	129	D
Doublefile Viburnum *Viburnum plicatum tomentosum*	4-8	149	P - D
Downy Jasmine *Jasminum multiflorum*	9-10	202	P - D
Dwarf Alberta Spruce *Picea glauca 'Conica'*	3-8	136	P - D
Dwarf Burford Holly *Ilex cornuta 'Burfordii Nana'*	6-9	128	P - D
Dwarf Burning Bush *Euonymus alatus 'Compacta'*	3-8	123	P - D
Dwarf Leucothoe *Leucothoe axillaris*	5-9	134	P
Dwarf Yaupon Holly *Ilex vomitoria 'Nana'*	7-10	130	P - D
Escallonia *Escallonia x exoniensis 'Frades'*	9-10	123	P
Gardenia *Gardenia jasminoides*	8-10	201	P - D
Glen Dale Azaleas *Azalea Glen Dale Hybrids*	6-9	116	P - D
Glossy Abelia *Abelia x grandiflora*	7-9	114	P - D
Golden Euonymus *Euonymus japonicus 'Aureus'*	7-9	124	P - D
Gruss an Aachen Rose *Rosa 'Gruss an Aachen'*	5-9	141	P - D
Gumpo Azalea *Azalea hybrida*	6-9	116	P
Heller Japanese Holly *Ilex crenata 'Helleri'*	5-8	128	P - D
Indian Hawthorn *Rhaphiolepis indica*	8-10	204	P - D
Inkberry *Ilex glabra 'Compacta'*	3-10	129	P - D
Ixora *Ixora coccinea*	10	202	P - D
Japanese Aucuba *Aucuba japonica*	7-10	114	P - D
Japanese Fatsia *Fatsia japonica*	8-10	124	P - D
King Sago *Cycas revoluta*	8-10	201	P - D
Kurume Azalea *Azalea obtusum*	6-9	118	P - D
Miss Kim Lilac *Syringa patula 'Miss Kim'*	3-7	148	P - D
Mountain Laurel *Kalmia latifolia*	4-9	133	P - D
Nandina *Nandina domestica*	6-9	135	P - D
Nellie R. Stevens Holly *Ilex x 'Nellie R. Stevens'*	6-9	130	P - D
New Zealand Tea Tree *Leptospermum scoparium*	9-10	133	P - D
Nikko Blue Hydrangea *Hydrangea macrophylla 'Nikko Blue'*	6-9	126	P - D
Oakleaf Hydrangea *Hydrangea quercifolia*	5-9	127	P
Otto Luyken Laurel *Prunus laurocerasus 'Otto Luyken'*	6-8	137	P - D
Pampas Grass *Cortaderia selloana*	7-10	121	P - D

Ixora
(Ixora coccinea)
Page 202

Japanese Maple
(Acer palmatum)
Page 71

Common Name	Zones	Page	Shade
PeeGee Hydrangea	3-8	127	P - D
Hydrangea paniculata 'Grandiflora'			
Pink Ruffles Azalea	9-10	118	P - D
Azalea Rutherford Hybrids 'Pink Ruffles'			
Pygmy Date Palm	9-10	204	P - D
Phoenix roebelenii			
Pyracantha	6-8	138	P - D
Pyracantha coccinea			
Redtip Photinia	6-9	136	P - D
Photinia x fraseri			
Rose of Sharon	5-9	125	P - D
Hibiscus syriacus			
Sasanqua Camellia	7-9	120	P
Camellia sasanqua			
Shibori Spirea	4-8	145	P - D
Spiraea japonica 'Shibori'			
Showy Jasmine	7-9	131	P - D
Jasminum floridum			
Southern Indian Azalea	8-10	117	P
Azalea indica			
Sweet Viburnum	8-10	205	P - D
Viburnum odoratissimum			
The Fairy Rose	4-9	144	P - D
Rosa 'The Fairy'			
Vanhoutte Spirea	3-8	146	P - D
Spiraea x vanhouttei			
Variegated Croton	10	200	P - D
Codiaeum variegatum var. pictum			
Variegated Pittosporum	8-10	204	P - D
Pittosporum tobira 'Variegata'			
Waxleaf Ligustrum	7-10	134	P - D
Ligustrum lucidum			

Groundcovers for shade

Common Name	Zones	Page	Shade
Aaron's Beard	5-9	164	P - D
Hypericum calycinum			
Ajuga	4-9	156	P
Ajuga reptans			
Alba Meidiland Rose	4-8	170	P - D
Rosa Alba Meidiland			
Arum	6-10	157	P - D
Arum italicum			
Asiatic Jasmine	7-10	173	P - D
Trachelospermum asiaticum			
Artillery Fern	8-10	169	P - D
Pilea serpyllacea 'Rotundifolia'			
Autumn Fern	6-9	160	P - D
Dryopteris erythrosora			
Bath's Pink	4-9	160	P - D
Dianthus gratianopolitanus 'Bath's Pink'			
Bearberry Cotoneaster	5-9	159	P - D
Cotoneaster dammeri			

Common Name	Zones	Page	Shade
Bloody Cranesbill	3-8	162	P - D
Geranium sanguineum			
Cast-Iron Plant	8-10	206	P - D
Aspidistra elatior			
Catmint	4-8	168	P - D
Nepeta x faassenii			
Coral Bells	3-8	163	P - D
Heuchera sanguinea			
Dwarf Lily of the Nile	9-10	206	P - D
Agapanthus africanus 'Peter Pan'			
English Ivy	5-9	162	P - D
Hedera helix			
Evergreen Candytuft	4-8	164	P - D
Iberis sempervirens			
Fleabane	2-10	160	P - D
Erigeron hybrid			
Holly Fern	8-10	159	P - D
Cyrtomium falcatum			
Hosta	3-8	163	P - D
Hosta species			
Japanese Ardisia	9-10	206	P - D
Ardisia japonica			
Japanese Blood Grass	5-9	164	P - D
Imperata cylindrica 'Red Baron'			
Japanese Painted Fern	4-9	158	P - D
Athyrium nipponicum 'Pictum'			
Japanese Primrose	5-8	170	D
Primula japonica			
Lady's Mantle	4-7	157	P
Alchemilla mollis			
Lenten Rose	4-8	163	P - D
Helleborus orientalis			
Lily-of-the-Valley	2-9	159	P - D
Convallaria majalis			
Liriope	7-10	167	P - D
Liriope muscari			
Littleleaf Periwinkle	4-8	173	P - D
Vinca minor			
Maidenhair Fern	3-8	156	P - D
Adiantum pedatum			
Mexican Heather	9-10	207	
Cuphea hyssopifola			
Mondo Grass	7-9	168	P - D
Ophiopogon japonicus			
Moneywort	3-8	167	P - D
Lysimachia nummularia			
Pachysandra	4-9	168	P - D
Pachysandra terminalis			
Pink Panda Strawberry	3-9	161	P - D
Fragaria 'Pink Panda'			
Snow-on-the-Mountain	3-9	156	P - D
Aegopodium podagraria 'Variegatum'			
Spotted Dead Nettle	3-9	167	P - D
Lamium maculatum			
Sweet Woodruff	4-8	158	P - D
Asperula odorata			
Variegated Algerian Ivy	7-10	208	D
Hedera canariensis 'Variegata'			
Variegated Japanese Sedge	6-9	158	P - D
Carex morrowii 'Variegata'			

Vines for shade

Common Name	Zones	Page	Shade
American Bittersweet	3-8	179	P - D
Celastrus scandens			
Boston Ivy	4-8	183	P - D
Parthenocissus tricuspidata			
Carolina Yellow Jessamine	7-9	181	P - D
Gelsemium sempervirens			
Chinese Wisteria	5-9	185	P - D
Wisteria sinensis			
Chocolate Vine	5-9	178	P - D
Akebia quinata			
Climbing Hydrangea	4-7	182	P - D
Hydrangea petiolaris			
Creeping Fig	8-10	211	P - D
Ficus pumila			
Cross-Vine	6-9	178	P - D
Bignonia capreolata			
Fatshedera	8-10	181	P - D
X Fatshedera lizei			
Hall's Honeysuckle	4-10	211	P - D
Lonicera japonica 'Halliana'			
Hybrid Clematis	3-9	180	P - D
Clematis hybrid			
Lady Bank's Climbing Rose	8-10	183	P - D
Rosa banksiae			
Madagascar Jasmine	10	213	P - D
Stephanotis floribunda			
Mandevilla	10	212	P - D
Mandevilla splendens 'Red Riding Hood'			
Passion Flower	7-10	213	P - D
Passiflora incarnata			
Silver Lace Vine	4-9	183	P - D
Polygonum aubertii			
Star Jasmine	8-10	213	P - D
Trachelospermum jasminoides			
Sweet Autumn Clematis	4-9	181	P - D
Clematis paniculata			
Trumpet Vine	4-9	179	P - D
Campsis radicans			
Virginia Creeper	4-9	182	P - D
Parthenocissus quinquefolia			

Sweet Woodruff
(Asperula odorata)
Page 158

Selection 2

Soil Conditions

K **nowing what kind of soil you have is the first step in choosing plants that will thrive.** Here are the basics; visit your county extension service if you want a specific soil analysis. No matter what condition you have, working the soil is beneficial to new plants, which need all the help you can offer them. Improving soil with amendments is a bonus for good growth (see pages 48-49), but don't think you can fool Mother Nature. Choose plants that thrive naturally in existing soil conditions.

Get Your Hands Dirty

Begin evaluating the soil in your yard by pushing up your sleeves and digging a few inches below the surface. You're looking for three indicators—water retention, nutrient content, and drainage or "percolation" rate. (See "Wisdom of the Aisles," below.) Scoop up a handful of soil and squeeze it to check for water content. If water dribbles out, it's wet. If it can't form a lump, it's dry. If the soil forms a lump that firmly holds its shape, you might have clay. If it forms a lump that easily crumbles again, the soil is moist. Next, roll it between your palms with light pressure.

Heavy Soil If it forms a snakelike form on rolling, the soil has a high clay content and is described as heavy. The pores between soil particles are very small. Nutrients do not leach out as quickly as in other soil types. However, water can be trapped in pores, resulting in sticky, wet soil. This situation creates standing water surrounding roots causing nonadapted plants to suffocate and die. When clay is dry, it is dense and hard, much like concrete. Roots can have difficulty penetrating these soils. Choose plants that can tolerate clay soil.

Porous Soil If the soil in your hand is too sandy or rocky to hold together well, it is porous. Water percolates quickly through such soil. There's no problem with water collecting around roots, but nutrients wash rapidly away. These soils are known as poor and dry. You'll need to water and fertilize plants regularly in porous soil. Select plants that tolerate poor, dry soils.

Moderate Soil Many soil types fall somewhere between these two extremes. You might be able to roll your soil into a ribbon, indicating some clay content, but it will break apart when just a few inches long. If you're able to crumble the soil easily between your fingers to its original state, your soil is moderate. Many

*River Birch
(Betula nigra)
Page 73*

different plants thrive in moderate soil, but they'll grow even better if you work the soil prior to planting.

Plants for Special Soil Conditions

Availability varies by area and conditions (see page 21). Check with your garden center.

Plants for wet, boggy soil

Common Name	Zones	Page
◆ **Trees**		
Bald Cypress	4-10	95
Taxodium distichum		
Eastern Red Cedar	3-9	81
Juniperus virginiana		
Green Ash	3-9	78
Fraxinus pennsylvanica		
Possum Haw	3-9	79
Ilex decidua		
River Birch	4-9	73
Betula nigra		
Royal Palm	10	197
Roystonea elata		
Southern Magnolia	6-10	83
Magnolia grandiflora		
Sweet Bay Magnolia	5-9	85
Magnolia virginiana		
Wax Myrtle	7-9	86
Myrica cerifera		
Weeping Willow	4-9	94
Salix babylonica		
Yaupon Holly	7-10	81
Ilex vomitoria		
◆ **Shrubs**		
Chinese Variegated Privet	7-10	135
Ligustrum sinense 'Variegatum'		
Escallonia	9-10	123
Escallonia x exoniensis 'Frades'		
European Cranberrybush	3-8	149
Viburnum opulus 'Roseum'		
Inkberry	3-10	129
Ilex glabra 'Compacta'		
Vanhoutte Spirea	3-8	146
Spiraea x vanhouttei		
◆ **Groundcovers**		
Bearberry Cotoneaster	5-9	159
Cotoneaster dammeri		
Japanese Primrose	5-8	170
Primula japonica		
Snow-on-the-Mountain	3-9	156
Aegopodium podagraria 'Variegatum'		

Wisdom
of the **A**isles

Do a Perc Test. Percolation is the way water drains through soil and is one of the guides for plant selection. Determine your soil's rate of percolation by digging test holes 12 to 18 inches deep in several spots around your yard. Fill them with water and measure the water depth with a stick. After 30 minutes measure the water depth again. If the hole empties or water levels drop an inch or more within half an hour, your soil drains very quickly. Choose plants that thrive in poor, dry soil. If water remains, check levels hourly. If the hole drains about an inch an hour, it's well-drained and should support many different plant types. Less than an inch an hour indicates poor drainage. Choose plants that grow well in wet, boggy areas or will tolerate compacted soil.

Plants for poor, dry soil

◆ Trees

Common Name	Zones	Page
Arizona Cypress *Cupressus arizonica*	7-9	194
Bailey Acacia *Acacia baileyana*	10	192
Bald Cypress *Taxodium distichum*	4-10	95
Bur Oak *Quercus macrocarpa*	2-8	91
Chinese Elm *Ulmus parvifolia*	5-9	97
Coast Live Oak *Quercus agrifolia*	9	90
Crimson Bottlebrush *Callistemon citrinus*	9-10	193
Deodar Cedar *Cedrus deodara*	6-9	74
Desert Willow *Chilopsis linearis*	8-10	194
Eastern Red Cedar *Juniperus virginiana*	3-9	81
Ginkgo *Ginkgo biloba*	3-9	79
Green Ash *Fraxinus pennsylvanica*	3-9	78
Japanese Pagoda Tree *Sophora japonica*	6-8	94
Laurel Oak *Quercus laurifolia*	7-10	197
Lilac Chaste Tree *Vitex agnus-castus*	6-10	199
Mediterranean Fan Palm *Chamaerops humilis*	8-10	193
Mesquite *Prosopis glandulosa*	10	197
Mexican Bird-of-Paradise *Caesalpinia mexicana*	10	192
Mexican Washington Palm *Washingtonia robusta*	9-10	199
Pecan *Carya illinoinensis*	5-9	74
Pin Oak *Quercus palustris*	4-8	92
Pindo Palm *Butia capitata*	8-10	192
Red Maple *Acer rubrum*	3-9	70
River Birch *Betula nigra*	4-9	73
Southern Live Oak *Quercus virginiana*	8-10	93
Southern Magnolia *Magnolia grandiflora*	6-10	83
Washington Hawthorn *Crataegus phaenopyrum*	3-9	77
Wax Myrtle *Myrica cerifera*	7-9	86
Weeping Willow *Salix babylonica*	4-9	94
White Oak *Quercus alba*	4-9	90
White Pine *Pinus strobus*	3-8	87
Willow Oak *Quercus phellos*	4-8	92
Yaupon Holly *Ilex vomitoria*	7-10	81
Yellowwood *Cladrastis lutea*	6-8	75

◆ Shrubs

Common Name	Zones	Page
Cape Honeysuckle *Tecomaria capensis*	10	205
Chinese Variegated Privet *Ligustrum sinense 'Variegatum'*	7-10	135
Dwarf Alberta Spruce *Picea glauca 'Conica'*	3-8	136
Dwarf Burford Holly *Ilex cornuta 'Burfordii Nana'*	6-9	128
Dwarf Yaupon Holly *Ilex vomitoria 'Nana'*	7-10	130
Escallonia *Escallonia x exoniensis 'Frades'*	9-10	123
Fru Dagmar Hastrup Rose *Rosa 'Fru Dagmar Hastrup'*	2-9	140
Golden Arborvitae *Thuja orientalis 'Aurea Nana'*	6-10	148
Golden Euonymus *Euonymus japonicus 'Aureus'*	7-9	124

Common Name	Zones	Page
Japanese Aucuba *Aucuba japonica*	7-10	114
King Sago *Cycas revoluta*	8-10	201
Nellie R. Stevens Holly *Ilex x 'Nellie R. Stevens'*	6-9	130
Old Gold Juniper *Juniperus chinensis 'Old Gold'*	4-10	131
Parson's Juniper *Juniperus chinensis 'Parsonii'*	3-9	132
Pyracantha *Pyracantha coccinea*	6-8	138
Sea Green Juniper *Juniperus chinensis 'Sea Green'*	4-8	132
Showy Jasmine *Jasminum floridum*	7-9	131
Texas Silverado Sage *Leucophyllum frutescens 'Silverado'*	8-9	202
Therese Bugnet Rose *Rosa 'Therese Bugnet'*	3-9	144
Thorny Elaeagnus *Elaeagnus pungens*	7-9	122
Waxleaf Ligustrum *Ligustrum lucidum*	7-10	134
White Rock Rose *Cistus x hybridus*	8-10	200

◆ Groundcovers

Common Name	Zones	Page
Artillery Fern *Pilea serpyllacea 'Rotundifolia'*	8-10	169
Bath's Pink *Dianthus gratianopolitanus 'Bath's Pink'*	4-9	160
Bearberry Cotoneaster *Cotoneaster dammeri*	5-9	159
Blanket Flower *Gaillardia x grandiflora*	2-9	161
Blue Chip Juniper *Juniperus horizontalis 'Blue Chip'*	3-9	165
Blue Pacific Shore Juniper *Juniperus conferta 'Blue Pacific'*	5-9	165
Cast-Iron Plant *Aspidistra elatior*	8-10	206
Creeping Thyme *Thymus leucotrichus*	5-9	173
Dwarf Coyote Brush *Baccharis pilularis*	7-10	207
Fountain Grass *Pennisetum alopecuroides*	5-9	169
Goldmoss *Sedum acre*	4-9	171
Hardy Ice Plant *Delosperma nubigenum*	6-9	207
Lily-of-the-Valley *Convallaria majalis*	2-9	159
Liriope *Liriope muscari*	7-10	167
Mondo Grass *Ophiopogon japonicus*	7-9	168
Moss Phlox *Phlox subulata*	2-9	169
Moss Verbena *Verbena pulchella*	8-10	209
Prostrate Rosemary *Rosmarinus officinalis 'Irene'*	7-10	171
Rock Rose *Helianthemum nummularium*	5-8	162
Snow-on-the-Mountain *Aegopodium podagraria 'Variegatum'*	3-9	156
Spotted Dead Nettle *Lamium maculatum*	3-9	167
Stonecrop *Sedum spectabile*	3-10	172

◆ Vines

Common Name	Zones	Page
American Bittersweet *Celastrus scandens*	3-8	179
Boston Ivy *Parthenocissus tricuspidata*	4-8	183
Carolina Yellow Jessamine *Gelsemium sempervirens*	7-9	181
Lady Bank's Climbing Rose *Rosa banksiae*	8-10	183
Porcelain Vine *Ampelopsis brevipedunculata*	4-8	178
Silver Lace Vine *Polygonum aubertii*	4-9	183
Sweet Autumn Clematis *Clematis paniculata*	4-9	181
Trumpet Vine *Campsis radicans*	4-9	179
Virginia Creeper *Parthenocissus quinquefolia*	4-9	182

Desert Willow
(*Chilopsis linearis*)
Page 194

Plants for heavy clay soil

◆ Trees

Common Name	Zones	Page
American Arborvitae *Thuja occidentalis*	3-9	95
Bald Cypress *Taxodium distichum*	4-10	95
Bur Oak *Quercus macrocarpa*	2-8	91
Dawn Redwood *Metasequoia glyptostroboides*	4-8	86
Eastern Red Cedar *Juniperus virginiana*	3-9	81
Ginkgo *Ginkgo biloba*	3-9	79
Green Ash *Fraxinus pennsylvanica*	3-9	78
Hollywood Juniper *Juniperus chinensis 'Torulosa'*	4-9	195
Littleleaf Linden *Tilia cordata*	3-7	96
Pin Oak *Quercus palustris*	4-8	92
Redbud *Cercis canadensis*	3-9	75
Saucer Magnolia *Magnolia x soulangiana*	5-9	84
Savannah Holly *Ilex opaca 'Savannah'*	5-9	80
Silver Maple *Acer saccharinum*	3-9	72

◆ Shrubs

Common Name	Zones	Page
Annabelle Hydrangea *Hydrangea arborescens 'Annabelle'*	3-9	126
Anthony Waterer Spirea *Spiraea japonica 'Anthony Waterer'*	3-9	145
Border Forsythia *Forsythia x intermedia*	6-9	125
Chinese Variegated Privet *Ligustrum sinense 'Variegatum'*	7-10	135
Dwarf Alberta Spruce *Picea glauca 'Conica'*	3-8	136
Escallonia *Escallonia x exoniensis 'Frades'*	9-10	123
Golden Arborvitae *Thuja orientalis 'Aurea Nana'*	6-10	148
Japanese Aucuba *Aucuba japonica*	7-10	114
Japanese Fatsia *Fatsia japonica*	8-10	124
Pyracantha *Pyracantha coccinea*	6-8	138
Thorny Elaeagnus *Elaeagnus pungens*	7-9	122
Vanhoutte Spirea *Spiraea x vanhouttei*	3-8	146

◆ Groundcovers

Common Name	Zones	Page
Bath's Pink *Dianthus gratianopolitanus 'Bath's Pink'*	4-9	160
Snow-on-the-Mountain *Aegopodium podagraria 'Variegatum'*	3-9	156

◆ Vines

Common Name	Zones	Page
Carolina Yellow Jessamine *Gelsemium sempervirens*	7-9	181
Sweet Autumn Clematis *Clematis paniculata*	4-9	181

Soil pH

Soil can be categorized three ways based on its pH: neutral, acidic, or alkaline. Knowing which category your yard fits into will help you choose the right plants to grow there. Most soil in a given geographic area will be similar in pH, so your local garden center associates will know what's typical of where you live. For a pH reading, purchase a soil testing kit or visit your county extension agent. Your results will show a number between 0 and 14. Neutral soils test around 7. Acidic soils are usually between 4 and 6. Alkaline soils yield readings higher than 7. Observing characteristics native to your area will also give you clues about soil pH. For example, areas where limestone is plentiful are naturally alkaline. Regions with high annual rainfall tend to have acidic soil because of nutrient washing. Areas with high amounts of decaying pine straw or oak leaves usually have acidic soil, too.

*Southern Indian Azalea
(Azalea indica)
Cultivar—Southern charm pink
Page 117*

Plants for Special Soil Conditions

Availability varies by area and conditions (see page 21). Check with your garden center.

Plants for acidic soil

Common Name	Zones	Page
◆ Trees		
American Beech	3-9	78
Fagus grandifolia		
Bristlecone Fir	7-8	70
Abies bracteata		
Canadian Hemlock	3-7	96
Tsuga canadensis		
Crepe Myrtle	7-9	82
Lagerstroemia indica		
Deodar Cedar	6-9	74
Cedrus deodara		
Eastern Red Cedar	3-9	81
Juniperus virginiana		
Flowering Dogwood	5-9	76
Cornus florida		
Fruitless American Sweetgum	5-9	83
Liquidambar styraciflua 'Rotundiloba'		
Ginkgo	3-9	79
Ginkgo biloba		
Green Ash	3-9	78
Fraxinus pennsylvanica		
Hollywood Juniper	4-9	195
Juniperus chinensis 'Torulosa'		
Japanese Zelkova	5-9	97
Zelkova serrata		
Kousa Dogwood	5-8	76
Cornus kousa		
Laurel Oak	7-10	197
Quercus laurifolia		
Littleleaf Linden	3-7	96
Tilia cordata		
Loquat	8-10	195
Eriobotrya japonica		
Lusterleaf Holly	7-9	80
Ilex latifolia		
Pin Oak	4-8	92
Quercus palustris		
Possum Haw	3-9	79
Ilex decidua		
Purple-Leaf Plum	4-8	88
Prunus cerasifera 'Atropurpurea'		
Queen Palm	10	198
Syagrus romanzoffianum		
Red Maple	3-9	70
Acer rubrum		
Redbud	3-9	75
Cercis canadensis		
River Birch	4-9	73
Betula nigra		
Saucer Magnolia	5-9	84
Magnolia x soulangiana		
Savannah Holly	5-9	80
Ilex opaca 'Savannah'		
Shumard Oak	5-9	93
Quercus shumardii		
Silver Maple	3-9	72
Acer saccharinum		
Southern Live Oak	8-10	93
Quercus virginiana		
Star Magnolia	4-9	84
Magnolia stellata		
Sugar Maple	4-8	72
Acer saccharum		
Sweet Bay Magnolia	5-9	85
Magnolia virginiana		

Common Name	Zones	Page
Washington Hawthorn	3-9	77
Crataegus phaenopyrum		
White Oak	4-9	90
Quercus alba		
Willow Oak	4-8	92
Quercus phellos		
Yaupon Holly	7-10	81
Ilex vomitoria		
◆ Shrubs		
American Beautyberry	7-10	120
Callicarpa americana		
Annabelle Hydrangea	3-9	126
Hydrangea arborescens 'Annabelle'		
Border Forsythia	6-9	125
Forsythia x intermedia		
Catawba Rhododendron	4-8	138
Rhododendron catawbiense		
Chinese Hibiscus	9-10	201
Hibiscus rosa-sinensis		
Chinese Variegated Privet	7-10	135
Ligustrum sinense 'Variegatum'		
Cleyera	7-10	121
Cleyera japonica		
Country Dancer Rose	4-9	140
Rosa 'Country Dancer'		
Dwarf Alberta Spruce	3-8	136
Picea glauca 'Conica'		
Dwarf Burford Holly	6-9	128
Ilex cornuta 'Bufordii Nana'		
Dwarf Burning Bush	3-8	123
Euonymus alata 'Compacta'		
Dwarf Leucothoe	5-9	134
Leucothoe axillaris		
Dwarf Yaupon Holly	7-10	130
Ilex vomitoria 'Nana'		
Escallonia	9-10	123
Escallonia x exoniensis 'Frades'		
Gardenia	8-10	201
Gardenia jasminoides		
Glen Dale Azaleas	6-9	116
Azalea Glen Dale Hybrids		
Glossy Abelia	7-9	114
Abelia x grandiflora		
Golden Arborvitae	6-10	148
Thuja orientalis 'Aurea Nana'		
Gruss an Aachen Rose	5-9	141
Rosa 'Gruss an Aachen'		
Gumpo Azalea	6-9	116
Azalea hybrida		
Indian Hawthorn	8-10	204
Rhaphiolepis indica		
Inkberry	3-10	129
Ilex glabra 'Compacta'		
Ixora	10	202
Ixora coccinea		
Japanese Fatsia	8-10	124
Fatsia japonica		
Korean Boxwood	5-9	119
Buxus microphylla koreana		
Kurume Azalea	6-9	118
Azalea obtusum		
Mountain Laurel	4-9	133
Kalmia latifolia		
Nellie R. Stevens Holly	6-9	130
Ilex x 'Nellie R. Stevens'		
New Zealand Tea Tree	9-10	133
Leptospermum scoparium		
Oakleaf Hydrangea	5-9	127
Hydrangea quercifolia		
Old Gold Juniper	4-10	131
Juniperus chinensis 'Old Gold'		
PeeGee Hydrangea	3-8	127
Hydrangea paniculata 'Grandiflora'		
Pink Ruffles Azalea	9-10	118
Azalea Rutherford Hybrids 'Pink Ruffles'		
Pyracantha	6-8	138
Pyracantha coccinea		
Sasanqua Camellia	7-9	120
Camellia sasanqua		
Showy Jasmine	7-9	131
Jasminum floridum		
Southern Indian Azalea	8-10	117
Azalea indica		
Sweet Viburnum	8-10	205
Viburnum odoratissimum		

Common Name	Zones	Page
Thorny Elaeagnus	7-9	122
Elaeagnus pungens		
Variegated Pittosporum	8-10	204
Pittosporum tobira 'Variegata'		

◆ Groundcovers

Common Name	Zones	Page
Asiatic Jasmine	7-10	173
Trachelospermum asiaticum		
Bath's Pink Dianthus	4-9	160
Dianthus gratianopolitanus 'Bath's Pink'		
Bearberry Cotoneaster	5-9	159
Cotoneaster dammeri		
Blue Pacific Shore Juniper	5-9	165
Juniperus conferta 'Blue Pacific'		
Dwarf Japanese Garden Juniper	4-9	166
Juniperus procumbens 'Nana'		
Japanese Primrose	5-8	170
Primula japonica		
Maidenhair Fern	3-8	156
Adiantum pedatum		
Mondo Grass	7-9	168
Ophiopogon japonicus		
Prostrate Rosemary	7-10	171
Rosmarinus officinalis 'Irene'		
Purple-Leaf Wintercreeper	4-8	161
Euonymus fortunei 'Coloratus'		
Snow-on-the-Mountain	3-9	156
Aegopodium podagraria 'Variegatum'		
Sweet Woodruff	4-8	158
Asperula odorata		

◆ Vines

Common Name	Zones	Page
Armand Clematis	7-9	179
Clematis armandii		
Blaze Climbing Rose	5-10	184
Rosa 'Blaze'		
Boston Ivy	4-8	183
Parthenocissus tricuspidata		
Carolina Yellow Jessamine	7-9	181
Gelsemium sempervirens		
Climbing Cecil Brunner Rose	6-10	185
Rosa 'Climbing Cecil Brunner'		
Climbing Iceberg Rose	4-10	184
Rosa 'Climbing Iceberg'		
Climbing Peace Rose	5-9	184
Rosa 'Climbing Peace'		
Cross-vine	6-9	178
Bignonia capreolata		
Joseph's Coat Climbing Rose	4-10	185
Rosa 'Joseph's Coat'		
Lady Bank's Climbing Rose	8-10	183
Rosa banksiae		
Porcelain Vine	4-8	178
Ampelopsis brevipedunculata		
Sweet Autumn Clematis	4-9	181
Clematis paniculata		
Virginia Creeper	4-9	182
Parthenocissus quinquefolia		

Purple-Leaf Plum
(Prunus cerasifera 'Atropurpurea)
Page 88

Plants for alkaline soil

Common Name	Zones	Page

◆ Trees

Common Name	Zones	Page
American Arborvitae	3-9	95
Thuja occidentalis		
Arizona Cypress	7-9	194
Cupressus arizonica		
Bur Oak	2-8	91
Quercus macrocarpa		
Chinese Elm	5-9	97
Ulmus parvifolia		
Chinese Pistache	6-9	87
Pistacia chinensis		
Deodar Cedar	6-9	74
Cedrus deodara		
Desert Willow	8-10	194
Chilopsis linearis		
Eastern Red Cedar	3-9	81
Juniperus virginiana		
Ginkgo	3-9	79
Ginkgo biloba		
Green Ash	3-9	78
Fraxinus pennsylvanica		
Hollywood Juniper	4-9	195
Juniperus chinensis 'Torulosa'		
Japanese Flowering Crabapple	4-8	85
Malus floribunda		
Japanese Pagoda Tree	6-8	94
Sophora japonica		
Japanese Zelkova	5-9	97
Zelkova serrata		
Lilac Chaste Tree	6-10	199
Vitex agnus-castus		
Littleleaf Linden	3-7	96
Tilia cordata		
Loquat	8-10	195
Eriobotrya japonica		
Mesquite	10	197
Prosopis glandulosa		
Olive	8-10	195
Olea europaea		
Paloverde	8-10	193
Cercidium texanum		
Possum Haw	3-9	79
Ilex decidua		
Purple-Leaf Plum	4-8	88
Prunus cerasifera 'Atropurpurea'		
Redbud	3-9	75
Cercis canadensis		
Shumard Oak	5-9	93
Quercus shumardii		
Silver Maple	3-9	72
Acer saccharinum		
Washington Hawthorn	3-9	77
Crataegus phaenopyrum		
Willow Oak	4-8	92
Quercus phellos		
Yaupon Holly	7-10	81
Ilex vomitoria		
Yellowwood	6-8	75
Cladrastis lutea		
Yoshino Cherry	5-8	88
Prunus x yedoensis		

◆ Shrubs

Common Name	Zones	Page
Border Forsythia	6-9	125
Forsythia x intermedia		
Chinese Variegated Privet	7-10	135
Ligustrum sinense 'Variegatum'		
Dwarf Burning Bush	3-8	123
Euonymus alatus 'Compacta'		
Dwarf Yaupon Holly	7-10	130
Ilex vomitoria 'Nana'		
Glossy Abelia	7-9	114
Abelia x grandiflora		
Golden Arborvitae	6-10	148
Thuja orientalis 'Aurea Nana'		
Indian Hawthorn	8-10	204
Rhaphiolepis indica		
Oakleaf Hydrangea	5-9	127
Hydrangea quercifolia		
Old Gold Juniper	4-10	131
Juniperus chinensis 'Old Gold'		
Pampas Grass	7-10	121
Cortaderia selloana		

Stonecrop
(Sedum spectabile)
Page 172

Common Name	Zones	Page
PeeGee Hydrangea	3-8	127
Hydrangea paniculata 'Grandiflora'		
Pyracantha	6-8	138
Pyracantha coccinea		
Rose of Sharon	5-9	125
Hibiscus syriacus		
Showy Jasmine	7-9	131
Jasminum floridum		
Texas Silverado Sage	8-10	202
Leucophyllum frutescens 'Silverado'		
Thorny Elaeagnus	7-9	122
Elaeagnus pungens		
Waxleaf Ligustrum	7-10	134
Ligustrum lucidum		

◆ Groundcovers

Common Name	Zones	Page
Andorra Compact Juniper	3-9	166
Juniperus horizontalis 'Plumosa Compacta'		
Asiatic Jasmine	7-10	173
Trachelospermum asiaticum		
Bar Harbor Juniper	3-9	165
Juniperus horizontalis 'Bar Harbor'		
Bath's Pink	4-9	160
Dianthus gratianopolitanus 'Bath's Pink'		
Bearberry Cotoneaster	5-9	159
Cotoneaster dammeri		
Blue Chip Juniper	3-9	165
Juniperus horizontalis 'Blue Chip'		
Blue Pacific Shore Juniper	5-9	165
Juniperus conferta 'Blue Pacific'		
Blue Rug Juniper	3-9	166
Juniperus horizontalis 'Wiltonii '		
Coral Bells	3-8	163
Heuchera sanguinea		
Creeping Thyme	5-9	173
Thymus leucotrichus		
Dwarf Coyote Brush	7-10	207
Baccharis pilularis		
Dwarf Japanese Garden Juniper	4-9	166
Juniperus procumbens 'Nana'		
Fountain Grass	5-9	169
Pennisetum alopecuroides		
Germander	4-9	172
Teucrium prostratum		
Goldmoss	4-9	171
Sedum acre		
Mondo Grass	7-9	168
Ophiopogon japonicus		
Prostrate Rosemary	7-10	171
Rosmarinus officinalis 'Irene'		
Purple-Leaf Wintercreeper	4-8	161
Euonymus fortunei 'Coloratus'		
Rock Rose	5-8	162
Helianthemum nummularium		
Snow-on-the-Mountain	3-9	156
Aegopodium podagraria 'Variegatum'		

◆ Vines

Common Name	Zones	Page
Armand Clematis	7-9	179
Clematis armandii		
Boston Ivy	4-8	183
Parthenocissus tricuspidata		
Carolina Yellow Jessamine	7-9	181
Gelsemium sempervirens		
Lady Bank's Climbing Rose	8-10	183
Rosa banksiae		
Porcelain Vine	4-8	178
Ampelopsis brevipedunculata		
Virginia Creeper	4-9	182
Parthenocissus quinquefolia		

Plants for Special Conditions

S pecial conditions require special plants. These selection guides will help you choose plants suitable for growing on slopes, in coastal areas, and on low-water sites. If parts of your yard suffer from car exhaust, reflected heat from paving, or confined root spaces, check out the list of Plants for Urban Areas on page 43. Availability varies by area and conditions (see page 21). Check with your garden center.

Porcelain vine
(Ampelopsis brevipedunculata)
Page 178

Plants for slopes

Common Name	Zones	Page
◆ Trees		
Bailey Acacia	10	192
Acacia baileyana		
Coast Live Oak	9	90
Quercus agrifolia		
Eastern Red Cedar	3-9	81
Juniperus virginiana		
Flowering Dogwood	5-9	76
Cornus florida		
Mesquite	10	197
Prosopis glandulosa		
Paloverde	8-10	193
Cercidium texanum		
Weeping Willow	4-9	94
Salix babylonica		
◆ Shrubs		
Border Forsythia	6-9	125
Forsythia x intermedia		
Chinese Variegated Privet	7-10	135
Ligustrum sinense 'Variegatum'		
Old Gold Juniper	4-10	131
Juniperus chinensis 'Old Gold'		
Pyracantha	6-8	138
Pyracantha coccinea		
Rockspray Cotoneaster	6-9	122
Cotoneaster horizontalis		
Sea Green Juniper	4-8	132
Juniperus chinensis 'Sea Green'		
Showy Jasmine	7-9	131
Jasminum floridum		
Texas Silverado Sage	8-10	202
Leucophyllum frutescens 'Silverado'		
Thorny Elaeagnus	7-9	122
Elaeagnus pungens		
White Rock Rose	8-10	200
Cistus x hybridus		
◆ Groundcovers		
Alba Meidiland Rose	4-8	170
Rosa Alba Meidiland		
Andorra Compact Juniper	3-9	166
Juniperus horizontalis 'Plumosa Compacta'		
Asiatic Jasmine	7-10	173
Trachelospermum asiaticum		
Bar Harbor Juniper	3-9	165
Juniperus horizontalis 'Bar Harbor'		
Bath's Pink	4-9	160
Dianthus gratianopolitanus 'Bath's Pink'		
Bearberry Cotoneaster	5-9	159
Cotoneaster dammeri		
Blanket Flower	2-9	161
Gaillardia x grandiflora		
Blue Chip Juniper	3-9	165
Juniperus horizontalis 'Blue Chip'		
Blue Pacific Shore Juniper	5-9	165
Juniperus conferta 'Blue Pacific'		
Blue Rug Juniper	3-9	166
Juniperus horizontalis 'Wiltonii '		
Dwarf Coyote Brush	7-10	207
Baccharis pilularis		
English Ivy	5-9	162
Hedera helix		
Evergreen Candytuft	4-8	164
Iberis sempervirens		
Freeway Daisy	10	209
Osteospermum fruticosum		
Goldmoss	4-9	171
Sedum acre		

Common Name	Zones	Page
Hardy Ice Plant	6-9	207
Delosperma nubigenum		
Liriope	7-10	167
Liriope muscari		
Littleleaf Periwinkle	4-8	173
Vinca minor		
Mondo Grass	7-9	168
Ophiopogon japonicus		
Moss Phlox	2-9	169
Phlox subulata		
Moss Verbena	8-10	209
Verbena pulchella		
Prostrate Rosemary	7-10	171
Rosmarinus officinalis 'Irene'		
Purple-Leaf Wintercreeper	4-8	161
Euonymus fortunei 'Coloratus'		
Rock Rose	5-8	162
Helianthemum nummularium		
Snow-on-the-Mountain	3-9	156
Aegopodium podagraria 'Variegatum'		
Stonecrop	3-10	172
Sedum spectabile		
Variegated Algerian Ivy	7-10	208
Hedera canariensis 'Variegata'		

Salt-tolerant plants

Common Name	Zones	Page
◆ Trees		
Eastern Red Cedar	3-9	81
Juniperus virginiana		
Hollywood Juniper	4-9	195
Juniperus chinensis 'Torulosa'		
Littleleaf Linden	3-7	96
Tilia cordata		
Sabal Palm	8-10	198
Sabal palmetto		
Sea Grape	10	194
Coccoloba uvifera		
Southern Live Oak	8-10	93
Quercus virginiana		
Southern Magnolia	6-10	83
Magnolia grandiflora		
Wax Myrtle	7-9	86
Myrica cerifera		
Yaupon Holly	7-10	81
Ilex vomitoria		
◆ Shrubs		
American Beautyberry	7-10	120
Callicarpa americana		
Cherry Laurel	6-9	137
Prunus caroliniana		
Dwarf Yaupon Holly	7-10	130
Ilex vomitoria 'Nana'		
Escallonia	9-10	123
Escallonia x exoniensis 'Frades'		
Golden Euonymus	7-9	124
Euonymus japonicus 'Aureus'		
Inkberry	3-10	129
Ilex glabra 'Compacta'		
Ixora	10	202
Ixora coccinea		
New Zealand Tea Tree	9-10	133
Leptospermum scoparium		
Nikko Blue Hydrangea	6-9	126
Hydrangea macrophylla 'Nikko Blue'		
Oleander	8-10	203
Nerium oleander		

Common Name	Zones	Page
Texas Silverado Sage	8-10	202
Leucophyllum frutescens 'Silverado'		
Thorny Elaeagnus	7-9	122
Elaeagnus pungens		
Variegated Pittosporum	8-10	204
Pittosporum tobira 'Variegata'		
White Rock Rose	8-10	200
Cistus x hybridus		
◆ Groundcovers		
Andorra Compact Juniper	3-9	166
Juniperus horizontalis 'Plumosa Compacta'		
Bar Harbor Juniper	3-9	165
Juniperus horizontalis 'Bar Harbor'		
Blanket Flower	2-9	161
Gaillardia x grandiflora		
Blue Chip Juniper	3-9	165
Juniperus horizontalis 'Blue Chip'		
Blue Pacific Shore Juniper	5-9	165
Juniperus conferta 'Blue Pacific'		
Blue Rug Juniper	3-9	166
Juniperus horizontalis 'Wiltonii '		
Dwarf Coyote Brush	7-10	207
Baccharis pilularis		
Freeway Daisy	10	209
Osteospermum fruticosum		
Gold Mound Lantana	9-10	208
Lantana camara 'Gold Mound'		
Liriope	7-10	167
Liriope muscari		
Silver Brocade Artemisia	3-9	157
Artemesia stelleriana 'Silver Brocade'		
◆ Vines		
Silver Lace Vine	4-9	183
Polygonum aubertii		
Virginia Creeper	4-9	182
Parthenocissus quinquefolia		

Plants for low-water sites

Common Name	Zones	Page
◆ Trees		
Arizona Cypress	7-9	194
Cupressus arizonica		
Coast Live Oak	9	90
Quercus agrifolia		
Date Palm	9-10	196
Phoenix dactylifera		
Desert Willow	8-10	194
Chilopsis linearis		
Hollywood Juniper	4-9	195
Juniperus chinensis 'Torulosa'		
Laurel Oak	7-10	197
Quercus laurifolia		
Mesquite	10	197
Prosopis glandulosa		
Olive	8-10	195
Olea europaea		
Paloverde	8-10	193
Cercidium texanum		
Pindo Palm	8-10	192
Butia capitata		
Sabal Palm	8-10	198
Sabal palmetto		
Sea Grape	10	194
Coccoloba uvifera		
Senegal Date Palm	9-10	196
Phoenix reclinata		

Common Name	Zones	Page
◆ **Shrubs**		
Bunny Ears Cactus	10	203
Opuntia microdasys		
Cape Honeysuckle	10	205
Tecomaria capensis		
Cherry Laurel	6-9	137
Prunus caroliniana		
Dwarf Yaupon Holly	7-10	130
Ilex vomitoria 'Nana'		
Fru Dagmar Hastrup Rose	2-9	140
Rosa 'Fru Dagmar Hastrup'		
Golden Arborvitae	6-10	148
Thuja orientalis 'Aurea Nana'		
Old Gold Juniper	4-10	131
Juniperus chinensis 'Old Gold'		
Oleander	8-10	203
Nerium oleander		
Parson's Juniper	3-9	132
Juniperus chinensis 'Parsonii'		
Pyracantha	6-8	138
Pyracantha coccinea		
Rockspray Cotoneaster	6-9	122
Cotoneaster horizontalis		
Rose of Sharon	5-9	125
Hibiscus syriacus		
Sea Green Juniper	4-8	132
Juniperus chinensis 'Sea Green'		
Showy Jasmine	7-9	131
Jasminum floridum		
Texas Silverado Sage	8-10	202
Leucophyllum frutescens 'Silverado'		
Therese Bugnet Rose	3-9	144
Rosa 'Therese Bugnet'		
Thorny Elaeagnus	7-9	122
Elaeagnus pungens		
White Rock Rose	8-10	200
Cistus x hybridus		
◆ **Groundcovers**		
Barrel Cactus	9-10	208
Echinocactus spp.		
Bath's Pink	4-9	160
Dianthus gratianopolitanus 'Bath's Pink'		
Catmint	4-8	168
Nepeta x faassenii		
Dwarf Coyote Brush	7-10	207
Baccharis pilularis		
Freeway Daisy	10	209
Osteospermum fruticosum		
Gold Mound Lantana	9-10	208
Lantana camara 'Gold Mound'		
Hens and Chicks	4-10	209
Sempervivum tectorum		
Moss Phlox	2-9	169
Phlox subulata		
Prostrate Rosemary	7-10	171
Rosmarinus officinalis 'Irene'		
Stonecrop	3-10	172
Sedum spectabile		
◆ **Vines**		
American Bittersweet	3-8	179
Celastrus scandens		
Boston Ivy	4-8	183
Parthenocissus tricuspidata		
Butterfly Vine	9-10	212
Mascagnia macroptera		
Carolina Yellow Jessamine	7-9	181
Gelsemium sempervirens		
Porcelain Vine	4-8	178
Ampelopsis brevipedunculata		
Silver Lace Vine	4-9	183
Polygonum aubertii		
Sweet Autumn Clematis	4-9	181
Clematis paniculata		
Trumpet Vine	4-9	179
Campsis radicans		
Virginia Creeper	4-9	182
Parthenocissus quinquefolia		

Plants for urban areas

Common Name	Zones	Page
◆ **Trees**		
Bradford Pear	4-8	89
Pyrus calleryana 'Bradford'		
Bur Oak	2-8	91
Quercus macrocarpa		
Chinese Elm	5-9	97
Ulmus parvifolia		
Ginkgo	3-9	79
Ginkgo biloba		
Green Ash	3-9	78
Fraxinus pennsylvanica		
Japanese Flowering Crabapple	4-8	85
Malus floribunda		
Japanese Pagoda Tree	6-8	94
Sophora japonica		
Japanese Zelkova	5-9	97
Zelkova serrata		
Littleleaf Linden	3-7	96
Tilia cordata		
Pin Oak	4-8	92
Quercus palustris		
Red Maple	3-9	70
Acer rubrum		
River Birch	4-9	73
Betula nigra		
Royal Palm	10	197
Roystonea elata		
Saucer Magnolia	5-9	84
Magnolia x soulangiana		
Savannah Holly	5-9	80
Ilex opaca 'Savannah'		
Shumard Oak	5-9	93
Quercus shumardii		
Washington Hawthorn	3-9	77
Crataegus phaenopyrum		
Wax Myrtle	7-9	86
Myrica cerifera		
Willow Oak	4-8	92
Quercus phellos		
Yoshino Cherry	5-8	88
Prunus x yedoensis		
◆ **Shrubs**		
African Iris	9-10	203
Moraea iridioides		
Anthony Waterer Spirea	3-9	145
Spiraea japonica 'Anthony Waterer'		
Border Forsythia	6-9	125
Forsythia x intermedia		
Butterfly Bush	5-9	119
Buddleia davidii		
Cherry Laurel	6-9	137
Prunus caroliniana		
Chinese Variegated Privet	7-10	135
Ligustrum sinense 'Variegatum'		
Cleyera	7-10	121
Cleyera japonica		
Dwarf Burning Bush	3-8	123
Euonymus alatus 'Compacta'		
Dwarf Yaupon Holly	7-10	130
Ilex vomitoria 'Nana'		
Glossy Abelia	7-9	114
Abelia x grandiflora		
Golden Arborvitae	6-10	148
Thuja orientalis 'Aurea Nana'		
Indian Hawthorn	8-10	204
Rhaphiolepis indica		
Ixora	10	202
Ixora coccinea		
Nandina	6-9	135
Nandina domestica		
Nellie R. Stevens Holly	6-9	130
Ilex x 'Nellie R. Stevens'		
Old Gold Juniper	4-10	131
Juniperus chinensis 'Old Gold'		
Oleander	8-10	203
Nerium oleander		
Parson's Juniper	3-9	132
Juniperus chinensis 'Parsonii'		
Pygmy Date Palm	9-10	204
Phoenix roebelenii		
Pyracantha	6-8	138
Pyracantha coccinea		

Asiatic Jasmine
(*Trachelospermum asiaticum*)
Page 173

Common Name	Zones	Page
Rockspray Cotoneaster	6-9	122
Cotoneaster horizontalis		
Sasanqua Camellia	7-9	120
Camellia sasanqua		
Sweet Viburnum	8-10	205
Viburnum odoratissimum		
Thorny Elaeagnus	7-9	122
Elaeagnus pungens		
Variegated Croton	10	200
Codiaeum variegatum var. pictum		
Waxleaf Ligustrum	7-10	134
Ligustrum lucidum		
◆ **Groundcovers**		
Andorra Compact Juniper	3-9	166
Juniperus horizontalis 'Plumosa Compacta'		
Asiatic Jasmine	7-10	173
Trachelospermum asiaticum		
Artillery Fern	8-10	169
Pilea serpyllacea 'Rotundifolia'		
Bar Harbor Juniper	3-9	165
Juniperus horizontalis 'Bar Harbor'		
Bearberry Cotoneaster	5-9	159
Cotoneaster dammeri		
Blanket Flower	2-9	161
Gaillardia x grandiflora		
Blue Chip Juniper	3-9	165
Juniperus horizontalis 'Blue Chip'		
Blue Pacific Shore Juniper	5-9	165
Juniperus conferta 'Blue Pacific'		
Blue Rug Juniper	3-9	166
Juniperus horizontalis 'Wiltonii '		
Catmint	4-8	168
Nepeta x faassenii		
Dwarf Japanese Garden Juniper	4-9	166
Juniperus procumbens 'Nana'		
Evergreen Candytuft	4-8	164
Iberis sempervirens		
Flower Carpet Rose	4-10	171
Rose 'Flower Carpet'		
Fountain Grass	5-9	169
Pennisetum alopecuroides		
Freeway Daisy	10	209
Osteospermum fruticosum		
Gold Mound Lantana	9-10	208
Lantana camara 'Gold Mound'		
Goldmoss	4-9	171
Sedum acre		
Hardy Ice Plant	6-9	207
Delosperma nubigenum		
Hens and Chicks	4-10	209
Sempervivum tectorum		
Liriope	7-10	167
Liriope muscari		
Mexican Heather	9-10	207
Cuphea hyssopifola		
Moss Phlox	2-9	169
Phlox subulata		
Moss Verbena	8-10	209
Verbena pulchella		
Prostrate Rosemary	7-10	171
Rosmarinus officinalis 'Irene'		
Purple-Leaf Wintercreeper	4-8	161
Euonymus fortunei 'Coloratus'		
Rock Rose	5-8	162
Helianthemum nummularium		
Spotted Dead Nettle	3-9	167
Lamium maculatum		
Stonecrop	3-10	172
Sedum spectabile		

Chapter 3
how-to

Bedlines create beauty and order, making beautiful spaces functional and easier to maintain. A well-conceived bedline anchors the house with the land around it and creates satisfying points of focus wherever the eye wanders.

Getting the Job Done

ere's where you'll learn to plant and care for your new landscape. We'll show you step-by-step how to get your carefully selected plants into the ground and keep them happy for years to come.

1) Begin with a Bedline

You can usually tell if a landscape was designed before planting or if trees and shrubs were put in without a great deal of thought. The first clue is the bedline. The bedline separates planting areas from lawns. How you draw the line determines the shape of the planting bed on one side and the shape of the lawn area on the other side of it.

Smooth, curving bedlines complement most homes. Such bedlines wrap around corners of houses, decks, patios, walkways, parking areas, and swimming pools. Curving bedlines nestle man-made structures within the landscape.

2) Keep It Simple

It's important to keep bedlines simple. Complicated lines with little curves will make the bedline appear unnatural and the lawn more difficult to mow. Part of your goal is functionality. You should be able to easily mow a perimeter strip around the edge of the bedline before cutting the lawn. Plants in a bed that grow to fill in a single, smooth curve will make your landscape attractive, neat, and easy to maintain.

3) Get It on Paper

Lay a piece of tracing paper over your site analysis and sketch bedline schemes. The sketch will show how planting areas in your yard connect. Leave some areas open for access to doorways and utility areas. Leave access to walk around your house. Build easy routes or pathways into your design to set out trash cans, move the mower from one lawn area to another, and receive deliveries.

Once you've designed a bedline that's both artistic and functional, you're ready to get to work.

STUFF YOU'LL NEED

✔ Garden hose that you don't mind getting paint on
✔ Sharp-shooter or trenching shovel
✔ Marking paint (not regular spray paint)
✔ Inexpensive gloves
✔ Old shoes

What to Expect

You'll probably try several patterns with the hose before you're satisfied with the bedline. Don't rush the process. You'll live with your choice for a long time.

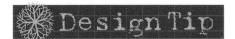

Design Tip

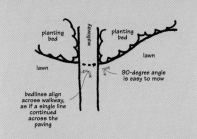

▲ **Right.** Aligning bedlines across a walkway makes the entrance lead into the landscape instead of interrupting it. Always make sure bedlines meet paving or structures at 90 degrees so that lawn areas are wide enough to mow easily.

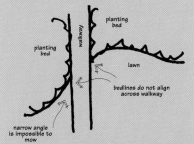

▲ **Wrong.** Bedlines that don't align across a walkway make the paving look like an afterthought. Bedlines that meet paving or structures at narrow angles create slivers of lawn that are difficult to mow, inviting weed growth.

1 Use a garden hose to create an outline. Spread a garden hose in the sun on a driveway or patio for about 15 minutes to make it flexible. Lay the garden hose on the ground in the shape of your proposed bedline. The area inside the hose will become the planting bed; the area outside the hose will remain unchanged.

2 Adjust the hose as needed. Reposition the hose until you like the outline. Smooth the hose to eliminate any dips that give the bedline an unnatural shape. The object is to create a gently flowing curve. If that curve connects to another bedline, flow them smoothly together.

Push your mower alongside the hose to see if you can cut the grass easily. This will help you make the final decision about the shape of your bedline.

3 Spray the grass or ground with marking paint. Don't use regular spray paint and don't spray paving, stones, or plants you want to keep. Remove the hose and examine the shape of the bedline. Make sure you're happy with it before you begin to dig. You can substitute flour for marking paint, but if you do, make sure you finish the job in a day. Flour will wash away if it rains.

Good idea! **Don't spray a thick line until you're sure.** You might change your mind. Try spraying small dashes and then standing back to look. Scuff out and correct areas you don't like, then connect the dashes into a digging line.

Making a Bed

Once you lay out your bedline, it's time to prepare the area inside it for planting. Chances are, the spot you want to convert to a lovely landscape is now full of grass and weeds. The first task is to get rid of plants you don't want.

1 **Spray the bed.** Pick a day for spraying when the weather is hot, sunny, dry, and still. (You don't want the spray to drift onto grass or plants you want to keep.) Using a pump sprayer, cover the area inside the bed with a systemic grass and weed killer. Follow sprayer directions and keep the spray head at the recommended distance above the grass and weeds. Coat all grass and weeds you want to kill. Wait three days for the product to do its work. If you notice green spots, respray as needed. If it rains, give the planting bed an extra day or two to dry out. If the grass and weeds don't appear to be dying, reapply the grass and weed killer on a sunny, still day and wait for it to do the job.

Good idea! **Don't do double duty with your garden sprayer.** Herbicides and fertilizers don't mix. No matter how carefully you wash out the sprayer, residue from the weed killer will remain and damage plants you want to keep. Mark sprayers carefully, and keep them separate in your garden shed.

2 **Shovel-cut the bedline when grass and weeds have turned brown.** Use a narrow-bladed shovel, such as a sharpshooter, to cut a nearly vertical edge along the grassed side of your planting bed. This line separates the new planting bed from existing lawn. Scrape soil away so that the opposite side of the trench rolls upwards into the bed area. Make your V-cut about 6 inches deep so it will hold a 3-inch layer of mulch. If you're planning to install edging, do so now. (See, "Edging Choices," page 47.)

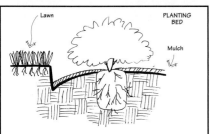

Lawn · PLANTING BED · Mulch

What to Expect

It's easier to keep track of where you've sprayed if you mix food coloring into the systemic herbicide before you start. Don't spray yourself into a corner; walking through fresh spray can leave footprints in your lawns.

Safety Alert!

Wear protective clothing, including eye protection and rubber gloves. Check product labels to see if a respirator is needed. Follow clean-up and disposal instructions.

Homer's Hindsight

It was a little windy the Saturday morning I had planned to work in the yard. I wanted to get things going, so I went ahead and sprayed herbicide on the grass I wanted to kill within my new planting bed. Did I feel foolish the next week when my wife's prize petunias in a nearby bed began to die. Now I know to wait for a still, calm day before spraying herbicide. Sometimes I even prop up a temporary cardboard shield around flowers and plants in adjacent beds before I go to work.

3 Using the same shovel, jab the blade under the roots of dead grass to separate them from the soil.

Scrape and remove all roots, grass, and weeds. If you're tempted to skip these three steps and till live grass under, make sure you're not dealing with a warm-season grass such as bermuda grass or St. Augustine grass. These deep-rooted spreading grasses will resprout if tilled into a new bed.

Get the *'Full Scoop'*

Improve Your Drainage: Good drainage is essential for a thriving bed.
—See page 51

TOOL TIP

A sharpshooter is another name for trenching shovel. It features a long, narrow blade that's straight and sharp. This light shovel is easy to use and good for digging straight down.

A sod lifter has a blade attached at an angle from the handle. It's easier to slide the sharp, flat end beneath grass roots.

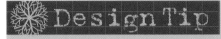

Edging Choices

You can keep bedlines neat by cutting the edges with a sharp shovel every few months. Or, install edging to form a barrier. The purposes of edging are to delineate the bedline, to make it more difficult for grass to grow into the bed or for groundcovers to spread into the lawn, and to provide a solid edge for mowing or trimming against. Brick, stone, or steel can do the job. Plastic edging is another choice. Install it carefully so the edging is inserted into the ground all the way to the rounded plastic lip. Pack soil firmly on both sides of the edging to keep it from popping out.

Edging creates neatly shaped bedlines to resist encroaching grass and weeds.

how-to **3**

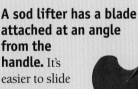

'Organic Grass Removal'

If you want to save the grass you're removing and it's dense, thick, and free of weeds, or you don't like the idea of using herbicides, rent a sod cutter. This machine uses sharp, scissors-action blades to cut sod so you can lift and remove sections of grass. Have the associate at the rental house teach you how to use the cutter before you go to work. Lawn pieces removed with a sod cutter are suitable for planting elsewhere. Keep cut sod moist. Replant as soon as possible and water thoroughly. Keep watering regularly until the sod has reestablished itself in its new location.

A well-prepared planting bed adds more than beauty and order to your landscape. The proper balance of nutrients and good drainage helps new plants succeed.

TOOL TIP

Prevention helps keeps weeds down, but you'll still need to do some digging. The classic garden hoe is a great weeder but here are some tools to make the job easier:

- **Warren hoe**—this hoe has a pointed blade for hooking into roots and pulling them out.

- **Hula hoe**— Use this hooped hoe to grub away weeds.

- **Hoe-Matic**— This hand tool has a rake on one end and and an ax head on the other.

- **Hoe mattock**—This hand tool has a claw on one end and and an ax head on the other.

Bed Preparation

Think of the soil in your yard as an aquarium and the plants you're adding as fish. They both have requirements for survival. Fish need the right kind of water, and plants need the right kind of soil. Prepare your bed correctly, and you'll give your landscape the right start.

The more you prep the soil prior to planting, the more hospitable it becomes for plants. Tilling, digging, and turning the ground loosens soil and makes it easier for water to percolate. Loose soil allows air to reach roots and makes it easier for them to spread.

Ideally, you should till your entire planting bed area before setting out the first plant. Prepping the entire bed is especially important when planting groundcover. Usually, these plants are set out at a smaller size than shrubs and are planted closer together. Tilling the whole bed is more efficient than digging lots of little holes and makes arranging the plants more efficient. Save the shovel for planting individual trees, shrubs, and vines. Though working the entire bed is preferable, you can improve the soil you use to fill planting holes— known as backfill—to give new trees and shrubs a good start. Whether you till or dig, mix in amendments prior to planting. Organic matter— such as well-composted manure, composted plant

debris, or leaf mold—is an excellent amendment for any soil type. When mixed into sandy or rocky soil, organic matter slows the flow of water, giving roots a chance to absorb moisture. Organic matter mixed into heavy clay soil does the opposite. It creates air spaces between the densely packed soil particles, improving drainage. Organic matter also supplies nutrients to roots.

Mix soil amendments with native soil at a ratio of 1:1. This helps plants adapt to native soil as roots spread. When you dig holes, pile the

Tilling the entire planting bed guarantees a consistent mixture of amendments in the soil. Tillers are available at most rental outlets. Get a lesson and safety tips from a qualified salesperson.

soil on a tarp or in a wheelbarrow. Mix in amendments, chopping and sifting lumps with your shovel before backfilling the hole around the roots of new plants. Without native soil as part of the mix, roots are discouraged from spreading beyond the backfill. In areas with high rainfall and heavy clay soil mix native soil with organic matter at a ratio of 4:1.

Keeping Weeds Down

Weeds will like your freshly prepared bed as much as your new plants do. Here's how to keep weeds down while your landscape gets started.

• **Apply preemergent herbicide.** Use on bare soil before you set out container-grown or balled-and-burlapped plants. (Follow product label instructions and don't use this kind of herbicide if you plan to sow your new bed with seeds.) Preemergents prevent seeds from germinating and will stop weed growth during the first growing season. Reapply each spring as needed by scratching into the soil around plants.

Preemergents won't hurt plants that are already growing.

• **Mulch, mulch, mulch.** The thicker the layer, the harder it is for weeds to penetrate and grow. Organic mulches such as shredded wood, bark, or compost are ideal because they also break down to supply nutrients to plants. Replenish mulch annually to keep layers about 3 inches thick. Tuck mulch carefully around stems of plants you want to keep; never pile mulch at the base of plants. Rock mulches also cover the ground, retarding weed growth. No matter what you do, tough weeds will eventually push their way upward. Plastic weed mats discourage weeds, but trap heat beneath them, raising soil temperatures higher than many plant roots prefer.

• **The best defense against plants you don't want is plenty of plants that you do want.** Bare soil is an invitation to weed growth. Crowd weeds out with groundcovers and shrubs. Leave some soil surface bare to allow new plants room to grow, fill in bare spots with groundcover as quickly as possible.

Raised Beds

Building the soil up is an alternative to digging down.
Raised beds offer the advantage of filling the entire planting area with good soil. Raised beds are good choices for spots with compacted or clay soils that don't drain well and for areas where the soil is full of tree roots. Make sure raised beds are open to the soil beneath. Sealing them with paving traps water.

Sweet and sour

Alkaline soil (sweet) and acidic soil (sour) occupy different ends of the pH scale and present different growing issues.

The easiest way to deal with sweet or sour soils is to grow plants that love them. You can also balance the pH to suit your needs. A pH reading of 7 (the pH of water) is considered neutral. Alkaline soils have pH numbers greater than 7. Acidic soils have pH numbers lower than 7. Average garden soil has a pH between 5 and 7. The ideal level for the largest range of plants is a pH reading between 6 and 7.

Peat moss is extremely acidic. Add it to reduce the pH of alkaline soils, such as arid desert soil.

Add **ground dolomitic limestone** to raise the pH of acidic soils. See pages 40-41 for plants that prefer alkaline or acidic soil.

Wisdom of the Aisles

Dealing with heavy clay:
• Gypsum is a valuable soil amendment for improving the structure of clay soils. (It also adds calcium; don't introduce it to soil with high calcium content.) Instead of adding gypsum to backfill, mix it into native soil first, tilling or digging it in deeply to separate sticky soil particles. This works little pockets of air into the soil, allowing water to flow through more freely instead of trapping it around roots, which can cause plants to drown. A couple of pounds of gypsum will amend about 100 square feet of bed area.
• When planting trees and shrubs in hard clay soil, use your shovel to scrape and roughen the sides of the hole. Slick-sided holes function much like clay pots, keeping the roots confined to the hole and trapping water.
• Some plants—such as azaleas and gardenias—are particularly sensitive to standing water collecting around their roots. When landscaping in clay soil, plant such shrubs high so root balls protrude an inch or two above the surface of the ground, ensuring that water will drain away from the roots.
• Gypsum does not affect soil pH.

A watering wand attached on a hose produces a spray similar to rainfall and gets in hard-to-reach places.

Keeping Plants Happy

M aking sure plants get the proper amount of water is critical. Rainfall is the best source of water for plants, but it isn't always plentiful. Here's the scoop on watering.

Deep Watering makes plants tougher. You can't actually drought-proof your plants, but you can prepare them for dry spells to give your landscape a fighting chance. To deep water, apply water slowly for long periods of time at infrequent intervals. Roots learn to follow water that seeps down into soil, making them less prone to suffering during dry spells. If you water often and quickly instead, you'll only dampen the top layer of soil. As a result, roots tend to stay within this area instead of digging deeper to seek moisture. Roots near the surface are more likely to wither during dry periods than roots that grow downward.

An automatic sprinkler system makes watering easy. Valves control water flow through pipes buried underground to sprinkler heads placed at ground level. Sprinklers are turned on and off by timers. Install automatic watering systems before you plant; trenching to lay pipes can damage existing plants.

Drip irrigation systems deliver water directly to the roots instead of through the air. Watering roots conserves water and prevents many fungal problems caused by wet foliage. Most drip systems are installed by burying flexible tubing beneath mulch. They can also be controlled by timers.

Hand watering works if you're diligent and patient. Many people enjoy the time spent watering their yards—it's therapeutic. The key to hand watering is consistency. If you get off schedule, your plants suffer, especially if you go away for an extended period of time. Trees and large shrubs need water too. A good soaking beneath the entire dripline is best, not just a quick spray while you're watering the flowers.

Troubleshooting is always a part of landscaping. Here are some common conditions and solutions to watering problems:

• **Too Much or Too Little** Those plants that prefer poor, dry soil will struggle with too much water. Plants requiring rich, moist soil will not thrive in dry locations.

Solution: Research plant needs thoroughly before you install.

• **Underwatering** Broad-leaved plants wilt in order to expose less leaf surface to sunshine. Foliage becomes crispy around the edges as though burned. Evergreens maintain their form but foliage becomes dry and discolored.

Solution: Check in-ground plants weekly and containerized plants daily for water needs. Poke a finger or dig a small hole a few inches below the soil surface near the plant. If the soil feels dry, the plant needs water. Apply a slow, gentle stream of water to the base, allowing the water to soak down to the roots.

• **Overwatering** Too much water produces the same symptoms as underwatering. Check the soil as above. If the soil is moist but still crumbly, lack of water is probably not the problem.

Solution: If the soil has any of the four "s" symptoms—soupy, sticky, soggy, or smelly—cut back on your watering schedule. Let the soil dry out between waterings.

Wisdom of the Aisles

When you water is as important as how you water.
The earlier in the day the better. (That's when timers come in handy.) If you wait until plants are struggling, watering becomes a form of first aid instead of a regular part of their care. Watering in the late afternoon or evening means your plants will have suffered during the hottest hours of the day. And, foliage might not have a chance to dry before nightfall, making conditions ripe for fungal problems. Soil and mulch that stay damp overnight invite soft-bodied pests, such as slugs and snails.

These simple timers attach directly to the hose and can be programmed to provide regular watering cycles.

Drainage Solutions

Too much water can harm plants by filling air pockets in the soil and drowning roots or by washing plants away. Here are some methods for making soggy soil drier, keeping storm water from blasting plants from their beds, and preventing puddles from forming. Keep in mind that it usually isn't legal to increase the amount of water that drains across property lines, so don't dump your excess water on your neighbor's property.

French Drains

French drains disperse water that becomes trapped in soil. They're used where pounding rain spills from roof edges, confined planting beds meet paving, or retaining walls cause groundwater to accumulate. To install:

- **Dig a trench that's 8 to 12 inches wide and deep.** Slope the trench downhill about one-eighth inch per foot. Extend as far from the problem area as possible.
- **Fill the trench with an inch or two of coarse gravel.** Rinse the gravel first to keep debris from clogging pipes later. Maintain the downward slope of the trench when adding gravel.
- **Place a 3- to 4-inch-wide perforated plastic pipe on top of the gravel bed.**
- **Wrap the pipe in a filter sleeve.** This will prevent holes from clogging. You can also buy perforated plastic pipe that's already wrapped in a filter sleeve. If the pipe has holes on just one side, lay this side face down.
- **Fill the rest of the trench with washed gravel, surrounding the pipe completely.** The top of the gravel in the trench should be level with the adjacent soil.

Downspouts

Downspouts are often the culprits when plants, topsoil, and mulch are washed away by a blast of water.

Solve the problem by connecting a flexible pipe to the end of the downspout. Bury the pipe in a trench. If you can, run the pipe to a lower spot in the yard where water can flow from the far end. Wedge a flat stone beneath the end of a drain pipe where it empties onto the ground. This helps prevent erosion. If it isn't possible to "daylight" the pipe—letting the low end open onto the soil's surface—build a long French drain to disperse the water, instead (see above).

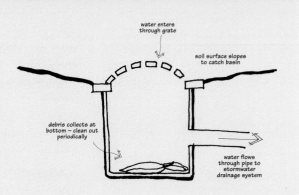

Catch Basins

Catch basins collect excess surface water so it can be moved elsewhere through underground pipes.

Set a catch basin at a low point where water puddles. Dig a hole just big enough to house the catch basin. This drainage device is topped with a grate to admit water. (Hint: domed grates help prevent mulch from washing into catch basins.) You'll need to dig a trench leading from your catch basin to an area where you want to release the water, such as a natural area or storm drainage system. Lay plastic drain pipe in the trench and connect it to the catch basin.

water enters through grate

soil surface slopes to catch basin

debris collects at bottom — clean out periodically

water flows through pipe to stormwater drainage system

Plants have varying nutritional needs. Choosing the right fertilizer and applying the right amount at the right time will keep your landscape a showplace.

Fertilizing

Fertilizing provides plants a good, balanced diet. Adding plenty of organic amendments at planting gives plants a healthy start. Properly applied fertilizers keeps them flourishing.

The Key is N-P-K.

Fertilizers are combinations of major elements, nitrogen (N), phosphorus (P), and potassium (K) along with other minor elements such as calcium (Ca), magnesium (Mn), and iron (Fe). N, P, and K are listed on the label in order. Bags labeled as complete fertilizers contain various percentages of N, P, and K and may contain minor elements as well. Balanced fertilizers contain equal amounts of N, P, and K. A label that reads 6-6-6 means there is 6 percent of each element; the remainder is inert matter. The larger the numbers, the higher the percentage of fertilizer. Use fertilizers with lower matching numbers in hot, dry weather to avoid chemical burns on plants. Higher matching numbers are good for cool, wet conditions when plants absorb elements easily. Different numbers indicate that the product contains N, P, and K in unequal amounts. Select fertilizers with higher percentages of specific elements to solve problems and match growing requirements. (See It's Elemental—Know Your N-P-K, right.) A fertilizer labeled 8-12-4 contains 8 percent nitrogen, 12 percent phosphorus, and 4 percent potassium. Always read labels on fertilizers before applying. If you're confused, look for plant lists on the label or a general description that fits the plant you want to feed.

Synthetic Fertilizers

are man-made. They may be dry—in granular, powder, or pellet form—or liquid. All come with instructions for proper use. Keep dry fertilizer away from foliage and avoid mounding it at the base of plants. Instead, scratch it into the soil around plants and water well. Slow-release fertilizers have coated pellets that disintegrate, releasing fertilizer over a longer period of time and are unlikely to burn plants. Mix them into the soil at planting or around established

Liquid or slow-release fertilizers are the best choice for tightly clustered plants to avoid burning foliage.

plants. Apply liquid fertilizers directly to plant leaves or spray onto moistened soil. Liquid fertilizers allow quick plant uptake.

Natural Fertilizers also

come in dry or liquid forms. Many provide only one nutrient and are not complete fertilizers. For example, bloodmeal supplies nitrogen that will quickly green up failing plants. Bonemeal provides phosphorus for root growth and flower formation. You might need to use more than one product to provide complete fertilization. Fish emulsion is a liquid fertilizer that can be applied to damp soil or directly to leaves. Benefits of natural fertilizers are listed on each product label. Natural fertilizers are more difficult to balance than synthetics. Natural products can also be used to amend the soil pH. Cottonseed meal makes soil more acidic, while limestone makes it more alkaline. Natural fertilizers work best on warm days.

Troubleshooting

• **Overfertilizing** Plants that are overfertilized compensate by shutting down and slowing growth. Foliage turns yellow or brown but remains on branches. Plants look burned. Flowering plants produce more leaves than blossoms.

Solution: Check the soil. You could have a watering problem. If the soil moisture is normal and you've been fertilizing frequently, stop immediately. Supply the plant with plenty of water to leach excess chemicals from the soil.

• **Underfertilizing** Foliage becomes discolored, turning a more yellowish hue. Growth becomes distorted or stunted.

Solution: Give the soil a finger-test first to find if it is too wet or too dry before fertilizing. Find a fertilizer that describes or lists your plant on the label. Follow directions carefully.

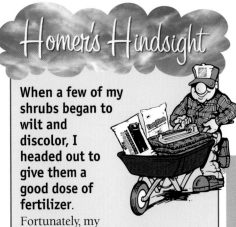

Homer's Hindsight

When a few of my shrubs began to wilt and discolor, I headed out to give them a good dose of fertilizer. Fortunately, my neighbor saw what I was up to and pointed out that the soil in the area was soggy. He went on to say that fertilizing overwatered shrubs is like shoving a cheeseburger in the mouth of a drowning man! I put the fertilizer back in my shed, temporarily raked the mulch away to speed up drying, and cut back on watering. These days my shrubs are in great shape.

It's Elemental–Know Your N-P-K

Understanding package labels is necessary for using fertilizers correctly.

You'll see the letters N-P-K on lots of fertilizer labels. Here's what they mean:

N is for Nitrogen. This element promotes green growth and lush foliage. But if you use too much of it, you could end up with more leaves than flowers. That's why a balanced fertilizer is a good idea.

P is for Phosphorus. Your plants need phosphorus for good root growth and strong production of flowers and fruit.

K is for Potassium. This element is vital for the general well-being of plants. Potassium helps neutralize ground salts that can make soil less than hospitable for growth.

You can feed at different speeds. The kind of granular fertilizer you choose affects the rate at which plants will absorb nutrients.

Slow-release. Fertilizers that are coated break down slowly, so plants don't get all the good stuff at one time. This is valuable because plants have access to a longer-lasting supply of nutrients. Because slow-release fertilizers are coated, there's no need to worry about burning plants when fertilizer is freshly applied.

Fast-release. These fertilizers are good for a quick fix. But they don't last long and must be "watered in" when applied to avoid burning plants. Keep away from foliage.

Saucer Magnolia (Magnolia X soulangiana) Page 84

Planting Bare-Root Roses

Whether you're planting bare-root roses or plants grown in containers, learn how to get new roses off to the best start.

Bare-root roses are shipped without soil, making them less expensive. They look like stubby sticks. You'll find these plants for sale in late winter or early spring. Plant them soon after purchasing.

1 Carefully open the packaging. Avoid cutting roots. Gently remove packing material from roots and discard. Place the roots in a bucket of water mixed with root stimulator. Allow them to soak in a dark, cool, dry location such as a garage. Soak roots no longer than eight hours.

2 Dig a hole in a spot that receives at least six hours of sun daily. The hole should be 12 to 18 inches deep. Mix bagged compost with some of the native soil in a wheelbarrow or on a tarp to create a mixture that's about two-thirds organic matter and one-third native soil. The soil mixture should appear dark and rich.

3 Shovel the good soil mixture into the hole until it's nearly full. Use your hands to form a cone of soil in the center of the hole. Make the top of the cone slightly below the level of adjacent undisturbed soil. Position the rose on top of the cone, spreading roots evenly around it.

4 Backfill around the rose with soil. Make sure the scion (the ridge where the rose was grafted to the rootstock) is still visible above the soil. Add a thick layer of compost for mulch. Use excess native soil to form a moat around the freshly planted rose. Fill moat with a slowly trickling hose.

Good idea!

Before planting, use a pair of good-quality hand pruners to trim away any roots that have jagged ends. This replaces rough edges with a good clean cut. Without overdoing it, remove any excessively long, dead, or broken roots.

Planting Containerized Roses

Roses grown in containers cost more than bare-root plants, but you get leaves and often buds right away.

1 **Dig a hole to the proper depth.** Check the depth by setting the rose, still in its container, into the hole. The soil in the container should be level with undisturbed soil around the hole. If the hole is too deep, remove the rose and add some soil to the bottom of the hole. If it's too shallow, you'll need to dig a little more.

2 **Gently slide the rose from its container and place it in the hole.** Remember, it's better to destroy the pot than the plant; cut the container with a utility knife if necessary. Don't pull on the plant.

3 **Fill the hole to the proper depth.** Mix bagged compost with native soil to create a mixture that's about two-thirds organic matter and one-third native soil and fill around the plant. Do not add any soil to the top of the root ball. Use excess soil to form a moat around the plant as wide as the depth of the hole. Mulch this area with compost before filling it slowly with a small, gentle stream from a hose. Mist newly planted roses frequently during the first week or so if the weather is hot and wilting occurs. Keep the soil around roots moist but not soggy while the plant adjusts to its new home.

Grafted and Nongrafted Roses

Keep the scion of grafted roses above ground. The scion is the ridge where the preferred variety was grafted onto sturdier rootstock. If buried, shoots may grow from the rootstock instead of the rose you want. When planting, keep the scion above the soil line. If a freeze is predicted, temporarily cover the scion with mulch.

Bury the crowns of nongrafted roses. The crown of the plant is the point where branches emerge from the main stem just above the roots. Make sure it's low enough to be covered with an inch or two of soil at planting.

Climbing Rose Care

• **When planting climbing roses, tilt the plant in the hole so that canes lean toward supports.** You'll get more blooms if you train climbers to grow horizontally, creating layers of greenery. Bend young flexible stems around supports or tie them with plant ties or rose clips.

• **Cut away dead canes in late winter, before new greenery appears.** This will encourage fresh growth in spring. Do not cut into main stems; always make cuts along the outer edges of the plant, leaving small stubs.

• **When leaves and blossoms appear,** some lower canes might be totally bare. Cut these about a foot above the ground to remove and encourage new growth.

Caring for Roses

Pruning roses is important to keep plants vigorous.

Prune roses at any time except before a freeze; trimming while plants are dormant makes it easier to see the structure of the plant and what you are doing.

What to Expect
Many roses have thorns; arm yourself with long sleeves and gloves while pruning.

1

Right:

Cut angles away from bud and about 1/4 inch above.

1 **Make the right cut.** The first order of business is making a proper cut. Cuts should be made on live canes about one-fourth inch above an outward facing bud. Angle your pruners so the tip is cut at a 45-degree slant away from the bud. Apply pruning sealer to fresh cuts to prevent damage from insects and diseases.

In the Zone

Why Prune?

Proper pruning keeps plants healthy. You'll need to trim roses each year to remove dead wood, improve air circulation, eliminate rubbing canes, reduce height, and encourage new, vigorous growth with plenty of blossoms..

Wrong:

Cut angles toward bud; rain washes to the bud.

Wrong:

Cut is too far above the bud and it's flat, not angled.

Wrong:

Cut is too close to the bud.

2

2 **Cut away darkened, dead wood.** Live canes will be green, and buds will be visible.

Wisdom of the Aisles

Preventative Medicine.
A few simple steps now will avoid problems later on. Dip cutting tools in rubbing alcohol or bleach after each cut. This helps prevent the spread of disease. Always collect rose clippings instead of letting them fall into garden beds. Clippings may harbor pests or diseases, so you'll need to destroy them. Do not compost rose clippings.

3

3 **Locate any canes that rub together.** Remove the one that is angling into the center of the plant near the base. Do not cut into the main stem; instead, prune the offending cane where it emerges from the main stem, leaving a little knob of growth known as a collar. If the cane is thicker than a pencil, use bypass loppers instead of hand pruners.

4 **Thin the center of thick shrub roses to improve air circulation.** Leave strong main stems uncut and prune away selected thin, twiggy canes. Remove canes from the center of the plant only, not the outside. Choose canes randomly from the plant's center, leaving nubs of growth so cuts don't go completely back to main stems. Reduce the overall size of a shrub rose if needed. Select your desired height and cut individual canes to that level.

5 **Remove individual fading blooms.** This encourages new buds for more flowers. A good rule of thumb is to remove spent flowers by cutting just above the first set of five healthy leaves.

6 **After pruning for winter, apply a dormant spray.** This preventative step makes sure that insects and diseases don't overwinter in your rose plants. Follow product directions. Dormant spray is the primary line of defense against rose mosaic, which causes leaves to appear skeletonized.

Rose Care—Symptoms & Solutions

Roses may require spraying to control problems.

If you know what to look for and what product to use, you've already won half the battle. Here are some common culprits. When seeking advice from a garden staffer, take a sample cutting with you. Begin your spray program as soon as first leaves appear.

Symptom: Orange powdery blemishes on foliage indicate rust.
Solution: Spray rust with a fungicide containing thiophanate-methyl.

Symptom: A grayish-white coating covers foliage, distorting young shoots.
Solution: Spray powdery mildew with a fungicide containing triforine, folpet, or thiophanate-methyl. Watering early in the day allows foliage to dry, preventing this problem.

Symptom: Black spots appear on foliage; leaves fall off.
Solution: Spray with a fungicide containing thiophante-methyl, chlorothalonil, mancozeb, or triforine. Allow foliage to dry by watering early in the day to prevent this problem. Rake up and destroy fallen leaves.

Symptom: Brown buds develop and flowers are few and oddly shaped, probably caused by tiny bugs such as thrips or mites.
Solution: Spray with a systemic insecticide containing acephate. Remove buds and blooms by hand and destroy.

Symptom: New leaves are curled and stunted; foliage is shiny and sticky. Little green bugs called aphids are visible.
Solution: Knock them off with a stiff spray of water. Control with insecticidal soap or a contact-killer spray. For long-term control, apply a systemic insecticide containing acephate.

Feeding Roses

Most roses are heavy feeders— they require more fertilizer than many other landscape plants. A fertilizer that contains higher amounts of phosphorus and potassium than nitrogen will encourage the growth of flowers instead of just leaves. Look for a fertilizer that lists a smaller first number (N) on its label than the next two numbers (P and K). Fertilizers identified as rose foods make it easy. They contain elements balanced to give roses just what they need. Slow-release fertilizers are coated to prevent all the nutrients from entering the soil at once. They supply benefits over a longer period of time than noncoated fertilizers. Some granular fertilizers also supply systemic insecticides for preventative care.

Feed roses each year when new growth is about 3 inches long. Rake away mulch and scratch dry fertilizers into the soil around plants, watering well before covering with mulch again. Feed roses again in autumn, at least a month before the first frost. In frost-free areas, continue feeding according to package directions. Fertilize again when pruning plants in late winter.

Foliar Feeding. Liquid fertilizer (foliar feed) can be applied directly to leaves. Temperatures should be below 90 degrees when applying. You can use liquid fertilizer as often as every week to correct nutrient deficiencies. Always apply liquid fertilizers in the early morning to allow leaves to dry thoroughly as quickly as possible. Damp leaves can lead to fungal problems, especially if foliage is left wet overnight.

Chapter 4
trees

Trees are the backbone of good design, providing color, texture, line, and form. They also offer shade, protection from wind and rain, and shelter for other plants in your yard. Because most trees take longer than other plants to mature, the sooner you get new trees started in your landscape, the better.

The Value of Trees

Start your landscape with trees. A single, well-placed tree impacts your yard more than any other landscaping item. Most trees are long-lasting and embody the elements of good design—color, texture, line, and form. Planting trees first shapes planting beds and gives them a head start on growth while you work on other parts of your landscape.

Trees Solve Problems

Look over the notes from your site analysis. Trees might solve the problem areas you identified. Carefully chosen trees put privacy where you need it, add shade, dress up patios and entries, deflect wind, and establish a background for your landscape. Good selection is more important than quantity. Picking the right trees to fill the right needs is more effective than planting whatever you happen to find on sale. Look at the selection guides on the following pages, then go to the tree encyclopedia later in this book to help make your final decisions.

Consider These Factors

Defining the jobs you want new trees to do helps identify desirable characteristics. Think about whether you need a tree that keeps its foliage year-round (evergreen) or sheds its leaves once a year (deciduous). Evergreen trees offer more privacy but usually grow more slowly than deciduous trees. Deciduous trees make good choices for producing summer shade.

Keep in mind that the right plant in the right place is critical to success. Before adding a tree to your yard, you need to know its ultimate size and how long it will take to reach maturity. After all, it's a shame to prune a tall, stately tree severely because you didn't take telephone or power lines into account at planting. Knowing how big a tree will get also helps you avoid the common problem of planting a tree that will grow large too close to your house. You'll also want to know if the tree has any characteristics that make it undesirable for the purpose you have in mind. For example, trees

Rapid Growers

Rapidly growing trees can improve your landscape in a hurry. Position new trees properly in the landscape, dig large-sized planting holes, provide good soil, water adequately (see page 50), and watch your trees take off. Find out all you can about the trees you are considering for your landscape. Growth rate is just one bit of information provided in the tree encyclopedia pages. Look on plant tags and ask garden associates for additional

Irregularly shaped trunks and limbs become unusual framing devices, creating points of interest in a landscape.

information if needed. Knowing the growth rate will help you decide the size of tree to purchase. If you've decided on a slow grower, consider planting one that's larger in size so you won't have to wait several years before enjoying it. A Japanese maple used as a focal point in an entry area or courtyard is a tree worth buying big. Other trees, such as river birches, grow so quickly that you needn't go to the expense of purchasing large ones. Remember that faster-growing trees usually have weaker wood and shorter lifespans than their slower-growing counterparts. Availability varies by area and conditions (see page 21). Check with your garden center.

Common Name	Zones	Page	Common Name	Zones	Page
Arizona Cypress	7-9	194	Mexican Washington Palm	9-10	199
Cupressus arizonica			*Washingtonia robusta*		
Bailey Acacia	10	192	Pecan	5-9	74
Acacia baileyana			*Carya illinoinensis*		
Bald Cypress	4-10	95	Pin Oak	4-8	92
Taxodium distichum			*Quercus palustris*		
Bradford Pear	4-8	89	Possum Haw	3-9	79
Pyrus calleryana 'Bradford'			*Ilex decidua*		
Chinese Elm	5-9	97	Purple-Leaf Plum	4-8	88
Ulmus parvifolia			*Prunus cerasifera 'Atropurpurea'*		
Crepe Myrtle	7-9	82	Red Maple	3-9	70
Lagerstroemia indica			*Acer rubrum*		
Crimson Bottlebrush	9-10	193	Redbud	3-9	75
Callistemon citrinus			*Cercis canadensis*		
Dawn Redwood	4-8	86	River Birch	4-9	73
Metasequoia glyptostroboides			*Betula nigra*		
Desert Willow	8-10	194	Saucer Magnolia	5-9	84
Chilopsis linearis			*Magnolia x soulangiana*		
Green Ash	3-9	78	Scarlet Oak	4-9	91
Fraxinus pennsylvanica			*Quercus coccinea*		
Japanese Pagoda Tree	6-8	94	Shumard Oak	5-9	93
Sophora japonica			*Quercus shumardii*		
Japanese Zelkova	5-9	97	Silver Maple	3-9	72
Zelkova serrata			*Acer saccharinum*		
Laurel Oak	7-10	197	Wax Myrtle	7-9	86
Quercus laurifolia			*Myrica cerifera*		
Leyland Cypress	6-9	77	Weeping Willow	4-9	94
X Cupressocyparis leylandii			*Salix babylonica*		
Lilac Chaste Tree	6-10	199	White Pine	3-8	87
Vitex agnus-castus			*Pinus strobus*		
Mesquite	10	197	Willow Oak	4-8	92
Prosopis glandulosa			*Quercus phellos*		
Mexican Bird-of-Paradise	10	192	Yaupon Holly	7-10	81
Caesalpinia mexicana			*Ilex vomitoria*		

with large root systems that buckle paving are poor choices for planting next to patios, sidewalks, parking areas, or streets. These areas need trees that have well-behaved roots. They should also thrive next to the reflected heat of paving. (Always check easements and right-of-way restrictions before planting.) Find out if trees have invasive roots so

you can avoid planting them around septic and drainage systems. Finally, know what it takes to care for your new trees before you plant them. Don't make high-maintenance choices if you desire a low-maintenance landscape. Throughout the following pages, you'll find the details to help you choose the right trees for your landscape.

Legacy Trees

Celebrating a major family event by planting a tree is a time-honored tradition. Trees that are known for slow growth and large size are also good choices for longevity. Ginkgos, Southern live oaks, and Southern magnolias are trees that will commemorate great moments for many generations to come.

Planting a legacy tree such as a Southern magnolia (Magnolia grandiflora) Page 83, connects generations, establishing a family home.

Wisdom of the Aisles

Trees can actually affect the climate around your home. Trees suitable for use as windbreaks make a big difference when positioned to deflect harsh northwestern winter winds. Deciduous trees planted along the southern and southeastern sides of your home offer cooling shade during the warm seasons. Then they shed their leaves, allowing winter rays to light and warm your home. Choosing trees known for providing leafy shade can make a big difference when positioned to block hot afternoon summer sun coming from the west.

trees

4

These Queen palms (Syagrus romanzoffianum), page 198, lend architectural interest even though they don't provide full shade.

Buying a Tree

C hoosing a good tree and getting it home from the store safely are the first steps in creating a landscape.

Trees are sold as container-grown, balled-and-burlapped, and bareroot. Containerized trees have lived their lives in nursery pots. Balled-and-burlapped trees—also known as B&B—start their lives in tree farm fields. After they're dug up with tree spades, their root balls are wrapped with fabric for shipping. Bare-root types (such as fruit trees) come with roots carefully surrounded with packing inside a plastic bag or set in sawdust.

Trees with big broad leaves provide shade and protection from the elements.

Container vs. B&B Trees grown in containers are often smaller than ones wrapped in burlap. Root growth is limited by the size of the container. Because they don't have to be removed from the ground, container-grown trees are less likely to go into shock and lose their leaves when planted. Garden shops, home centers, and nurseries carry wide selections of container-grown trees. They are often easier for most consumers to handle and are available for a longer period of time during the growing season. B&B trees are for sale only during early spring or late fall.

Shopping Tips

• **Choose a tree with bigger caliper.** A thick trunk is sturdier than a tall, skinny-trunked tree.

• **Check the firmness of the root ball.** If the tree and root ball move as one, it has developed a good, firm root ball. If the tree is loose within the soil in the container, it has only recently been "stepped up" from a smaller pot into the larger container. Roots are the most important thing you buy when you purchase any plant. Bypass a tree that hasn't been in its container long enough to develop roots to fill the container. If the root ball of a B&B tree is cracked or crumbling, find another tree.

• **Look at the tree roots.** A tree that has long, white roots protruding from the bottom drainage hole has been in its container too long and is root-bound. Though you can grow such a tree successfully, it shouldn't be your first choice. A root-bound tree takes longer to put out fresh feeder roots in its new home.

- **Avoid trees that have nicks or wounds to their trunks.** These trees are damaged and may attract insects or develop disease problems.
- **Know the form of the mature tree.** If a tree is supposed to have multiple trunks, that's one thing. But if a particular kind of tree normally has a single, straight trunk, don't purchase one that divides into a double trunk. Water collecting in the crotch can cause splitting because of rot or the formation of ice. High winds may damage an improperly formed tree, too. It pays to know what form is correct before you buy.
- **Check the tree container.** Trees with burlap-wrapped root balls are sometimes set in containers for easier handling. A layer of bark is then added to cover the burlap and keep the root ball moist. These are good trees, just not container grown. Check beneath the mulch to see what you're getting. If you see

Rich fall colors make trees desirable additions to any landscape. Even in hotter climates seasonal changes make beautiful transitions.

burlap, the tree was dug from a nursery field and is balled-and-burlapped, not container grown.

Fall is for Planting
Autumn is an excellent time to plant woody trees and shrubs. Cold weather slows growth above ground, so a plant's energy is put into expanding roots beneath the ground. Cool weather puts less stress on new trees than hot weather does. Regular watering is not as critical. Insect and disease problems are fewer in fall and winter than in spring and summer. Planting in the fall gives you a jump start on next spring.

Tree Mortality

Plants that have been transported from one location to another and then replanted are under a great deal of stress. Some will die through no fault of yours. If the plant is mishandled at any point during the shipping process, the damage has been done before you buy it.

Newly planted trees and shrubs that turn completely brown and hold their leaves instead of dropping them are not going into transplant shock (see page 64). This symptom usually indicates that the plant has died. To test whether your tree is dead or alive, use your fingernail to scratch the thin bark of a branch. If you see green, your tree is alive. If you see brown or gray beneath the bark, try again on other branches or even on the trunk. If none are green, your tree is dead.

Trunk damage is one of the leading reasons that healthy trees die. Trunk wounds destroy the tissues that transport water and nutrients from the roots to the upper portions of the tree. Wounds also invite insects and disease. In the landscape, string trimmers and mowers often cause this damage. Avoid planting grass near tree trunks to eliminate potential problems.

Don't ignore mature trees. They can suffer during the stress of drought. Shallow-rooted trees such as dogwoods are particularly vulnerable during prolonged periods of extremely hot, dry weather. Curling leaves that turn crispy brown along the edges are a sign that a tree needs water. Foliage may also drop prematurely. Water trees by turning a hose on to a slow trickle and placing it around the base of the tree and at various places under the dripline for several hours at a time to give the tree a good soaking. If water flows across the surface of the ground, your hose is turned on too hard.

Homer's Hindsight

I bought a new tree and was eager to get it home. My first mistake was putting it in the trunk with the top sticking out. The tree was destroyed by the time I got home. Even though I'd driven slowly, the wind shredded the leaves and dried them out. Next time, I'll get a tarp and bungie cords to bundle up the tree, or at least lay it down in the bed of a pickup truck to give it some wind protection during the ride home.

Planting a Container-Grown Tree

It's easy to add trees to your landscape. Follow these guidelines for planting the container-grown variety.

1 **Dig a hole that's one-and-a-half to two times as wide as the tree's container.** The hole should be as deep as the container is tall. Use a shovel handle to take a rough measurement; if your hole is too deep, add soil to the bottom and tamp it in place to keep the tree from settling. If you're planting in an area with heavy clay soil, scrape the sides of the hole with a shovel to roughen them. A slick-sided hole acts like a big clay pot and restricts root growth. Add gypsum to clay soil (see page 49).

Good idea! → **Have a tarp or wheelbarrow handy.** As you shovel, place soil onto a tarp or in a wheelbarrow instead of on your lawn. This will make it easier to mix amendments into the soil before putting it back into the hole around the root ball. This trick also makes cleaning up easier.

2 **Mix amendments into the removed soil.** Amendments vary according to existing soil conditions and plant requirements. Bagged organic matter is a good amendment to use. The amended mixture should contain half native soil and half organic matter. The use of native soil helps the tree adapt to its new home and spread roots out into the soil beyond the planting hole.

3 **Gently slide the tree from its container.** Cut the container with a utility knife if you can't get it off without tugging. (Pulling on the trunk can damage roots.) When the container is off, lay the tree on its side. Gently score the root ball with a sharp shovel or utility knife to encourage the growth of new roots outside the pot-shaped mass of roots. It's important to keep the root ball intact; limit the scores on the root ball.

STUFF YOU'LL NEED

✔ Round-point shovel
✔ Hose connected to water supply within reach of work site
✔ Organic matter (such as bagged compost)
✔ Wheelbarrow
✔ Mulch
✔ Gypsum (for clay soil)

What to Expect

Your newly planted tree will look shorter than it did at the garden center because the container itself seems to add height. When the tree is planted, the roots are buried beneath the soil surface.

Wisdom
of the Aisles

Moving a tree correctly

▲ **Right** Support the heavy root ball from below to prevent damaging tree roots.

▲ **Wrong** Transport trees to the planting site by the container, not the tree trunk.

4 **Position the tree in its hole.** The top of the root ball should be level with adjacent, undisturbed soil. In areas with heavy clay soil, trees should be planted higher so the root ball protrudes an inch or two above the soil surface. This prevents water from puddling around roots. Before filling the hole, gently swivel the tree so it looks best at the angle from which you'll see it the most. Check to make sure the tree is straight from all directions.

5 **Fill the hole with amended soil mixture.** Add soil around the root ball, pressing it firmly with your hands as you go. If planting during hot weather, water the soil as you fill in the hole. Avoid stomping on the soil to tamp it down. This destroys soil porosity, making it difficult for water and air to reach plant roots. Because you have dug the hole only as deep as the container is tall, the tree should be sitting on a firm base that won't settle.

Unless your yard has heavy clay soil, use the excess soil to form a moat around the tree. Make the moat as wide as the hole. Pat the soil firmly in place with your hands. The moat walls should be 3 inches wide and tall. Mulch the area inside the moat and fill with water from a slowly trickling hose. Place the hose at the base of the tree's trunk to soak the root ball; otherwise, the water will run past the root ball into the looser soil in the hole. The moat allows the water to seep down to the roots instead of running off the soil's surface. Weather will eventually melt your moat; but by then, your tree will no longer need it.

Planting a Tree on a Slope

Hilly terrain can make growing trees difficult. If a new tree is not properly secured, gravity will cause the root ball to pivot in its hole before roots grow into the adjacent soil. When this happens, the tree leans downhill and grows at an angle instead of straight up and down. Use a tree-staking kit to secure the tree on the uphill side. (To secure a newly planted tree on level soil in areas prone to high winds, use three cables to anchor the tree from all sides.) Watering is also a major concern. Here's how to solve both potential problems:

1) Form a moat on the downhill side of the tree. Now the soil is level, preventing water runoff (see A). Deep watering (see page 50) is particularly important for trees planted on slopes. Roots growing downward to seek water give the tree stability.

2) Pass the roping through plastic tubes. Loop tubes around the trunk above a limb, and position the hose to prevent wire from cutting into the tree (see B).

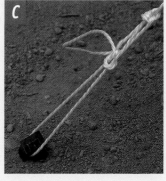

3) Secure each rope to a stake driven into the soil on the uphill side. (The two stakes should form the points of a triangle, with the tree at the apex.) Wrap the ropes around the hook in each stake, pulling until taut. Make sure the tree is straight from all angles. Tie a brightly colored flag to each rope (see C).

Remove the ropes after the tree has been in place for one complete growing season. If your area is prone to high winds, leave trees—even those not planted on slopes—roped for a year. Check the lines periodically and tighten as needed. As the root system develops, the tree becomes securely anchored in the ground.

Planting a B&B Tree

Trees that come from the store with balled-and-burlapped root balls are known as B&B trees. Planting them is slightly different than planting container-grown trees.

1 **Dig a hole that's twice as wide as the tree's root ball.** The hole should be as deep as the root ball is tall. Use a shovel handle to take a rough measurement. If your hole is too deep, add soil to the bottom and tamp it in place to keep the tree from settling. If you're planting in an area with heavy clay soil, scrape the sides of the hole with a shovel to roughen them. A slick-sided hole acts like a big clay pot and restricts root growth.

2 **Mix amendments into the removed soil.** The resulting mixture is usually half native soil and half organic matter. Amendments vary according to existing soil conditions and plant requirements. In areas with high rainfall and heavy clay soil, mix native soil with organic matter at a reduced ratio of 4:1. Organic materials such as bagged compost make excellent soil additions.

3 **Cut back all metal or plastic fasteners from the root ball and peel back the top third of the burlap after the tree is set in the hole.** It's important to remove metal or plastic fasteners wrapped around the burlap at the base of the trunk. Leaving these will eventually girdle the tree, killing it. However, if the B&B root ball is sitting in a wire basket, do not remove it. This helps keep the root ball intact. The roots will grow through the wire and the wire will eventually rust away.

Wisdom of the Aisles

Topping trees. Don't flat-top your trees. Cutting branches so they're all the same level encourages the development of many fast-growing sprouts from the tips of remaining stubs. Though the tree's canopy will appear dense and bushy for a while, the sprouts will shoot upward, requiring more pruning. Thick, gnarled scars can appear after cuts are made in the same place year after year. Cutting branches off to make the tree resemble a lollipop prohibits the development of the tree's natural form. Instead, shoots angle upward, close to the trunk. Narrow crotches result, which may accumulate water and rot wood or form ice that will split the branches from the tree. Topping trees also severely limits the size of a tree's canopy; eventually, the trunk grows thicker, making it appear out of proportion to the limited canopy. Topping is also known as pollarding or dehorning.

STUFF YOU'LL NEED

✔ Round-point shovel
✔ Water supply and hose within reach of work site
✔ Organic matter such as bagged compost
✔ Tarp (optional)
✔ Gypsum for clay soil

What to Expect

It may be difficult to pry fasteners from root balls with your fingers; try using a flat-head screwdriver, instead.

TOOL TIP

A digging bar is essential when you're digging holes in rocky, compacted, or hard clay soil. Use a sledgehammer to drive it into the soil to pry chunks loose and get your hole started.

In the Zone

Transplant Shock

If your new tree drops all its leaves shortly after planting, don't give it up for dead. A balled-and-burlapped tree has many roots severed when it is dug from the ground. It is more likely to experience transplant shock than a container-grown tree. Trees in shock shed their foliage and go into a survival mode. Given enough time and water, such trees will most likely recover. Keep the soil lightly moist. Though it appears a little silly to be watering something that looks dead, keep doing it!

BUYER'S GUIDE

If you want a larger tree than those in stock, ask a garden associate about ordering a B&B tree for you. Some stores stock balled-and-burlapped trees only upon request. Inquire about the approximate measurements of the root ball and dig the proper-sized hole before the tree arrives. Ask if delivery is available for a fee when you order your tree. If so, find out where the tree will be left—don't be surprised if the delivery driver will take it no farther than the curb. You'll probably need to have a sturdy wheelbarrow waiting to get the tree to the hole. You may want to hire a professional or get a friend to help with a big tree; B&B trees are heavy.

Design Tip

Plan your bedlines around existing or future trees

Though you shouldn't plant right up to the trunks of trees, you can surround them with a bed of shrubs and groundcovers. Keep lawns away from the base of trees to avoid trunk damage from mowers and string trimmers and to avoid problems caused by different watering needs for trees and grass.

4 Position the tree in its hole. Peel back the fabric to reveal the top third of the root ball. Leave the fabric in place unless it is nonbiodegradable plastic which will need to be removed before the ball goes in the hole. The top of the root ball should be level with adjacent, undisturbed soil. This is easily checked with the handle of a shovel. In clay soil, trees need to be planted so the root ball is an inch or two above the soil surface so water won't puddle around roots. Make sure the tree is straight from all sides.

5 Fill the hole with the amended soil mixture. Add soil around the root ball, pressing it firmly with your hands as you go. If planting during hot weather, water the soil as you fill in the hole. Avoid stomping on the soil to tamp it down. This destroys soil porosity, and makes it difficult for water and air to reach plant roots. Because you have dug the hole only as deep as the root ball is tall, the tree is sitting on a firm base and shouldn't settle.

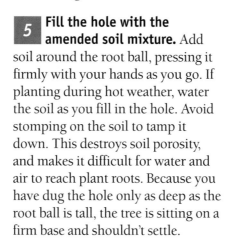

Good idea! **Capture a wonderful family occasion by taking pictures as you plant your new tree.** Everyone will treasure the memories, and the moment will become part of your family history.

6 Use the excess soil to form a moat around the tree. The moat should be as wide as the hole and 3 inches wide and tall. Pat it in place with your hands to make it sturdy. Mulch the inside and fill the area with water from a trickling hose placed at the base of the trunk. The moat allows the water to seep down to the roots instead of running off the surface of the soil. Fill the moat slowly several times, letting the water soak in each time. Weather will eventually wear away your moat; but after establishment, your tree will no longer need it.

trees

4

Trees 65

Lush summer foliage provides a rich backdrop for the spray from a fountain in a backyard pond.

Choosing Trees for Seasonality

Decorate the seasons. Choose trees for beauty throughout the year. You'll find plenty of different kinds with attractive flowers, foliage, berries, or bark. The selection guides on these pages offer a range of choices. Eliminate any trees that don't include your planting zone within their range. Turn to the pages listed for photographs and more information.

Dogwoods welcome spring with drifts of snowy petals on bare branches.

Autumn has arrived when the fan-shaped leaves of a Ginkgo turn golden.

Paloverde
(Cercidium texanum)
Page 193

Trees with colorful fall foliage

Common Name	Zones	Page
American Beech	3-9	78
Fagus grandifolia		
Bradford Pear	4-8	89
Pyrus calleryana 'Bradford'		
Chinese Elm	5-9	97
Ulmus parvifolia		
Chinese Pistache	6-9	87
Pistacia chinensis		
Crepe Myrtle	7-9	82
Lagerstroemia indica		
Flowering Dogwood	5-9	76
Cornus florida		
Fruitless American Sweetgum	5-9	83
Liquidambar styraciflua 'Rotundiloba'		
Ginkgo	3-9	79
Ginkgo biloba		
Green Ash	3-9	78
Fraxinus pennsylvanica		
Japanese Maple	5-8	71
Acer palmatum		
Japanese Zelkova	5-9	97
Zelkova serrata		
Kousa Dogwood	5-8	76
Cornus kousa		
Littleleaf Linden	3-7	96
Tilia cordata		
Pin Oak	4-8	92
Quercus palustris		
Possum Haw	3-9	79
Ilex decidua		
Red Maple	3-9	70
Acer rubrum		
Redbud	3-9	75
Cercis canadensis		
Scarlet Oak	4-9	91
Quercus coccinea		
Shumard Oak	5-9	93
Quercus shumardii		
Star Magnolia	4-9	84
Magnolia stellata		
Sugar Maple	4-8	72
Acer saccharum		
Washington Hawthorn	3-9	77
Crataegus phaenopyrum		
White Oak	4-9	90
Quercus alba		
Yellowwood	6-8	75
Cladrastis lutea		
Yoshino Cherry	5-8	88
Prunus x yedoensis		

Availability varies by area and conditions (see page 21). Check with your garden center.

Spring-flowering trees

Common Name	Zones	Page
Bailey Acacia	10	192
Acacia baileyana		
Bradford Pear	4-8	89
Pyrus calleryana 'Bradford'		
Crimson Bottlebrush	9-10	193
Callistemon citrinus		
Desert Willow	8-10	194
Chilopsis linearis		
Flowering Dogwood	5-9	76
Cornus florida		
Japanese Flowering Crabapple	4-8	85
Malus floribunda		
Kousa Dogwood	5-8	76
Cornus kousa		
Mesquite	10	197
Prosopis glandulosa		
Mexican Bird-of-Paradise	10	192
Caesalpinia mexicana		
Paloverde	8-10	193
Cercidium texanum		
Purple-Leaf Plum	4-8	88
Prunus cerasifera 'Atropurpurea'		
Red Maple	3-9	70
Acer rubrum		
Redbud	3-9	75
Cercis canadensis		
Saucer Magnolia	5-9	84
Magnolia x soulangiana		
Sea Grape	10	194
Coccoloba uvifera		
Star Magnolia	4-9	84
Magnolia stellata		
Sweet Bay Magnolia	5-9	85
Magnolia virginiana		
Washington Hawthorn	3-9	77
Crataegus phaenopyrum		
White Bird-of-Paradise	9-10	198
Strelitzia nicolai		
Yellowwood	6-8	75
Cladrastis lutea		
Yoshino Cherry	5-8	88
Prunus x yedoensis		

Summer-flowering trees

Common Name	Zones	Page
Crimson Bottlebrush	9-10	193
Callistemon citrinus		
Desert Willow	8-10	194
Chilopsis linearis		
Japanese Pagoda Tree	6-8	94
Sophora japonica		
Lilac Chaste Tree	6-10	199
Vitex agnus-castus		
Littleleaf Linden	3-7	96
Tilia cordata		
Mexican Bird-of-Paradise	10	192
Caesalpinia mexicana		
Olive	8-10	195
Olea europaea		
Sea Grape	10	194
Coccoloba uvifera		
Southern Magnolia	6-10	83
Magnolia grandiflora		
Yellowwood	6-8	75
Cladrastis lutea		

Trees for winter interest

Common Name (Special Feature)		Zones	Page
American Beech	(bark)	3-9	78
Fagus grandifolia			
Bald Cypress	(bark)	4-10	95
Taxodium distichum			
Canadian Hemlock	(shape)	3-7	96
Tsuga canadensis			
Chinese Elm	(bark)	5-9	97
Ulmus parvifolia			
Coast Live Oak	(bark)	9	90
Quercus agrifolia			
Crepe Myrtle	(bark/shape)	7-9	82
Lagerstroemia indica			
Dawn Redwood	(bark)	4-8	86
Metasequoia glyptostroboides			
Eastern Red Cedar	(shape)	3-9	81
Juniperus virginiana			
Hollywood Juniper	(shape)	4-9	195
Juniperus chinensis 'Torulosa'			
Japanese Maple	(shape)	5-8	71
Acer palmatum			
Lusterleaf Holly	(berries)	7-9	80
Ilex latifolia			
Olive	(shape)	8-10	195
Olea europaea			
Paloverde	(bark)	8-10	193
Cercidium texanum			
Possum Haw	(berries)	3-9	79
Ilex decidua			
River Birch (bark/multiple trunks)		4-9	73
Betula nigra			
Savannah Holly	(berries)	5-9	80
Ilex opaca 'Savannah'			
Washington Hawthorn (berries)		3-9	77
Crataegus phaenopyrum			
Windmill Palm	(bark)	8-10	199
Trachycarpus fortunei			
Yaupon Holly	(berries)	7-10	81
Ilex vomitoria			

Peeling bark on a River Birch trunk becomes more noticeable in winter when leaves are gone.

trees 4

Trees 67

Queen Palms are good for filling garden corners or planting in rows along streets or driveways.

Kousa Dogwood (Cornus kousa) Page 76

Streetside trees

Common Name	Zones	Page
Canary Island Date Palm	9-10	196
Phoenix canariensis		
Chinese Elm	5-9	97
Ulmus parvifolia		
Chinese Pistachio	6-9	87
Pistacia chinensis		
Common Bald Cypress	4-10	95
Taxodium distichum		
Date Palm	9-10	196
Phoenix dactylifera		
Dawn Redwood	4-8	86
Metasequoia glyptostroboides		
Fruitless American Sweetgum	5-9	83
Liquidambar styraciflua 'Rotundiloba'		
Ginkgo	3-9	79
Ginkgo biloba		
Green Ash	3-9	78
Fraxinus pennsylvanica		
Japanese Zelkova	5-9	97
Zelkova serrata		
Laurel Oak	7-10	197
Quercus laurifolia		
Littleleaf Linden	3-7	96
Tilia cordata		
Pin Oak	4-8	92
Quercus palustris		
Pindo Palm	8-10	192
Butia capitata		
Queen Palm	10	198
Syagrus romanzoffianum		
Red Maple	3-9	70
Acer rubrum		
River Birch	4-9	73
Betula nigra		
Royal Palm	10	197
Roystonea elata		
Sabal Palm	8-10	198
Sabal palmetto		
Savannah Holly	5-9	80
Ilex opaca 'Savannah'		
Shumard Oak	5-9	93
Quercus shumardii		
Southern Live Oak	8-10	93
Quercus virginiana		
Willow Oak	4-8	92
Quercus phellos		
Yoshino Cherry	5-8	88
Prunus x yedoensis		

Trees for Every Need

Some trees are better suited for special jobs than others. Use these selection guides as a starting point for choosing the right tree for the right place. You may find other choices for sale, too. Availability varies by area and conditions (see page 21). Check with your garden center.

Patio trees

Common Name	Zones	Page
Bald Cypress	4-10	95
Taxodium distichum		
Bradford Pear	4-8	89
Pyrus calleryana 'Bradford'		
Chinese Elm	5-9	97
Ulmus parvifolia		
Chinese Pistache	6-9	87
Pistacia chinensis		
Crepe Myrtle	7-9	82
Lagerstroemia indica		
Crimson Bottlebrush	9-10	193
Callistemon cirtrinus		
Flowering Dogwood	5-9	76
Cornus florida		
Fruitless American Sweetgum	5-9	83
Liquidambar styraciflua 'Rotundiloba'		
Japanese Flowering Crabapple	4-8	85
Malus floribunda		
Japanese Maple	5-8	71
Acer palmatum		
Japanese Zelkova	5-9	97
Zelkova serrata		
Kousa Dogwood	5-8	76
Cornus kousa		
Lilac Chaste Tree	6-10	199
Vitex agnus-castus		
Littleleaf Linden	3-7	96
Tilia cordata		
Mexican Bird-of-Paradise	10	192
Caesalpinia mexicana		
Olive	8-10	195
Olea europaea		
Purple-Leaf Plum	4-8	88
Prunus cerasifera 'Atropurpurea'		
Queen Palm	10	198
Syagrus romanzoffianum		
Red Maple	3-9	70
Acer rubrum		
Redbud	3-9	75
Cercis canadensis		
River Birch	4-9	73
Betula nigra		
Sabal Palm	8-10	198
Sabal Palmetto		
Savannah Holly	5-9	80
Ilex opaca 'Savannah'		
Shumard Oak	5-9	93
Quercus shumardii		
Sweet Bay Magnolia	5-9	85
Magnolia virginiana		
Washington Hawthorn	3-9	77
Crataegus phaenopyrum		
Wax Myrtle	7-9	86
Myrica cerifera		
Willow Oak	4-8	92
Quercus phellos		
Yaupon Holly	7-10	81
Ilex vomitoria		
Yellowwood	6-8	75
Cladrastis lutea		
Yoshino Cherry	5-8	88
Prunus x yedoensis		

Japanese Maples grow well in confined spaces, making them good choices for planting beside patios.

Trees for open areas

Common Name	Zones	Page
Bur Oak	2-8	91
Quercus macrocarpa		
Date Palm	9-10	196
Phoenix dactylifera		
Deodar Cedar	6-9	74
Cedrus deodara		
Eastern Red Cedar	3-9	81
Juniperus virginiana		
Ginkgo	3-9	79
Ginkgo biloba		
Japanese Pagoda Tree	6-8	94
Sophora japonica		
Mexican Washington Palm	9-10	199
Washingtonia robusta		
Pecan	5-9	74
Carya illinoinensis		
River Birch	4-9	73
Betula nigra		
Royal Palm	10	197
Roystonea elata		
Saucer Magnolia	5-9	84
Magnolia x soulangiana		
Silver Maple	3-9	72
Acer saccharinum		
Southern Live Oak	8-10	93
Quercus virginiana		
Southern Magnolia	6-10	83
Magnolia grandiflora		
Sugar Maple	4-8	72
Acer saccharum		
Weeping Willow	4-9	94
Salix babylonica		

Shade trees

Common Name	Zones	Page
Bur Oak	2-8	91
Quercus macrocarpa		
Coast Live Oak	9	90
Quercus agrifolia		
Fruitless American Sweetgum	5-9	83
Liquidambar styraciflua 'Rotundiloba'		
Green Ash	3-9	78
Fraxinus pennsylvanica		
Japanese Pagoda Tree	6-8	94
Sophora japonica		
Japanese Zelkova	5-9	97
Zelkova serrata		
Laurel Oak	7-10	197
Quercus laurifolia		
Littleleaf Linden	3-7	96
Tilia cordata		
Loquat	8-10	195
Eriobotrya japonica		
Mesquite	10	197
Prosopis glandulosa		
Mexican Bird-of-Paradise	10	192
Caesalpinia mexicana		
Olive	8-10	195
Olea europaea		
Paloverde	8-10	193
Cercidium texanum		
Pecan	5-9	74
Carya illinoinensis		
Pin Oak	4-8	92
Quercus palustris		
Red Maple	3-9	70
Acer rubrum		
Redbud	3-9	75
Cercis canadensis		
Saucer Magnolia	5-9	84
Magnolia x soulangiana		
Scarlet Oak	4-9	91
Quercus coccinea		
Sea Grape	10	194
Coccoloba uvifera		
Shumard Oak	5-9	93
Quercus shumardii		
Silver Maple	3-9	72
Acer saccharinum		
Southern Live Oak	8-10	93
Quercus virginiana		
Sugar Maple	4-8	72
Acer saccharum		
White Oak	4-9	90
Quercus alba		
Willow Oak	4-8	92
Quercus phellos		
Yellowwood	6-8	75
Cladrastis lutea		

Pink Flowering Dogwoods offer a touch of spring color to this front yard.

Abies bracteata

Bristlecone Fir

Zones: 3-9

Light Needs:

Mature Size:

50'-70'

15'-20'

Growth Rate: slow

evergreen tree

Needs: Grow in well-drained soil that's neutral to acidic. Rocky soils are fine. Plant in partial to deep shade. Humidity and wet soil are not good for this tree.

Good for: Northern California landscapes, mountainsides, rock gardens, specimen trees, providing a background for deciduous plants, specimen tree, screening

More Choices: pages 30, 36, and 40

Outstanding Features:

- Stiff, dark green needles have silvery undersides
- The most heat-tolerant fir grown
- Its columnar form adds a formal look

Who says you can't grow a fir tree in a warm climate? Try Bristlecone Fir for a fluffy evergreen if your area is warm and dry. Its symmetrical shape, especially in youth, adds a formal look to the landscape. Leave lowest branches all the way to the ground for best appearance. This tree is also sold as Santa Lucia Fir and may be listed as *A. venusta*. Cones are rounded.

Acer rubrum

Red Maple

Zones: 3-9

Light Needs:

Mature Size:

40'-50'

30'-40'

Growth Rate: rapid

deciduous tree

Needs: Grow in any kind of soil, from alkaline to acidic, rich to poor, or wet to dry. Grow in full sun or partial shade. Water new trees regularly for the first growing season; after that, trees rarely need water. Tolerates heat and car exhaust.

Good for: shade trees, parking areas, street trees, lining long driveways, woodlands, patios, decks, fast-growing deciduous screens, beside ponds or creeks, in boggy areas or in hot, dry spots, natural areas

More Choices: pages 31, 39, 40, 43, 59, 67, 68, and 69

Outstanding Features:

- Leafy shade gives way to bright fall color
- Tolerant of a range of soil conditions
- Flowers and seeds appear before leaves

Grow this tough, native tree for a delicate blush of red in spring, leafy shade in summer, and brightly colored foliage in fall. Red maples adapt to a variety of growing conditions. These trees grow naturally in swamps but are equally at home in a hot, dry parking area. Known as a hard maple. Try these cultivars: 'Autumn Flame'—leaves turn vivid red in early fall; 'October Glory'—brilliant orange or red fall foliage; 'Red Sunset'—foliage turns red in early fall; 'Bowhall'—symmetrical, narrow canopy; yellow to red fall leaves; 'Columnare'—narrow canopy about 10' wide, red fall foliage; 'Indian Summer'—vigorous, very cold-hardy; leaves turn red-orange in fall.

Japanese Maple

Zones: 5-8

Light Needs:

Mature Size:

15'-20'
10'-15'

Growth Rate:
slow

deciduous tree

Needs: Plant in fertile soil that's moist but well-drained. Add compost at planting; mulch roots well to keep them cool. Grow in full sun or partial shade; protect selections with fine-textured leaves from afternoon sun in hotter months. Young trees in particular benefit from shade and water in summer. Grow green-leaved varieties in sun for brilliant fall color. Trees tolerate confined spaces if watered.

Good for: specimen planting, accents and focal points, winter interest, patios, decks, entries, courtyards, understory trees, adding human scale, small gardens

More Choices: pages 36, 67, and 69

Options: 'Atropupurea'—red-purple summer foliage turns brighter red in autumn; medium-textured leaves
Upright—tree size:
'Bloodgood'—red-purple summer foliage turns brighter red in autumn; fine-textured leaves
'Linearilobum'—bright green, fine-textured leaves turn yellow in fall
'Burgundy Lace'—red-purple leaves are deeply cut for a lacy look
'Shishio'—new leaves and autumn foliage are red; summer leaves are green
var. heptalobum—broader leaves have coarser texture; green foliage turns bright orange to red in fall
'Sango Kaku'—green leaves with coral bark; good winter interest
'Oshio Beni'—bright red foliage during the growing season
Weeping—smaller size:
'Dissectum' (threadleaf)—very fine-textured foliage; mounding form
'Crimson Queen'—reddish purple leaves; fine-textured foliage
'Ever Red'—very fine-textured foliage, dark red-purple in color; mounding form
'Inaba Shidare'—red leaves
'Viridis'—green leaves

'Bloodgood'

This tree is so graceful, it's an accent even in winter when it's as bare as a bone. Delicate leaves vary among named selections in shape, color, size, and texture; all are shaped somewhat like a hand. Green-leaved selections tend to have the best fall color, turning brilliant shades of orange, gold, or crimson. Trees are often multitrunked. Picturesque form shows best against solid backgrounds such as walls or tall evergreen shrubs.

trees 4

Acer saccharinum

Silver Maple

Zones: 3-9

Light Needs:

Mature Size:

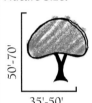

50'-70'

35'-50'

Growth Rate:
rapid

deciduous tree

Needs: Plant in full sun or partial shade. Tolerates a variety of soils, from acidic to alkaline and sandy loam to clay. Plant away from buildings, paving, and pipes.

Good for: shading, screening, adding quick shade and height to new yards while longer-lived trees mature; large open spaces.

More Choices: pages 31, 34, 36, 39, 40, 41, 59, and 61

Options: 'Silver Queen'—oval form, bears fewer seeds; 'Skinneri'—stronger wood, deeply cut leaves

Outstanding Features:

- Grows quickly; transplants easily
- Large leaves cast abundant shade
- Grows in a wide variety of soil conditions

Plant a silver maple to provide quick shade in broad, open areas. Silvery-back leaves turn lemon yellow in autumn. Because of its rapid growth, wood is weak and trees will break apart during storms; keep trees away from powerlines or houses for this reason. Plant where roots can't invade septic or drainage systems. Keep roots away from paving. Short-lived compared to other maples. Known as a soft maple.

Acer saccharum

Sugar Maple

Zones: 4-7

Light Needs:

Mature Size:

60'-75'

40'-50'

Growth Rate:
slow

deciduous tree

Needs: Plant in acidic soil that's moist but well-drained; avoid compacted clay, wet soil, or city conditions. Grow in full sun or partial shade. Fall color is best in sun.

Good for: shade trees, lawn trees, lining driveways and streets, large open spaces, seasonal accent, natural areas, large estates, formal landscapes, mountainsides

More Choices: pages 34, 36, 40, 67, and 69

Options: 'Green Mountain'—thick, deep green foliage
'Bonfire'—grows slightly faster
'Green Column'—leaves turn yellow-orange

Outstanding Features:

- 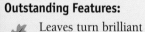Leaves turn brilliant colors in autumn
- 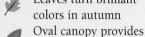Oval canopy provides deep shade
- 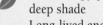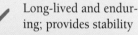Long-lived and enduring; provides stability

Leafy summer shade followed by traffic-stopping fall color makes Sugar Maple an excellent choice for growing in large lawns or in rows along streets or driveways. Roots require large open spaces rather than restricted growing areas. Plants will grow well in the cooler areas of Zone 8. Known as a hard maple. Try these cultivars: 'Legacy'—drought-resistant; 'Flax Mill Majesty'—faster growing, red-orange leaves.

Betula nigra

River Birch

Zones: 4-9

Light Needs:

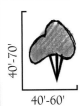

Mature Size:

40'-70'

40'-60'

Growth Rate:
rapid

deciduous tree

Needs: Plant in almost any soil from dry to soggy, poor or fertile. Acidic pH suits it best. Grow in full sun or partial shade. Prune only to remove obstructing low-hanging branches.

Good for: boggy areas, watersides, natural areas, beside patios and decks, along walkways, groves, open areas, deciduous screens, winter interest

More Choices: pages 31, 34, 38, 39, 40, 43, 59, 67, 68, and 69

Options: 'Heritage'—outstanding peely bark

Outstanding Features:

- Coarse-textured, peeling bark
- Fast-growing and adaptable
- Multiple trunks have instant presence

The best way to make a brand-new or flat landscape look better is to add a fast-growing tree. River Birch adds height, shade, and texture quickly. Peeling bark adds to its ornamental value throughout the year. River Birch is tolerant of a variety of growing conditions; it will even tolerate standing in water. Heat-tolerant too, this is the best birch tree for the South. Other birches become stressed when temperatures rise, making them more susceptible to damaging and potentially deadly pests. River Birch is NOT susceptible to borers; definitely an added landscaping bonus.

Calocedrus decurrens

California Incense Cedar

Zones: 5-8

Light Needs:

Mature Size:

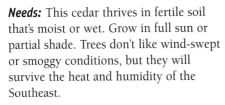

30'-60'

8'-10'

Growth Rate:
slow

evergreen tree

Needs: This cedar thrives in fertile soil that's moist or wet. Grow in full sun or partial shade. Trees don't like wind-swept or smoggy conditions, but they will survive the heat and humidity of the Southeast.

Good for: specimen use, windbreaks, planting in groves beside large lawns and formal estates

More Choices: pages 34 and 36

Outstanding Features:

- Evergreen branches are attractive year-round
- Columnar shape provides formal look
- Towering size is great for large landscapes

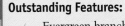
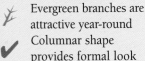

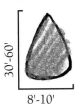

These trees stand like soldiers at attention, lending an air of formality to the large landscape. Their height complements the larger landscapes but may prove too large for small lots or single-story homes. Though it prefers moist sites, California Incense Cedar is adaptable to the heat and drought found in Southern growing areas. Makes a beautiful large specimen tree.

trees

4

Carya illinoensis

Pecan

Zones: 5-9

Light Needs:

Mature Size:

70'-100'

40'-75'

Growth Rate:
medium to rapid

deciduous tree

Needs: For best growth, plant in soil that's moist and well-drained. However, this tree can adapt to dry conditions and poor soil. Grow in full sun. Prune to remove dead or damaged limbs before they fall.

Good for: shade in hot, dry areas, producing edible pecans; growing in large, open areas

More Choices: pages 34, 39, 59, and 69

Outstanding Features:

✔ Tolerant of high temperatures and drought
🌿 Large leaves provide dense shade
🥜 Edible nuts for humans and wildlife

Where hot, dry conditions make shade tree pickings slim, pecans make the easy switch from farm to landscape. Low branching and wide spreading, trees produce an added bonus of tasty nuts in the fall. Overall an attractive tree though it can be messy and require picking up after. Trees drop catkins, leaves, limbs, and nuts at various times throughout the year. Seedlings often appear in planting beds where squirrels have buried nuts. Trees grow easily from seed but are difficult to transplant.

Cedrus deodara

Deodar Cedar

Zones: 6-9

Light Needs:

Mature Size:

40'-70'

25'-30'

Growth Rate:
medium

evergreen tree

Needs: Plant in any well-drained or dry soil, from acidic to alkaline. Grow in full sun and provide protection from sweeping winds that can deform the tree.

Good for: specimen use, screening to block poor views and add year-round privacy, provide background for deciduous trees and shrubs, winter interest; large, open areas

More Choices: pages 30, 34, 39, 40, 41, and 69

Outstanding Features:

🌿 Green foliage is silvery with hints of blue
🌲 Pyramidal form; branches pendulous
🪴 Tolerates dry soil that's alkaline or acidic

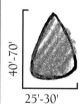

Even if you live where it's too hot to grow most wintery-looking evergreen trees, you can grow this one. Graceful Deodar Cedar tolerates heat and poor, dry soils. Trees make excellent specimen plantings with graceful, pendulous branching. As trees mature, they widen out and become flat-topped. Older trees also produce green cones that turn reddish brown at maturity. Cones take two years to mature. Option: 'Aurea'—golden foliage.

Redbud

Zones: 3-9

Light Needs:

Mature Size:

20'-30'

25'-35'

Growth Rate:
medium

deciduous flowering tree

Needs: Will tolerate many soil types from sandy to clay and soil pH from acidic to alkaline. Prefers dry over soggy soil. Grow in full sun to partial shade. Prune to remove dead wood and open the canopy for light penetration.

Good for: specimen, patio, understory, small lawn tree use, seasonal accent, in groundcover, shrub beds, woodland areas

More Choices: pages 31, 34, 36, 39, 40, 41, 59, 67, and 69

Options: 'Alba'—white flowers
'Forest Pansy'—leaves are purple in spring and fall

Outstanding Features:

Purplish pink flowers appear before leaves
Heart-shaped leaves turn yellow in fall
Native tree proves tough and adaptable

Spring arrives early if you have a Redbud in your yard. April blooms appear on trees just a few years old. Older trees actually form flower buds on tree trunks and provide a conversation topic through the entire neighborhood. Attractive, heart-shaped leaves turn yellow in fall; color quality varies with genetics and light. Tree trunks divide close to the ground and then develop graceful, ascending branches.

Cladrastis lutea

Yellowwood

Zones: 3-8

Light Needs:

Mature Size:

30'-50'

40'-55'

Growth Rate:
medium

deciduous flowering tree

Needs: Plant in fertile, well-drained soil. Alkaline soils are ideal but not required. Shelter from hot sun by planting in partial shade. This tree is not drought-tolerant and requires adequate moisture throughout the growing season. Protect from strong winds. Prune in the summer to reduce bleeding sap.

Good for: Single specimen use or as a shade tree for small yards. Group several together for a grove of bloom. Plant near outdoor seating areas to enjoy the fragrance of flowers.

More Choices: pages 34, 36, 39, 41, 67, and 69

Outstanding Features:

Dangling white flowers in late spring
Coarse-textured leaves turn yellow in fall
Upright form with spreading lower limbs

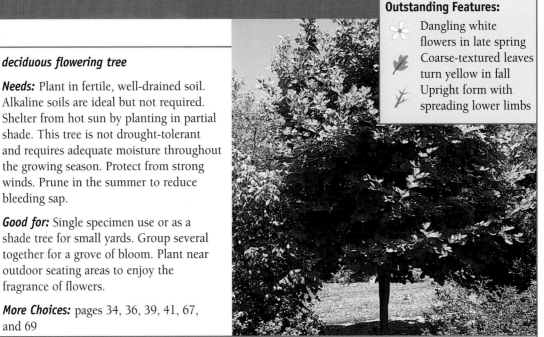

trees

4

Fragrant blossoms appear to drip like white rain when this tree blooms in late spring and early summer. Foliage emerges a bright yellow-green in the spring and provides a nice contrast with the dark green leaves of maples and oaks. Fall color is yellow though not as outstanding as maple. Gray-colored bark is smooth and resembles that of beech. Try the cultivar 'Rosea' if you prefer pink flowers.

4

Cornus florida

Flowering Dogwood

Zones: 5-9

Light Needs:

Mature Size:

20'-25'

20'-25'

Growth Rate:
slow to medium

deciduous flowering tree

Needs: Plant in rich, acidic soil that's moist but well-drained. Grow in partial to dense shade. Trees bloom best in sun, but require afternoon shade in hotter climates unless watered regularly. Supply all dogwoods with extra water during droughts.

Good for: specimen trees, seasonal accents, understory plantings, natural areas, edges of woodlands, filling empty corners of yards, near patios, decks, or benches, corners of houses, attracting birds in fall and winter

More Choices: pages 36, 40, 42, 67, and 69

Outstanding Features:
- Showy white flowers in early spring
- Scarlet fall leaf color followed by red fruit
- Graceful tiered branch habit; irregular form

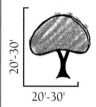

Plant a single dogwood or several together to welcome spring with drifts of white. Flowers appear before the foliage. The leaves of these graceful trees turn varying shades of red to purple in autumn. Bare trees form interesting silhouettes in winter. Pink-flowering selections are not as heat-tolerant as white flowering cultivars. Try these cultivars: 'Cherokee Chief'—dark pink flowers and reddish-colored new foliage; 'Plena'—white, double flowers

Cornus kousa

Kousa Dogwood

Zones: 5-8

Light Needs:

Mature Size:

20'-30'

20'-30'

Growth Rate:
slow to medium

deciduous flowering tree

Needs: Plant in well-drained, acidic soil with some organic matter. Grow in partial shade or full sun with regular watering. Roots are shallow; all dogwoods will need extra water during droughts.

Good for: specimen trees, seasonal accents, courtyard and patios, edges of woodlands, natural areas, shrub and groundcover beds

More Choices: pages 34, 36, 40, 67, and 69

Options: *C. alternifolia*—small white flowers, blue-black fruit, horizontal branching

Outstanding Features:
- Pointy, white flowers in late spring
- Leaves turn bright scarlet in autumn
- Horizontal layers of foliage and flowers

Kousa Dogwood extends spring by blooming later than the flowering dogwoods. Horizontal layers of leaves are in place before the flowers appear. White in color they remain attractive for more than six weeks. Edible, pinkish colored fruit develops in late summer through fall. Fall foliage is eye-catching in shades of red and purple. Plant form and attractive peeling bark provide winter interest for the landscape. Named selections are more pest-resistant than many cultivars of *C. florida*.

Crataegus phaenopyrum

Washington Hawthorn

Zones: 3-9

Light Needs:

Mature Size:

25'-30'

20'-25'

Growth Rate:
medium

deciduous flowering tree

Needs: Plant in any soil, from acidic to alkaline, dry to moist, or poor to fertile. Grow in full sun or partial shade. Tolerates urban pollution and paving. Remove low-hanging branches for clearance if desired. Avoid planting in high-traffic areas because of the thorns.

Good for: specimen trees, seasonal accents, natural areas, growing in clusters, attracting birds, winter interest, narrow spaces, and hedges

More Choices: pages 34, 36, 39, 40, 41, 43, 67, and 69

Outstanding Features:

- Clusters of white flowers in spring
- Leaves turn orange or red in autumn
- Red berries provide winter interest

Here's a small tree that isn't picky about its growing conditions. Plant a few anywhere you want to add year-round color in the yard. White flowers tinged with pink start off the spring season followed by glossy green summer foliage. Colorful fall foliage raises the curtain for red fruit that persist throughout the winter. Thorny twigs add fine texture during the winter as well.

X Cupressocyparis leylandii

Leyland Cypress

Zones: 6-9

Light Needs:

Mature Size:

60'-70'

10'-15'

Growth Rate:
rapid

evergreen tree

Needs: Grow in any soil that's well-drained. Plant in full sun and water regularly for fastest growth. Supply extra water during dry spells.

Good for: quick screening of unwanted views, provide privacy, evergreen background for deciduous trees and shrubs, tolerant of salt spray

More Choices: pages 30, 34, and 59

Options: If you can't water regularly, substitute Eastern or Southern Red Cedar, *Juniperus virginiana* or *J. silicicola*, in areas with long, hot summers and sandy soils.

Outstanding Features:

- Dense, fluffy foliage stays green year-round
- Fast-growing; more than 3 feet a year
- Low maintenance; tolerant of soil extremes

Feathery foliage and columnar form make a graceful, airy addition to the landscape. Bluish green color provides interesting contrast. Leyland Cypress will block poor views or add privacy in a hurry. Perfect for use as a living fence. Trees may decline in hot climates without regular watering. Design tip: When planting a screen, stagger trees so they form a zigzag pattern. This will provide a thicker planting and add depth to the area.

trees

4

Trees   77

Fagus grandifolia

American Beech

Zones: 3-9	

Light Needs:

Mature Size:

50'-70'

50'-70'

Growth Rate:

slow to medium,

deciduous tree

Needs: Plants thrive in moist, well-drained, acidic soil. Avoid heavy clay or where construction equipment has compacted the planting site. Trees grow best in full sun or partial shade.

Good for: specimen use, woodland plantings, natural areas, attracting birds and wildlife, providing winter interest

More Choices: pages 34, 36, 40, and 67

Options: *Fagus sylvatica pendula*—weeping branches; full sun; zones 5-7
Fagus sylvatica 'Purpurea Tricolor'—purple leaves, edged striped with pink and pink-ish white; full sun; zones 5-7

Smooth, gray trunks, golden fall foliage, and dried brown leaves that linger through the long winter months make American Beech an attractive landscape addition. Low, wide branching makes a beautiful specimen in large open areas. The root system is very shallow and the canopy dense; growing a thick stand of grass can be a challenge. Mulch instead for improved tree health and less work for you. Nuts are edible and enjoyed by several species of birds and squirrels.

Fraxinus pennsylvanica

Green Ash

Zones: 3-9	

Light Needs:

Mature Size:

50'-60'

25'-30'

Growth Rate:

rapid

deciduous tree

Needs: Plant in soils ranging from acidic to alkaline, wet to dry, compacted or loose. Tolerates drought, reflected heat from paving, and car exhaust. Roots won't buckle paving.

Good for: providing shade; lining walkways, driveways, or roadsides; planting in open lawns and parking areas

More Choices: pages 31, 38, 39, 40, 41, 43, 59, 67, 68, and 69

Options: 'Marshall's Seedless'—rapid growth, seedless, insect-resistant
F. americana Autumn Purple—purple to chocolate brown fall color

Need shade? Grow Green Ash. This tree grows fast, lives a long life, and tolerates whatever growing conditions are thrown its way. Roots are well-behaved and will not buckle paving, though they will clog drains if given the opportunity. Trees are widely planted because of their ease of growth. Choose seedless varieties for less mess in the landscape. For a tree with a narrow, egg-shaped crown, choose 'Summit'.

Ginkgo

Zones: 3-9

Light Needs:

Mature Size:

50'-80'

30'-50'

Growth Rate:
slow

deciduous tree

Needs: Plant in a range of soils including acidic, alkaline, sandy, or clay. Ginkgo grows best in full sun. Trees are drought-resistant but grow faster with regular watering and a spring feeding of balanced fertilizer. No pruning is necessary except to remove lower limbs for clearance beneath the tree. Tolerates urban conditions, confined root spaces, heat, and cold.

Good for: specimen use, seasonal accents, street trees, lining walkways or drives, parking areas, open lawns, large estates

More Choices: pages 34, 39, 40, 41, 43, 67, 68, and 69

Hold that rake; let the fallen leaves stay on the ground awhile. When Ginkgo's fan-shaped leaves turn golden in autumn, they hold their color even after dropping to the ground. This tree is considered to be one of the most attractive deciduous trees grown. Female trees produce messy fruit with an objectionable odor. There are several male clones available that do not produce fruit, including 'Autumn Gold', and the narrow-formed 'Fastigiata'.

Possum Haw

Zones: 3-9

Light Needs:

Mature Size:

15'-25'

8'-20'

Growth Rate:
rapid

deciduous tree

Needs: Plant in soil that's well-drained or swampy, acidic or alkaline. Provide a location with full sun or partial shade. Trees require little if any pruning; they look best when maintained in their naturally irregular form.

Good for: small specimen use, winter interest, natural areas, understory use, parking areas, soggy locations, courtyards and entries

More Choices: pages 34, 36, 38, 40, 41, 59, and 67

Options: 'Warren's Red'—upright form, profuse berries

This tough holly is different from most; it loses its leaves in the winter and grows well in swampy, alkaline soils. Irregular in form, the branches are horizontal and ascending. Yellow fall foliage color provides beautiful color contrast to the red fruit before dropping. Berries show off against bare branches providing winter interest for the landscape. Plant female trees in showy locations, but be sure to include a male tree nearby for pollination purposes.

Ilex latifolia

Lusterleaf Holly

Zones: 7-9

Light Needs:

Mature Size:

20'-25'

10'-12'

Growth Rate:
slow

evergreen tree

Needs: Grow in moist, well-drained acidic soil; established plants will tolerate drought. Grow in sun or shade. Little if any pruning is required. Leave lower limbs to maintain attractive pyramidal tree form.

Good for: screening to provide privacy or block poor views; an evergreen background for deciduous plants; winter interest, specimen use, windbreaks, and woodland gardens

More Choices: pages 30, 34, 36, 40, and 67

Outstanding Features:

- Foliage stays glossy green year-round
- Clusters of bright red berries surround stems
- Dense, pyramidal form provides background

If you have acidic soil, you can't go wrong in planting Lusterleaf Holly. Trees form dense pyramids of shiny green leaves highlighted by the formation of bright red berries in fall that persist through the winter months. Female plants produce the showy red berries if properly pollinated; separate male plants are necessary for pollination, but will not form fruit.

Ilex opaca 'Savannah'

Savannah Holly

Zones: 5-9

Light Needs:

Mature Size:

20'-25'

10'-15'

Growth Rate:
slow

evergreen tree

Needs: Plant in full sun or partial shade. Soil conditions should be fertile, acidic, moist, yet well-drained. Prune trees in the winter if they need shaping up. Female plants produce showy red berries. Males are necessary for pollination. Plant one male for every two to three females.

Good for: specimen use, low-growing street tree, providing winter interest, patio plantings, parking areas, screening, background plantings in shrub beds

More Choices: pages 30, 34, 36, 39, 40, 43, 67, 68, and 69

Outstanding Features:

- Pyramidal form, yellow-green foliage
- Prolific red fruit in winter
- Tolerates air pollution and paving

This versatile holly produces bumper crops of berries that last from late fall through the winter. Trees have naturally pyramidal forms. Leave lower branches all the way to the ground or prune them to expose a portion of the trunk. Foliage is normally a yellow-green color; if leaves turn noticeably yellow, fertilize with acid-loving plant food.

Yaupon Holly

Zones: 7-10

Light Needs:

Mature Size:

15'-20'

6'-8'

Growth Rate:
medium to rapid

evergreen tree

Needs: Plant in any soil from dry to wet, acidic to alkaline. Very adaptable. Grows in sun or shade. Tolerates salt spray, wind, heat, and pruning.

Good for: seaside landscapes including dune plantings, screening, specimen trees, planting beside patios, in natural areas or woodland gardens, attracting birds, foundation plantings, espalier

More Choices: pages 30, 34, 36, 38, 39, 40, 41, 42, 59, 67, and 69

Options: Weeping yaupon, *I. vomitoria* 'Pendula'—narrow shape, attractive drooping branches

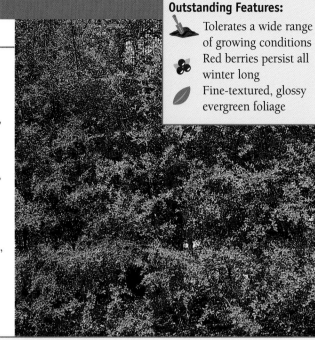

Outstanding Features:

 Tolerates a wide range of growing conditions
Red berries persist all winter long
Fine-textured, glossy evergreen foliage

Yaupon Holly will live anywhere you put it. A very obliging member of the holly family. Glossy, gray-green leaves provide a change in texture that lasts year-round. Stems are whitish to gray in color; young stems are covered with down. Scarlet red berries cover trees fall through winter and are great for attracting flocks of birds into the landscape. Plants can be grown as a small tree or large shrub. Dwarf cultivars are a better choice for shrub use.

Juniperus virginiana

Eastern Red Cedar

Zones: 3-9

Light Needs:

Mature Size:

40'-50'

8'-20'

Growth Rate:
medium

evergreen tree

Needs: Grow in any soil from acidic to alkaline, sandy to clay, wet to dry. Plant in full sun for densest growth. Trees grown in partial shade will be more open. Tolerates wind, salt, and drought. Water new trees regularly the first year to help them establish.

Good for: screening, privacy, windbreaks, shelter belts, seaside landscapes, hillsides, natural areas, providing background for deciduous trees and shrubs, attracting birds, hedges, topiaries

More Choices: pages 30, 34, 38, 39, 40, 41, 42, 67, and 69

Outstanding Features:

Dense foliage stays green year-round
Withstands wind, salt, and dry conditions
Conical form becomes pendulous with age

trees

4

Grow this durable native to block winds and screen poor views, provide a background for your garden, or to add needed privacy in the landscape. Trees are tough enough to plant at the beach and anywhere else you need its wide adaptability. Numerous cultivars are available with varying sizes, forms, and foliage color.

Lagerstroemia indica

Crepe Myrtle

Zones: 7-9

Light Needs:

Mature Size:

15'-25'

15'-25'

Growth Rate:
rapid

deciduous flowering tree

Needs: Plant in full sun in any moist, well-drained soil. Add peat moss or organic matter to soil at planting time. Remove dead wood when it occurs. For larger blooms, remove suckers from the base.

Good for: specimen, patio tree, poolside, parking areas, entries, courtyards, providing privacy, seasonal accent, winter interest, massed plantings, or hedge rows

More Choices: pages 31, 40, 59, 67, and 69

Grown for its fabulous summer flowers, autumn foliage color, attractive peeling bark, and sculptural form. Flowers bloom from mid to late summer in white, red, and all shades in between. Glossy green foliage turns orange, red, and yellow before dropping in the fall. Smooth gray bark peels off to reveal an underbark of various colors. Many superior selections are named after Native American tribes.

Pruning Crepe Myrtle

Crepe Myrtles are commonly the victims of overzealous pruning. Crepe Myrtles that have been pruned sparingly form attractive trees with sturdy, sculptural trunks and spreading canopies. Here's how to prune Crepe Myrtles correctly.

1 **Pinch flexible green suckers by hand.** Remove them from the base of trunks. Suckers are little sprouts that appear at the base of plants. Leaving them on diverts energy from flowering. Suckers can also grow into woody stems, ruining the form of your tree.

2 **Cut away woody stems.** Reach into trees to cut away woody stems that cross other branches. Cut stems no thicker than a pencil with bypass hand pruners; use bypass loppers for larger stems.

STUFF YOU'LL NEED

✔ Bypass hand pruners
✔ Bypass loppers

What to Expect

Maintenance companies often incorrectly advise cutting your Crepe Myrtle back severely, leaving a few thick stubs. Now you know the right way!

Bad Pruning Technique

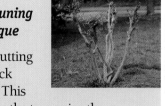

Avoid cutting into thick trunks. This damages the tree, ruins the sculptural form, and makes it an eyesore in winter. The tree will send out long, weak shoots in an attempt to regain health and stability. The shoots will droop under the weight of summer blossoms.

Liquidambar styraciflua 'Rotundiloba'

Fruitless American Sweetgum

Zones: 5-9

Light Needs: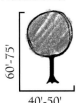

Mature Size:

60'-75'

40'-50'

Growth Rate: medium

deciduous tree

Needs: Plant in full sun. Moist, slightly acidic soil is required for growth. Trees do not tolerate pollution, city life, or areas where its fleshy roots are limited. Remove lower branches in late winter if needed to walk or park beneath trees.

Good for: shading lawns, parking areas, or decks; street tree use

More Choices: pages 34, 40, 67, 68, and 69

More Choices: pages 34, 40, 67, 68, and 69

Outstanding Features:
- Summer and fall foliage color
- Fruitless; no messy gumballs to pick up
- Pyramidal in youth, rounded with age

Large lobed leaves turn various hues in fall, from yellow to red to dark purple. Young trees have a distinctly pyramidal outline that becomes more rounded as they mature. Neat in appearance and because this variety is fruitless, it is neat all the way around. Give roots room to spread—avoid planting areas surrounded by paving. In milder climates, fall color may not be as showy as those which bear fruit. Also try 'L. Styraciflua'—produces spiny gumballs, bright fall foliage; *L. formosana*—leaves are five-lobed, tree shape is conical, bright fall foliage.

Magnolia grandiflora

Southern Magnolia

Zones: 6-10

Light Needs:

Mature Size:

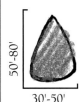

50'-80'

30'-50'

Growth Rate: slow to medium

evergreen flowering tree

Needs: Grows best in well-drained rich soil, but trees tolerate poor soils and wet locations. Soil should be acidic. Plant in full sun or partial shade. Protect from winter winds in northern areas.

Good for: specimen tree, open lawn areas, large estates, screening, soggy soil, espalier blank walls

More Choices: pages 34, 36, 38, 39, 42, 67, and 69

More Choices: pages 34, 36, 38, 39, 42, 67, and 69

Options: 'Bracken's Brown Beauty'— cold-tolerant, brown-backed leaves 'Little Gem'—shrubby form, small sizes D.D. Blancher—tree with upright form

Outstanding Features:
- Large, cream-colored, fragrant flowers
- Dark, coarse-textured leaves
- Broad pyramidal form; low branching

Everything about this magnolia is big—its size, its foliage, its flowers, and its fruit. Blooms up to 12 inches across appear in late spring emitting a scent better than almost any perfume. Rose-red fruit ripens in late fall. Trees need plenty of room to grow and develop their stately form. Avoid planting this tree in small areas. Look for trees that are named; they are generally superior in strength and quality to unnamed varieties.

trees

4

Trees   83

Magnolia x soulangiana

Saucer Magnolia

Zones: 5-9

Light Needs:

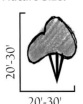

Mature Size:

20'-30'
20'-30'

Growth Rate:
medium

deciduous flowering tree

Needs: Plant in rich soil high in organic matter. Slightly acidic soil is best, but trees tolerate some alkalinity. Mulch well and water regularly in summer to keep soil moist. Prune after flowering and only as needed because cuts heal slowly.

Good for: specimen use, seasonal accents, open lawn areas, large planting beds, groupings, near buildings

More Choices: pages 31, 34, 36, 39, 40, 43, 59, 67, and 69

Options: Northern Japanese Magnolia, *M. kobus*—blooms in midspring

Outstanding Features:

- Big, five- to ten-inch flowers in early spring
- Coarse-textured leaves provide dense shade
- Sculptural form for specimen use

Big, beautiful blooms in shades of white to pink and purple accent this ornamental tree. Often jumping the gun on spring, it blooms during the slightest warm spell often resulting in flower loss due to frost. Flowering occurs before leaves emerge. Planting on a northern exposure may help to delay flowering and reduce flower loss. Hybrids with girls' names bloom a bit later as well. Branches emerge low on the trunk and spread widely to form a crown with an attractive rounded outline.

Magnolia stellata

Star Magnolia

Zones: 5-9

Light Needs:

Mature Size:

15'-20'
10'-15'

Growth Rate:
slow

deciduous flowering tree

Needs: Plant in moist, well-drained soil that's rich in organic matter and acidic. Mulch trees well and water regularly to keep soil moist during summer months. Grows best in partial shade. Plant in warmer parts of Zone 4.

Good for: small specimen trees, seasonal accent, foundation planting, narrow spaces, beside walkways or steps, natural areas, understory trees, woodlands, shaded courtyards

More Choices: pages 36, 40, and 67

Outstanding Features:

- Fragrant, white starry blooms in early spring
- Neat, small size for foundation planting
- Green summer foliage turns yellow in fall

Starry white blooms brighten shady spots during the gray days between winter and spring. This tree stays small and tidy. This is the earliest-blooming magnolia. Planting on a northern exposure may delay flowering and reduce flower loss due to freezing temperatures. Trees look great planted against red brick walls and buildings.

Magnolia virginiana

Sweet Bay Magnolia

Zones: 5-9

Light Needs:

Mature Size:

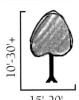

10'-30'+

15'-20'

Growth Rate:
medium

semievergreen tree

Needs: Plant in highly organic, acidic soil that's moist or even wet and boggy. It will not tolerate drought. Grow in sun or partial shade. Protect from winds where winters are cold. Roots will not buckle paving.

Good for: specimen tree use, patios, courtyards, damp locations, naturalized areas, narrow spaces, shrub beds, coastal areas, and screening where winters are warm and mild, confined spaces

More Choices: pages 30, 34, 36, 38, and 40

This magnolia is a good choice if you're looking for a tidy tree with foliage, flowers, and form. Blooming begins in late spring and continues sporadically through the summer months. Foliage is glossy green above with a silvery underside. Trees are highly variable depending on the climate in which they are grown. Trees in Zone 9 may reach up to 50' tall with time and be completely evergreen. A tree in Zone 5 may reach just 10' tall and lose all its foliage in the fall.

Malus floribunda

Japanese Flowering Crabapple

Zones: 3-8

Light Needs:

Mature Size:

15'-25'

15'-25'

Growth Rate:
medium

deciduous flowering tree

Needs: Plant in moist, well-drained, slightly acidic soil. Grow in full sun. Prune new shoots to shape trees by late spring.

Good for: specimen tree, suitable for small yards, seasonal accent, lining driveways, framing patios, low decks, or shrub beds

More Choices: pages 34, 41, 43, 67, and 69

Options: M. 'Pink Spires'—Zones 3-8
M. x *robusta* 'Red Siberian'—Zones 3-8
Selections known for disease-resistance and persistent fruit.
M. 'Red Splendor'—dark foliage, Zone 3
M. 'Royalty'—Zone 3
M. 'Profusion'—Zone 4

Outstanding Features:

Scented flowers open before leaves

Ornamental red fruit in fall

Broad, rounded form; multitrunked

trees

4

Crabapples are known for their spring beauty especially when they burst into bloom. Japanese Flowering Crabapple has deep pink to red buds that open into fading white flowers. Developing fruits are yellow to red in color and add another season of show. They do not persist on the tree during the winter. This selection may be sold as Showy Crabapple. Numerous species, cultivars, and varieties of crabapples are available. Look for those that are disease-resistant and those with persistent fruit for added seasonal enjoyment.

Metasequoia glyptostroboides

Dawn Redwood

Zones: 4-8

Light Needs:

Mature Size:

70'-100'

20'-25'

Growth Rate: rapid

deciduous conifer tree

Needs: Plant in moist—but not soggy—soil. Acidic soils are preferred over alkaline. Grow in full sun. Seldom requires any pruning.

Good for: Large, open lawns or natural areas; groves, lining streets or long driveways, large estates

More Choices: pages 34, 39, 59, 67, and 68

More Choices: pages 34, 39, 59, 67, and 68

Outstanding Features:

✔ Impressive size with conical form

🍃 Fine-textured, feathery bright green foliage

❧ Reddish bark peeling off in long strips

If you have room for a big tree, look no further. Dawn Redwoods can top 100 feet. Feathery foliage turns bronze in autumn before dropping. The large size of this tree will dwarf most single-story houses. Plant away from smaller buildings to avoid comparison or place near larger structures. Trunks of older trees develop buttressed, fluted bases, and possess exfoliating bark.

Myrica cerifera

Wax Myrtle

Zones: 7-9

Light Needs:

Mature Size:

10'-15'

10'-15'

Growth Rate: rapid

evergreen tree

Needs: Plant in wet or dry soil, including poor, sandy soils. Grow in full sun or partial shade. Tolerates heat, salt spray, and high humidity. Trees will perform best with regular watering and fertilization. Prune lower limbs to develop tree form.

Good for: screening, privacy, poolside, parking areas, patios, along walkways, city conditions, seaside landscapes, berms, or areas surrounded by paving, small specimen tree in planting beds

More Choices: pages 30, 34, 36, 38, 39, 42, 43, 59, and 69

More Choices: pages 30, 34, 36, 38, 39, 42, 43, 59, and 69

Outstanding Features:

🍃 Glossy, olive-green leaves year-round

⛏ Tolerates harsh growing conditions,

✔ Fast-growing, pest- and problem-free

Got a black thumb? Plant Wax Myrtle; it'll turn your thumb green no matter where you plant it. Add just a little water and fertilizer, myrtle will soar along with your gardening ego. The dense canopy of this little tree stays green year-round, unless hit with a blast of cold temperatures. Trees take pruning well; easy to trim exposing multiple trunks and developing as small trees. Can also be grown as large shrubs. Thin canopies in ice-prone areas to prevent trees from splitting. Also try: 'Fairfax'—dwarf selection, 6' to 8' tall.

White Pine

Zones: 3-8

Light Needs:

Mature Size:

50'-80'
20'-40'

Growth Rate:
rapid

Outstanding Features:
- Fluffy, soft needles have a bluish hue
- Grows quickly for screen and hedge use
- Full-skirted, graceful, pyramidal form

evergreen tree

Needs: Plant in any well-drained soil; trees thrive in many extremes except heavy clay soil. Grow in full sun. Trees transplant easily into the landscape. Trees are not tolerant of high pollution levels.

Good for: screening for privacy and blocking poor views, filling large empty areas, background plantings, clustering together or planting in rows or groves

More Choices: pages 30, 34, 38, 39, and 59

It's hard to find a screening tree that grows as quickly or is as pretty as White Pine. Bluish green needles are three to five inches long, soft, and touchable. Given room to grow, trees may reach 150' in height. They can also be sheared for hedging use. Allow fallen needles to accumulate as water-conserving, weed-controlling mulch. Water during dry spells. In colder areas, protect from sweeping winds and road salt. Options: 'Nana'—dwarf globe white pine, a rounded shrub.

Chinese Pistache

Zones: 6-9

Light Needs:

Mature Size:

30'-35'
25'-35'

Growth Rate:
medium

Outstanding Features:
- Manageable size and rounded canopy
- Outstanding fall colors of orange to red
- Roots won't buckle paving

deciduous tree

Needs: Plant in full sun. Trees grow best in moist, well-drained soils, but they adapt to less than ideal conditions. Chinese pistache is drought-resistant and tolerant of moderately alkaline conditions. Prune and stake young trees to encourage the growth of a strong, central trunk.

Good for: street, lawn, and patio use; entries, parking areas, city conditions; anchoring the corner of a yard

More Choices: pages 34, 41, 67, 68, and 69

Don't be deterred by ungainly young plants; with a little training and care they mature into neatly rounded shade trees known for brilliant fall color. These are the closest trees providing the colors of Sugar Maple for the South. Summer foliage is dark green. Trees are disease- and pest-free.

trees 4

Prunus cerasifera 'Atropurpurea'

Purple-Leaf Plum

Outstanding Features:
- Light pink flowers in early spring
- Dark purple foliage in summer
- Grows quickly to provide seasonal color

Zones: 4-8

Light Needs:

Mature Size:

15'-30'

15'-25'

Growth Rate: rapid

deciduous flowering tree

Needs: Plant in any soil that is well-drained. They will not tolerate wet feet. Trees aren't particular about soil pH. Grow in full sun for best color development. Prune after flowering. Keep plants growing vigorously for best pest resistance.

Good for: specimen trees, seasonal accent, lining driveways, patio trees, planting in clusters at entries to property, groves

More Choices: pages 31, 34, 40, 41, 59, 67, and 69

Options: 'Thundercloud'—dark pink, fragrant flowers; deep purple foliage; 20' high and wide; Zones 5-8.

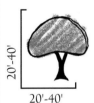

Fast growth and colorful foliage makes Purple-Leaf Plum a popular plant for landscapes. Pink flowers appear in early spring before the foliage; spring foliage emerges ruby-red changing to the summer color of dark purple. Trees are usually short-lived, surviving about 20 years under good growing conditions. Trees will spread by suckering. Plant them where you can easily control sucker growth through mowing or pruning. Purple foliage may clash with some house colors. Also try: 'Versuvias'—double light pink flowers, purple foliage; *P. bireiana*—ruffled pink flowers, greenish-red foliage.

Prunus x yedoensis

Yoshino Cherry

Outstanding Features:
- Light pink buds open to white flowers
- Yellow fall foliage provides seasonality
- Sturdy trunks with spreading canopies

Zones: 5-8

Light Needs:

Mature Size:

20'-40'

20'-40'

Growth Rate: medium

deciduous flowering tree

Needs: Plant in moist, well-drained soil that's moderately fertile. Grow in full sun and provide protection from harsh winds. Keep trees growing vigorously by watering during drought and fertilizing annually.

Good for: specimen trees, seasonal accent, planting near patios, entries, courtyards, street trees, city conditions

More Choices: pages 34, 41, 43, 67, 68, and 69

Options: 'Shidare Yoshino'—weeping, dwarf tree

You too can grow the famous cherry trees of Washington, D.C. Yoshino Cherry opens with clouds of white blooms in early spring before the foliage appears; falling petals resemble snowflakes. Blooms possess a slight fragrance and are not overpowering. Rounded crowns form trees of spectacular spring beauty. Occasionally up to 50' high.

Pyrus calleryana 'Bradford'

Bradford Pear

Zones: 4-8

Light Needs:

Mature Size:

30'-50'
20'-35'

Growth Rate:
rapid

deciduous tree

Needs: Plant in any soil that's well-drained and receives full sun. Trees tolerate city conditions including polluted air and reflected heat from paving. Roots are well-behaved and won't buckle paving. Prune in late winter or early spring.

Good for: Parking, lawns, and street trees, specimens, patios, courtyards, entries, lining driveways, growing in large planting beds, providing seasonal accent

More Choices: pages 31, 34, 43, 59, 67, and 69

Bradford Pear combines all the features desired in an ornamental tree—rapid growth, spring bloom, summer shade, no fruit, and autumn color. Tends to be weak-wooded. Flowers have an unpleasant odor. See pruning information below to minimize winter damage. Look at these cultivars as well for use in the landscape. 'Aristocrat'—less prone to splitting, 30' to 35' high, 20' to 25' wide; 'Capital'—fall leaves coppery, 40' high, 15' wide; 'Chanticleer'—less susceptible to freeze damage than 'Bradford', 30' high, 20' wide; 'Cleveland Select'—blooms very young, 30' to 35' high, 20' wide.

Pruning Bradford Pear

These ornamental pear trees are known for their uniformly shaped canopies. Pruning to remove narrow crotch angles is essential to keep trees from splitting apart during icy weather.

1 **To remove branches,** make the first cut with a pruning saw from the underside of the branch, about a foot from the trunk. Saw about a third of the way through. This cut stops the branch from ripping and splitting the bark.

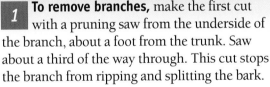

2 **Make the second cut** about an inch farther out along the branch than the first one. Cut from the top of the branch until it comes off.

3 **Remove the remaining branch stub** by cutting upward from the bottom. Make your cut on the outside of the branch bark ridge (where the branch joins the trunk and bark is slightly raised). Trees heal best when pruned here.

4 **Watersprouts are vigorous shoots** that grow straight up from larger branches. They cross other branches and rub against them causing damage to both. Remove them with loppers or hand pruners in either spring or summer.

Quercus agrifolia

Coast Live Oak

Zones: 8-10

Light Needs:

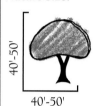

Mature Size:

40'-50'
40'-50'

Growth Rate:
medium

evergreen tree

Needs: Plant in well-drained soil; trees can't tolerate wet soil. Grow in full sun or partial shade. Cover root zones beneath canopies with mulch, not grass or flowers, which require additional water. Overly wet roots may develop oak root fungus.

Good for: shade trees (not in lawn), natural areas, arid landscapes, Xeriscaping, hillsides

More Choices: pages 34, 36, 39, 42, 67, and 69

If you have dry soil and low humidity, this is the shade tree for you. Small leaves make a thick crown for branches that twist with age. Sheds leaves in spring.

Outstanding Features:

- Irregular, picturesque form with age
- Grows in dry soil
- Small hollylike leaves are evergreen

Quercus alba

White Oak

Zones: 3-9

Light Needs:

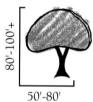

Mature Size:

80'-100'+
50'-80'

Growth Rate:
slow to medium

deciduous tree

Needs: Plant in acidic soil that's moist and well-drained. Grow in full sun. Avoid planting in areas where construction has compacted soils. Make any pruning cuts in late winter or early spring.

Good for: shade trees, large specimen trees, natural areas, woodlands

More Choices: pages 34, 39, 40, 67, and 69

Large landscapes deserve at least one White Oak to provide generations of leafy shade. Dark green summer foliage turns in the fall to a reddish wine and finally to brown. Leaves are large, coarse, and may remain on the tree throughout the winter. Wood is sturdy.

Outstanding Features:

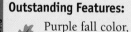

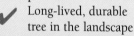

- Purple fall color, leaves remain on tree
- Spreading canopies provide dense shade
- Long-lived, durable tree in the landscape

Quercus coccinea

Scarlet Oak

Zones: 4-9

Light Needs:

Mature Size:

70'-75'

40'-50'

Growth Rate:
medium to rapid

deciduous tree

Needs: Plant in acidic soil that's moist and well-drained. It will tolerate dry, sandy soils. Grow in full sun. Prune in late winter or early spring to prevent spread of disease.

Good for: shade tree, large specimen tree, lawn tree, natural areas, woodland landscapes

More Choices: pages 31, 34, 59, 67, and 69

Outstanding Features:

- Rounded, spreading canopies with age
- Leaves turn bright red in fall
- Impressive size is best suited for large areas

For dense summer shade and bright fall color, add Scarlet Oak to your yard. Trees grow to an impressive size that works well with multistory homes and buildings. Young trees have a pyramidal form with a strong central leader and pendulous lower branches that drop off as the tree matures.

Quercus macrocarpa

Bur Oak

Zones: 2-8

Light Needs:

Mature Size:

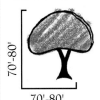

70'-80'

70'-80'

Growth Rate:
slow

deciduous tree

Needs: Plant in just about any soil, including alkaline, dry clay, or sand. Grow in full sun. Tolerates polluted air and a wide range of temperatures. One of the most tolerant oaks to life in the city.

Good for: large specimen or shade tree use, open prairie and natural areas, parks

More Choices: pages 34, 39, 41, 43, and 69

Outstanding Features:

- Tolerates a wide range of growing conditions
- Big tree, long-lived in the landscape
- Coarse-textured leaves offer dense shade

trees

4

This shady oak will grow in difficult conditions where many other oak trees can't. The only requirement: Make sure you have the room for a long-lived, massive tree sometimes reaching over 100' tall. Glossy green leaves turn yellow in the fall. Large acorns, with distinctly fringy cups, provide the other common name of Mossycup Oak.

Quercus palustris

Pin Oak

Zones: 4-8

Light Needs:

Mature Size:

60'-70'

25'-40'

Growth Rate:
rapid

deciduous tree

Needs: Plant in moist, acidic soil—dry soil is okay, but not alkaline. Grow in full sun or partial shade. Endures confined roots, reflected heat from paving, and air pollution.

Good for: shade and street tree use, lining driveways, parking areas, urban conditions, parks, and golf courses

More Choices: pages 31, 34, 39, 40, 41, 43, 59, 68, and 69

Outstanding Features:
- One of the fastest-growing oaks
- Tolerates a range of difficult conditions
- Pyramidal form; pendulous lower branches

In acidic soils there is nothing better than Pin Oak for a big, fast-growing shade tree. Roots won't buckle paving. Foliage turns scarlet in fall; brown leaves remain until spring. Surround with shade-tolerant groundcover, mulch, or paving; shade is too dense for a nice lawn. Remove lower branches for parking or walking beneath trees. Iron chlorosis is a common ailment of trees grown in alkaline soils. It is difficult to nearly impossible to remedy on a long-term basis. Select another tree species more suited to alkaline locations.

Quercus phellos

Willow Oak

Zones: 4-8

Light Needs:

Mature Size:

40'-60'+

30'-40'

Growth Rate:
rapid

deciduous tree

Needs: Grow in fertile, moist acidic soil. Wet clays and loams are not a problem. Trees will tolerate dry, slightly alkaline soil though not the ideal. City conditions don't pose a problem. Transplants easily.

Good for: large specimen, shade, and street tree use; lining long driveways, large patio trees

More Choices: pages 31, 34, 39, 40, 41, 43, 59, 68, and 69

Outstanding Features:
- Fine-textured foliage; unusual in large trees
- Wide, shady canopy; oval form with age
- Behaved roots won't buckle paving

Majestic in size, this oak is big enough to shade your house and your landscape. Long narrow leaves provide fine-textured appearance different from most oaks. Leaves turn varying shades of yellow in the fall. Remove lower limbs to park or walk beneath your tree safely. Iron chlorosis may develop in alkaline soils. Check your pH before planting. Acorns produce numerous seedlings for transplanting.

Quercus shumardii

Shumard Oak

Zones: 5-9

Light Needs:

Mature Size:

80'-100'

50'-60'

Growth Rate:
rapid

deciduous tree

Needs: Plant in soil that's acidic or alkaline, well-drained or damp. Grow in full sun. Roots won't buckle paving. Tolerates reflected heat and air pollution. Easy to grow.

Good for: shade, lawn, or street tree use, lining long driveways, parking areas, large patios, natural areas, damp locations

More Choices: pages 31, 34, 40, 41, 43, 59, 67, 68, and 69

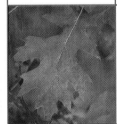

If you need a shade tree that's tough, try this one; it'll grow just about anywhere. Shumard Oaks feature big canopies and red fall color.

Quercus virginiana

Southern Live Oak

Zones: 8-10

Light Needs:

Mature Size:

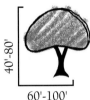

40'-80'

60'-100'

Growth Rate:
slow to medium

evergreen tree

Needs: Grow in almost any soil, including poor, dry, sandy, and alkaline. Slightly acidic, moist soil is optimum. Tolerates wind, heat, salt spray, and compacted soil. Prune to develop suitable leader if needed.

Good for: shade, street, and large specimen use; large estates, coastal locations, open areas, new yards

More Choices: pages 39, 40, 42, 68, and 69

If you want to grow a legacy, plant a Southern Live Oak in your landscape. These broad, spreading trees become massive and live for generations. Horizontal, arching branches grow more picturesque with age. It's not for the small landscape though; trees are best used where they can spread out to their fullest.

trees

4

trees

4

Salix babylonica

Weeping Willow

Zones: 4-8

Light Needs:

Mature Size:

30'-40'

30'-40'

Growth Rate:
rapid

deciduous tree

Needs: Plant in soil that's wet or dry, fertile or poor. Lush, fast growth occurs when grown in moist locations. Grow in full sun. Leaves will shed prematurely during droughts.

Good for: specimen trees, beside ponds or streams, damp, boggy areas, hillsides, large spaces

More Choices: pages 34, 38, 39, 42, 59, and 69

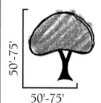

If you have a large pond, you need a weeping willow to reflect on the water's surface. Streamer-like stems dangle to the water; roots love the soggy soil. Roots are invasive; don't plant this tree near waterlines, swimming pools, drain lines, or septic fields. Though they grow quickly, trees may be short-lived. Leaves, twigs, and branches drop frequently resulting in the need for constant cleanup.

Outstanding Features:
- Pendulous branches sweep the ground
- Grows quickly to provide screening
- Large, dramatic form in the landscape

Sophora japonica

Japanese Pagoda Tree

Zones: 6-8

Light Needs:

Mature Size:

50'-75'

50'-75'

Growth Rate:
medium to rapid

deciduous flowering tree

Needs: Plant in loamy, well-drained soil. Tolerates polluted conditions of the city and poor soil. Once established, can tolerate heat and drought. Prune young trees to encourage the development of a main, central trunk.

Good for: large specimen, shade, and lawn tree use; urban landscapes, open areas, large estates, golf courses, parks

More Choices: pages 31, 34, 39, 41, 43, 59, 67, and 69

Options: 'Pendula'—weeping form for accent use

When most trees are plain green, Japanese Pagoda Tree puts on a summer spectacular with its show of scented, creamy flowers. Trees get big; give them room to grow and develop their broad, rounded crown. Can be messy when petals, leaves, and pods drop throughout the year, but summer flowers and leafy shade make it worth planting, even beside patios.

Outstanding Features:
- Creamy white, fragrant flowers in summer
- Rounded canopy produces filtered shade
- Seedpods turn yellow in autumn and persist

Taxodium distichum

Bald Cypress

Zones: 4-10

Light Needs:

Mature Size:

50'-70'

20'-30'

Growth Rate:
rapid

deciduous conifer tree

Needs: Grow in soil that's poor and dry, rich and moist, or just plain wet. Acidic soils are preferred; chlorosis develops on alkaline sites. Grow in full sun. Plants are very wind tolerant.

Good for: Wet areas, compacted soils of newly constructed homes, streetside trees, natural areas, beside ponds or streams, swampy sites, specimen use

More Choices: pages 31, 34, 38, 39, 59, 67, 68, and 69

Outstanding Features:

- Fine-textured feathery foliage; rusty fall color
- Tolerates adverse growing conditions
- Conical form and massive trunk

This swamp native can tolerate the extremes: from soggy soils to hot areas surrounded with paving. Trees form towering cones of feathery foliage. Bright green spring foliage matures to a soft, sage green in summer; fall color is a rusty brown before dropping. Trunks become buttressed with age. When grown in water or in damp, marshy spots, trees develop knobby, protruding roots known as knees. Cones are green to purple in color and mature to brown in a single growing season.

Thuja occidentalis

American Arborvitae

Zones: 2-8

Light Needs:

Mature Size:

40'-60'

10'-15'

Growth Rate:
slow to medium

evergreen tree

Needs: Plant in full sun in moist, well-drained soil; tolerates alkaline soils well. Protect from winter winds, snow, and ice. Prune to shape shrubs during the warm season.

Good for: A specimen shrub, screen, or hedge. Anchor the corner of a planting bed, foundation plantings

More Choices: pages 30, 39, and 41

Options: 'Pyramidalis'-narrow pyramid shape easily maintained by shearing; new leaves bright green; 12' to 15' high, 3' to 4' wide; Zones 3-8

Outstanding Features:

- Easy to prune into desired shape
- Tolerates a variety of soil conditions
- Excellent used for screening and privacy

These low-care evergreens come in an assortment of shapes and sizes, so there's easily one to fit every yard. Most arborvitae leaves turn yellow-brown in winter, which is unappealing to some. Cultivars are available that maintain a good green color even in winter. Heavy snow or ice can break shrubs and disfigure plantings; knock snow away with a broom if this is a problem in your growing area.

trees

4

Tilia cordata

Littleleaf Linden

Zones: 4-7

Light Needs:

Mature Size:

60'-70'

30'-50'

Growth Rate:
medium

deciduous tree

Needs: Plant in any soil that's moist, including acidic or alkaline, fertile or poor. Trees can withstand the compacted soils of new construction as well as pollution and paving. Grow in full sun.

Good for: lawn, specimen, shade, and street tree use; parking areas, lining driveways, formal landscapes, patio trees

More Choices: pages 34, 39, 40, 41, 42, 43, 67, 68, and 69

This tree's uniform shape makes it a good choice for planting in neat rows or squares and to add symmetry to the landscape. Glossy green foliage turns yellow-green in fall. Small summer flowers aren't showy but they're fragrant. Several cultivars are available that differ in form and growth rate. Trees can be grown in the warmer parts of Zone 3.

Tsuga canadensis

Canadian Hemlock

Zones: 3-7

Light Needs:

Mature Size:

40'-70'

25'-35'

Growth Rate:
medium

evergreen tree

Needs: Plant in acidic soil that's moist but well-drained. Grow in sun or partial shade in areas protected from the wind. Water new trees for two growing seasons to ensure good establishment. Afterwards, water during severe droughts. Trees are not tolerant of pollution.

Good for: screening, background, hedging along property lines, natural areas, woodlands, mountainsides, large estates

More Choices: pages 30, 34, 36, and 67

Options: 'Pendula'—slow-growing; gracefully drooping branches

Give your garden a look reminiscent of a cool, green mountainside by planting Canadian Hemlock. They will form a screen concealing undesirable views or a backdrop for other shrubs in the planting bed. Plants can tolerate heavy pruning and are often planted in hedges. Trees look best when lower branches can remain in place all the way to the ground.

Ulmus parvifolia

Chinese Elm

Zones: 5-9

Light Needs:

Mature Size:

35'-45'

20'-25'

Growth Rate:
rapid

deciduous tree; evergreen in frost-free areas

Needs: Plant in moist, loamy soil for best results, though trees will also grow in dry, sandy, or alkaline soils. Grow in full sun. Roots will not buckle paving. Trees endure heat, drought, and pollution.

Good for: Shading small areas such as decks, patios, courtyards, and entries; streetside trees, parking areas, sideyards, narrow spaces, urban landscapes

More Choices: pages 31, 34, 39, 41, 43, 59, 67, 68, and 69

Options: 'Sempervirens'—pedulous canopy 'Drake'—good heat tolerance

This just may be the ultimate patio tree. Its small size, neat habit, fast-growth, and leafy shade makes it ideal for sitting areas. Dark green summer foliage changes to yellow and finally to reddish purple in the fall. Ample root system makes growing grass beneath this tree difficult. Bark is a mottled combination of gray, green, orange, and brown. Very ornamental.

Zelkova serrata

Japanese Zelkova

Zones: 6-9

Light Needs:

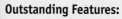

Mature Size:

50'-80'

50'-80'

Growth Rate:
medium to rapid

deciduous tree

Needs: Plant in fertile soil that's moist but well-drained. Soil pH isn't a problem. Trees grow in acidic or alkaline soils. They tolerate wind and drought once established. Reflected heat from paving and pollution don't pose a problem. Prune as needed to keep limbs overhead.

Good for: street, shade, and lawn tree use, lining walkways or drives, beside decks, entries, or patios

More Choices: pages 31, 40, 43, 59, 67, 68, and 69

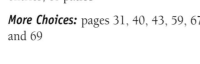

Consider this tree as a replacement for the disease-prone American Elm. Leafy shade, upright branches and sturdy trunks make it perfect for patios, yards, or lining streets. Tree trunks exfoliate in old age revealing colorful inner bark. Plants are resistant to many of the insects and diseases that plague elms.

trees 4

shrubs

Chapter 5
shrubs

*Vanhoutte Spirea
(Spiraea x vanhouttei)
Page 146*

Shrubs add beauty to your
landscape throughout the seasons.
Plant groupings of the same shrubs
together to show them at their
best. For year-round interest,
choose shrubs with various seasonal
characteristics for grouping in
different areas of your yard.

*Dwarf Burning Bush
(Euonymus alatus)
Page 123*

Depend on Shrubs

Whether you're new to landscaping or have been working in your yard
for years, this chapter helps you select, plant, and care for shrubs.
The following pages offer tips and techniques. Landscaping decisions
are a challenge because of the variety of available shrubs. But this chapter—
complete with selection guides listing shrubs for specific purposes and growing
conditions—makes it easier to buy the right shrub, plant it in the right place,
and keep it thriving.

Provide the Framework

Rely on shrubs to supply the
framework your landscape needs.
Shrubs define spaces and hold the
composition together. Use them to
establish unity (see pages 12-13),
provide background, screen
unwanted views, complement your
house, enhance privacy, and provide
attractive accents. The selection
guides help you select a palette of
shrubs to beautify your landscape.
They also provide ideas about solving

problems identified when you made
your site analysis. The guides match
plants to the growing conditions of
your yard and orchestrate a changing
seasonal show of form and color.

Prepare to Purchase

After you've chosen your shrubs for
planting, you'll need to determine
their arrangement in your planting
beds. Start by finding out the growth
rate and mature plant size. Shrub
descriptions begin on page 114.
Knowing these facts helps you space

your shrubs correctly. As a general
rule, set plants so that the distance
between them—measuring from the
center of one plant to the center of
the next plant—is equal to or
slightly less than the plant's mature
spread. This gives shrubs room to
grow and provides the desired
massed effect without large gaps at
maturity. Space slow-growing
species a little closer together.

Draw your planting beds to scale
on paper. Fill in with circles that
touch slightly (also drawn to scale).

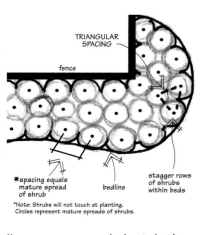

TRIANGULAR SPACING

fence

*spacing equals mature spread of shrub

bedline

stagger rows of shrubs within beds

*Note: Shrubs will not touch at planting. Circles represent mature spreads of shrubs.

How you arrange your shrubs at planting time has a big influence on how evident your bedlines become. The front row of the bed is the most important, so start there.

The circles represent your shrubs at maturity; they won't touch at planting time. Count the circles to determine how many shrubs of each type you will need before going to the store.

Prepare to Plant

Arrange shrubs in the actual planting bed while still in their containers. You can finalize their spacing without worrying about shrubs drying out. (Always remove

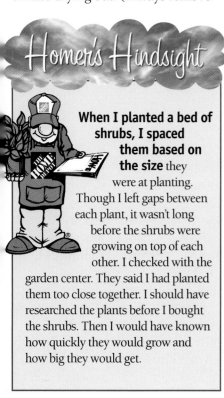

Homer's Hindsight

When I planted a bed of shrubs, I spaced them based on the size they were at planting. Though I left gaps between each plant, it wasn't long before the shrubs were growing on top of each other. I checked with the garden center. They said I had planted them too close together. I should have researched the plants before I bought the shrubs. Then I would have known how quickly they would grow and how big they would get.

pots just before planting. Take only one plant out of its pot at a time.) First, position shrubs to follow the bedlines. This reinforces the shape of the bedline you spent so much time designing. Next, place shrubs in the back of the bed to follow elements that define this area, such as a fence or the wall of your home. Finally, fill the center by setting a second row behind the shrubs following the bedline. Stagger their placement in a triangular pattern (see diagram) so that no two shrubs line up. Work front to back, making adjustments and rearranging rows to avoid gaps. Before digging holes, move containers around until you're completely satisfied. Turn each shrub so that its best side faces the most important angle of view. Professionals take time with this phase. You should, too. You'll live with your decisions for a long time.

Curving paths of lawn set off attractive planting beds. Make such paths equal to at least one mower width, preferably two.

Hedges

Hedges are as functional as they are great-looking. Will yours be formal or informal, tall growing for screening and privacy, or low growing for outlining a planting bed? Use this list to help guide your selections. On the pages referenced, look for photos and information about shrubs that include your growing zone.

Evergreen shrubs suitable for hedging:

Common Name	Zones	Page	Common Name	Zones	Page
Cape Honeysuckle *Tecomaria capensis*	10	205	Korean Boxwood *Buxus microphylla koreana*	5-9	119
Cherry Laurel *Prunus caroliniana*	6-9	137	Oleander *Nerium oleander*	8-10	203
Chinese Hibiscus *Hibiscus rosa-sinensis*	9-10	201	Parson's Juniper *Juniperus chinensis 'Parsonii'*	3-9	132
Chinese Variegated Privet *Ligustrum sinense 'Variegatum'*	7-10	135	Pyracantha *Pyracantha coccinea*	6-8	138
Country Dancer Rose *Rosa 'Country Dancer'*	4-9	140	Redtip Photinia *Photinia x fraseri*	6-9	136
Downy Jasmine *Jasminum multiflorum*	9-10	202	Sasanqua Camellia *Camellia sasanqua*	7-9	120
Dwarf Burford Holly *Ilex cornuta 'Burfordii Nana'*	6-9	128	Sweet Viburnum *Viburnum odoratissimum*	8-10	205
Dwarf Yaupon Holly *Ilex vomitoria 'Nana'*	7-10	130	Texas Silverado Sage *Leucophyllum frutescens 'Silverado'*	8-9	202
Glossy Abelia *Abelia x grandiflora*	7-9	114	Thorny Elaeagnus *Elaeagnus pungens*	7-9	122
Gruss an Aachen Rose *Rosa 'Gruss an Aachen'*	5-9	141	Variegated Pittosporum *Pittosporum tobira 'Variegata'*	8-10	204
Indian Hawthorn *Rhaphiolepis indica*	8-10	204	Waxleaf Ligustrum *Ligustrum lucidum*	7-10	134
Ixora *Ixora coccinea*	10	202	White Rock Rose *Cistus x hybridus*	8-10	200

Availability varies by area and conditions (see page 21). Check with your garden center.

Shrubs 5

Well-chosen shrubs marry
the house to the yard,
making the architecture a
natural fit with the land.

Foundation Planting

Plants growing close to your house are known as foundation
plantings. Their primary functions are hiding the base of the house
and connecting your home to the rest of the landscape. Shrubs
provide numerous options for dressing up your home. Break out of the old
mold—think about ways other than planting a straight hedge across the front
of your home.

Use plants with contrasting
forms or colors to create
entry accents.

Bedlines First Your house
should seem nestled into the
landscape. For all but the most
contemporary styles of architecture,
which might call for angular lines,
smoothly curving bedlines soften
the straight lines of houses. This
complements architecture, making
houses become part of their settings.

Start planning your foundation
planting by laying out and installing
the planting bed (see pages 44-45).
A design plan results in a much
more attractive project than if you
limit yourself to following the shape
of the house or keeping an old
landscape. After drawing a rough
sketch for the bedlines around your

home, take a step back and look at
your house. You'll want to enhance
attractive features such as windows,
stone chimneys, and the front-door
area. Things you wish you didn't
see—exposed foundations, meters,
blank walls, and dingy siding—are
candidates for screening.

Next, go inside your home and
look out the windows. Do you keep
the blinds shut to block glare or
provide privacy? Use landscaping to
solve such problems. Windows that
you frequently look through should
offer an attractive view. It's important
that everyday living spaces such as
the kitchen, breakfast room, and den
have views. Make notes about what
you see from them. If there's nothing
to look at, it's time to add fresh
landscaping for an attractive view.
Remember this as you fine-tune
your sketches of bedlines, making
the necessary adjustments.

Filling Beds Shrubs are the primary ingredient of most foundation plantings. If properly selected, they fit well beneath windows and grow together to form neat groups. Groups of shrubbery, known as masses, grow to form a single unit where individual plants are not noticed. Massing shrubs complements house size better than separate plants do. Resist the urge to prune each shrub into an individual plant; instead, let the shrubs grow together and trim only as needed to shape the mass.

Position shrubs in foundation plantings to follow bedlines, not the house. Fill curved beds with a curving arrangement of plants. If you already have a straight-line foundation planting, add more of the same shrubs in front of the hedge to stagger its shape. Then, add front layers of shorter plants arranged to follow the bedlines. Let the architecture of your house influence where you put accent plants. Fill in niches, frame attractive windows and doors, or add charming touches to porch posts and walls with trees, shrubs, groundcovers, and vines. (See page 175 to select appropriate vines that will grow on your home without damaging it.)

Foundation Shrubs

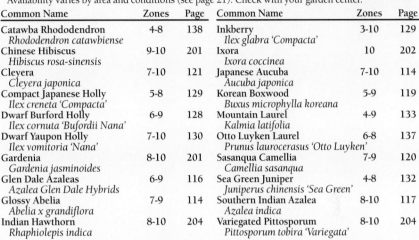

Select shrubs that include your range within their zones. Then, find more information on the pages specified. You'll need to know the mature size, rate of growth, and natural form of any plant you select to grow near your house. Don't choose naturally arching plants if what you want is a tightly clipped look.

Evergreen shrubs for foundation planting:

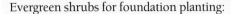

Availability varies by area and conditions (see page 21). Check with your garden center.

Common Name	Zones	Page	Common Name	Zones	Page
Catawba Rhododendron *Rhododendron catawbiense*	4-8	138	Inkberry *Ilex glabra 'Compacta'*	3-10	129
Chinese Hibiscus *Hibiscus rosa-sinensis*	9-10	201	Ixora *Ixora coccinea*	10	202
Cleyera *Cleyera japonica*	7-10	121	Japanese Aucuba *Aucuba japonica*	7-10	114
Compact Japanese Holly *Ilex creneta 'Compacta'*	5-8	129	Korean Boxwood *Buxus microphylla koreana*	5-9	119
Dwarf Burford Holly *Ilex cornuta 'Bufordii Nana'*	6-9	128	Mountain Laurel *Kalmia latifolia*	4-9	133
Dwarf Yaupon Holly *Ilex vomitoria 'Nana'*	7-10	130	Otto Luyken Laurel *Prunus laurocerasus 'Otto Luyken'*	6-8	137
Gardenia *Gardenia jasminoides*	8-10	201	Sasanqua Camellia *Camellia sasanqua*	7-9	120
Glen Dale Azaleas *Azalea Glen Dale Hybrids*	6-9	116	Sea Green Juniper *Juniperus chinensis 'Sea Green'*	4-8	132
Glossy Abelia *Abelia x grandiflora*	7-9	114	Southern Indian Azalea *Azalea indica*	8-10	117
Indian Hawthorn *Rhaphiolepis indica*	8-10	204	Variegated Pittosporum *Pittosporum tobira 'Variegata'*	8-10	204

Some trees are not good near your home. Trees that grow large or have weak wood or invasive roots are poor choices for foundation planting. However, many small ornamental trees are just right for creating attractive focal points seen from main windows. They also offer a sense of shelter to people nearing your house along a walkway. The need to establish a transition between indoor and outdoor spaces is important, too; the sheltering effect of small trees helps do just that. Lastly, well-placed small trees help bring tall, multistory homes into human scale, making people feel more comfortable coming to your door.

Underplant such trees with shrubs and groundcovers to give your foundation planting a layered look that's sure to be an improvement over the single-row hedge style. Layers of shorter plants help to define your bedline plan and wrap your home with broad and generous sweeps of plantings. Layering allows you to build a framework of evergreen plants for a solid background that enhances your home year-round, and provide an anchor for the landscape composition. Deciduous shrubs and small trees as well as annuals and perennials can be added for seasonal interest in the foreground.

Foundation planting is important for backyards, too. Include paving in your design for entertaining.

Planting a Container Shrub

Planting shrubs correctly isn't difficult. Follow these steps to give your new plant the best possible start. Don't worry if you have an entire bed to fill. The more shrubs you plant, the more efficient and quicker you'll become at planting them.

What to Expect
Workers hired to dig these holes might try to talk you out of making the holes wide. Remain firm and your shrubs will thrive as a result.

1 **Pick a spot to plant your new shrub.** Make sure growing conditions match the needs of your plant. There should be enough space around the area for the shrub to grow undisturbed for many years to come.

Dig a hole twice as wide as the plant's container. This will give roots room to grow into the good, loosened soil before venturing through into native soil. Dig the hole only as deep as the container is tall to prevent planting too deep.

2 **Carefully remove the shrub from its plastic pot and lay it on the ground.** (Don't tug on the plant to pull it out.) Using the shovel blade, score the root ball gently to loosen the roots. The root ball should continue to retain the shape of the container. Scoring encourages feeder roots to grow beyond the root ball, establishing the plant in your yard faster.

In the Zone

New plants may need daily watering for the first few weeks, especially during hot weather.
In cooler seasons, you can water every other day for the first week. After that, cut back to once a week for 2 to 3 months, then reduce to once a month, until shrubs have weathered a full growing season. Water faithfully unless nature supplies at least one-half inch of water during the week. Once established, properly sited plants will need supplemental water only during hot, dry spells.

3 **Set the shrub in the hole to check the depth.** The top of the root ball—where stems emerge from the soil—should be level with the surface of the undisturbed ground around the hole. If your shrub sits too low, the hole is too deep. Planting your shrub at this level may cause stems to rot. Remove the plant and shovel additional soil into the bottom of the hole. Press loose soil firmly to prevent settling later. Put the plant into the hole to check the depth again.
If the top of the root ball sits too high, remove the plant and dig the hole deeper. An exception to this step occurs when planting in heavy clay soils. In these locations, plant shrubs an inch or two higher than the level of the undisturbed soil to prevent water from collecting around roots.

Handling Your Shrub

▲ **Good** Always carry new plants by their nursery containers.

▲ **Not Good** Holding shrubs by their branches can stress and break roots and stems.

4 **Mix topsoil or composted organic matter** with the soil you dug from the hole, usually at a ratio of 1:1. In areas with high rainfall and heavy clay soil, reduce the amount of organic matter in the mix to 4:1.

Shovel the mixed soil around the plant, filling the hole completely. Don't tamp the soil in place because that can destroy porosity. Water to settle the soil. Add additional soil mixture as needed after settling occurs.

Use excess soil to form a moat 3 to 4 inches high around the perimeter of the hole. Pat firmly in place to keep water from running off.

Good idea! → **Putting the Best Face on Things** Before backfilling, turn your shrub so that its best side is facing the direction from which it will be viewed. Once the dirt's in the hole, it's harder to adjust the shrub's direction.

5 **Mulch the area inside the moat with a 2- to 3-inch layer of organic mulch.** Mulching retains moisture, cools the soil, and prevents weeds around the plant. Hay, pine straw, ground bark, compost, or shredded leaves are ideal. (Avoid bark nuggets, which float and wash away.) Use less mulch around stems. Mulch that fills the crotches of low stems can cause fungal problems.

Water your new shrub thoroughly. Lay a garden hose at the base of the plant and turn the water on to a gentle stream. Fill the moat slowly several times, letting water soak in.

Planting Shrubs on Slopes

Shrubs should always be planted upright, even if they're on sloping ground. Most upright stems will naturally reach for the vertical position as they grow, even if they have to bend to do so. Dig holes for shrubs on sloping sites much the way you would on a level site. Make sure plants are positioned straight up and down once they are placed in the hole. Build the soil moat only on the downhill side of the plant. The top of the moat should be level with the uphill soil. This prevents water from rushing down past the shrub before getting a chance to soak in. If your soil is heavy clay, omit the moat but build up the soil to form a level planting area before setting your new shrub in place.

Pruning Evergreen Shrubs

Hold those clippers! There are things you need to know before pruning your evergreen shrubs.

First, determine what types of evergreens you have planted. Needled evergreens have needles surrounding plant stems. They may be short or long, soft or stiff depending on the plant. Broad-leaf evergreens have leaves ranging from the large leaves of rhododendrons to the small leaves of boxwood.

Pruning Style

Next, decide if the plant is going to or should have an informal or formal look. Plants informally pruned are not sheared into shapes the way shrubbery is in formal gardens. Both needled and broad-leaf evergreens can be pruned to maintain a natural, informal style. Shrubs with small leaves and naturally compact forms are good choices for shearing into a formal style, as are many needled shrubs.

STUFF YOU'LL NEED

✔ Hand pruners for pencil-thick branches
✔ Loppers for bigger branches
✔ Hedge trimmers for shearing
✔ Sharpening stone
✔ Garden gloves

What to Expect

If you find it necessary to trim your shrubs late in the growing season, don't be surprised if fresh growth appears and then turns brown during a cold snap. While unsightly, the plant is unharmed.

Selective pruning

When you're finished pruning selectively, all cuts will be concealed by foliage.

Selective pruning removes wayward branches while retaining a plant's natural form.

Why: Keep shrubs neat and control their size while maintaining natural, informal forms.

When: Prune needled evergreen shrubs in late winter or early spring. Prune flowering, broad-leaf evergreens right after bloom.

How: Reach inside shrubs and find where each long shoot emerges from stiff, older wood. Make pruning cuts here, inside the shrub, removing only the flexible shoot. (Cuts on stiff, older wood will not sprout again.) Do not leave any stubs. Make cuts toward the tops of plants where sunlight prompts the most new growth. Avoid pruning evergreens severely at the bottom where there's less sunlight.

Shearing

Shearing cuts the surface of a plant instead of individual branches.

To give shrubs a tightly clipped, formal look, shear them on the surface, shaping them into the desired form. Plants suitable for shearing grow new twigs and leaves from each cut, making foliage thick and dense.

Why: Create a formal, sculpted look in the landscape.

When: Shear in warm weather, promoting fresh growth. Clip frequently to keep shrubs neatly trimmed and to control the size of evergreen shrubs.

How: Angle the blades of sharpened hedge trimmers as needed to cut the surface and to shape it. Stand back frequently to assess your work. Electric hedge trimmers make shearing large hedges easy. Use care to avoid overdoing it and whittling your shrubs away to bare branches.

Pinching

Pinching soft, new growth controls the size of evergreen shrubs.

Bright green sprouts on pines, spruce, and fir are called candles. Pinching by hand is the best way to control plant size and keep these evergreens neat without browning the tips.

Why: Control size and shape quickly and neatly during the early part of the growing season.

When: Pinch soft, new growth on nonflowering evergreens in late spring or early summer before the shoots "harden off," becoming stiff and woody.

How: Clasp the stem of the plant where the new growth is attached to the older wood. Pinch off the portion of new growth you want removed, even the entire shoot. Buds for next year's growth will form at this point.

Design Tip

Before pruning your plant, determine its natural form at maturity. Check the shrub encyclopedia or ask a garden staffer to describe its natural mature form. Many beautiful plants have been ruined by improper pruning.

The larger the leaf, the less pruning an evergreen shrub requires. Broad-leaf evergreens with big leaves aren't well suited for shearing. Ragged, brown-edged foliage and blunted stems producing few leaves will result. If you want shrubs that can be clipped neatly into smooth forms, choose evergreens with naturally compact shapes. These shrubs may have either needled foliage or very small leaves.

Trim flowering evergreen shrubs when flowers fade. Use hand pruners to cut off the dead blooms and tips of small branches. This keeps plants from becoming shaggy and overgrown. Trimming prompts fresh growth and flower bud development for next year.

Homer's Hindsight

I pruned my azaleas in autumn one year, long after they had finished blooming. The next spring, my shrubs had no flowers! Without realizing it, I had cut off all the new flower buds. Now I've learned that azaleas bloom on "old wood." They form buds on this year's stems for next year. Pruning my azaleas immediately after flowering ensures a beautiful display of flowers every spring.

Rule of Thumb in Pruning Hedges

▲ **Right** A hedge pruned narrower at the top than the bottom will stay lush and full from the ground up.

▲ **Wrong** Pruning hedges wider at the top than at the bottom results over time in lower branches with thin, spindly foliage.

Pruning Rhododendrons

When the flowers of these evergreen shrubs fade, bend and snap them off at their bases. (Be careful to remove only the soft flower part, not the stiff wood from which it grew.) Getting rid of old flowers is called deadheading. When you deadhead a rhododendron, you encourage the plant to produce new leaves and form fresh flower buds for next year's show.

Prune dead, leafless branches from rhododendrons during any season. Make the cuts on dead wood just above its connection to the main, live stem. Sterilize tools with rubbing alcohol between cuts in order to avoid spreading possible disease.

Dead leaves on the branches indicate dieback, a fungal problem. Cut away dead branches, making each cut a few inches below the problem to avoid cutting into and leaving infected wood. Sterilize tools between pruning cuts. Destroy cuttings. The following spring, after blooming, spray a fungicide containing basic copper sulfate. Repeat applications twice at two-week intervals.

Pruning Flowering Shrubs

Flowering shrubs need occasional shaping. Keep them under control without sacrificing flowers or form.

Selective Pruning

Prune spring-flowering shrubs when blossoms fade to avoid cutting off next year's flowers.

Prune spring-flowering shrubs as soon as flowers fade. Many spring-flowering shrubs, such as azaleas, bloom on "old wood." They develop next year's flower buds on this year's growth. If you wait too late in the season to prune, you will remove next spring's show of blossoms. Summer-blooming shrubs can be pruned in the spring before new growth begins.

Unless a shrub is severely overgrown and warrants hard pruning, make selective pruning your goal. Selective pruning reduces size and refines shape. No cuts are evident.

Reaching into shrubs to make cuts will hide unsightly stubs and preserve natural forms.

To prune selectively, locate an overgrown branch. Reach into the center of the plant so the cut is made deep within the shrub. Make your cut just above a leaf or where the stem emerges from a main branch. New growth will begin at this point. Pruning this way achieves three things. First, foliage hides ugly stubs from view. Second, removal of individual branches preserves the plant's natural form. Finally, selective pruning encourages prolific flowering. Sunlight reaches the center of the plant, promoting growth of new buds and leaves.

Give flowering shrubs a light pruning whenever you notice stray stems that have gone awry, giving your plant a hairy look. Use selective pruning methods to remove such branches so the natural form of the plant is preserved.

Shearing a flowering shrub—cutting the outer edge of a branch to change a shrub's size and shape—eventually damages the plant. Dense, twiggy growth emerges from the multiple cuts, shading the center of the shrub. In time, leaves and flowers grow only along the outside edges of the plant, giving it a thin, scalped look. Some flowering shrubs send up long, stray shoots in protest, making trimming necessary all over again to eliminate the odd appearance of the plant. (Don't cut too much if flowering is finished.)

What to Expect

Avoid the temptation to switch from hand tools to electric trimmers. Unless you're trimming a big, formally clipped hedge, you'll be disappointed if you use them on most shrubs.

Wisdom of the Aisles

Rubbing alcohol is a bargain shopper's dream for plant disease prevention. Fill a spray bottle with the alcohol and make it a habit to spritz pruning tools to sterilize them between cuts, even when you're working on just a single plant. Nonsterilized tools can transfer diseases from one branch to another and spread infections throughout your entire landscape.

Pruning Hydrangeas

Hydrangeas can be trimmed in fall. Hydrangeas hold their big, beautiful blooms well into autumn. Flowers fade from white, pink, or blue to various shades of cream, pinkish brown, or tan. Leave them on shrubs to enjoy them in your yard. If you need to give your shrub a trim, wait until flowers have completely dried on their stems before pruning. The dried flowers make wonderful arrangements in your home. You should still plan to do major pruning on most hydrangeas in spring to avoid cutting off next year's flowers.

Annabelle Hydrangea (Hydrangea arborescens 'Annabelle') Page 126

Some plants are naturally arching, loose and airy. Resist the urge to cut them into tight shapes.

Hard Pruning

Overgrown shrubs have big, healthy root systems, making them worth renovating.

There are times when drastic measures are justified. Neglected shrubs become large and develop poor shape. You could just start over with a new plant, but don't let your eyes convince you that the old shrub is hopeless. What you can't see is the most valuable part of the plant.

Overgrown shrubs have had time to establish big, healthy root systems. It will take years for a replacement plant to do as well.

You can start over and still save the most valuable part of the shrub. But in doing so, you have to be ruthless. Prune individual branches nearly to the ground. Stagger cutting heights some so that all branches won't be at the same level. This will make the new growth appear to fill out faster.

Late winter or early spring, before new growth emerges, is the ideal time for hard pruning. (You can do it any time of year except just before a freeze.) Pruning this severely might result in no flowers for a season or two. In the meantime, you'll be amazed and pleased at how quickly your shrub can recover and how much better it looks despite your apparent abuse.

Hard pruning is not for the soft-hearted. Cut overgrown shrubs drastically to start over.

Shrubs 5

Oakleaf Hydrangea
(Hydrangea quercifolia)
Page 127

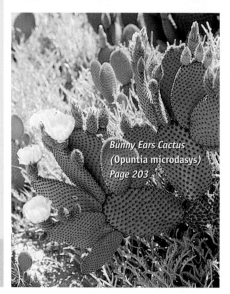

Bunny Ears Cactus
(Opuntia microdasys)
Page 203

Low shrubs suitable for clipping, such as this Korean Boxwood (page 119), lend structure and a tidy touch to small gardens containing lots of color.

Choosing Shrubs by Characteristics

Identify particular plant characteristics that meet your needs. A plant's growth rate, its mature form, and foliage texture are other traits to consider when selecting shrubs. Availability varies by area and site conditions (see page 21). Check with your garden center.

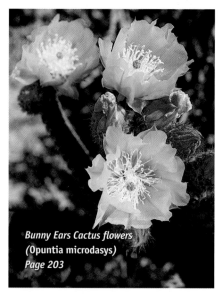

Bunny Ears Cactus flowers
(Opuntia microdasys)
Page 203

Fine-textured shrubs

Common Name	Zones	Page
Bouvardia	9-10	200
Bouvardia longiflora 'Albatross'		
Cape Honeysuckle	10	205
Tecomaria capensis		
Dwarf Yaupon Holly	7-10	130
Ilex vomitoria 'Nana'		
Heller Japanese Holly	5-8	128
Ilex crenata 'Helleri'		
Ixora	10	202
Ixora coccinea		
Korean Boxwood	5-9	119
Buxus microphylla koreana		
Nandina	6-9	135
Nandina domestica		
New Zealand Tea Tree	9-10	133
Leptospermum scoparium		
Pampas Grass	7-10	121
Cortaderia selloana		
Pygmy Date Palm	9-10	204
Phoenix roebelenii		
White Rock Rose	8-10	200
Cistus x hybridus		

Coarse-textured shrubs

Common Name	Zones	Page
American Beautyberry	7-10	120
Callicarpa americana		
Annabelle Hydrangea	3-9	126
Hydrangea arborescens 'Annabelle'		
Bird-of-Paradise	9-10	205
Strelitzia reginae		
Bunny Ears Cactus	10	203
Opuntia microdasys		
Chinese Hibiscus	9-10	201
Hibiscus rosa-sinensis		
Doublefile Viburnum	4-8	149
Viburnum plicatum tomentosum		
European Cranberrybush	3-8	149
Viburnum opulus 'Roseum'		
Japanese Fatsia	8-10	124
Fatsia japonica		
Nikko Blue Hydrangea	6-9	126
Hydrangea macrophylla 'Nikko Blue'		
Oakleaf Hydrangea	5-9	127
Hydrangea quercifolia		
Oleander	8-10	203
Nerium oleander		
PeeGee Hydrangea	3-8	127
Hydrangea paniculata 'Grandiflora'		
Sweet Viburnum	8-10	205
Viburnum odoratissimum		
Variegated Croton	10	200
Codiaeum variegatum var. pictum		

5 shrubs

Upright shrubs

Common Name	Zones	Page
African Iris *Moraea iridioides*	9-10	203
Bird-of-Paradise *Strelitzia reginae*	9-10	205
Bunny Ears Cactus *Opuntia microdasys*	10	203
Butterfly Bush *Buddleia davidii*	5-9	119
Dwarf Burning Bush *Euonymus alatus 'Compacta'*	3-8	123
Golden Euonymus *Euonymus japonicus 'Aureus'*	7-9	124
Japanese Aucuba *Aucuba japonica*	7-10	114
Mountain Laurel *Kalmia latifolia*	4-9	133
Nandina *Nandina domestica*	6-9	135
Oleander *Nerium oleander*	8-10	203
Redtip Photinia *Photinia x fraseri*	6-9	136
Rose of Sharon *Hibiscus syriacus*	5-9	125
Sweet Viburnum *Viburnum odoratissimum*	8-10	205
Waxleaf Ligustrum *Ligustrum lucidum*	7-10	134

Pyramidal shrubs

Common Name	Zones	Page
Cherry Laurel *Prunus caroliniana*	6-9	137
Cleyera *Cleyera japonica*	7-10	121
Dwarf Alberta Spruce *Picea glauca 'Conica'*	3-8	136
Nellie R. Stevens Holly *Ilex x 'Nellie R. Stevens'*	6-9	130

Slow-growing shrubs

Common Name	Zones	Page
Catawba Rhododendron *Rhododendron catawbiense*	4-8	138
Dwarf Alberta Spruce *Picea glauca 'Conica'*	3-8	136
Dwarf Burning Bush *Euonymus alatus 'Compacta'*	3-8	123
Dwarf Yaupon Holly *Ilex vomitoria 'Nana'*	7-10	130
Gumpo Azalea *Azalea hybrida*	6-9	116
King Sago *Cycas revoluta*	8-10	201
Miss Kim Lilac *Syringa patula 'Miss Kim'*	3-7	148
Pygmy Date Palm *Phoenis roebelenii*	9-10	204
Texas Silverado Sage *Leucophyllum frutescens 'Silverado'*	8-9	202

Baby's Breath Spirea (*Spiraea thunbergii*), page 147, has an arching form that's attractive even when flowering is finished.

Arching shrubs

Common Name	Zones	Page
Baby's Breath Spirea *Spiraea thunbergii*	4-8	147
Border Forsythia *Forsythia x intermedia*	6-9	125
Bridalwreath Spirea *Spiraea prunifolia*	5-8	146
Chinese Variegated Privet *Ligustrum sinense 'Variegatum'*	7-10	135
Dwarf Leucothoe *Leucothoe axillaris*	5-9	134
Glossy Abelia *Abelia x grandiflora*	7-9	114
New Zealand Tea Tree *Leptospermum scoparium*	9-10	133
Peegee Hydrangea *Hydrangea paniculata 'Grandiflora'*	3-8	127
Sea Green Juniper *Juniperus chinensis 'Sea Green'*	4-8	132
Showy Jasmine *Jasminum floridum*	7-9	131
Thorny Elaeagnus *Elaeagnus pungens*	7-9	122
Vanhoutte Spirea *Spiraea x vanhouttei*	3-8	146

Rapid-growing shrubs

Common Name	Zones	Page
Baby's Breath Spirea *Spiraea thunbergii*	4-8	147
Border Forsythia *Forsythia x intermedia*	6-9	125
Bridalwreath Spirea *Spiraea prunifolia*	5-8	146
Cape Honeysuckle *Tecomaria capensis*	10	205
Cherry Laurel *Prunus caroliniana*	6-9	137
Chinese Hibiscus *Hibiscus rosa-sinensis*	9-10	201
Chinese Variegated Privet *Ligustrum sinense 'Variegatum'*	7-10	135
Escallonia *Escallonia x exoniensis 'Frades'*	9-10	123
Pampas Grass *Cortaderia selloana*	7-10	121
PeeGee Hydrangea *Hydrangea paniculata 'Grandiflora'*	3-8	127
Redtip Photinia *Photinia x fraseri*	6-9	136
Rose of Sharon *Hibiscus syriacus*	5-9	125
Showy Jasmine *Jasminum floridum*	7-9	131
Thorny Elaeagnus *Elaeagnus pungens*	7-9	122
Vanhoutte Spirea *Spiraea x vanhouttei*	3-8	146
Waxleaf Ligustrum *Ligustrum lucidum*	7-10	134

Rounded/Mounded shrubs

Common Name	Zones	Page
Annabelle Hydrangea *Hydrangea arborescens 'Annabelle'*	3-9	126
Compact Japanese Holly *Ilex creneta 'Compacta'*	5-8	129
Doublefile Viburnum *Viburnum plicatum tomentosum*	4-8	149
Dwarf Yaupon Holly *Ilex vomitoria 'Nana'*	7-10	130
Glen Dale Azaleas *Azalea Glen Dale Hybrids*	6-9	116
Golden Arborvitae *Thuja orientalis 'Aurea Nana'*	6-10	148
Limemound Spirea *Spiraea japonica Limemound*	4-9	147
Indian Hawthorn *Rhaphiolepis indica*	8-10	204
Inkberry *Ilex glabra 'Compacta'*	3-10	129
Korean Boxwood *Buxus microphylla koreana*	5-9	119
New Zealand Tea Tree *Leptospermum scoparium*	9-10	133
Variegated Pittosporum *Pittosporum tobira 'Variegata'*	8-10	204

Fragrant flowering shrubs

Common Name	Zones	Page
Betty Prior Rose *Rosa 'Betty Prior'*	4-9	139
Bouvardia *Bouvardia longiflora 'Albatross'*	9-10	200
Carefree Beauty Rose *Rosa 'Carefree Beauty'*	4-8	139
Country Dancer Rose *Rosa 'Country Dancer'*	4-9	140
Fru Dagmar Hastrup Rose *Rosa 'Fru Dagmar Hastrup'*	2-9	140
Gardenia *Gardenia jasminoides*	8-10	201
Graham Thomas Rose *Rosa Graham Thomas*	5-9	141
Gruss an Aachen Rose *Rosa 'Gruss an Aachen'*	5-9	141
Iceberg Rose *Rosa 'Iceberg'*	4-9	142
Margo Koster Rose *Rosa 'Margo Koster'*	5-8	142
Miss Kim Lilac *Syringa patula 'Miss Kim'*	3-7	148
Rosa Rubrifolia *Rosa rubrifolia*	4-9	143
Sweet Viburnum *Viburnum odoratissimum*	8-10	205
Therese Bugnet Rose *Rosa 'Therese Bugnet'*	3-9	144
Thorny Elaeagnus *Elaeagnus pungens*	7-9	122
Variegated Pittosporum *Pittosporum tobira 'Variegata'*	8-10	204

Doublefile Viburnum
(*Viburnum plicatum tomentosum*)
Page 149

Golden Arborvitae (page 148) adds a distinctive shape to the landscape year-round.

Choose shrubs to add color, texture, line, and form to your landscape.

Pink Ruffles Azalea
(Azalea Rutherford Hybrids 'Pink Ruffles')
Page 118

Dwarf Burning Bush
(Euonymus alatus 'Compacta')
Page 123

Choosing Shrubs by Needs

Put shrubs to work in your landscape. The guides on these pages are organized by different landscaping needs. (See pages 30-31 to find lists of shrubs for privacy.) Go to the shrub encyclopedia for detailed information about individual shrubs. Availability varies by area and conditions (see page 21). Check with your garden center.

Nandina
(Nandina domestica)
Page 135

Shrubs for mass planting

Common Name	Zones	Page
American Beautyberry	7-10	120
Callicarpa americana		
Annabelle Hydrangea	3-9	126
Hydrangea arborescens 'Annabelle'		
Betty Prior Rose	4-9	139
Rosa 'Betty Prior'		
Doublefile Viburnum	4-8	149
Viburnum plicatum tomentosum		
Dwarf Burning Bush	3-8	123
Euonymus alatus 'Compacta'		
Dwarf Leucothoe	5-9	134
Leucothoe axillaris		
Escallonia	9-10	123
Escallonia x exoniensis 'Frades'		
Glen Dale Azaleas	6-9	116
Azalea Glen Dale Hybrids		
Graham Thomas Rose	5-9	141
Rosa Graham Thomas		
Iceberg Rose	4-9	142
Rosa 'Iceberg'		
Inkberry	3-10	129
Ilex glabra 'Compacta'		

Common Name	Zones	Page
Kurume Azalea	6-9	118
Azalea obtusum		
Mountain Laurel	4-9	133
Kalmia latifolia		
Nandina	6-9	135
Nandina domestica		
Nikko Blue Hydrangea	6-9	126
Hydrangea macrophylla 'Nikko Blue'		
Otto Luyken Laurel	6-8	137
Prunus laurocerasus 'Otto Luyken'		
Pink Meidiland Rose	5-8	143
Rosa Pink Meidiland		
Pink Ruffles Azalea	9-10	118
Azalea Rutherford Hybrids 'Pink Ruffles'		
Pyracantha	6-8	138
Pyracantha coccinea		
Showy Jasmine	7-9	131
Jasminum floridum		
Southern Indian Azalea	8-10	117
Azalea indica		
Thorny Elaeagnus	7-9	122
Elaeagnus pungens		

Shrubs for entries, courtyards, and patios

Common Name	Zones	Page	Common Name	Zones	Page
African Iris *Moraea iridioides*	9-10	203	Ixora *Ixora coccinea*	10	202
Anthony Waterer Spirea *Spiraea japonica 'Anthony Waterer'*	3-9	145	Japanese Fatsia *Fatsia japonica*	8-10	124
Baby's Breath Spirea *Spiraea thunbergii*	4-8	147	King Sago *Cycas revoluta*	8-10	201
Bird-of-Paradise *Strelitzia reginae*	9-10	205	Korean Boxwood *Buxus microphylla koreana*	5-9	119
Bouvardia *Bouvardia longiflora 'Albatross'*	9-10	200	Kurume Azalea *Azalea obtusum*	6-9	118
Bridalwreath Spirea *Spiraea prunifolia*	5-8	146	Limemound Spirea *Spiraea japonica Limemound*	4-9	147
Chinese Hibiscus *Hibiscus rosa-sinensis*	9-10	201	Nandina *Nandina domestica*	6-9	135
Compact Japanese Holly *Ilex creneta 'Compacta'*	5-8	129	Nikko Blue Hydrangea *Hydrangea macrophylla 'Nikko Blue'*	6-	126
Country Dancer Rose *Rosa 'Country Dancer'*	4-9	140	Otto Luyken Laurel *Prunus laurocerasus 'Otto Luyken'*	6-8	137
Dwarf Alberta Spruce *Picea glauca 'Conica'*	3-8	136	Pink Ruffles Azalea *Azalea Rutherford Hybrids 'Pink Ruffles'*	9-10	118
Escallonia *Escallonia x exoniensis 'Frades'*	9-10	123	Pygmy Date Palm *Phoenix roebelenii*	9-10	204
Golden Arborvitae *Thuja orientalis 'Aurea Nana'*	6-10	148	Shibori Spirea *Spiraea japonica 'Shibori'*	4-8	145
Gruss an Aachen Rose *Rosa 'Gruss an Aachen'*	5-9	141	Vanhoutte Spirea *Spiraea x vanhouttei*	3-8	146
Gumpo Azalea *Azalea hybrida*	6-9	116	Variegated Croton *Codiaeum variegatum var. pictum*	10	200
Indian Hawthorn *Rhaphiolepis indica*	8-10	204			

Otto Luyken Laurel.
(Prunus laurocerasus 'Otto Luyken')
Page 137

Shrubs for formal gardens

Common Name	Zones	Page
Annabelle Hydrangea *Hydrangea arborescens 'Annabelle'*	3-9	126
Bird-of-Paradise *Strelitzia reginae*	9-10	205
Cherry Laurel *Prunus caroliniana*	6-9	137
Cleyera *Cleyera japonica*	7-10	121
Compact Japanese Holly *Ilex creneta 'Compacta'*	5-8	129
Country Dancer Rose *Rosa 'Country Dancer'*	4-9	140
Dwarf Alberta Spruce *Picea glauca 'Conica'*	3-8	136
Dwarf Yaupon Holly *Ilex vomitoria 'Nana'*	7-10	130
European Cranberrybush *Viburnum opulus 'Roseum'*	3-8	149
Golden Arborvitae *Thuja orientalis 'Aurea Nana'*	6-10	148
Gruss an Aachen Rose *Rosa 'Gruss an Aachen'*	5-9	141
Inkberry *Ilex glabra 'Compacta'*	3-10	129
Japanese Fatsia *Fatsia japonica*	8-10	124
Korean Boxwood *Buxus microphylla koreana*	5-9	119
Kurume Azalea *Azalea obtusum*	6-9	118
Nikko Blue Hydrangea *Hydrangea macrophylla 'Nikko Blue'*	6-9	126
Pink Ruffles Azalea *Azalea Rutherford Hybrids 'Pink Ruffles'*	9-10	118
Pygmy Date Palm *Phoenix roebelenii*	9-10	204

Shrubs for accent

Common Name	Zones	Page	Common Name	Zones	Page
African Iris *Moraea iridioides*	9-10	203	Golden Euonymus *Euonymus japonicus 'Aureus'*	7-9	124
American Beautyberry *Callicarpa americana*	7-10	120	Gruss an Aachen Rose *Rosa 'Gruss an Aachen'*	5-9	141
Annabelle Hydrangea *Hydrangea arborescens 'Annabelle'*	3-9	126	Ixora *Ixora coccinea*	10	202
Baby's Breath Spirea *Spiraea thunbergii*	4-8	147	Japanese Aucuba *Aucuba japonica*	7-10	114
Bird-of-Paradise *Strelitzia reginae*	9-10	205	Japanese Fatsia *Fatsia japonica*	8-10	124
Border Forsythia *Forsythia x intermedia*	6-9	125	King Sago *Cycas revoluta*	8-10	201
Bouvardia *Bouvardia longiflora 'Albatross'*	9-10	200	Limemound Spirea *Spiraea japonica Limemound*	4-9	147
Cape Honeysuckle *Tecomaria capensis*	10	205	Nandina *Nandina domestica*	6-9	135
Chinese Hibiscus *Hibiscus rosa-sinensis*	9-10	201	New Zealand Tea Tree *Leptospermum scoparium*	9-10	133
Chinese Variegated Privet *Ligustrum sinense 'Variegatum'*	17-10	135	Old Gold Juniper *Juniperus chinensis 'Old Gold'*	4-10	131
Country Dancer Rose *Rosa 'Country Dancer'*	4-9	140	Pampas Grass *Cortaderia selloana*	7-10	121
Doublefile Viburnum *Viburnum plicatum tomentosum*	4-8	149	PeeGee Hydrangea *Hydrangea paniculata 'Grandiflora'*	3-8	127
Dwarf Burning Bush *Euonymus alatus 'Compacta'*	3-8	123	Pink Ruffles Azalea *Azalea Rutherford Hybrids 'Pink Ruffles'*	9-10	118
European Cranberrybush *Viburnum opulus 'Roseum'*	3-8	149	Pygmy Date Palm *Phoenix roebelenii*	9-10	204
Gardenia *Gardenia jasminoides*	8-10	201	Pyracantha *Pyracantha coccinea*	6-8	138
Glen Dale Azaleas *Azalea Glen Dale Hybrids*	6-9	116	Sasanqua Camellia *Camellia sasanqua*	7-9	120
Golden Arborvitae *Thuja orientalis 'Aurea Nana'*	6-10	148	Variegated Croton *Codiaeum variegatum var. pictum*	10	200

Shrubs for woodland gardens

Common Name	Zones	Page
American Beautyberry *Callicarpa americana*	7-10	120
Cherry Laurel *Prunus caroliniana*	6-9	137
Doublefile Viburnum *Viburnum plicatum tomentosum*	4-8	149
Dwarf Leucothoe *Leucothoe axillaris*	5-9	134
European Cranberrybush *Viburnum opulus 'Roseum'*	3-8	149
Glen Dale Azaleas *Azalea Glen Dale Hybrids*	6-9	116
Mountain Laurel *Kalmia latifolia*	4-9	133
Showy Jasmine *Jasminum floridum*	7-9	131
Southern Indian Azalea *Azalea indica*	8-10	117
Thorny Elaeagnus *Elaeagnus pungens*	7-9	122

Japanese Fatsia
(Fatsia japonica)
Page 124

Spring-flowering azaleas are available in colors ranging from shades of red, pink, and white to lavender.

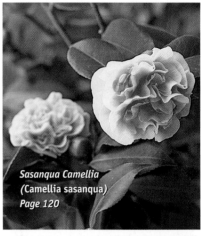

Sasanqua Camellia
(Camellia sasanqua)
Page 120

Southern Indian Azalea
(Azalea indica)
Page 117

Choosing Shrubs for Seasonal Interest

Decorate your yard throughout the seasons with shrubs. Fragrant flowers, colorful foliage, and desireable fruit add interest to the landscape throughout spring, summer, fall, and winter.

Spring-flowering shrubs

Common Name	Zones	Page
African Iris	9-10	203
Moraea iridioides		
Annabelle Hydrangea	3-9	126
Hydrangea arborescens 'Annabelle'		
Baby's Breath Spirea	4-8	147
Spiraea thunbergii		
Border Forsythia	6-9	125
Forsythia x intermedia		
Bouvardia	9-10	200
Bouvardia longiflora 'Albatross'		
Bridalwreath Spirea	5-8	146
Spiraea prunifolia		
Catawba Rhododendron	4-8	138
Rhododendron catawbiense		
Doublefile Viburnum	4-8	149
Viburnum plicatum tomentosum		
Downy Jasmine	9-10	202
Jasminum multiflorum		
Dwarf Leucothoe	5-9	134
Leucothoe axillaris		
European Cranberrybush	3-8	149
Viburnum opulus 'Roseum'		
Gardenia	8-10	201
Gardenia jasminoides		

Common Name	Zones	Page
Glen Dale Azaleas	6-9	116
Azalea Glen Dale Hybrids		
Iceberg Rose	4-9	142
Rosa 'Iceberg'		
Indian Hawthorn	8-10	204
Rhaphiolepis indica		
Ixora	10	202
Ixora coccinea		
Kurume Azalea	6-9	118
Azalea obtusum		

Cape Honeysuckle
(Tecomaria capensis)
Page 205

Common Name	Zones	Page
Miss Kim Lilac	3-7	148
Syringa patula 'Miss Kim'		

Common Name	Zones	Page
Mountain Laurel	4-9	133
Kalmia latifolia		
Nandina	6-9	135
Nandina domestica		
New Zealand Tea Tree	9-10	133
Leptospermum scoparium		
Oleander	8-10	203
Nerium oleander		
Otto Luyken Laurel	6-8	137
Prunus laurocerasus 'Otto Luyken'		
Pyracantha	6-8	138
Pyracantha coccinea		
Rockspray Cotoneaster	6-9	122
Cotoneaster horizontalis		
Showy Jasmine	7-9	131
Jasminum floridum		
Texas Silverado Sage	8-9	202
Leucophyllum frutescens 'Silverado'		
Vanhoutte Spirea	3-8	146
Spiraea x vanhouttei		
White Rock Rose	8-10	200
Cistus x hybridus		

Bird-of-Paradise
(Strelitzia reginae)
Page 205

Summer-flowering shrubs

Common Name	Zones	Page
African Iris *Moraea iridioides*	9-10	203
Annabelle Hydrangea *Hydrangea arborescens 'Annabelle'*	3-9	126
Anthony Waterer Spirea *Spiraea japonica 'Anthony Waterer'*	3-9	145
Betty Prior Rose *Rosa 'Betty Prior'*	4-9	139
Bouvardia *Bouvardia longiflora 'Albatross'*	9-10	200
Carefree Beauty Rose *Rosa Carefree Beauty*	4-8	139
Chinese Hibiscus *Hibiscus rosa-sinensis*	9-10	201
Dwarf Leucothoe *Leucothoe axillaris*	5-9	134
Escallonia *Escallonia x exoniensis 'Frades'*	9-10	123
Fru Dagmar Hastrup Rose *Rosa 'Fru Dagmar Hastrup'*	2-9	140
Gardenia *Gardenia jasminoides*	8-10	201
Glen Dale Azaleas *Azalea Glen Dale Hybrids*	6-9	116
Glossy Abelia *Abelia x grandiflora*	7-9	114
Graham Thomas Rose *Rosa Graham Thomas*	5-9	141
Gruss an Aachen Rose *Rosa 'Gruss an Aachen'*	5-9	141
Gumpo Azalea *Azalea hybrida*	6-9	116
Iceberg Rose *Rosa 'Iceberg'*	4-9	142
Ixora *Ixora coccinea*	10	202
Margo Koster Rose *Rosa 'Margo Koster'*	5-8	142
Miss Kim Lilac *Syringa patula 'Miss Kim'*	3-7	148
Nikko Blue Hydrangea *Hydrangea macrophylla 'Nikko Blue'*	6-9	126
Oakleaf Hydrangea *Hydrangea quercifolia*	5-9	127
Oleander *Nerium oleander*	8-10	203
Pampas Grass *Cortaderia selloana*	7-10	121
Peegee Hydrangea *Hydrangea paniculata 'Grandiflora'*	3-8	127
Pink Meidiland Rose *Rosa Pink Meidiland*	5-8	143
Pyracantha *Pyracantha coccinea*	6-8	138
Rosa Rubrifolia *Rosa rubrifolia*	4-9	143
Rose of Sharon *Hibiscus syriacus*	5-9	125
The Fairy Rose *Rosa 'The Fairy'*	4-9	144
Therese Bugnet Rose *Rosa 'Therese Bugnet'*	3-9	144
White Rock Rose *Cistus x hybridus*	8-10	200

Shrubs with autumn interest

Colorful fall foliage

Common Name	Zones	Page
American Beautyberry *Callicarpa americana*	7-10	120
Baby's Breath Spirea *Spirea thunbergii*	4-8	147
Bridalwreath Spirea *Spiraea prunifolia*	5-8	146
Doublefile Viburnum *Viburnum plicatum tomentosum*	4-8	149
Dwarf Burning Bush *Euonymus alatus 'Compacta'*	3-8	123
Dwarf Leucothoe *Leucothoe axillaris*	5-9	134
Limemound Spirea *Spiraea japonica Limemound*	4-9	147
Nandina *Nandina domestica*	6-9	135
Oakleaf Hydrangea *Hydrangea quercifolia*	5-9	127

Flowers in fall

Common Name	Zones	Page
Annabelle Hydrangea *Hydrangea arborescens 'Annabelle'*	3-9	126
Bird-of-Paradise *Strelitzia reginae*	9-10	205
Bouvardia *Bouvardia longiflora 'Albatross'*	9-10	200
Butterfly Bush *Buddleia davidii*	5-9	119
Cape Honeysuckle *Tecomaria capensis*	10	205
Escallonia *Escallonia x exoniensis 'Frades'*	9-10	123
Glossy Abelia *Abelia grandiflora*	7-9	114
Graham Thomas Rose *Rosa Graham Thomas*	5-9	141
Gruss an Aachen Shrub Rose *Rosa 'Gruss an Aachen'*	5-9	141
Iceberg Rose *Rosa 'Iceberg'*	4-9	142
Ixora *Ixora coccinea*	10	202
Oakleaf Hydrangea *Hydrangea quercifolia*	5-9	127
Oleander *Nerium oleander*	8-10	203
PeeGee Hydrangea *Hydrangea paniculata 'Grandiflora'*	3-8	127
Pink Meidiland Rose *Rosa Pink Meidiland*	5-8	143
Sasanqua Camellia *Camellia sasanqua*	7-9	120
The Fairy Rose *Rosa 'The Fairy'*	4-9	144
Therese Bugnet Rose *Rosa 'Therese Bugnet'*	3-9	144

Oleander
(Nerium oleander)
Page 203

Shrubs with winter interest

Winter flowers

Common Name	Zones	Page
Bird-of-Paradise *Strelitzia reginae*	9-10	205
Cape Honeysuckle *Tecomaria capensis*	10	205
Downy Jasmine *Jasminum multiflorum*	9-10	202
Indian Hawthorn *Rhaphiolepis indica*	8-10	204
Sasanqua Camellia *Camellia sasanqua*	7-9	120

Winter fruit

Common Name	Zones	Page
Carefree Beauty Rose *Rosa Carefree Beauty*	4-8	139
Dwarf Burford Holly *Ilex cornuta 'Bufordii Nana'*	6-9	128
Nandina *Nandina domestica*	6-9	135
Pink Meidiland Rose *Rosa Pink Meidiland*	5-8	143
Rosa Rubrifolia *Rosa rubrifolia*	4-9	143

Spring flowers are pretty but don't overlook fall color when choosing shrubs for your yard.

Abelia x grandiflora

Glossy Abelia

Zones: 7-9

Light Needs:

Mature Size:

4'-6'

3'-5'

Growth Rate:
medium

semievergreen shrub

Needs: Plant in sun or part shade in well-drained soil ranging from acid to alkaline. Pinch new growth to maintain compact plants. Informal settings suit it best.

Good for: informal hedge, mass planting, or bank cover

More Choices: pages 30, 34, 36, 40, 41, 43, 99, 101, 109, and 113

Options: 'Edward Goucher'—4' high, lavender flowers
'Francis Mason'—pinkish white flowers
'Prostrata'—2' high, white flowers
'Sherwood'—2'-3' high cascading form; white flowers

Outstanding Features:

- Glossy Abelia is heat-tolerant
- Shrubs bloom summer through fall
- Low-maintenance plants are easy to grow

Here's a low maintenance shrub that blooms in sun or part shade. Hot weather promotes flowering; pink, white, or lavender blossoms occur summer through fall. Put it with broad-leaf evergreens for a textural contrast.

Aucuba japonica

Japanese Aucuba

Zones: 7-10

Light Needs:

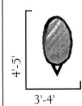

Mature Size:

4'-5'

3'-4'

Growth Rate:
slow to medium

evergreen shrub

Needs: Plant in partial sun or shade in rich to poor soil. The hotter the climate, the shadier your planting spot should be. Prune in spring. Variegated forms brighten dark, shady spots but use them sparingly, it is easy to overdo.

Good for: shady corners, foundation planting, background, accent

More Choices: pages 35, 36, 39, 101, 109, and 111
Options: 'Crassofolia'—dark green leaves
'Crotonifolia'—leaves gold and white
'Longfolia'—bright green, narrow leaves
'Nana'—2' tall

Outstanding Features:

- Foliage stays green year-round
- Variegated forms add color contrast
- Thrives in poor soil conditions

Japanese Aucuba thrives in poor soil, partial sun or deep shade. Leaves range from solid green to speckled, to mostly yellow depending on variety. Neat in appearance and dense even in heavy shade.

Azalea carolinianum

Carolina Azalea

Zones: 5-9

Light Needs:

Mature Size:

3'-6'

3'-6'

Growth Rate:
slow

Evergreen flowering shrub

Needs: Grow in full sun. Plant in fertile, acidic, moist, and well-drained soil. Set new shrubs slightly higher to prevent water from collecting around roots. Mulch to keep roots moist. Provide extra water in autumn. Prune as soon as flowering finishes by reaching into plants to remove woody stems; do not shear.

Good for: seasonal accents, background planting, foundation planting, along fences, entries, along walkways, beside patios, massing in planting beds

Outstanding Features:
- Wide range of flower colors
- Foliage stays green year-round
- Provides seasonal accent

Welcome spring to your yard with Carolina Azaleas. These shrubs feature flowers in springtime shades. Leaves stay shiny green throughout the year. Can grow in Zone 4 with winter protection. Avoid planting azaleas where they'll be exposed to harsh winds or strong winter sun. Also try: var. *album*—white flowers; var. *luteum*—yellow flowers.

Planting Azaleas

Azaleas are especially sensitive to "wet feet." Here's how to plant them to keep roots from drowning, even in heavy clay soil.

1 **Dig a hole** that is not quite as deep as the nursery container. Set the azalea, still in its pot, into the hole to check the depth. The rim of the pot should protrude about 2 inches above the soil level. Remove the plant and widen the hole so it is at least one-and-a-half times as wide as the nursery container. If your soil is heavy clay, roughen the sides of the hole with a shovel. If the hole is too deep, remove the plant and add some soil back to the bottom of the hole. Tamp to prevent the shrub from settling later on.

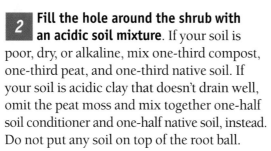

2 **Fill the hole around the shrub with an acidic soil mixture.** If your soil is poor, dry, or alkaline, mix one-third compost, one-third peat, and one-third native soil. If your soil is acidic clay that doesn't drain well, omit the peat moss and mix together one-half soil conditioner and one-half native soil, instead. Do not put any soil on top of the root ball.

STUFF YOU'LL NEED

- ✔ Round-point shovel
- ✔ Organic matter
- ✔ Peat moss for poor, dry soil
- ✔ Soil conditioner for clay soil
- ✔ Mulch

What to Expect
If leaves turn yellow and the root area feels wet, allow plants to dry out more between waterings.

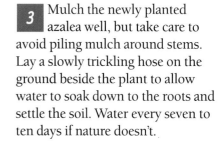

3 Mulch the newly planted azalea well, but take care to avoid piling mulch around stems. Lay a slowly trickling hose on the ground beside the plant to allow water to soak down to the roots and settle the soil. Water every seven to ten days if nature doesn't.

Glen Dale Azaleas

Zones: 6-9

Light Needs:

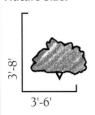

Mature Size:

3'-8'

3'-6'

Growth Rate:
medium

evergreen flowering shrub

Needs: Plant in acidic soil that's moist but well-drained. These plants won't tolerate wet soils. Grow in partial or dense shade. Hand-prune after flowering; do not shear. Cold-hardy.

Good for: shrub borders, woodland edges, foundation plantings, massing, beside patios, surrounding lawns, accents

More Choices: pages 36, 40, 101, 109, 110, 111, 112, and 113

These evergreen azaleas were bred with cold-hardiness in mind. Choose from a range of flower colors and bloom times, from mid-April to mid-June. Flowers may be white, pink, purple, red, or orange-red. If you chose a speckled or striped selection, remove branches which bear solid-colored flowers. May be listed botanically as Rhododendron.

Gumpo Azalea

Zones: 6-9

Light Needs:

Mature Size:

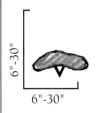

6"-30"

6"-30"

Growth Rate:
slow to medium

evergreen flowering shrub

Needs: Gumpo azaleas need partial shade and well-drained soil. Mix organic matter such as compost into the hole. If planting near concrete—which raises soil pH—mulch with pine bark or pine straw to increase acidity.

Good for: entries, planters, parking areas, beneath low windows, or planted as the front layer of shrub beds

More Choices: pages 36, 40, 109, 111, and 113

Options: Gumpo pink—pink flowers
Gumpo white—white flowers
Gumpo rose—reddish flowers

This little azalea blooms when it's hot. Though it requires acidic soil to grow optimally, very little care is needed beyond that. Plants come in the colors of white, red, pink, lavender, salmon, and rose.

Southern Indian Azalea

Zones: 8-10

Light Needs:

Mature Size:

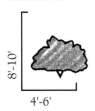

8'-10'

4'-6'

Growth Rate:
medium to rapid

evergreen flowering shrub

Needs: Plant in acidic soil that's moist but well-drained. Shrubs grow rapidly with regular watering but can't tolerate soggy soil. Morning sun with afternoon shade is ideal. Hand-prune after flowering; do not shear. Feed with acid-loving plant food after bloom. Mulch to conserve moisture and increase acidity.

Good for: shrub borders, entries, woodland edges, foundation plantings, massing, seasonal accents, planting beside patios and driveways, growing beneath tall trees

More Choices: pages 37, 40, 101, 110, and 111

Options: 'Du de Rohan'—bright pink flowers with purplish blotches
'Formosa'—vivid purplish red flowers
'George Lindley Tabor'—white to soft pink blooms
'Mrs. G.G. Gerbing'—white flowers
'President Clay'—red flowers
'Pride of Mobile'—strong pink blossoms with darker blotches

Outstanding Features:
- Large spring flowers in a variety of colors
- Tolerates heat and humidity
- Layers of foliage stay green year-round

BUYER'S GUIDE

Though fall is the best time to plant woody shrubs, it's worth waiting until spring for azaleas. Doing so will allow you to buy azaleas while they're in bloom so you can be sure of the color you're getting and match all the plants. Unintended colors will stick out like a sore thumb in an otherwise well-planned landscape.

Spring isn't official throughout much of the warmer climates until these evergreen shrubs are covered with blossoms. Flowers come in white, and shades of salmon, pink, red to purple. Southern Indian Azaleas aren't hard to grow if your soil is acidic. Also sold as Southern Indian Hybrid Azaleas. May be referred to as "Southern Indicas." May be listed botanically as Rhododendron. If the soil in your yard is alkaline, don't try to grow azaleas. They'll require major soil amendments and endless fertilizer.

Shrubs

5

Azalea obtusum

Kurume Azalea

Zones: 6-9

Light Needs:

Mature Size:

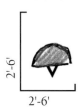

2'-6'

2'-6'

Growth Rate:
slow

evergreen flowering shrub (semievergreen in cool climates)

Needs: Plant in acidic soil that's moist but well-drained. Shrubs grow faster with regular watering but can't tolerate soggy soil. Grow in full sun to partial shade. Feed with acid-loving plant food after blooming ceases.

Good for: massing in planting beds, bordering taller shrubs, entries, courtyards, beside patios and walkways, accents

More Choices: pages 35, 36, 40, 110, 111, and 112

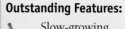

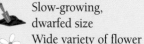

Outstanding Features:

- Slow-growing, dwarfed size
- Wide variety of flower colors available
- With proper watering, tolerates heat and sun

Grow these compact azaleas where you want dense shrubs covered with green leaves year-round and blankets of blossoms in spring. Kurumes are slow-growing, so they stay small longer than Southern Indian Azaleas. Other cultivars you might be interested in: 'Hinode Giri'—purplish red, very hardy; 'Appleblossom'—white to pink flowers with darker blotches, occasional red stripes; 'Christmas Cheer'—red blooms; 'Coral Bells'—strong pink flowers.

Azalea Rutherford Hybrids 'Pink Ruffles'

Pink Ruffles Azalea

Zones: 9-10

Light Needs:

Mature Size:

2'-3'

2'-3'

Growth Rate:
slow

evergreen flowering shrub (semievergreen in cool climates)

Needs: Plant in acidic soil that's moist but well-drained. Shrubs grow rapidly with regular watering but can't tolerate soggy soil. Grow in partial sun to dense shade. Feed with acid-loving plant food after blooming ceases.

Good for: massing in planting beds, bordering tall shrubs, entries, courtyards, beside patios and walkways, seasonal accents, planting beneath low windows

More Choices: pages 35, 37, 40, 110, and 111

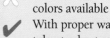

Outstanding Features:

- Deep pink, semidouble flowers
- Compact shape and size
- Tolerates heat, sun, and humidity

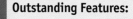

These slow-growing, wide plants are easy to keep neat and low. They thrive in hotter climates, often blooming in early to late winter and repeating bloom in the fall. Leaves stay green year-round. Also try: 'Red Ruffles'—strong red; 'Alaska'—white blooms.

Buddleia davidii

Butterfly Bush

Zones: 5-9

Light Needs:

Mature Size:

4'-8'

3'-6'

Growth Rate:
rapid

Outstanding Features:
- Flowers attract butterflies to landscape
- Excellent vase life for cut flower use
- Easily grown in hot, sunny locations

perennial or semievergreen shrub

Needs: Give plants a good start by mixing organic matter such as compost into the planting hole. Full sun yields the most flowers. Prune in either spring or fall to encourage blooming.

Good for: sunny flower beds or natural areas. Plant beside patios or decks to enjoy butterflies and blossoms. Enjoy cut flowers indoors.

More Choices: pages 35, 43, 109, and 113

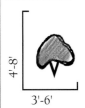

Butterfly Bush is easy to grow; hot sun and limited water do little to discourage abundant flowers in shades of pink, white, purple, or red. Blooms attract butterflies. Cultivars of interest include: 'Empire Blue'—large dark blue flowers; 'Fascination'—salmon pink blossoms; 'Harlequin'—variegated leaves, maroon flowers; 'Royal Red'—dark purple-red flowers; 'Black Knight'—deep purple flowers; 'White Bouquet'—white blossoms; 'Wilsonii'—drooping, light pink-purple flower spikes.

Buxus microphylla koreana

Korean Boxwood

Zones: 5-9

Light Needs:

Mature Size:

1'-2'

2'-3'

Growth Rate:
slow

Outstanding Features:
- Fine-textured foliage is bright green all year
- Tolerates cold, heat, and humidity
- Grows slowly and stays low

evergreen shrub

Needs: Plant in fertile soil that's moist but well-drained. Slightly acidic soil is best. Mulch well to keep shallow roots cool; peat or compost is good for mulching. Protect shrubs from strong, drying winds. Prune to shape in early or midsummer.

Good for: low hedges, massing, surrounding vegetable, rose, or herb gardens; formal landscapes, courtyards, entries, winter interest, edging planting beds

More Choices: pages 40, 99, 101, 108, 109, and 111

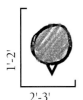

The toughest of all boxwoods, this one withstands hot or cold climates. Shrubs grow slowly, stay low, and take pruning well. Plants are easily trimmed into a variety of shapes for formal landscapes. Also sold as Korean Littleleaf Boxwood. This is the best boxwood for Zones 8 and 9. Cultivar options: 'Wintergreen'—4' to 5' high, 3' to 4' wide; Zones 4-9; 'Suffructicosa' (edging boxwood)—3' high, 12" wide; Zones 6-8; 'Tide Hill'—15" high, 5' wide; Zones 4-9.

Callicarpa americana

American Beautyberry

Zones: 7-10

Light Needs:

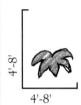

Mature Size:

4'-8'

4'-8'

Growth Rate:
medium to rapid

deciduous shrub

Needs: Plant in full sun to partial shade. Moist, slightly acidic soil is best, but established shrubs can thrive with neglect in wet or dry soils. Salt-tolerant.

Good for: specimen plants, seasonal accents, seaside landscapes, natural areas, woodlands, shrub borders, massing, attracting birds

More Choices: pages 34, 36, 40, 42, 108, 110, 111, and 113

Options: var. *lactea*—white fruit

If you see this plant in fruit, you'll have to have one for your own yard. Magenta berries circle stems like thick wreaths in autumn. Cut berried stems for use in indoor arrangements. Sprawling, arching form makes this shrub a poor choice for formal gardens.

Camellia sasanqua

Sasanqua Camellia

Zones: 7-9

Light Needs:

Mature Size:

7'-12'

5'-7'

Growth Rate:
medium to rapid

evergreen shrub

Needs: Plant in partial shade. This shrub needs good drainage and acidic soil. Plants rarely need pruning.

Good for: corners of houses and porches, accents, background, or trimmed into small trees. Group plants together to grow hedges or set alone for a specimen plant.

More Choices: pages 30, 37, 40, 43, 99, 101, 111, and 113

Options: *C. japonica* (Common Camellia), blooms fall, winter, or spring. Dozens of colors in single or double flowers from which to choose.

This dark green shrub adds elegant flowers to the landscape at an unexpected time of year. Large blooms, in an array of colors, open in late fall and early winter. Aged camellias can be pruned to form small trees like the one shown here. Camellia blossoms are lovely in flower arrangements, holding their color and shape well.

Cleyera

Zones: 7-10

Light Needs:

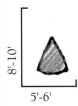

Mature Size:

8'-10'
5'-6'

Growth Rate:
medium to rapid

evergreen shrub

Needs: Plant in sun or shade in acidic, moist soil. Prune to shape any time of year. Plants must be protected from salt spray to prevent desiccation.

Good for: formal or informal landscapes, tight spots and city conditions, backgrounds, near corners of houses

More Choices: pages 34, 36, 40, 43, 101, 109, and 111

Outstanding Features:

- Thick, glossy evergreen foliage
- ✓ New foliage growth is bronze colored
- ✓ Adaptable to formal and informal yards

As long as your soil isn't alkaline or boggy, you can grow Cleyera. This upright shrub keeps its dark glossy leaves year-round. It may also be sold as *Ternstromia gymnatheria*.

Pampas Grass

Zones: 7-10

Light Needs:

Mature Size:

6'-10'
6'-10'

Growth Rate:
rapid

perennial grass used as a shrub

Needs: Plant in full sun to partial shade in any kind of soil as long as it's well-drained. Cut clumps to the ground in early spring. Pampas grass is insect and disease-resistant.

Good for: large areas, summer screening, accents, or background problems. This big plant is not for small spaces.

More Choices: pages 35, 36, 41, 108, 109, 111, and 113

Outstanding Features:

- Feathery plumes in white to pink
- Fine-textured leaves lend a tropical effect
- ✓ Tall, fast-growing screen to block views

Shrubs 5

Clumps of arching foliage reach 6 feet or more in height and grow as big across. Tall plumes of flowers top Pampas Grass in late summer. Cultivar options: 'Argenteum'—grows to 12' high with silvery plumes; 'Gold Band—yellow striped foliage; 'Pumila'—reaches just 4' to 6' high; 'Rendatleri'—matures at 8' to 10' tall with large, pink, feathery flowers. Avoid planting Pampas Grass where people may brush against the foliage. Grass blades are sharply serrated and can cause injury. Use in large areas.

Rockspray Cotoneaster

Zones: 6-9

Light Needs:

Mature Size:

2'-3'

5'-8'

Growth Rate: slow to medium

evergreen shrub

Needs: Plant in full sun and well-drained soil. Susceptible to fireblight. Remove and destroy affected branches. Sprays containing streptomycin prevent infection, which occurs during blooming.

Good for: slopes, planters, behind retaining walls, in sunny, dry beds and as groundcover

More Choices: pages 35, 42, 43, and 112

Options: 'Little Gem'—12" high
'Robusta'—vigorous, upright growth, heavy fruiting
'Saxatilis'—compact, few berries
'Tom Thumb'—broad spreading, dense

Outstanding Features:
- Clusters of white flowers open in April
- Numerous red berries in fall
- Horizontal branches; evergreen leaves

Rockspray Cotoneaster offers effortless seasonal interest. Showy spring flowers are followed by red berries in fall; leaves stay green year-round. Branches have interesting fish bone pattern and create a layered effect. The level of "evergreen" depends upon the location in which it is grown. Plants are deciduous in cooler regions. *C. dammeri* 'Coral Beauty' has bigger pink flowers and a spreading form.

Thorny Elaeagnus

Zones: 7-9

Light Needs:

Mature Size:

8'-11'

6'-10'

Growth Rate: rapid

evergreen shrub

Needs: Plant in full sun in any kind of soil, including sand, clay, acid, alkaline, or poor and dry. Choose a spot where plants will have room to grow. Size is not easy to control. Pruning promotes long unattractive shoots. This is not a plant for a formal garden.

Good for: hillsides, large informal hedges, screening, background planting, and natural areas

More Choices: pages 30, 35, 39, 41, 42, 43, 99, 109, 110, and 111

Options: 'Aurea'— leaves have yellow coloration around their edges

Outstanding Features:
- Evergreen leaves with silvery undersides
- Fragrant flowers; fruit attracts birds
- Tolerates pollution and salt spray

If you give it room to grow, you couldn't ask for an easier shrub. Arching branches bearing silvery foliage stay green year-round; tiny fall flowers are fragrant with a scent similar to that of gardenia.

Escallonia x exoniensis 'Frades'

Escallonia

Zones: 9-10

Light Needs:

Mature Size:

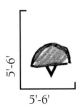

5'-6'

5'-6'

Growth Rate:
rapid

evergreen flowering shrub

Needs: Plant in any soil except alkaline. Water regularly. Grow in partial shade. After flowers fade, prune lightly to keep plants compact. Tolerates salt and wind.

Good for: coastal areas, massing, shrub borders, entries, patio planting or around semishaded decks, screening, low windbreaks, espalier

More Choices: pages 30, 36, 38, 39, 40, 42, 109, 110, 111, and 113

Options: 'Newport Dwarf'—less than 3' high, about 4' wide; dark pink to red flowers

As long as your soil isn't alkaline, you can't go wrong with this tidy shrub. Small glossy leaves have a fine-texture; pink flowers bloom nearly all year. Plants damaged by hard freezes will often recover. Prune dead branches after new growth emerges. Will grow in costal areas of Zone 8.

Euonymus alatus 'Compacta'

Dwarf Burning Bush

Zones: 5-7

Light Needs:

Mature Size:

5'-10'

5'-10'

Growth Rate:
slow

deciduous shrub

Needs: Plant in any well-drained soil, acidic or alkaline. Grow in full sun or partial shade. Pruning is seldom needed or desired. Maintain plants in their natural rounded form.

Good for: specimen shrubs, seasonal accents, deciduous screens, massing, parking areas, beside patios, along walkways or paths, hedges

More Choices: pages 31, 34, 36, 40, 41, 43, 109, 110, 111, and 113

Options: Burning Bush (not dwarf; no 'Compacta' in botanical name)—12' to 15' high, 10' to 12' wide

Outstanding Features:

Flame red fall foliage color

Leaves grow in horizontal layers

Naturally dense, rounded outline

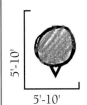

If you enjoy fall color, you ought to plant some Burning Bush. Leaves on these shrubs turn brilliant red in autumn. Also sold as Dwarf Winged Euonymus, so named for corky ridges present on stems.

Shrubs 5

Euonymus japonicus 'Aureus'

Golden Euonymus

Zones: 7-9

Light Needs:

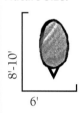

Mature Size:

8'-10'

6'

Growth Rate:
medium to rapid

evergreen shrub

Needs: Golden Euonymus thrives in sunny or shady spots with good air circulation. Heat, poor soil, and coastal conditions are no problem. Plants can withstand heavy pruning.

Good for: accents, coastal gardens, and specimen plants

More Choices: pages 34, 36, 39, 42, 109, and 111

Outstanding Features:

- Bright golden and green variegated leaves
- Rapid-growing and tough
- Tolerant of salt spray and coastal locations

With leaves brighter than many flowers, Golden Euonymus is a real head-turner. This evergreen shrub is very easy to grow, working as well in a container as it does in the ground. A little of this plant goes a long way in the landscape. Avoid placing it where the bright foliage will clash with house colors or other plants. To help prevent powdery mildew, space plants growing in shade far enough apart to keep air circulating. Remove branches that revert to solid green.

Fatsia japonica

Japanese Fatsia

Zones: 8-10

Light Needs:

Mature Size:

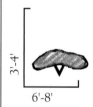

3'-4'

6'-8'

Growth Rate:
medium

evergreen shrub

Needs: Plant in moist, acidic soil that's rich with organic matter for ideal growing conditions. Shrubs also tolerate soils from sandy to heavy clay, but not soggy soils. Grow in partial to dense shade; protect from afternoon or winter sun. Water regularly for optimal growth.

Good for: courtyards, against walls, poolside, shaded entries or patios, contrasting with fine-textured plants

More Choices: pages 36, 39, 40, 108, and 111

Outstanding Features:

- Big, glossy, dark green leaves
- Thrives in deep or partial shade
- Excellent for bold textural effects

Grow this shade-loving shrub for its leaves, not its flowers. Large, glossy foliage is lobed and adds a noticeably coarse texture to landscape compositions. White flowers appear in October and November. Protect plants from extreme wind. May be sold as Japanese Aralia.

Border Forsythia

Zones: 6-9

Light Needs:

Mature Size:

8'-10'

7'-10'

Growth Rate: rapid

deciduous shrub

Needs: Plant in a well-drained, sunny spot in a wide range of soils. Tolerant to variable levels of soil pH. Give this plant room to grow. Large, arching form is not appropriate for formal gardens or shaping.

Good for: informal hedge or screen, massed plantings, and banks

More Choices: pages 31, 34, 39, 40, 41, 42, 43, 109, 111, and 112

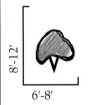

This big, arching shrub welcomes spring with sunshine-yellow blooms. It's easy to grow but give it plenty of room. Prune after flowering by removing oldest wood to the ground. Tolerant of city conditions.

Rose of Sharon

Zones: 5-9

Light Needs:

Mature Size:

8'-12'

6'-8'

Growth Rate: medium to rapid

deciduous shrub

Needs: Plant in full sun to partial shade in any soil that's well-drained, from acidic to alkaline. Trim only as needed to shape plants; make cuts in winter to avoid removing flower buds. Underplant with shorter shrubs.

Good for: informal shrub bed or screen, narrow areas or beside paving and swimming pools, single specimen in beds and containers

More Choices: pages 31, 35, 37, 41, 43, 109, and 113

Large flowers in pinks, reds, whites, and blues dress up this old-fashioned shrub. Rose of Sharon is a fast-growing plant that withstands poor soil, heat, and drought. May also be sold as Althea. Cultivar options: 'Aphrodite'—dark pink petals with dark red centers; 'Blue Bird'—large lavender flowers with red centers; 'Diana'—large, pure white flower; 'Oiseau Bleu'—azure-blue flower with purple veining; 'Paeoniflora'—flowers double, light pink from June to September.

Shrubs 5

Hydrangea arborescens 'Annabelle'

Annabelle Hydrangea

Zones: 3-9

Light Needs:

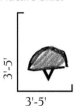

Mature Size:

3'-5'

3'-5'

Growth Rate:
rapid

deciduous shrub

Needs: Plant in fertile, slightly acidic soil that's well-drained but moist. Water regularly. Grow in full sun or partial shade—blooms best in sun but may require afternoon shade in hotter regions. Prune in late winter or early spring, cutting stems just above a bud to remove one-quarter of stem length.

Good for: specimen shrubs, seasonal accent, massing, entries, courtyards, beside patios, include in flower or shrub beds, fill in narrow spaces between walkways and walls

More Choices: pages 34, 36, 39, 40, 108, 109, 110, 111, 112, and 113

Outstanding Features:

- Big, showy flowers last from spring into fall
- Grows quickly to fill in planting beds
- Tolerates both cold and hot temperatures

Get the soil right and this shrub is easy to grow. Big blossoms are showy from spring into fall and change colors with the seasons. They start off apple green in late spring, then become white, then back to green, and finally fade to pink-blushed beige in cool weather. Position these shrubs where you can enjoy them throughout the growing season. Flowers may reach nearly a foot in diameter. Cut blossoms dry well.

Hydrangea macrophylla 'Nikko Blue'

Nikko Blue Hydrangea

Zones: 6-9

Light Needs:

Mature Size:

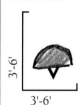

3'-6'

3'-6'

Growth Rate:
rapid

deciduous flowering shrub

Needs: Plant in fertile soil that's moist but well-drained. Grow in full sun in cooler regions, afternoon shade in hotter areas. Water regularly; plants wilt when roots are dry. Tolerates salt. Remove flower heads after color fades. Grow in sheltered spots in colder parts of Zone 6.

Good for: specimen shrubs, massing, brightening shady beds, entries, courtyards, coastal landscapes, planting in shrub beds, including in perennial beds

More Choices: pages 35, 36, 42, 108, 110, 111, and 113

Options: 'Pia'—pink flowers

Outstanding Features:

- Big, rounded flowers in late summer
- Large, coarse-textured green leaves
- Fast growth with salt tolerance

Bigleaf hydrangeas will make you look like a gardening genius. Big, showy blue or pink flowers appear in warm weather set against rich green leaves. Acidic soil yields blue flowers, while plants grown in alkaline soil bloom pink. Add aluminum sulfate to soil for blue, lime for pink. Treat plants individually within a bed for a medley of blue and pink flowers.

Hydrangea paniculata 'Grandiflora'

PeeGee Hydrangea

Zones: 3-8

Light Needs:

Mature Size:

10'-20' (height)
10'-20' (width)

Growth Rate:
rapid

deciduous flowering shrub

Needs: Plant in rich soil that's moist but well-drained. Slightly acidic soils are best. Shrubs will adapt to any soil condition except soggy. Grow in full sun or partial shade. Avoid pruning by giving plants plenty of room; shrubs grow vigorously and get large enough to be trained into small trees.

Good for: specimen shrub, seasonal accent, informal deciduous screen, coarse-textured background, beside blank walls or fences

More Choices: pages 31, 35, 37, 40, 41, 108, 109, 111, and 113

H. paniculata 'Tardiva'

Outstanding Features:
- Large, cone-shaped white flowers
- Blossoms fade to pink, beige, and then to rust
- Grows quickly and tolerates cold

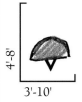

Plant this tough, fast-growing shrub where it has room to get big. Plants fade into the background until midsummer flowers put them in the spotlight. Flowers are produced on new wood. Flower heads can reach 12 to 18 inches in length. Plants should be pruned to five or ten main shoots to produce the largest heads. Ultimate plant size is quite variable. Also try: 'Tardiva'—flowers in fall.

Hydrangea quercifolia

Oakleaf Hydrangea

Zones: 3-8

Light Needs:

Mature Size:

4'-8' (height)
3'-10' (width)

Growth Rate:
slow to medium

deciduous flowering shrub

Needs: Plant in moist, acidic or alkaline soil that's rich in organic matter. Grow in full sun in cooler regions, partial shade in hotter areas. Shrubs grow best with regular watering but will tolerate drought.

Good for: specimen shrubs, planting beneath trees, massing, coarse-textured backgrounds, shrub borders, edges of woodlands, natural areas

More Choices: pages 36, 40, 41, 108, and 113

Outstanding Features:
- Big, drooping cones of creamy flowers
- Large, coarse leaves turn scarlet in autumn
- Mounded, irregular plant form

Shrubs 5

Brighten empty spots in dappled shade with Oakleaf Hydrangea. These shrubs are big, their flowers are big, and so are their leaves. Prune after flowering if necessary. Plants look best when grown into their naturally irregular form. Not a good choice for formal landscapes.

Design Tip Oakleaf Hydrangea is a good companion plant to Mountain Laurels and Rhododendrons. It also grows well in beds of Hostas.

Ilex cornuta 'Burfordii Nana'

Dwarf Burford Holly

Zones: 6-9

Light Needs:

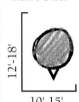

Mature Size:

12'-18'

10'-15'

Growth Rate:
medium to rapid

evergreen shrub

Needs: Plant in full sun to partial shade in acidic soil that's either rich or poor but not too wet. Prune as needed to control size. Allow plants to form dense mass instead of individual shapes.

Good for: foundation planting, parking areas, hedges, barriers, or use as a background plant

More Choices: pages 34, 36, 39, 40, 99, 101, and 113

Outstanding Features:

- Glossy green leaves remain year-round
- Attractive red berries in winter
- Adaptable to a range of soil conditions

This tough shrub gets much larger than its name implies. You can keep hedges trimmed between 4 and 6 feet tall. Or, let single specimen plants grow tall enough to form small trees (remove lower branches to reveal trunks), as shown here. Foliage stays a glossy dark green year-round. Heavy crops of red berries appear in winter.

Ilex crenata 'Helleri'

Heller Japanese Holly

Zones: 5-8

Light Needs:

Mature Size:

2'-3'

3'-5'

Growth Rate:
slow

evergreen shrub

Needs: Plant in sun or shade in soil of medium fertility and moisture. Requires acidic soil and will not thrive in alkaline or sandy soil. Pick a shadier spot if your soil is poor. Water regularly during hot, dry spells. Space new plants 2 feet apart and let them grow together to form a dense mass.

Good for: use in front of low windows or taller plants, filling large shrub beds, edging around patios and decks

More Choices: pages 35, 36, and 108

Outstanding Features:

- Low maintenance; no pruning required
- Fine-textured foliage stays green all year
- Dwarf, naturally mounded form

If you hate pruning, here's the plant for you. Heller Japanese Holly stays low and tidy all by itself. This evergreen shrub grows slowly. Start with larger plants if you want instant impact. Transplants easily into the landscape. Tolerant of city conditions.

Compact Japanese Holly

Zones: 5-8

Light Needs:

Mature Size:

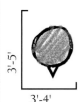

3'-5'

3'-4'

Growth Rate:
rapid

evergreen shrub

Needs: Plant in sun or shade in well-drained soil. Prune if desired to maintain compact form. This disease-resistant shrub is easy to transplant.

Good for: entries, specimen use, formal gardens, foundation or background planting in shrub beds

More Choices: pages 34, 36, 101, 109, and 111

Outstanding Features:
- Round, dense form, dark green leaves
- Resembles boxwood but grows more rapidly
- Tolerates frequent and repeated pruning

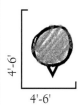

Consider this shrub a substitute for boxwood. Though inexpensive and fast-growing in comparison, the dense form of this disease-resistant shrub has similar classic appeal. Plants are easily trimmed into formal shapes.

Inkberry

Zones: 3-10

Light Needs:

Mature Size:

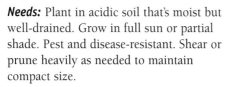

4'-6'

4'-6'

Growth Rate:
slow to medium

evergreen shrub

Needs: Plant in acidic soil that's moist but well-drained. Grow in full sun or partial shade. Pest and disease-resistant. Shear or prune heavily as needed to maintain compact size.

Good for: foundation planting, screening, massing, winter interest, providing background, seaside landscapes, formal or informal gardens, parking areas, poolside, planting beside patios, and walkways

More Choices: pages 30, 35, 36, 38, 40, 42, 101, 109, 110, and 111

Outstanding Features:
- Glossy leaves stay dark green year-round
- Tolerates heat, snow, salt, and pruning
- Dense, compact form; tight branching

Shrubs 5

Few shrubs are as adaptable as glossy-leaved Inkberry. You can grow it at the beach, in snow, in alkaline or acidic soils, in sunny or shady spots. Also sold as Gallberry. Compact varieties are more desired for home landscape use. Choose these selections unless you want a 10' tall shrub. Also try: 'Nigra'—3' to 4' tall; 'Shamrock'—5' to 6' tall. Thrives in the Eastern United States.

Ilex x *'Nellie R. Stevens'*

Nellie R. Stevens Holly

Zones: 6-9

Light Needs:

Mature Size:

15'-20'

10'-15'

Growth Rate: medium

large evergreen shrub

Needs: Plant in full sun or partial shade in well-drained, acidic soil. Give new plants plenty of room to grow. Mature plants can withstand drought.

Good for: corners of tall houses, screening poor views, privacy, windbreaks, or as specimen plants

More Choices: pages 30, 35, 36, 39, 40, 43, and 109

With its naturally broad, pyramidal form and dark, glossy green leaves, Nellie R. Stevens Holly is a long-time favorite in the landscape. Plants get big, so give them plenty of room. They resemble a fat Christmas tree growing in the yard. Female plants fruit heavily.

Ilex vomitoria 'Nana'

Dwarf Yaupon Holly

Zones: 7-10

Light Needs:

Mature Size:

3'-4'

3'-5'

Growth Rate: slow to medium

evergreen shrub

Needs: Plant in sun or shade and in just about any soil, including acidic, alkaline, poor, or sandy. Established plants are drought-tolerant. No pruning is needed unless old plants outgrow their space. Then, cut back severely.

Good for: foundation planting, low hedges, formal gardens, coastal areas, xeriscaping, massed plantings

More Choices: pages 34, 36, 39, 40, 41, 42, 43, 99, 101, 108, 109, and 111

Options: 'Schilling's Dwarf'—good for hotter climates (Zones 9 and 10).

Sun or shade, wet or dry—this plant is happy anywhere. Dwarf Yaupon Holly is slow-growing and compact, though plants eventually get big with age. Fruit is hidden by the foliage.

Showy Jasmine

Zones: 7-9

Light Needs:

Mature Size:

4'-6'

4'-6'

Growth Rate:
  medium

semievergreen flowering shrub

Needs: Plant in any soil—including acidic or alkaline—that doesn't stay wet. Grow in full sun to partial shade. Prune to control plant size.

Good for: xeriscaping, slopes and banks, massing, trailing over walls

More Choices: pages 35, 37, 39, 40, 41, 42, 43, 109, 110, 111, and 112

Options: Winter jasmine, *J. nudiflorum*— yellow flowers occur in late winter on bare, green, arching stems

Here's a vigorous shrub that's just right for hillsides. Stems arch gracefully downhill; roots don't mind the dry conditions. Tiny yellow flowers produced over several months are a bonus. May be sold as Florida Jasmine. Evergreen in hotter areas.

Old Gold Juniper

Zones: 4-10

Light Needs:

Mature Size:

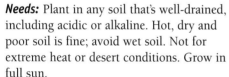

2'-3'

3'-4'

Growth Rate:
  slow to medium

evergreen shrub

Needs: Plant in any soil that's well-drained, including acidic or alkaline. Hot, dry and poor soil is fine; avoid wet soil. Not for extreme heat or desert conditions. Grow in full sun.

Good for: specimen plants, dry areas, hillsides, winter interest, xeriscaping, arid landscapes

More Choices: pages 35, 39, 40, 41, 42, 43, and 111

Options: 'Spartan'—20' tall pyramidal shrub, green foliage, fast-growing

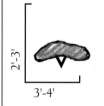

Not every plant must flower to add color to your landscape. Old Gold Juniper features foliage as bright as its name implies. A little of this plant goes a long way, due to its strong color. Locate near dark or neutral backgrounds. Foliage may clash with house color or the foliage of other variegated plants.

Shrubs   5

Juniperus chinensis 'Parsonii'

Parson's Juniper

Zones: 3-9

Light Needs:

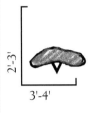

Mature Size:

2'-3'

3'-4'

Growth Rate:
slow to medium

evergreen shrub

Needs: Plant in full sun in moist, well-drained soil. Junipers will also grow in chalky, sandy soils that are dry. Little pruning is needed.

Good for: low growing hedge, low plantings along a walkway, or surrounding a patio or deck

More Choices: pages 35, 39, 43, and 99

Outstanding Features:

- Forms a low-growing mound of grey-green
- ✓ Maintains leaf color through the seasons
- ✓ Low maintenance and adaptability

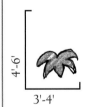

Junipers earn their keep in the landscape. Once established, they are care-free. Occasional pruning to remove any dead or damaged growth is all that is needed. Don't overwater.

Juniperus chinensis 'Sea Green'

Sea Green Juniper

Zones: 4-8

Light Needs:

Mature Size:

4'-6'

3'-4'

Growth Rate:
slow to medium

evergreen shrub

Needs: Plant in full sun in moist to dry, well-drained soil. Junipers will also grow in chalky, sandy soils that are dry. Little pruning is needed.

Good for: foundation plantings around homes or decks or porches

More Choices: pages 35, 39, 42, 43, 101, and 109

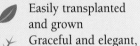
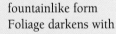
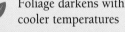

Outstanding Features:

- Easily transplanted and grown
- Graceful and elegant, fountainlike form
- Foliage darkens with cooler temperatures

Easy and evergreen—that pretty much sums up Sea Green Juniper. Grow it for year-round frothy foliage in moist or poor soils in full sun.

Mountain Laurel

Outstanding Features:
- Clusters of spring flowers
- Large leaves stay green year-round
- Great for moist areas in the landscape

Zones: 4-9

Light Needs:

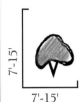

Mature Size:

7'-15'

7'-15'

Growth Rate: slow

evergreen shrub

Needs: Plant in acidic, moist soil in sun or shade. Fewer flowers are produced in dense shade. No pruning is needed. Mulch plants well and provide water during hot, dry spells. Plants will not thrive in alkaline or very dry soil.

Good for: natural areas, large planting beds, and foundations, good background for summer perennials

More Choices: pages 35, 36, 40, 101, 109, 110, 111, and 112

If you have the right soil condition for Mountain Laurel in your yard, don't miss the opportunity to grow this large-leaved evergreen shrub. You'll enjoy clusters of blossoms from May to June in white and shades of pink and red. Desirable cultivars include: 'Alba'—white flowers; 'Myrtifolia'—stays under 6' high; 'Ostbo Red'—deep red flower buds; 'Pink Charm'—pink flower; 'Polypetala'—double feathery pink flowers; 'Sharon Rose'—deep red buds and light pink flowers, compact growth habit.

New Zealand Tea Tree

Outstanding Features:
- White, pink, or red blooms in spring
- Tolerates heat and salty air
- Dense foliage stays green year-round

Zones: 9-10

Light Needs:

Mature Size:

6'-10'

6'-10'

Growth Rate: medium

evergreen flowering shrub

Needs: Plant in fertile, acidic soil that's moist but well drained; root rot may develop in wet soil. Grow in full sun or partial shade. Protect from harsh winds.

Good for: coastal areas, specimen shrubs, seasonal accent, background planting, screening, shrub beds

More Choices: pages 30, 35, 36, 40, 42, 108, 109, 111, and 112

Options: 'Pink Pearl'—pink to white double flowers; 6'-10' high
'Snow White'—white double flowers; 2'-4' high

Here's a big shrub with a soft look. Grow it to enjoy early summer flowers with white, pink, or red petals. May be grown as a small tree. Alkaline soil can lead to chlorosis; offset with supplemental iron. Thrives in Southern California.

Shrubs 133

Shrubs 5

Leucothoe axillaris

Dwarf Leucothoe

Zones: 5-9

Light Needs:

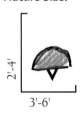

Mature Size:

2'-4'

3'-6'

Growth Rate:
slow

evergreen flowering shrub

Needs: Plant in acidic, deep soil that's rich in organic matter. Water regularly to establish plants. Plants are not drought-tolerant. They will tolerate damp soils. Grow in partial shade.

Good for: natural areas, woodlands, massed plantings, damp areas, low layer in front of taller shrubs, beside shady patios, along shady paths

More Choices: pages 36, 40, 109, 110, 111, 112, and 113

Outstanding Features:

- Glossy leaves turn bronze-purple in fall
- Dense, graceful form is compact
- Drooping clusters of creamy flowers

Grow groups of this graceful little shrub to fill in damp or shady spots in your yard. Glossy foliage stays green year-round; creamy flowers decorate stems in spring. Not as susceptible to leaf spot diseases as Drooping Leucothoe. Transplants easily into the landscape. May be sold as Coastal Leucothoe. Also try: *L. fontanesiana*, Drooping Leucothoe—arching branches.

Ligustrum lucidum

Waxleaf Ligustrum

Zones: 7-10

Light Needs:

Mature Size:

8'-12'

5'-10'

Growth Rate:
rapid

evergreen shrub

Needs: Plant in medium fertility soil in sun or shade. Prune stems as needed to shape; remove lower limbs if you want to train into a small tree. Leaves are too large to clip plants into formal shapes.

Good for: tree-form specimen, confined areas beside parking, swimming pools, or in large planters. Shrubs make thick, dense hedges

More Choices: pages 30, 35, 37, 39, 41, 43, 99, and 109

Outstanding Features:

- Thick, glossy foliage green year-round
- Adapts to a variety of soil conditions
- Useful in many landscape situations

Easy-to-grow Waxleaf Ligustrum isn't known for showy flowers or brightly colored fruit. But it is invaluable for year-round greenery that thrives just about anywhere, shaped as a shrub or a small tree. Privet flower fragrance is offensive to some.

Chinese Variegated Privet

Zones: 7-10

Light Needs:

Mature Size:

6'-12'

6'-12'

Growth Rate:
rapid

Outstanding Features:

- Leaves are edged in creamy white
- Forms thickets of arching stems
- Grows anywhere it is planted

evergreen shrub (semievergreen in cool climates)

Needs: Plant in any kind of soil. Grow in any level of light. Mow over seedlings or pull them by hand. Prune to shape into desired forms.

Good for: informal hedges, screening for privacy or to block poor views, specimen shrubs, accents

More Choices: pages 30, 34, 36, 38, 39, 40, 41, 42, 43, 99, 109, and 111

This shrub displays clusters of white flowers with a fragrance described as both pleasant and unpleasant. Most widely used for hedges. Can be clipped into shapes for large containers. Remove any branches bearing solid green leaves. Seedlings will bear green leaves. This plant is hard to kill; make sure you want it where you plant it.

Nandina domestica

Nandina

Zones: 6-9

Light Needs:

Mature Size:

6'-8'

4'-6'

Growth Rate:
medium

Outstanding Features:

- Leaflets add fine texture to the landscape
- Clusters of shiny berries fall into winter
- New foliage or winter leaves may turn reddish

evergreen shrub

Needs: Plant in moist, fertile soil but plants can adapt to any soil. Grow in full sun for best color; partial shade is okay.

Good for: massing, growing in narrow spaces, adding fine texture, seasonal accents, screening, entries, beside driveways, walkways, or patios; screening the area beneath low decks

More Choices: pages 30, 35, 36, 43, 108, 109, 110, 111, 112, and 113

Options: 'Harbour Dwarf'—compact 2' to 3' high; reddish purple in winter
'Moon Bay'—smaller leaves, 18" to 30" high; bright red in winter

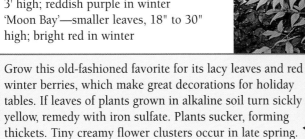

Grow this old-fashioned favorite for its lacy leaves and red winter berries, which make great decorations for holiday tables. If leaves of plants grown in alkaline soil turn sickly yellow, remedy with iron sulfate. Plants sucker, forming thickets. Tiny creamy flower clusters occur in late spring. Plants look best planted in drifts or massed.

Wisdom of the Aisles

Keep Nandina bushy by pruning in late winter each year. Cut two-thirds of randomly selected stalks at staggered heights. Allow the remaining third to remain at full height.

Shrubs 5

Photinia x fraseri

Redtip Photinia

Zones: 6-9

Light Needs:

Mature Size:

10'-15'

5'-7'

Growth Rate:
rapid

evergreen shrub

Needs: Plant in full sun or partial shade in well-drained soil. Fertilize regularly with Nitrogen to prevent deficiency. Prune heavily in late winter or early spring by cutting woody stems at their bases.

Good for: hedging or screening, single-stemmed tree

More Choices: pages 30, 35, 37, 99, and 109

Outstanding Features:

- Early spring growth is bright red
- Summer leaves are a lustrous deep green
- Upright growth for hedging use

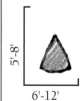

Redtip Photinia grows quickly. New growth unfolds bright red at the tops of shrubs. If left unpruned, this shrub will get very large, so give it room to grow or plan to prune. Flowers have an unpleasant smell. Die-back can kill an entire hedge quickly. Remove diseased branches as soon as they appear, rinsing loppers between cuts to avoiding spreading the problem. Redtip Photinia suffers in areas with high humidity.

Picea glauca 'Conica'

Dwarf Alberta Spruce

Zones: 2-8

Light Needs:

Mature Size:

5'-8'

6'-12'

Growth Rate:
slow

evergreen shrub

Needs: Plant in neutral to acidic soil that's moist but well-drained. Grow in full sun or partial shade. Provide regular watering in hot areas. If growing in containers, make sure pots drain well. Rarely needs pruning; cut stray branches on occasion to maintain shape.

Good for: single specimens, matched pairs, anchoring corners of flower beds, formal gardens, entries, courtyards, beside walkways, gates, and patios; growing in containers or confined spaces

More Choices: pages 34, 36, 39, 40, 109, and 111

Outstanding Features:

- Tidy, conical shape adds contrast
- Small and slow-growing
- Bluish green foliage stays fresh year-round

If you want a topiary but don't have time to train one, this is the plant for you. Slow-growing dwarf shrubs resemble tidy, miniature trees. These little shrubs often stay as small as 2 or 3 feet tall for many years. Easily grown.

Cherry Laurel

Zones: 6-9

Light Needs:

Mature Size:

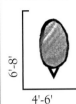

6'-8'

4'-6'

Growth Rate:
rapid

evergreen shrub

Needs: Plant in average soil. After the first summer, plants don't require watering. Grow in full sun or partial shade. Prune anytime. Shears well. Can train shrubs as small trees.

Good for: hedges, screening, informal or formal gardens, coastal areas, quick background, attracting birds, xeriscaping, natural areas

More Choices: pages 30, 34, 36, 42, 43, 99, 109, and 111

Outstanding Features:
- Bronze new growth turns glossy green
- Tolerates heat, salt, and drought
- Grows quickly into large hedge

Grow this tough shrub when you need an easy hedge or green background. Plants can be left natural or pruned into shapes. Do not plant near paving; falling berries and leaves are messy. Plants grown in alkaline soil may require iron sulfate to keep foliage from yellowing. Sometimes sold as Carolina Cherry Laurel or Laurelcherry.

Otto Luyken Laurel

Zones: 6-8

Light Needs:

Mature Size:

5'-6'

6'-8'

Growth Rate:
medium

evergreen shrub

Needs: Plant in moist, well-drained soil in partial or dense shade. Mulch roots well and water regularly. Protect from afternoon sun in hot climates. No pruning required.

Good for: foundation planting, massing beneath trees, shrub beds, background to shade gardens and perennial borders, entries, low hedges

More Choices: pages 36, 101, 110, 111, and 112

Options: Schip Laurel, 'Schipkaensis'— very similar, a little hardier; 10' to 15' high, good for screening; Zones 5 to 8

Outstanding Features:
- Rich, dark green pointed leaves
- Compact form with upright branches
- White spring flowers will bloom in shade

Shrubs 5

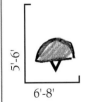

You'll love this plant for its glossy, dark green foliage. The large leaves add coarse texture to compositions as neat, spreading plants fill in shady spots. Do not prune to separate plants. Allow shrubs to grow together to form a mass of dark green. Flowers profusely even in heavy shade.

Pyracantha coccinea

Pyracantha

Zones: 6-8

Light Needs:

Mature Size:

6'-18'

6'-18'

Growth Rate:
medium to rapid

evergreen shrub

Needs: Plant in any well-drained soil; dry soil is fine, so is alkaline or acidic. Grow in full sun or partial shade.

Good for: hedges, barriers, espalier, slopes, massing, specimen plants, seasonal accents, attracting birds, filling in hot, dry areas in yards

More Choices: pages 35, 37, 39, 40, 41, 42, 43, 99, 110, 111, 112, and 113

Outstanding Features:

- Orange-red fruit ripens in fall
- Multitudes of tiny flowers in spring
- Sprawling form, stiff branches

Pyracantha boasts orange-red berries in September and October. Plants adapt to any kind of dry soil. Stems are thorny. Berries are produced on two-year-old wood; over-pruning will reduce fruiting. Also try: 'Scarlet Firethorn'—profuse berries.

Wisdom of the Aisles

Fireblight turns Pyracantha twigs black and kills them. Remove infected branches about 18" below affected areas, sterilizing between cuts. Use steptomycin or copper sulfate spray before buds open in spring. Repeat weekly until blooming ceases.

Rhododendron catawbiense

Catawba Rhododendron

Zones: 4-8

Light Needs:

Mature Size:

6'-10'

5'-8'

Growth Rate:
slow

evergreen shrub

Needs: Plant in moist, well-drained, acidic, fertile soil. Rhododendrons can take full sun in colder areas; in warmer climates, partial shade is best. Water plants in fall. Mulch beneath shrubs to help soil stay moist. Prune to remove dead branches after new growth has emerged. Snap off flowers after they fade.

Good for: specimen shrub, screen, massed, or foundation planting

More Choices: pages 30, 34, 36, 40, 101, 109, and 112

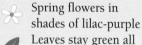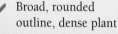

Outstanding Features:

- Spring flowers in shades of lilac-purple
- Leaves stay green all year-round
- Broad, rounded outline, dense plant

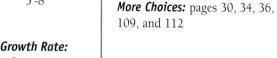

The bright lilac-purple blossoms of Catawba Rhododendron are breathtaking against the dark green leaves. Catawba Rhododendron can take cold weather without sacrificing flower buds, but protect it from drying winter winds. Cultivar options: 'P.J.M.'—lavender-pink flowers; shade- and drought-tolerant; 6' high to 4' wide; Zones 4-8; 'P.J.M. White'—white flowers; leaves turn burgundy in winter; 3' to 4' high and wide; Zones 4-8; 'Mollis' Hybrids—large, waxy blooms; many flower colors; deciduous; 4' to 5' high and wide; Zones 4-8.

Betty Prior Rose

Zones: 4-9

Light Needs:

Mature Size:

3'-4'

2'-3'

Growth Rate:
medium

deciduous shrub

Needs: Plant roses in full sun in moist, well-drained, fertile soil. Prune to remove dead branches and to shape shrubs after buds swell in spring. Clip faded blooms for nonstop flowers until late summer. Fertilize with rose food when blooming starts.

Good for: specimen shrub, hedge, or massed planting. Space plants 18 inches apart for a hedge of bloom. It will also grow well in a large container.

More Choices: pages 34, 109, 110, and 113

Outstanding Features:
- Large flowers are deep pink and fragrant
- ✔ Cold-hardy and easy care
- ✔ Compact size and form

Want a hedge that is as beautiful as it is functional? Plant a row of 'Betty Prior' roses. Pink blossoms are 2 to 3 inches wide and appear from summer until frost. When planting roses, it's helpful to add super phosphate or bonemeal to the soil in the planting hole to promote root growth.

Carefree Beauty Rose

Zones: 4-8

Light Needs:

Mature Size:

3'-4'

2'-3'

Growth Rate:
medium

deciduous shrub

Needs: Plant in full sun in moist, well-drained, fertile soil. Prune to remove dead branches after buds swell in spring. Clip spent blooms to encourage ongoing flowering. Fertilize with rose food when blooming starts.

Good for: specimen shrub, hedge, or foundation planting. To grow as a hedge, space plants 18 inches apart.

More Choices: pages 34, 109, and 113

Outstanding Features:
- Clusters of fragrant pink blooms
- ✔ Bright orange hips persist all winter
- ✔ Winter-hardy and disease-free

Shrubs 5

The name says it all: Carefree Beauty. Flowers open continually from summer until frost—large, double, rose-pink blooms packed with perfume. No spraying needed; they are completely disease-free. When planting roses, it's helpful to add super phosphate or bonemeal to the soil in the planting hole to promote root growth. This is probably the most famous of Griffith Buck's roses.

Rosa 'Country Dancer'

Country Dancer Rose

Zones: 4-9

Light Needs:

Mature Size:

3'-4'

3'-4'

Growth Rate:
rapid

deciduous shrub

Needs: Plant in well-drained, slightly acidic soil. Grow in full sun. Water generously during the growing season, taking care not to wet foliage. Fertilize with rose food when blooming starts.

Good for: specimen shrubs, seasonal accents, informal hedges, filling planting beds, layering against taller shrubs, poolside, entries, courtyards, beside patios and along walkways

More Choices: pages 34, 40, 99, 109, and 111

Outstanding Features:

✔ Compact size and form
❋ Clusters of large, pink, double blooms
✔ Cold-hardy and carefree

You don't need to know much about roses to grow this pink-blooming beauty. Give it good soil, full sun, and regular moisture, and you'll be rewarded with effortless flowers. Modern shrub; a Dr. Griffith Buck rose. Blossoms are lightly fragrant, bubble gum pink in color. Repeat bloomer.

Wisdom of the Aisles

Prune roses in winter when leaves are gone and you can see what you're doing. Remove diseased, weak, or dead canes. Spring pruning can remove blooms. Fall pruning can reduce flowering.

Rosa 'Fru Dagmar Hastrup'

Fru Dagmar Hastrup Rose

Zones: 2-9

Light Needs:

Mature Size:

3'-4'

3'-4'

Growth Rate:
medium

deciduous flowering shrub

Needs: Fru Dagmar Hastrup prefers sandy, light soil. It will survive in warm, coastal climates as well as cold. Prune in early spring each year only to remove old, worn-out stems that have stopped bearing blooms. Fertilize with rose food when blooming starts.

Good for: specimen shrub or hedge. It's also a good plant to include in the back of a perennial bed.

More Choices: pages 34, 39, 43, 109, and 113

Outstanding Features:

• One of the most disease-resistant roses
❋ Single flowers in shades of silvery pink
✔ Flowers have a rich clove scent

Large, single, pale pink blooms first appear in June and continue opening all summer long. At the end of the season, large scarlet hips cover the bush. Leaves are a deep green in summer, then develop shades of maroon and gold in the fall. It is a highly disease-resistant rose.

Graham Thomas Rose

Zones: 5-9

Light Needs:

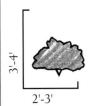

Mature Size:

3'-4'

2'-3'

Growth Rate:
medium

deciduous shrub

Needs: Plant roses in full sun in moist, well-drained, fertile soil. The only required pruning is removing nonflowering stems in spring. Remove faded blooms to get more flowers.

Good for: specimen shrub, hedge, or mass planting. Good for planting near sitting areas to enjoy fragrance.

More Choices: pages 34, 109, 110, and 113

Outstanding Features:
- 3-inch-wide, golden yellow, double blooms
- ✔ Old-fashioned rose fragrance
- ✔ Compact size and form

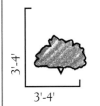

This David Austin rose boasts the fragrance of an old-fashioned rose in a shrub form that blooms repeatedly during the growing season. Flowers are golden yellow and double-petalled; they appear all through the growing season, including during the heat of summer. Grow where the fragrance can be enjoyed to the fullest. When grown in ideal conditions, plants may become large with age.

Rosa 'Gruss an Aachen'

Gruss an Aachen Rose

Zones: 5-9

Light Needs:

Mature Size:

3'-4'

3'-4'

Growth Rate:
medium to rapid

deciduous flowering shrub

Needs: Plant in well-drained, slightly acidic soil. Grow in full sun; shrubs bloom reasonably well in partial shade, too. Water generously during the growing season, taking care not to wet foliage. Fertilize with rose food when blooming starts. Disease-resistant.

Good for: specimen shrubs, seasonal accents, informal hedges, filling in planting beds, layering against taller shrubs, entries, courtyards, beside patios and walkways

More Choices: pages 35, 36, 40, 99, 109, 111, and 113

Outstanding Features:
- Large blush pink flowers mature to cream
- ✔ Compact, bushy form for garden use
- Dark, leathery foliage is disease-resistant

The peaches-and-cream complexion of this rose is irresistible. Compact shrubs are easy to grow; flowers are fragrant. Floribunda. Fragrant, double blossoms open summer and fall. Flowers profusely.

Shrubs 5

Iceberg Rose

Zones: 4-9

Light Needs:

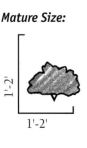

Mature Size:

1'-2'

1'-2'

Growth Rate:
medium

deciduous shrub

Needs: Plant roses in full sun in moist, well-drained, fertile soil. Prune to remove dead branches and to shape plants after buds swell in spring. Clip faded blooms to keep flowers coming. Fertilize with rose food when blooming starts.

Good for: specimen shrub, hedge, or massed planting, good cut flowers

More Choices: pages 35, 109, 110, 112, and 113

Outstanding Features:
- Fragrant flowers in pure white clusters
- Canes are nearly thornless
- Clean, dark green foliage

Volumes of pure white flowers open in clusters that are borne at the end of growing stems. Like all floribunda roses, Iceberg can take cold winters (to 30 degrees below zero). Iceberg is easy-care beauty at its best—you won't be disappointed with this rose. Some gardeners have had success getting this rose to bloom in partial shade.

Margo Koster Rose

Zones: 5-8

Light Needs:

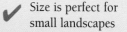

Mature Size:

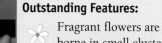

12"

12"-24"

Growth Rate:
medium

deciduous flowering shrub

Needs: Plant roses in full sun in moist, well-drained, fertile soil. Fertilize with rose food when blooming starts.

Good for: an edging plant, a low hedge, or a specimen. Use it to edge a perennial border, skirt evergreen shrubs, or in well-drained soil near a water garden.

More Choices: pages 35, 109, and 113

Outstanding Features:
- Fragrant flowers are borne in small clusters
- Blooms fade in shades of salmon as they age
- Size is perfect for small landscapes

Growing a mere 12 inches high, Margo Koster is a perfect choice to edge a walkway, patio, or shrub border. The stems are nearly thornless and flowers open in shades of salmon all summer long. This rose is a low-maintenance plant. Also try: 'Nearly Wild'—nearly nonstop pink blossoms.

Pink Meidiland Rose

Zones: 5-8

Light Needs:

Mature Size:

3'-4'

3'-4'

Growth Rate:
medium

deciduous flowering shrub

Needs: Plant roses in full sun in moist, well-drained, fertile soil. The only required pruning is removing nonflowering stems in spring. Remove spent blooms to encourage flowering. Do not plant roses where they will be exposed to heavy winds or strong winter sun. Fertilize with rose food when blooming starts.

Good for: specimen shrub, low hedge, or massed planting

More Choices: pages 35, 110, and 113

The Meidiland roses are French-bred beauties that are tough as nails. Pink Meidiland tosses open shell pink blooms from summer until frost. The flowers are single and look like a Dogwood blossom. This rose will grow in shade and still bloom.

Rosa Rubrifolia

Zones: 4-9

Light Needs:

Mature Size:

4'-6'

3'-5'

Growth Rate:
medium

deciduous flowering shrub

Needs: Plant roses in full sun in moist, well-drained, fertile soil. Prune stray stems as needed. Fertilize with rose food when blooming starts.

Good for: specimen shrub or hedge. Plant it where you can see it from inside your home for year-round view.

More Choices: pages 35, 109, and 113

Outstanding Features:

❋ Bright pink flowers are fragrant

✔ Nearly thornless purple-red stems

✔ Scarlet hips linger through winter

Shrubs 5

Single flowers open to a bright flamingo pink in early summer. Petal tips are pink with white bases. After they fade, the purple-tinged leaves take center stage, highlighted against bright, purple-red arching stems. In fall, hips ripen to a scarlet red color and last all winter. May be sold as *Rosa glauca*.

Rosa 'The Fairy'

The Fairy Rose

Zones: 4-9

Light Needs: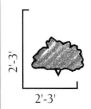

Mature Size:

2'-3'

2'-3'

Growth Rate:
medium

deciduous flowering shrub

Needs: Plant in moist, well-drained fertile soil in full sun or partial shade. Fertilize with rose food when blooming starts.

Good for: specimen shrub or low hedge. The Fairy is a perfect rose to grow in large container such as a whiskey barrel planter.

More Choices: pages 35, 37, and 113

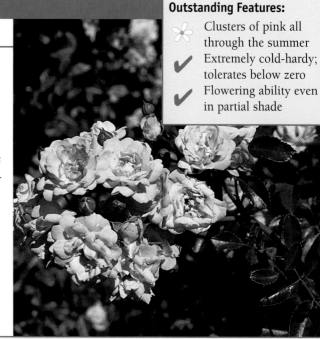

Outstanding Features:

- Clusters of pink all through the summer
- ✔ Extremely cold-hardy; tolerates below zero
- ✔ Flowering ability even in partial shade

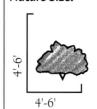

Though dainty flowers appear delicate, this rose is hardy to 40 degrees below zero. Small, double pink blossoms open summer through fall. This rose will even bloom in partial shade.

Rosa 'Therese Bugnet'

Therese Bugnet Rose

Zones: 3-9

Light Needs:

Mature Size:

4'-6'

4'-6'

Growth Rate:
medium

deciduous flowering shrub

Needs: Therese Bugnet tolerates sandy, light, poor soils. Prune sparingly in early spring each year only to remove old, worn-out stems that have stopped bearing blooms. Fertilize with rose food when blooming starts.

Good for: a hedge or specimen shrub

More Choices: pages 35, 39, 43, 109, and 113

Outstanding Features:

- Pink, ruffled flowers are 4 inches wide
- Wonderfully fragrant flowers
- Dark green foliage turning red in fall

Large, fully double pink blooms are rich with fragrance. Leaves are a lustrous green in summer and then deep red in the fall. Therese Bugnet can grow and bloom in poor soil and even in shade. If your yard is hard on roses, Therese Bugnet is the choice for you.

Anthony Waterer Spirea

Zones: 3-9

Light Needs:

Mature Size:

3'-5'

3'-5'

Growth Rate:
medium to rapid

deciduous flowering shrub

Needs: Plant in full sun to partial shade in any well-drained soil. Prune back in spring before new growth begins.

Good for: parking areas, entries, specimen plants, beside patios, background to summer flowerbeds, facing for taller shrubs, massed plantings, low hedges

More Choices: pages 34, 36, 39, 43, 111, and 113

Options: 'Little Princess'—rounded shape, about 30" high, pink flowers
'Alpina'—12" to 30" high

S. japonica 'Little Princess'

Outstanding Features:

- Dark pink blooms in late spring and summer
- New foliage is reddish purple in color
- Durable and adaptable in any setting

Not all spireas have white flowers in early spring. This one boasts dark pink blooms when spring is fading into summer. For durability nothing can take the place of spirea in home landscapes. May be sold as *S. x bumalda* 'Anthony Waterer'

Shibori Spirea

Zones: 4-8

Light Needs:

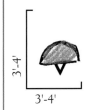

Mature Size:

3'-4'

3'-4'

Growth Rate:
medium

deciduous flowering shrub

Needs: Plant in full sun to partial shade in well-drained soil. Spirea will not tolerate wet sites. Prune in spring before new growth begins. Blooms best in sun.

Good for: entries, groups behind flower beds, specimen plants, beside patios and low decks, low hedges

More Choices: pages 35, 37, and 111

Outstanding Features:

- Pink and white flowers blooming together
- Easy to grow, very adaptable
- Wide range of landscape use

Shrubs 5

Can't decide between pink or white flowers? This spirea blooms in both colors at the same time. Like all spirea, Shibori is adaptable for a variety of uses in the home landscape.

shrubs

Spiraea prunifolia

Bridalwreath Spirea

Zones: 5-8

Light Needs:

Mature Size:

5'-7'

4'-6'

Growth Rate:
rapid

deciduous flowering shrub

Needs: Plant in full sun to partial shade in soil that's moderately fertile and doesn't stay wet. Prune with a light hand, over-pruning spoils the naturally arching form. Give plants room to grow.

Good for: entries, informal hedges, specimen plants, or as a background to spring flowerbeds

More Choices: pages 31, 34, 36, 109, 111, 112, and 113

Little white flowers cover the arching branches early each spring. A perfect backdrop for spring flowering bulbs. Shiny dark green foliage turns orange-red in fall. Best used in informal areas.

Spiraea x vanhouttei

Vanhoutte Spirea

Zones: 3-8

Light Needs:

Mature Size:

6'-8'

10'-12'

Growth Rate:
rapid

deciduous flowering shrub

Needs: Plant in full sun to partial shade in soil that's moderately fertile and doesn't stay wet. Blooms best in sun. Set it where you have room for a big, arching shrub. Plants are not a choice for formal areas.

Good for: entry areas, informal hedges, specimen plants, or as a background to spring flowerbeds

More Choices: pages 31, 35, 37, 38, 39, 109, 111, and 112

The flowers of Vanhoutte Spirea look like tiny white bouquets in late spring and early summer. This shrub is easy to grow no matter where you put it. Not for small areas.

Spiraea japonica Limemound

Limemound Spirea

Zones: 4-9

Light Needs:

Mature Size:

2'-3' (height)
2'-3' (width)

Growth Rate:
rapid

deciduous flowering shrub

Needs: Plant in full sun and well-drained soil. No pruning is needed.

Good for: entries, parking areas, accents, or the front layer of shrub beds

More Choices: pages 35, 109, 111, and 113

Options: 'Golden Princess'—golden yellow leaves
'Goldmound'—heat-tolerant, 30" to 40" high, pink flowers

S. japonica

True to its name, Limemound Spirea is a little lump of bright, lime-green foliage. Tiny blooms cover plants in late spring and leaves turn bright orange in fall. Plants provide interest no matter what the season. If desired, prune plants back in the spring before new growth begins.

Spiraea thunbergii

Baby's Breath Spirea

Zones: 4-8

Light Needs:

Mature Size:

3'-5' (height)
3'-5' (width)

Growth Rate:
rapid

deciduous flowering shrub

Needs: Plant in full sun to partial shade in soil that's moderately fertile and doesn't stay very wet. Give plants room to grow. Prune as needed, but maintain naturally arching form.

Good for: entries, accent plants, informal hedges, beside patios, or plant as a background to beds of spring-blooming bulbs

More Choices: pages 31, 34, 36, 109, 111, 112, and 113

Options: 'Compacta'—grows 2' to 4' tall

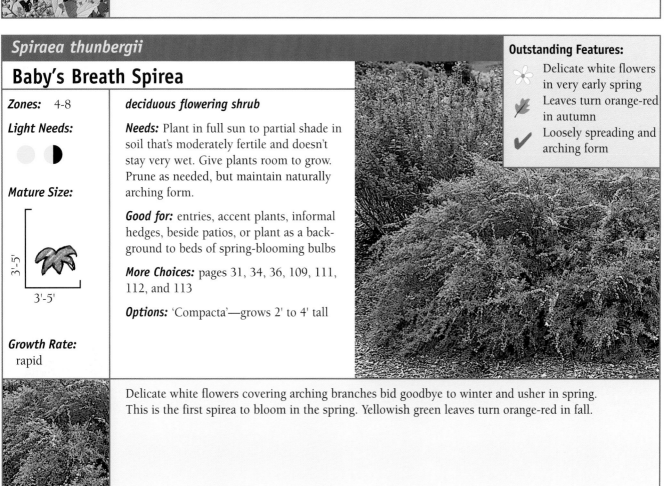

Delicate white flowers covering arching branches bid goodbye to winter and usher in spring. This is the first spirea to bloom in the spring. Yellowish green leaves turn orange-red in fall.

Shrubs 5

5

shrubs

Syringa patula 'Miss Kim'

Miss Kim Lilac

Zones: 3-7

Light Needs:

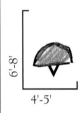

Mature Size:

6'-8'
4'-5'

Growth Rate:
slow

deciduous flowering shrub

Needs: Plant in full sun to partial shade in well-drained, fertile soil. Clip off blooms after they fade. Prune only if needed, after flowering, to shape the shrub.

Good for: shrub border, informal hedge, screen, specimen shrub, near outdoor seating areas to enjoy the fragrance

More Choices: pages 31, 35, 36, 109, 112, and 113

Outstanding Features:

- Purple flowers are very fragrant
- ✔ Leaves resist powdery mildew
- ✔ Plants are cold-hardy and durable

This late-blooming lilac features single, pale lavender flowers that are rich with perfume. Leaves are glossy green in summer, then turn a burgundy-red in fall. Miss Kim Lilac can survive winter temperatures of 40 degrees below zero. A nice lilac for smaller areas.

Thuja orientalis 'Aurea Nana'

Golden Arborvitae

Zones: 6-10

Light Needs:

Mature Size:

5'-8'
3'-4'

Growth Rate:
slow to medium

evergreen shrub

Needs: Plant in any soil that isn't extremely wet. Poor, dry soil is fine. Grow in full sun for best color development.

Good for: specimen plants, accents, anchoring the corners of flowerbeds, entries, formal gardens

More Choices: pages 34, 39, 40, 41, 43, 109, and 111

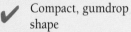

BUYER'$ GUIDE

This plant has more aliases than any criminal. It may also be sold as Berckman's Golden Arborvitae, Golden American Arborvitae. It may bear botanical labels including *T. occidentalis* 'Aurea Nana' or *Playtycladus orientalis* 'Aurea Nana.'

Outstanding Features:

- Green-golden foliage keeps its color
- ✔ Compact, gumdrop shape
- ✔ Tolerates heat and poor, dry soil

Add this bright-colored plant where you need year-round accent and tidy growth. A matched pair or a single plant will catch the eye without overdoing it. Foliage may clash with house colors so use carefully near your home.

148   Shrubs

European Cranberrybush

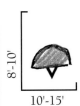

Viburnum opulus 'Roseum'

Zones: 3-8

Light Needs:

Mature Size:

8'-10'

10'-15'

Growth Rate:
medium

deciduous flowering shrub

Needs: Plant in wet or well-drained soil. This cold-hardy plant doesn't tolerate heat well; grow in afternoon shade in hotter climates, full sun elsewhere.

Good for: specimen plants, seasonal accents, focal points, large courtyards or entries, anchoring planting beds, contrasting with evergreen backgrounds, corners of houses, or yards

More Choices: pages 34, 38, 108, 111, and 112

Outstanding Features:
- Flowers resemble large snowballs
- Coarse, dark foliage provides background
- Large, irregular to mounding form

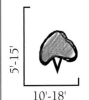

Grow, don't throw, snowballs in the spring. A blizzard of blossoms—puffy, white, and round—covers this large shrub, commanding attention in the spring. Shrubs tolerate wet soil. Very easy to grow in almost any soil. Susceptible to aphids. Spray with insecticide or insecticidal soap to control. Sometimes sold as Snowball Viburnum or 'Sterile.'

Viburnum plicatum tomentosum

Doublefile Viburnum

Zones: 5-8

Light Needs:

Mature Size:

5'-15'

10'-18'

Growth Rate:
rapid

deciduous flowering shrub

Needs: Plant in fertile soil that's moist but well-drained. Grow in full sun to partial shade. Water regularly.

Good for: specimen plants, seasonal accents, massing, corners of houses or yards, in front of fences, balancing vertical plants, beside patios, natural areas

More Choices: pages 34, 36, 108, 109, 110, 111, 112, and 113

Outstanding Features:
- Lacy white flowers in spring
- Clusters of red berries late summer to fall
- Branches grow in horizontal layers

For layers of branches covered with white spring flowers, plant Doublefile Viburnum. You'll also enjoy red berries as the hot season fades and scarlet foliage in the fall. Leaves are coarse-textured. Blooms as well in partial shade as it does in full sun. Shrubs can be pruned to form a small tree. May be planted in warmer parts of Zone 4.

Shrubs 5

Chapter 6
groundcovers
and vines

Ever wonder why some landscapes have a gardenlike feeling while others seem to be basic and dull? Groundcovers and vines add lush layers and finishing touches to your yard. These plants also have a problem-solving, practical side too. Vines screen views and add privacy. Groundcovers anchor slopes, fill planting beds, and cover bare spots where grass won't grow.

Adding the Final Layers

This section explains how to add the final layers to your planting beds. Groundcovers and vines refine landscape compositions and make them appear filled out and complete. This chapter helps you choose groundcovers to control erosion, add texture and seasonal interest, and cover bare areas where grass won't grow. Selection guides indicate which groundcovers are best for growing in large beds and which are suitable for growing in confined areas, such as courtyards and entryways. For groundcovers suitable for growing in sun or shade, see pages 35 and 37.

Add pockets of groundcover for finishing touches at steps.

You'll find information about vines, too. Adding vines and climbers puts color and texture at eye level and above. They can also be used to shelter a location, enhance privacy, screen poor views, and add shade. The inclusion of vines in a landscape is an extra step professional designers take to make new landscape installations look natural and more mature.

Groundcover

Any plant that grows close to the ground—spreading vines, prostrate plants, dwarf shrubs, and low perennials— is considered a groundcover. The selection guides and detailed information within individual plant descriptions enable you to find the plants best suited to your purpose. Local garden center staff can help, too.

Plant groundcovers after all your trees and shrubs are in place. Low-growing plants fill in empty spaces beneath taller plants, giving planting beds a finished look and preventing weeds from taking over. However, groundcovers are more than just fillers. Planting an entire bed with nothing but groundcover gives the landscape a simple, sophisticated look. To achieve this effect, make sure that bedlines are smooth and well-defined. Beds of groundcover are excellent for framing lawns with foliage that differs from grass in color, texture, or height.

Groundcovers are also handy for edging walkways, patios, and planting beds containing taller plants. Grow them in neat rows or let them spill over the edges of paving for a softer look. Some groundcovers are suitable for tucking into the crevices of rock gardens or between stepping-stones. Others look best in beds all alone, set in front of a background of trees and shrubs. When you're laying out bedlines and adding trees and shrubs to your landscape, remember to save room for the last layer of the planting bed.

Slopes

When planting groundcovers on slopes, cover the soil surface with landscape fabric to keep topsoil from washing away while plants are young. (Avoid plastic which heats the soil and must be removed later.) Use any landscape fabric that will decompose over time. Lay it on the slope and cut slits through the fabric where you want the new plants to grow. For steep angles or windy areas, nail the fabric in place with spikes. Water new groundcovers thoroughly at planting and apply supplemental irrigation if necessary until plants are established.

Plant groundcover through slits in landscape fabric on steep slopes.

Planting Groundcovers

Though you don't have to dig deep holes, planting groundcover is labor-intensive.

Planting small plants means getting down on your hands and knees. If possible, till the bed area to make planting easier and establishment quicker. Spread soil amendments such as organic matter on the surface and work it into the soil. A loose planting bed is best for small plants sold in 4-inch pots or cell packs. Planting groundcover is labor-intensive. If you hire someone to do the planting, you might find yourself paying more for the work than for the plants.

Dig individual holes just as you would for a shrub if you're planting groundcovers grown in 1- or 3-gallon containers. Regardless of container size, arrange the plants to fill an area before you remove them from their pots. This keeps them from drying out. Set plants in a staggered formation—like laying bricks. Avoid lining plants in perfect rows. The goal is to fill the bed with greenery, not to create a geometrical pattern that will remain recognizable for months or even years. Always set the first row of groundcover plants to follow the shape of the bedline. Set plants back from the edge of the bed a distance equal to half their mature spread. Plants then have room to grow without crossing the bedline.

Replace worn paths with stepping-stones and groundcovers.

Large-leafed Hostas (page 163) add coarse texture to the front of a planting bed.

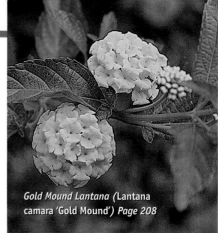

Gold Mound Lantana (Lantana camara 'Gold Mound') Page 208

Blue Pacific Shore Juniper (Juniperus conferta 'Blue Pacific') Page 165

Choosing Groundcovers by Characteristics

The more you know about groundcovers that grow in your area, the more likely you are to pick ones with characteristics desirable for your yard. Groundcovers listed as evergreen keep their foliage year-round. Perennial groundcovers go dormant in late fall or early winter and come back in spring. Coarse-textured groundcovers frame lawns, add depth to the foreground of small, confined spaces, and contrast with finer textured plants, including fine-textured groundcovers. If you want seasonal color in your yard, look at the grouped list of flowering groundcover in this chapter.

Availability varies by area and conditions (see page 21). Check with your garden center.

Sweet Woodruff (Asperula odorata) Page 158

Evergreen groundcover

Common Name	Zones	Page
Aaron's Beard	5-9	164
Hypericum calycinum		
Ajuga	4-9	156
Ajuga reptans		
Andorra Compact Juniper	3-9	166
Juniperus horizontalis 'Plumosa Compacta'		
Asiatic Jasmine	7-10	173
Trachelospermum asiaticum		
Autumn Fern	6-9	160
Dryopteris erythrosora		
Bar Harbor Juniper	3-9	165
Juniperus horizontalis 'Bar Harbor'		
Barrel Cactus	9-10	208
Echinocactus spp.		
Bearberry Cotoneaster	5-9	159
Cotoneaster dammeri		
Blue Chip Juniper	3-9	165
Juniperus horizontalis 'Blue Chip'		
Blue Pacific Shore Juniper	5-9	165
Juniperus conferta 'Blue Pacific'		
Blue Rug Juniper	3-9	166
Juniperus horizontalis 'Wiltonii'		
Cast-Iron Plant	8-10	206
Aspidistra elatior		

Common Name	Zones	Page
Coral Bells	3-8	163
Heuchera sanguinea		
Creeping Phlox	2-9	169
Phlox subulata		
Creeping Thyme	5-9	173
Thymus leucotrichus		
Dwarf Coyote Brush	7-10	207
Baccharis pilularis		
Dwarf Japanese Garden Juniper	4-9	166
Juniperus procumbens 'Nana'		
Dwarf Lily of the Nile	9-10	206
Agapanthus africanus 'Peter Pan'		
English Ivy	5-9	162
Hedera helix		
Evergreen Candytuft	4-8	164
Iberis sempervirens		
Germander	4-9	172
Teucrium prostratum		
Gold Mound Lantana	9-10	208
Lantana camara 'Gold Mound'		
Goldmoss	4-9	171
Sedum acre		
Hens and Chicks	4-10	209
Sempervivum tectorum		

Common Name	Zones	Page
Holly Fern	8-10	159
Cyrtomium falcatum		
Japanese Ardisia	9-10	206
Ardisia japonica		
Lenten Rose	4-8	163
Helleborus orientalis		
Liriope	7-10	167
Liriope muscari		
Littleleaf Periwinkle	4-8	173
Vinca minor		
Mexican Heather	9-10	207
Cuphea hyssopifola		
Mondo Grass	7-9	168
Ophiopogon japonicus		
Prostrate Rosemary	7-10	171
Rosmarinus officinalis 'Irene'		
Purple-Leaf Wintercreeper	4-8	161
Euonymus fortunei 'Coloratus'		
Rock Rose	5-8	162
Helianthemum nummularium		
Silver Brocade Artemisia	3-9	157
Artemisia stelleriana 'Silver Brocade'		
Variegated Japanese Sedge	6-9	158
Carex morrowii 'Variegata'		

Flowering groundcover

Common Name	Zones	Page
Aaron's Beard	5-9	164
Hypericum calycinum		
Ajuga	4-9	156
Ajuga reptans		
Alba Meidiland Rose	4-8	170
Rosa Alba Meidiland		
Arum	6-10	157
Arum italicum		
Barrel Cactus	9-10	208
Echinocactus spp.		
Bath's Pink	4-9	160
Dianthus gratianopolitanus 'Bath's Pink'		
Bearberry Cotoneaster	5-9	159
Cotoneaster dammeri		
Blanket Flower	2-9	161
Gaillardia x grandiflora		
Bloody Cranesbill	3-8	162
Geranium sanguineum		
Catmint	4-8	168
Nepeta x faassenii		
Coral Bells	3-8	163
Heuchera sanguinea		
Creeping Thyme	5-9	173
Thymus leucotrichus		
Dwarf Lily of the Nile	9-10	206
Agapanthus africanus 'Peter Pan'		
Evergreen Candytuft	4-8	164
Iberis sempervirens		
Fleabane	2-10	160
Erigeron hybrid		
Flower Carpet Rose	4-10	171
Rose 'Flower Carpet'		
Freeway Daisy	10	209
Osteospermum fruticosum		
Germander	4-9	172
Teucrium prostratum		
Gold Mound Lantana	9-10	208
Lantana camara 'Gold Mound'		
Goldmoss	4-9	171
Sedum acre		
Hardy Ice Plant	6-9	207
Delosperma nubigenum		
Japanese Primrose	5-8	170
Primula japonica		
Lady's Mantle	4-7	157
Alchemilla mollis		
Lamb's Ears	4-8	172
Stachys byzantina		
Lenten Rose	4-8	163
Helleborus orientalis		
Lily-of-the-Valley	2-9	159
Convallaria majalis		
Liriope	7-10	167
Liriope muscari		
Littleleaf Periwinkle	4-8	173
Vinca minor		
Memorial Rose	4-9	170
Rosa wichuraiana		
Mexican Heather	9-10	207
Cuphea hyssopifola		
Moneywort	3-8	167
Lysimachia nummularia		
Moss Phlox	2-9	169
Phlox subulata		
Moss Verbena	8-10	209
Verbena pulchella		
Pachysandra	4-9	168
Pachysandra terminalis		
Pink Panda Strawberry	3-9	161
Fragaria 'Pink Panda'		
Prostrate Rosemary	7-10	171
Rosmarinus officinalis 'Irene'		
Rock Rose	5-8	162
Helianthemum nummularium		
Snow-on-the-Mountain	3-9	156
Aegopodium podagraria 'Variegatum'		
Spotted Dead Nettle	3-9	167
Lamium maculatum		
Stonecrop	3-10	172
Sedum spectabile		
Sweet Woodruff	4-8	158
Asperula odorata		
Variegated Japanese Sedge	6-9	158
Carex morrowii 'Variegata'		

Perennial groundcover

Common Name	Zones	Page
Arum	6-10	157
Arum italicum		
Artillery Fern	8-10	169
Pilea serpyllacea 'Rotundifolia'		
Autumn Fern	6-9	160
Dryopteris erythrosora		
Bath's Pink	4-9	160
Dianthus gratianopolitanus 'Bath's Pink'		
Blanket Flower	2-9	161
Gaillardia x grandiflora		
Bloody Cranesbill	3-8	162
Geranium sanguineum		
Cast-Iron Plant	8-10	206
Aspidistra elatior		
Catmint	4-8	168
Nepeta x faassenii		
Coral Bells	3-8	163
Heuchera sanguinea		
Dwarf Coyote Brush	7-10	207
Baccharis pilularis		
Dwarf Lily of the Nile	9-10	206
Agapanthus africanus 'Peter Pan'		
Evergreen Candytuft	4-8	164
Iberis sempervirens		
Fleabane	2-10	160
Erigeron hybrid		
Fountain Grass	5-9	169
Pennisetum alopecuroides		
Freeway Daisy	10	209
Osteospermum fruticosum		
Goldmoss	4-9	171
Sedum acre		
Hardy Ice Plant	6-9	207
Delosperma nubigenum		
Hens and Chicks	4-10	209
Sempervivum tectorum		
Holly Fern	8-10	159
Cyrtomium falcatum		
Hosta	3-8	163
Hosta species		
Japanese Blood Grass	5-9	164
Imperata cylindrica 'Red Baron'		
Japanese Painted Fern	4-9	158
Athyrium nipponicum 'Pictum'		
Japanese Primrose	5-8	170
Primula japonica		
Lamb's Ears	4-8	172
Stachys byzantina		
Lenten Rose	4-8	163
Helleborus orientalis		
Lily-of-the-Valley	2-9	159
Convallaria majalis		
Liriope	7-10	167
Liriope muscari		
Maidenhair Fern	3-8	156
Adiantum pedatum		
Moneywort	3-8	167
Lysimachia nummularia		
Moss Phlox	2-9	169
Phlox subulata		
Moss Verbena	8-10	209
Verbena pulchella		
Pachysandra	4-9	168
Pachysandra terminalis		
Pink Panda Strawberry	3-9	161
Fragaria 'Pink Panda'		
Rock Rose	5-8	162
Helianthemum nummularium		
Silver Brocade Artemisia	3-9	157
Artemesia stelleriana 'Silver Brocade'		
Snow-on-the-Mountain	3-9	156
Aegopodium podagraria 'Variegatum'		
Spotted Dead Nettle	3-9	167
Lamium maculatum		
Stonecrop	3-10	172
Sedum spectabile		
Sweet Woodruff	4-8	158
Asperula odorata		
Variegated Japanese Sedge	6-9	158
Carex morrowii 'Variegata'		

Coarse-textured groundcover

Common Name	Zones	Page
Barrel Cactus	9-10	208
Echinocactus spp.		
Cast-Iron Plant	8-10	206
Aspidistra elatior		
Dwarf Lily of the Nile	9-10	206
Agapanthus africanus 'Peter Pan'		
English Ivy	5-9	162
Hedera helix		
Holly Fern	8-10	159
Cyrtomium falcatum		
Hosta	3-8	163
Hosta species		
Japanese Ardisia	9-10	206
Ardisia japonica		
Lenten Rose	4-8	163
Helleborus orientalis		
Lily-of-the-Valley	2-9	159
Convallaria majalis		
Variegated Algerian Ivy	7-10	208
Hedera canariensis 'Variegata'		

Fine-textured groundcover

Common Name	Zones	Page
Andorra Compact Juniper	3-9	166
Juniperus horizontalis 'Plumosa Compacta'		
Asiatic Jasmine	7-10	173
Trachelospermum asiaticum		
Artillery Fern	8-10	169
Pilea serpyllacea 'Rotundifolia'		
Bar Harbor Juniper	3-9	165
Juniperus horizontalis 'Bar Harbor'		
Bearberry Cotoneaster	5-9	159
Cotoneaster dammeri		
Blue Chip Juniper	3-9	165
Juniperus horizontalis 'Blue Chip'		
Blue Rug Juniper	3-9	166
Juniperus horizontalis 'Wiltonii '		
Dwarf Coyote Brush	7-10	207
Baccharis pilularis		
Dwarf Japanese Garden Juniper	4-9	166
Juniperus procumbens 'Nana'		
Evergreen Candytuft	4-8	164
Iberis sempervirens		
Littleleaf Periwinkle	4-8	173
Vinca minor		
Maidenhair Fern	3-8	156
Adiantum pedatum		
Mexican Heather	9-10	207
Cuphea hyssopifola		
Mondo Grass	7-9	168
Ophiopogon japonicus		
Moss Verbena	8-10	209
Verbena pulchella		
Purple-Leaf Wintercreeper	4-8	161
Euonymus fortunei 'Coloratus'		
Variegated Japanese Sedge	6-9	158
Carex morrowii 'Variegata'		

Moneywort
(*Lysimachia nummularia*)
Page 167

Groundcovers can help you turn problem places into favorite spots in your yard.

Hardy Ice Plant
(Delosperma nubigenum)
Page 207

Littleleaf Periwinkle
(Vinca minor)
Page 173

Choosing Groundcovers for Special Areas

Use these lists to find groundcovers that will fulfill your needs.
Photographs of plants and detailed information can be found on the page numbers listed. Look for plants that include your growing zone within their range. To find your climate zone, turn to page 5.

Availability varies by area and conditions (see page 21). Check with your garden center.

Sweet Woodruff
(Asperula odorata)
Page 158

Groundcover for woodland areas

Common Name	Zones	Page
Arum	6-10	157
Arum italicum		
Autumn Fern	6-10	160
Dryopteris erythrosora		
Bearberry Cotoneaster	5-9	159
Cotoneaster dammeri		
English Ivy	5-9	162
Hedera helix		
Holly Fern	8-10	159
Cyrtomium falcatum		
Hosta	3-8	163
Hosta species		
Japanese Painted Fern	4-9	158
Athyrium nipponicum 'Pictum'		
Lenten Rose	4-8	163
Helleborus orientalis		
Lily-of-the-Valley	6-8	159
Convallaria majalis		
Littleleaf Periwinkle	4-8	173
Vinca minor		
Maidenhair Fern	3-8	156
Adiantum pedatum		
Snow-on-the-Mountain	3-9	156
Aegopodium podagraria 'Variegatum'		
Sweet Woodruff	4-8	158
Asperula odorata		

Groundcover for rock gardens

Common Name	Zones	Page
Ajuga	4-9	156
Ajuga reptans		
Bath's Pink	4-9	160
Dianthus gratianopolitanus 'Bath's Pink'		
Bearberry Cotoneaster	5-9	159
Cotoneaster dammeri		
Catmint	4-8	168
Nepeta x faassenii		
Evergreen Candytuft	4-8	164
Iberis sempervirens		
Germander	4-9	172
Teucrium prostratum		
Goldmoss	4-9	171
Sedum acre		
Hardy Ice Plant	6-9	207
Delosperma nubigenum		
Hens and Chicks	4-10	209
Sempervivum tectorum		
Liriope	7-10	167
Liriope muscari		
Moss Phlox	2-9	169
Phlox subulata		
Prostrate Rosemary	7-10	171
Rosmarinus officinalis 'Irene'		
Rock Rose	5-8	162
Helianthemum nummularium		
Silver Brocade Artemisia	3-9	157
Artemisia stelleriana 'Silver Brocade'		
Stonecrop	3-10	172
Sedum spectabile		

Groundcover for edging patios, entries, garden beds

Common Name	Zones	Page
Ajuga	4-9	156
Ajuga reptans		
Alba Meidiland Rose	4-8	170
Rosa Alba Meidiland		
Andorra Compact Juniper	3-9	166
Juniperus horizontalis 'Plumosa Compacta'		
Arum	6-10	157
Arum italicum		
Artillery Fern	8-10	169
Pilea serpyllacea 'Rotundifolia'		
Autumn Fern	6-9	160
Dryopteris erythrosora		
Bar Harbor Juniper	3-9	165
Juniperus horizontalis 'Bar Harbor'		
Bath's Pink	4-9	160
Dianthus gratianopolitanus 'Bath's Pink'		
Blanket Flower	2-9	161
Gaillardia x grandiflora		
Bloody Cranesbill	3-8	162
Geranium sanguineum		
Blue Chip Juniper	3-9	165
Juniperus horizontalis 'Blue Chip'		
Blue Rug Juniper	3-9	166
Juniperus horizontalis 'Wiltonii'		
Catmint	4-8	168
Nepeta x faassenii		
Coral Bells	3-8	163
Heuchera sanguinea		
Creeping Thyme	5-9	173
Thymus leucotrichus		
Dwarf Japanese Garden Juniper	4-9	166
Juniperus procumbens 'Nana'		
Dwarf Lily of the Nile	9-10	206
Agapanthus africanus 'Peter Pan'		
Evergreen Candytuft	4-8	164
Iberis sempervirens		
Fleabane	2-10	160
Erigeron hybrid		
Fountain Grass	5-9	169
Pennisetum alopecuroides		
Germander	4-9	172
Teucrium prostratum		
Holly Fern	8-10	159
Cyrtomium falcatum		
Hosta	3-8	163
Hosta species		
Lady's Mantle	4-7	157
Alchemilla mollis		
Lamb's Ears	4-8	172
Stachys byzantina		
Lenten Rose	4-8	163
Helleborus orientalis		
Lily-of-the-Valley	2-9	159
Convallaria majalis		
Liriope	7-10	167
Liriope muscari		
Memorial Rose	4-9	170
Rosa wichuraiana		
Mexican Heather	9-10	207
Cuphea hyssopifola		
Moss Phlox	2-9	169
Phlox subulata		
Moss Verbena	8-10	209
Verbena pulchella		
Pink Panda Strawberry	3-9	161
Fragaria 'Pink Panda'		
Silver Brocade Artemisia	3-9	157
Artemisia stelleriana 'Silver Brocade'		
Variegated Japanese Sedge	6-9	158
Carex morrowii 'Variegata'		

Artemisia
(*Artemisia* spp.)
Page 157

Groundcover for small, confined spaces

Common Name	Zones	Page
Ajuga	4-9	156
Ajuga reptans		
Andorra Compact Juniper	3-9	166
Juniperus horizontalis 'Plumosa Compacta'		
Arum	6-10	157
Arum italicum		
Artillery Fern	8-10	169
Pilea serpyllacea 'Rotundifolia'		
Autumn Fern	6-9	160
Dryopteris erythrosora		
Bar Harbor Juniper	3-9	165
Juniperus horizontalis 'Bar Harbor'		
Bath's Pink	4-9	160
Dianthus gratianopolitanus 'Bath's Pink'		
Blanket Flower	2-9	161
Gaillardia x grandiflora		
Bloody Cranesbill	3-8	162
Geranium sanguineum		
Blue Chip Juniper	3-9	165
Juniperus horizontalis 'Blue Chip'		
Blue Pacific Shore Juniper	5-9	165
Juniperus conferta 'Blue Pacific'		
Blue Rug Juniper	3-9	166
Juniperus horizontalis 'Wiltonii'		
Cast-Iron Plant	8-10	206
Aspidistra elatior		
Catmint	4-8	168
Nepeta x faassenii		
Coral Bells	3-8	163
Heuchera sanguinea		
Creeping Thyme	5-9	173
Thymus leucotrichus		
Dwarf Coyote Brush	7-10	207
Baccharis pilularis		
Dwarf Japanese Garden Juniper	4-9	166
Juniperus procumbens 'Nana'		
Dwarf Lily of the Nile	9-10	206
Agapanthus africanus 'Peter Pan'		
Evergreen Candytuft	4-8	164
Iberis sempervirens		
Fleabane	2-10	160
Erigeron hybrid		
Germander	4-9	172
Teucrium prostratum		
Gold Mound Lantana	9-10	208
Lantana camara 'Gold Mound'		
Goldmoss	4-9	171
Sedum acre		
Hens and Chicks	4-10	209
Sempervivum tectorum		
Holly Fern	8-10	159
Cyrtomium falcatum		
Hosta	3-8	163
Hosta species		
Japanese Blood Grass	5-9	164
Imperata cylindrica 'Red Baron'		
Japanese Painted Fern	4-9	158
Athyrium nipponicum 'Pictum'		
Lamb's Ears	4-8	172
Stachys byzantina		
Lenten Rose	4-8	163
Helleborus orientalis		
Liriope	7-10	167
Liriope muscari		
Maidenhair Fern	3-8	156
Adiantum pedatum		
Mexican Heather	9-10	207
Cuphea hyssopifola		
Mondo Grass	7-9	168
Ophiopogon japonicus		
Moss Phlox	2-9	169
Phlox subulata		
Moss Verbena	8-10	209
Verbena pulchella		
Silver Brocade Artemisia	3-9	157
Artemisia stelleriana 'Silver Brocade'		
Stonecrop	3-10	172
Sedum spectabile		
Variegated Japanese Sedge	6-9	158
Carex morrowii 'Variegata'		

Japanese Painted Fern
(*Athyrium nipponicum* 'Pictum')
Page 158

Groundcover for hillsides

Common Name	Zones	Page
Alba Meidiland Rose	4-8	170
Rosa Alba Meidiland		
Andorra Compact Juniper	3-9	166
Juniperus horizontalis 'Plumosa Compacta'		
Asiatic Jasmine	7-10	173
Trachelospermum asiaticum		
Bar Harbor Juniper	3-9	165
Juniperus horizontalis 'Bar Harbor'		
Bath's Pink	4-9	160
Dianthus gratianopolitanus 'Bath's Pink'		
Bearberry Cotoneaster	5-9	159
Cotoneaster dammeri		
Blanket Flower	2-9	161
Gaillardia x grandiflora		
Blue Chip Juniper	3-9	165
Juniperus horizontalis 'Blue Chip'		
Blue Pacific Shore Juniper	5-9	165
Juniperus conferta 'Blue Pacific'		
Blue Rug Juniper	3-9	166
Juniperus horizontalis 'Wiltonii'		
Dwarf Coyote Brush	7-10	207
Baccharis pilularis		
English Ivy	5-9	162
Hedera helix		
Evergreen Candytuft	4-8	164
Iberis sempervirens		
Freeway Daisy	10	209
Osteospermum fruticosum		
Goldmoss	4-9	171
Sedum acre		
Hardy Ice Plant	6-9	207
Delosperma nubigenum		
Hens and Chicks	4-10	209
Sempervivum tectorum		
Liriope	7-10	167
Liriope muscari		
Littleleaf Periwinkle	4-8	173
Vinca minor		
Mondo Grass	7-9	168
Ophiopogon japonicus		
Moss Phlox	2-9	169
Phlox subulata		
Moss Verbena	8-10	209
Verbena pulchella		
Prostrate Rosemary	7-10	171
Rosmarinus officinalis 'Irene'		
Purple-Leaf Wintercreeper	4-8	161
Euonymus fortunei 'Coloratus'		
Rock Rose	5-8	162
Helianthemum nummularium		
Snow-on-the-Mountain	3-9	156
Aegopodium podagraria 'Variegatum'		
Stonecrop	3-10	172
Sedum spectabile		
Variegated Algerian Ivy	7-10	208
Hedera canariensis 'Variegata'		
Variegated Japanese Sedge	6-9	158
Carex morrowii 'Variegata'		

Adiantum pedatum

Maidenhair Fern

Zones: 3-8

Light Needs:

Mature Size:

8"-10"

12"-24"

Growth Rate: medium

perennial

Needs: Plant in moist soil that's rich in organic matter. Soil should be neutral or slightly acidic. Grow in partial to dense shade; protect from afternoon sun in hotter climates. Mulch for winter.

Good for: natural areas, damp sites, woodland paths, shady courtyards and entries, textural contrast among plants or stones, narrow confined spaces, shady ponds, creeks, or water downspouts

More Choices: pages 37, 41, 153, 154, and 155

Outstanding Features:

- Bright green fine-textured foliage
- Thrives in damp, shady locations
- Comes back every year in the spring

Add this plant to shady, damp spots and you'll be rewarded with bright green, delicate fronds. Leaflets seem to hover above dark, purplish stems. May be sold as Northern Maidenhair Fern.

Aegopodium podagraria 'Variegatum'

Snow-on-the-Mountain

Zones: 4-9

Light Needs:

Mature Size:

4"-6"

indefinite

Growth Rate: rapid

perennial

Needs: Plant in any kind of soil. Grow in full sun, partial shade, or dense shade; protect from afternoon sun in hotter climates. Tolerates full sun where summers are cool.

Good for: Filling in where grass won't grow, massing, erosion control, hillsides, dry shade around tree roots, natural areas, large planting beds, brightening dim, shaded areas

More Choices: pages 37, 38, 39, 41, 42, 153, 154, and 155

Outstanding Features:

- Lustrous green leaves are edged with white
- Grows rapidly to cover ground completely
- Small white flowers in early summer

Here's a groundcover good in sun or shade. Green-and-white foliage spreads quickly; vigorous growth is a hallmark of this plant. Also sold as Variegated Bishop's Weed or Goutweed. Remove any solid green foliage that appears.

Ajuga reptans

Ajuga

Zones: 4-9

Light Needs:

Mature Size:

3"-5"

indefinite

Growth Rate: rapid

evergreen groundcover

Needs: Plant in any soil that's moist but well-drained. Plants won't thrive in soggy soil or in drought conditions. Grow in partial shade.

Good for: rock gardens, edging patios, stepping-stone paths, formal or informal gardens, as the front layer of planting beds

More Choices: pages 37, 152, 153, 154, and 155

Options: 'Alba'—white flowers
'Burgundy Lace'—dark pink flower
'Atropurpurea'—blue flowers, bronze
'Tricolor'—pink, cream, green leaves

Outstanding Features:

- Low-growing mats of flat foliage
- Blue to purple blossoms in late spring
- Grows quickly and stays low

Planted in the right conditions, Ajuga easily forms a thick carpet of rosettelike leaves. Little blue flower spikes are an added bonus. Install a solid edging to separate from lawns. Crown rot and weediness are two possible problems.

Alchemilla mollis

Lady's Mantle

Zones: 4-7

Light Needs:

Mature Size:

12"–18"
20"–24"

Growth Rate:
medium

Perennial

Needs: Plant in well-drained fertile, moist soil. Partial shade is best in hotter areas; plants can take full sun in cooler regions.

Good for: Edging a planting bed, planting beneath shrubs, lining a walkway

More Choices: pages 37, 153, and 155

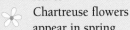
Lady's Mantle is a good, low plant for in-between areas that are both shady and sunny. Chartreuse blooms are set off by silky gray-green leaves. Morning dew or rain caught by the leaves is a beautiful site.

Artemisia stelleriana

Silver Brocade Artemisia

Zones: 3-9

Light Needs:

Mature Size:

18"–24"
12"–24"

Growth Rate:
medium

evergreen perennial

Needs: Plant in well-drained soil in full sun. Poor, sandy soil and coastal conditions are fine. Remove flower stalks to keep plants bushy. This is grown more for its foliage. Dig and divide plants in spring or fall when centers of crowded clumps die.

Good for: entry areas, fronts of beds, near colorful or dark green plants. Leaves complement white gardens.

More Choices: pages 35, 42, 152, 153, 154, and 155

Artemisia

Outstanding Features:

- Silvery foliage combines with white
- Tolerates dry, sandy soil conditions
- Soft texture is great for touching

Choose this low-growing plant for a sandy, sunny yard. There are several types, each boasting silvery leaves year-round. **Options:** 'Powis Castle' Zones 7-9; *Artemisia schmidtiana*; 'Silver Mound, Zones 4-10; *Artemisia ludoviciana* Zones 4-7.

Arum italicum

Arum

Zones: 6-10

Light Needs:

Mature Size:

12"–18"
6"–8"

Growth Rate:
medium

perennial

Needs: Plant in well-drained soil that's rich in organic matter. Grow in shade or sun.

Good for: planting beside patios, shady pathways, and beneath covered porticoes and courtyards. Arum multiplies readily in woodland plantings.

More Choices: pages 35, 37, 153, 154, and 155

Options: 'Marmoratum'—large leaves with silvery veins
'Pictum'—leaves with gray and cream

Outstanding Features:

- Arrow-shaped leaves add interest
- Red or orange berries in fall
- Unusual growth cycle, dormant in spring

Arum is a contrary plant: Leaves emerge in fall, last through winter, and wither in spring. Summer flowers are followed by cool-season red berries.

groundcovers 6

Asperula odorata(also listed as Galium odoratum)

Sweet Woodruff

Zones: 3-8

Light Needs:

Mature Size:

4"-12"
12"

Growth Rate:
medium to rapid

perennial

Needs: Plant in well-drained, humus-rich, acidic soil—increase soil acidity by adding peat moss, composted oak leaves, or by mulching with pine straw. Sweet Woodruff grows in full sun or partial shade. The hotter the climate, the more shade is required.

Good for: planting in groups beneath shade trees, along walkways, or in the front of flowerbeds

More Choices: pages 35, 37, 41, 153, and 154

This groundcover grows quickly in rich soil, making it a good choice to fill in bare areas. Little white blossoms spread like snowflakes across a blanket of green in spring.

Athyrium nipponicum 'Pictum'

Japanese Painted Fern

Zones: 4-9

Light Needs:

Mature Size:

12"-18"
12"-18"

Growth Rate:
slow

perennial

Needs: Plant in moist soil that's rich in organic matter. Grow in partial or dense shade. Mulch for winter. Don't remove freeze-damaged foliage until new leaves begin to emerge.

Good for: shady areas, front layer of planting beds, growing beneath trees or tall shrubs, beside shady creeks, ponds, or downspouts, at the foot of a shaded bench, woodlands

More Choices: pages 37, 153, 154, and 155

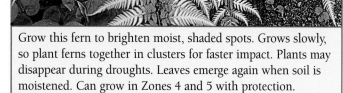

Grow this fern to brighten moist, shaded spots. Grows slowly, so plant ferns together in clusters for faster impact. Plants may disappear during droughts. Leaves emerge again when soil is moistened. Can grow in Zones 4 and 5 with protection.

Carex morrowii 'Variegata'

Variegated Japanese Sedge

Zones: 6-9

Light Needs:

Mature Size:
18"-20"
12"

Growth Rate:
rapid

evergreen perennial

Needs: Plant in well-drained, fertile, moist soil in full sun or partial shade. Remove dead leaves during the growing season.

Good for: planting along walkways, on hillsides, or in front of bigger, dark green shrubs. Plant in groups of three or more for best effect.

More Choices: pages 35, 37, 152, 153, and 155

Options: 'Fisher'—cream-striped, cream-edged leaves

Cream-and-green weeping foliage sways in the slightest breeze adding movement in the garden. The fine texture and bright color of Variegated Japanese Sedge contrasts nicely with the larger, dark green leaves of many shrubs.

Convallaria majalis

Lily-of-the-Valley

Zones: 2-9

Light Needs:

Mature Size:

6"-8" × 12"-16"

Growth Rate: slow to rapid

perennial

Needs: Plant in any soil that's moist or receives regular watering. Grow in partial to dense shade; protect from afternoon sun in hotter climates. Tolerates full sun where summers are cool and moisture is adequate. Mulch.

Good for: shady beds, growing beneath trees or shrubs, filling in bare spots, beside shady patios, entries, or courtyards, woodland gardens, natural areas

More Choices: pages 37, 39, 153, 154, and 155

Outstanding Features:
- Bell-shaped, very fragrant spring flowers
- Coarse-textured, dark green foliage
- Fast growing, tolerates moist conditions

This easy-to-grow perennial spreads to cover plenty of bare ground. Delicate spring flowers show off against coarse-textured leaves. Dig and divide crowded beds in fall. Share extras with friends.

Cotoneaster dammeri

Bearberry Cotoneaster

Zones: 5-9

Light Needs:

Mature Size:

12"-18" × 3'-6'

Growth Rate: slow to medium

semievergreen shrub

Needs: Plant in any soil, acidic or alkaline, wet or dry. Grow in full sun or partial shade.

Good for: hillsides, ditches, rock gardens, planters, filling bare planting beds, cascading over retaining walls, natural areas, parking areas, winter interest, adding fine texture

More Choices: pages 35, 37, 38, 39, 41, 42, 43, 152, 153, 154, and 155

Outstanding Features:
- Prostrate form needs no pruning
- Fine-textured foliage adds contrast
- White flowers in summer; red berries in fall

Grow this shrubby groundcover on slopes or in raised planters. Clusters of white flowers cover branches in spring and develop red berries in autumn. Extreme heat and excess fertilization makes them vulnerable to fire blight.

Cyrtomium falcatum

Holly Fern

Zones: 8-10

Light Needs:

Mature Size:

18"-24" × 24"-30"

Growth Rate: medium

evergreen perennial

Needs: Plant in soil that's moist but well-drained and rich in organic matter. Set plants high in planting holes; plants can't stand water around roots. Grow in partial or dense shade. Mulch for winter.

Good for: shady areas where grass won't grow, edging shady walkways, planting beds, or patios; courtyards, entries, beside benches

More Choices: pages 37, 152, 153, 154, and 155

Outstanding Features:
- Glossy, coarse-textured foliage is dark green
- Thrives in both partial and deep shade
- Low maintenance in moist areas

Fill moist, shady beds with Holly Fern. Glossy, dark green leaves seem to shine in dim light; their coarse texture contrasts well with smaller-leaved plants. Not a plant for poor, dry soils.

groundcovers 6

Groundcovers 159

6

groundcovers

Dianthus gratianopoliatanus 'Bath's Pink'

Bath's Pink

Zones: 4-9

Light Needs:

Mature Size:

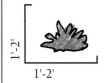
9"-12"
18"-24"

Growth Rate: medium to rapid

perennial

Needs: Plant in well-drained soil; plants won't thrive in soggy soil. Grow in full sun or partial shade. Too much shade discourages flowering. Pluck or shear wilted blooms to extend flowering and tidy up plants.

Good for: hillsides, growing over retaining walls, raised beds, berms, rock gardens, bordering planting beds, patios, or walkways, courtyards, xeriscaping

More Choices: pages 35, 37, 39, 41, 42, 43, 153, 154, and 155

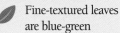**Outstanding Features:**
- Fine-textured leaves are blue-green
- Pink, fringed flowers cover foliage in spring
- Tolerates heat, humidity, and drought

Plant this fragrant groundcover in sloping soil where water can drain quickly away. Pink flowers adorn blue-green mats of foliage each spring. If deadheaded, flowering will continue for more than six weeks. Almost indestructible.

Dryopteris erythrosora

Autumn Fern

Zones: 6-9

Light Needs:

Mature Size:

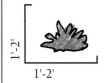
1'-2'
1'-2'

Growth Rate: slow

evergreen perennial

Needs: Moist soil, rich with organic matter; mix compost into planting holes. Grow in partial or dense shade. Plants tolerate some drought. Mulch for winter. Protect from wind in winter.

Good for: filling shady areas where grass won't grow, edging walkways, planting beds, or patios, courtyards, entries, beside benches, massing, woodlands, winter interest

More Choices: pages 37, 152, 153, 154, and 155

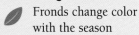**Outstanding Features:**
- Fronds change color with the season
- Red spores visible on fronds in winter
- Great for covering moist, shady areas

Here's a fern with seasonal color. Fronds are pink or yellow in spring, green in summer, and brown in fall. Red spores are visible in winter. Performs best where soil never dries out.

Erigeron hybrid

Fleabane

Zones: 2-10

Light Needs:

Mature Size:

9"-30"
24"

Growth Rate: rapid

perennial

Needs: Plant in full sun in well-drained, fertile soil. Soil should not dry out between waterings. Site plants in midday shade in warmer climates. Remove spent blooms to increase flowering. Shape plants by cutting stems back to just above a leaf.

Good for: entries, beside patios, along walkways, in front of taller shrubs, in mixed flowerbeds

More Choices: pages 35, 37, 153, and 155

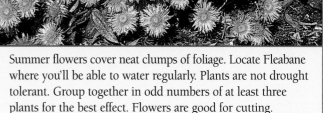
E. speciósus

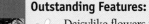**Outstanding Features:**
- Daisylike flowers with bright yellow centers
- Grows in neat clumps of mounded foliage
- Suitable for moist growing areas

Summer flowers cover neat clumps of foliage. Locate Fleabane where you'll be able to water regularly. Plants are not drought tolerant. Group together in odd numbers of at least three plants for the best effect. Flowers are good for cutting.

Euonymus fortunei 'Coloratus'

Purple-Leaf Wintercreeper

Zones: 4-8

Light Needs:

Mature Size:

6"-24"

indefinite

Growth Rate:
rapid

evergreen

Needs: Plant in full sun in any soil that is well-drained. Tolerant of high and low soil pH. Trim midspring to keep it in bounds and to remove dead or damaged stems. Underplant with spring bulbs. Mulch for winter in colder growing zones.

Good for: filling in bare spots beneath trees, on hills, or dry areas surrounded with paving

More Choices: pages 35, 41, 42, 43, 152, 153, and 155

Outstanding Features:
- Leaves turn purplish red in fall and winter
- Foliage is dark green during warm months
- Tough, durable and fast-spreading

This sprawling groundcover isn't picky about soil. Plant it in full sun so green foliage will turn wine-red in fall and winter. Control scale with an insecticide spray labeled for Euonymus. This plant spreads fast, so be sure you want it.

Fragaria 'Pink Panda'

Pink Panda Strawberry

Zones: 3-9

Light Needs:

Mature Size:

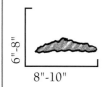

6"-8"

8"-10"

Growth Rate:
rapid

perennial

Needs: Plant in full sun or partial shade in fertile, well-drained soil. Divide by digging up tiny rooted plants and clipping connecting stems. In spring, remove any dead or winter-damaged leaves before new growth emerges. Mulch plants in cold winters to help keep them evergreen.

Good for: Entries, beside patios, along walkways, or grow in containers

More Choices: pages 35, 37, 153, and 155

Outstanding Features:
- Pink flowers through warm months
- Small, edible berries are sweet and tasty
- Glossy green foliage spreads rapidly

If you have fertile, well-drained soil in partial shade, consider Pink Panda Strawberry. Enjoy pink flowers, miniature berries, and spreading foliage. Plants spread by runners that root wherever they touch soil. Needs room.

Gaillardia x grandiflora

Blanket Flower

Zones: 2-9

Light Needs:

Mature Size:

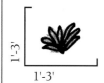

1'-3'

1'-3'

Growth Rate:
rapid

perennial

Needs: Plant in any soil that's well-drained. Poor, dry, and sandy soil is fine. Grow in full sun. Tolerates heat and drought. Divide every few years in the spring. Salt-tolerant.

Good for: seaside gardens, hillsides, ditches, raised beds, berms, parking areas, seasonal accent, along sunny walkways or patios, containers, covering bare, dry hot spots

More Choices: pages 35, 39, 42, 43, 153, and 155

Outstanding Features:
- Bright yellow, maroon, and reddish flowers
- Blooms nonstop throughout hot weather
- Thrives in hot, dry areas; tolerates cold

You can grow this bright bloomer anywhere soil stays dry. Hot, warm, or cold climates, it doesn't matter. Fiery flowers appear summer through frost. Flowers well even without regular deadheading.

groundcovers

6

Geranium sanguineum

Bloody Cranesbill

Zones: 3-8

Light Needs:

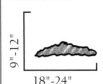

Mature Size:

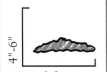
9"-12"
18"-24"

Growth Rate:
medium

perennial

Needs: Plant in any soil that's well-drained; fertile soil is best. Grow in full sun or partial shade. Protect from afternoon sun in hotter climates. Trim plants after first bloom to extend flowering. Pest- and disease-resistant.

Good for: planting beds, growing beneath shrubs or roses, beside patios, along walkways, in small spaces, formal or informal gardens, seasonal accents

More Choices: pages 35, 37, 153, and 155

This long-lived perennial—available in magenta, pink, and lavender—is perfect for small gardens or for covering ground beneath shrubs. Foliage grown in full sun turns red in autumn. Moist soil aids plants in spreading.

Hedera helix

English Ivy

Zones: 5-9

Light Needs:

Mature Size:

4"-6"
indefinite

Growth Rate:
slow to rapid

evergreen

Needs: Grow in any soil that's moist or damp. Plant in full sun or partial shade where summers are cool; plant in partial or dense shade where summers are hot (protect from afternoon sun). Vines will adapt to poor, dry soil in shade.

Good for: hillsides, shady areas, planting beds, natural areas, formal gardens, aging new structures, clinging to and covering solid walls

More Choices: pages 35, 37, 42, 152, 153, 154, and 155

Grow English Ivy to blanket shady beds or slopes with layers of dark, glossy foliage. Frame a lawn with an ivy-filled bed for a classic look. In areas with high rainfall, English Ivy is a nuisance plant that may climb and choke trees.

Helianthemum nummularium

Rock Rose

Zones: 5-8

Light Needs:

Mature Size:

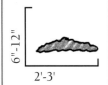
6"-12"
2'-3'

Growth Rate:
medium

evergreen shrub

Needs: Plant in full sun in well-drained, alkaline to neutral soil. Work lime into soil to increase alkalinity. Shear plants after the flowers fade to keep plants neat and promote new growth.

Good for: rock gardens, raised beds, planters, hillsides, rock walls, and the front layer of shrub beds

More Choices: pages 35, 39, 41, 42, 43, 152, 153, 154, and 155

Options: 'Buttercup'—golden yellow flowers

H. grandiflorum

Rock Rose is a heavy bloomer needing full sun and well-drained soil. Plants perform best in poor soils. Little care is required if good drainage is present. Water around roots can freeze, killing Rock Rose in colder climates.

Helleborus orientalis

Lenten Rose

Zones: 4-8

Light Needs:

Mature Size:

12"-18"

Growth Rate:
medium

evergreen perennial

Needs: Plant in moist soil and grow in partial shade. Protect from afternoon sun in hotter climates. Plants will fail in extreme heat or drought. Water regularly when conditions are dry. Mulch each spring to help conserve moisture.

Good for: winter interest, pathways, shady patios, natural areas, beneath trees, in raised beds or woodsy slopes

More Choices: pages 37, 152, 153, 154, and 155

Tuck Lenten Rose in the shade for clusters of coarse-textured leaves to contrast with other plants. You'll enjoy delicate pink-to cream-colored blossoms from January to March. Tolerates cold temperatures as well as warm.

Heuchera sanguinea

Coral Bells

Zones: 3-8

Light Needs:

Mature Size:

12"-18"

Growth Rate:
medium to rapid

evergreen perennial

Needs: Plant in well-drained, fertile soil. Coral Bells will not thrive in acidic soil; add lime to raise soil pH. In hotter climates, give plants partial shade. Grow in full sun elsewhere, but keep plants moist.

Good for: perennial beds, edging planting beds and walks, filling in narrow areas, combining with spring-blooming bulbs, foliage effect

More Choices: pages 35, 37, 41, 152, 153, and 155

Forming tidy mounds of heart-shaped leaves, this is grown more for the foliage than the flowers. Numerous cultivars are available with variations of foliage color. Delicate blooms in red, pink, or white open on stalks in spring or summer.

Hosta species

Hosta

Zones: 3-8

Light Needs:

Mature Size:

3"-48"

Growth Rate:
rapid

perennial

Needs: Plant in rich, moist soil. Mix compost at planting and mulch with humus each spring. Grow in partial or dense shade. Sun tolerance varies with the cultivar grown. Supply extra water during dry periods.

Good for: shade gardens, front layer of beds, natural areas, massing, specimen plants, coarse-textured accent, shady courtyards, entries, or patio areas

More Choices: pages 37, 153, 154, and 155

If you find composing with textures to be an elusive concept, plant beds filled with Hostas. These large-leaved plants add coarse texture, a variety of hues, and erect stems of often fragrant flowers. Use variegation with care to avoid clashing.

groundcovers **6**

Hypericum calycinum

Aaron's Beard

Zones: 5-9

Light Needs:

Mature Size:

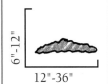

12"–18"

indefinite

Growth Rate:
rapid

shrub

Needs: Plant in partial to dense shade in well-drained, fertile soil. In small gardens, divide plants every 2 to 3 years to keep in bounds. For best flowering, cut plants to the ground early each spring. Plants are quite drought-tolerant.

Good for: filling in bare, shady areas, growing beneath trees or as a low layer in front of shrubs

More Choices: pages 37, 152, and 153

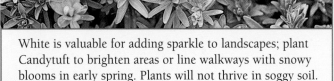

Outstanding Features:
- Bright yellow flowers in summer
- Dark green leaves—evergreen/deciduous
- Covers the ground in dry shady areas

Don't give up on flowers in the shade. Aaron's Beard produces bright yellow puffs of bloom with little sunlight, filling in bare spaces with layers of leaves. Plants spread quickly through stolons and can take over a planting bed.

Iberis sempervirens

Evergreen Candytuft

Zones: 4-8

Light Needs:

Mature Size:

6"–12"

12"-36"

Growth Rate:
slow to medium

evergreen perennial

Needs: Plant in any well-drained soil, fertile is best. Grow in full sun or partial shade. Every few years, prune heavily after blooming to encourage vigorous new growth.

Good for: rock gardens, edging walkways, patios, courtyards, narrow, confined spaces, raised planters, retaining walls, slopes, perennial beds, stone pathways, entries, moonlight gardens

More Choices: pages 35, 37, 42, 43, 152, 153, 154, and 155

Outstanding Features:
- White flowers cover plants in early spring
- Fine-textured foliage stays green year-round
- Forms low, spreading mats

White is valuable for adding sparkle to landscapes; plant Candytuft to brighten areas or line walkways with snowy blooms in early spring. Plants will not thrive in soggy soil.

Imperata cylindrica 'Red Baron'

Japanese Blood Grass

Zones: 5-9

Light Needs:

Mature Size:

18"–24"

18"-24"

Growth Rate:
medium

perennial

Needs: Plant in well-drained, fertile soil that's moist. Foliage color is best in full sun, but plants need afternoon shade in hotter climates. Mulch well. Cut plants back to the ground in spring before new growth emerges.

Good for: accents and planting beds in front of walls, fences, and evergreen shrubs, massed plantings

More Choices: pages 35, 37, 153, and 155

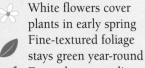

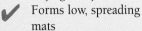

Outstanding Features:
- Leaves are green at the bottom, and red above
- Texture contrasts with other plants
- Very attractive massed planting

Though it dislikes hot, dry areas, Japanese Blood Grass will quickly fill an area with bright red foliage if conditions are right. Most effective when planted in groups. Avoid poorly drained sites with this plant.

Juniperus conferta 'Blue Pacific'

Blue Pacific Shore Juniper

Zones: 5-9

Light Needs:

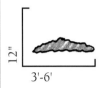

Mature Size:

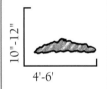

12"

3'-6'

Growth Rate:
slow to medium

evergreen shrub

Needs: Plant in full sun and any well-drained soil, from acidic to alkaline. Little pruning required—remove dead or damaged branches as needed.

Good for: parking areas, entries, planting beds, hillsides, planter boxes, or as a low layer in front of taller shrubs

More Choices: pages 35, 39, 41, 42, 43, 152, and 155

Options: 'Emerald Sea'—emerald green leaves
'Silver Mist'—silvery foliage

Outstanding Features:
- Blue-green foliage lasts year-round
- Spreads to form very low, neat mats
- Tolerates salt and drought

Keep extra watering to a minimum and this sun-loving groundcover will thrive. Blue-green foliage stays fresh looking year-round and provides great contrast with other foliage and flowers.

Juniperus horizontalis 'Bar Harbor'

Bar Harbor Juniper

Zones: 3-9

Light Needs:

Mature Size:

10"-12"

4'-6'

Growth Rate:
slow

evergreen shrub

Needs: Plant in full sun in well-drained soil. Slightly alkaline soil is preferred. Little pruning required—remove dead or damaged branches as needed. Supplemental water is not needed.

Good for: parking areas, coastal gardens, raised planters, hillsides, beside patios, and filling in hot, dry beds, bare spots, and foundations

More Choices: pages 35, 41, 42, 43, 152, 153, and 155

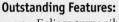

Outstanding Features:
- Foliage turns silvery plum shades in winter
- Tolerant of salt spray and rocky locations
- Low-growing, groundcovering form

This spreading shrub tolerates heat, salt, and drought plus turns shades of plum in winter. Makes a handsome groundcover. Twig blight can be a problem. Remove affected branches and destroy. Rinse pruners in alcohol between cuts.

Juniperus horizontalis 'Blue Chip'

Blue Chip Juniper

Zones: 3-9

Light Needs:

Mature Size:

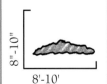

8"-10"

8'-10'

Growth Rate:
slow

evergreen shrub

Needs: Plant in full sun in any well-drained soil, including alkaline. Little pruning required. Extra water usually isn't needed.

Good for: parking areas, coastal gardens, raised planters, hillsides, beside patios, and filling in hot, dry beds, bare spots, and foundations

More Choices: pages 35, 39, 41, 42, 43, 152, 153, and 155

Options: 'Prince of Wales'—bright green leaves turn purplish in winter

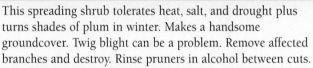

Outstanding Features:
- Blue summer foliage, ornamental in winter
- Plants stay low and grow wide
- Tolerant of drought and salt

Grow Blue Chip Juniper for its blue needlelike summer foliage that becomes tipped with purple during winter months. This plant loves sunny, dry locations and doesn't mind salt.

groundcovers 6

Juniperus horizontalis 'Plumosa Compacta'

Andorra Compact Juniper

Zones: 3-9

Light Needs:

Mature Size:

12"-18"

6'-10'

Growth Rate:
slow

evergreen shrub

Needs: Plant in full sun in any well-drained soil, including alkaline. Little pruning required—remove dead or damaged branches as needed. Extra water usually isn't needed.

Good for: parking areas, coastal gardens, raised planters, hillsides, beside patios, and filling in hot, dry beds and bare spots, and foundations

More Choices: pages 35, 41, 42, 43, 152, 153, and 155

Outstanding Features:

- Low plumes of foliage are blue- to gray-green
- Forms a dense mat of evergreen foliage
- Drought- and salt-tolerant

If you're looking for a groundcover for a bed surrounded by paving, look no further. This juniper won't mind the reflected heat as long as the soil drains well. Plants stay full in the center. Susceptible to Kabatina twig blight.

Juniperus horizontalis 'Wiltonii'

Blue Rug Juniper

Zones: 3-9

Light Needs:

Mature Size:

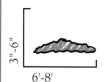

3"-6"

6'-8'

Growth Rate:
slow

evergreen shrub

Needs: Plant in full sun in any well-drained soil, including alkaline. Little pruning required—remove dead or damaged branches as needed. Extra water usually isn't needed.

Good for: parking areas, coastal gardens, dry planting beds, beside walkways and patios, behind retaining walls

More Choices: pages 35, 41, 42, 43, 152, 153, and 155

Outstanding Features:

- Flat, spreading growth creeps along ground
- Blue foliage turns purplish in winter
- Drought- and salt-tolerant

Here's a plant that's aptly named. Its intense blue foliage is flat just like a rug. Grow this juniper in hot, dry soil to carpet difficult spots or drape over retaining walls. This plant is susceptible to Kabatina twig blight.

Juniperus procumbens 'Nana'

Dwarf Japanese Garden Juniper

Zones: 4-9

Light Needs:

Mature Size:

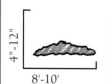

4"-12"

8'-10'

Growth Rate:
slow to medium

evergreen shrub

Needs: Plant in full sun in any well-drained soil, including acidic or alkaline. Little pruning required—remove dead or damaged branches as needed. Extra water is usually required.

Good for: parking areas, planting beds, growing beside walkways and patios

More Choices: pages 35, 41, 152, 153, and 155

Options: 'Nana Greenmound'—resembles bright green cushions, 4" to 6" tall, 6' to 8' wide

Outstanding Features:

- Fine-textured bluish green foliage
- Tolerates heat and car exhaust
- Stays low with dense growth

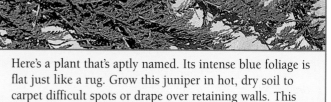

This ground-hugging juniper has branches that are densely packed with blue-green foliage. Plants thrive in heat and dry soil; they'll even tolerate pollution. The brighter the sunlight, the better for this sun-loving plant.

Lamium maculatum

Spotted Dead Nettle

Zones: 3-9

Light Needs:

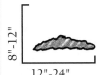

Mature Size:

8"-12" / 12"-24"

Growth Rate: rapid

perennial

Needs: Plant in deep or partial shade in any soil that's well-drained. Plants will grow in full sun in colder climates if soil stays consistently moist.

Good for: planting beneath trees and covering bare, shady spots—even places with dry soil

More Choices: pages 37, 39, 43, 152, and 153

Options: 'White Nancy'—white flowers 'Beacon Silver'—pale pink blooms 'Pink Pewter'—pink flowers

Outstanding Features:
- Leaves have white or silvery centers
- Pink or purple blooms in spring to summer
- Trailing stems cover shady ground quickly

Even shady spots kept dry by thirsty tree roots are no problem for this plant. Choose Spotted Dead Nettle for its silvery leaves and durability. Plants can be very vigorous and may outgrow some garden situations.

Liriope muscari

Liriope

Zones: 7-10

Light Needs:

Mature Size:

12"-18" / 12"-18"

Growth Rate: rapid

evergreen

Needs: Plant in any kind of soil except soggy. Grow in sun or shade. Mow or trim grassy blades every few years in late winter before new growth emerges.

Good for: filling empty areas, massing, edging beds, walkways, or patios; entries, courtyards, slopes, narrow, confined spaces, parking areas, rock gardens, coastal areas

More Choices: pages 37, 39, 42, 43, 152, 153, 154, and 155

Outstanding Features:
- Thick clumps of green, grassy foliage
- Adaptable and easy to grow in sun or shade
- Lavender flower spikes in summer

Often called Monkey Grass, this clumping cover will grow like crazy just about anywhere you plant it. Plant solid beds or neat rows. Also sold as Lilyturf. Divide thick clumps in spring or fall to make new plants. Variegated forms in white or yellow.

Lysimachia nummularia

Moneywort

Zones: 3-8

Light Needs:

Mature Size:

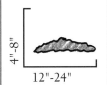

4"-8" / 12"-24"

Growth Rate: rapid

perennial

Needs: Plant in well-drained, fertile, moist soil. Choose a spot in dense or partial shade. Cut plants back after flowering to promote compact growth. For low maintenance, let plants grow.

Good for: shady, damp areas where grass won't grow, beside ponds and water features, and near downspouts

More Choices: pages 37 and 153

Options: 'Aurea'—lime-green to yellow leaves

Outstanding Features:
- Grows quickly to fill in shaded, damp areas
- Yellow flowers in early summer
- Useful along streams, lakes, pools

Moneywort thrives in wet shade. Plants spread quickly and can take over small areas in no time. Plants are adaptable to sun or shade as long as moisture is available. Also known as Creeping Jennie.

Nepeta x faassenii

Catmint

Zones: 4-8

Light Needs:

Mature Size:

12"-18"

18"-24"

Growth Rate:
rapid

perennial

Needs: Plant in well-drained, sandy soil in full sun or partial shade. Cut plants back after bloom to encourage a second flowering later. Dig and divide plants in early spring to make new plants.

Good for: xeriscaping, rock gardens, filling in hot spots, and edging planting beds, walkways, entries, or patios

More Choices: pages 35, 37, 43, 153, 154, and 155

Options: 'Six Hills Giant'—violet-blue blooms; 24" to 36" tall, 24" wide

Outstanding Features:

- Grows in hot sun and dry, sandy soil
- Great in combination with yellow and pink
- Cascading gray-green foliage is aromatic

Plant Catmint where you need a low-growing bloomer to tumble over the edges of patios, walkways, and rock walls. Purple-blue flowers bloom steadily in summer sun forming a ribbon of blue where they are used.

Ophiopogon japonicus

Mondo Grass

Zones: 7-9

Light Needs:

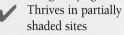

Mature Size:

6"-10"

spreading clumps

Growth Rate:
rapid to medium

evergreen

Needs: Plant in any soil that isn't soggy. Tolerates varying levels of soil pH. Mow every few years in late winter before new growth emerges. Grow in full sun, partial shade, or dense shade.

Good for: filling in shady areas, hillsides, planting beneath trees and shrubs, narrow confined areas, forming the front layer of planting beds

More Choices: pages 35, 37, 39, 41, 42, 152, 153, and 155

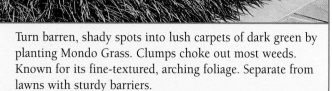

Outstanding Features:

- Fine-textured, narrow foliage stays green
- Thrives in partially shaded sites
- Turflike clumps form a soft, thick carpet

Turn barren, shady spots into lush carpets of dark green by planting Mondo Grass. Clumps choke out most weeds. Known for its fine-textured, arching foliage. Separate from lawns with sturdy barriers.

Pachysandra terminalis

Pachysandra

Zones: 4-9

Light Needs:

Mature Size:

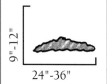

9"-12"

24"-36"

Growth Rate:
rapid

perennial

Needs: Plant in dense to partial shade—protect from afternoon sun in hotter climates. Moist, fertile soil is essential. Mix in peat moss or composted leaves at planting and tuck around plants each spring. Mulch new plantings for their first and second winters in colder areas.

Good for: filling in shady spots where grass won't grow, planting beneath trees, raised beds, growing in shade gardens

More Choices: pages 37 and 153

Outstanding Features:

- Covers shady, bare areas
- Rich green leaves stay low and neat
- Small white flowers in late spring

This groundcover fills in bare shady spots where grass won't grow—but only if the soil is moist. Makes a good companion to Hostas. Both are coarse-textured, grow in shade, and like the same type of soil.

Pennisetum alopecuroides

Fountain Grass

Zones: 5-9

Light Needs:

Mature Size:

18"–48"
24"-36"

Growth Rate:
rapid

perennial

Needs: Plant in average soil (dry is better than wet) and full sun. Allow leaves and seedheads to remain on plants through the winter. Cut them off in spring just as new growth is emerging.

Good for: growing in masses to fill bare, sunny spots, adding winter color to landscapes, growing as accent plants, edging patios, and containers

More Choices: pages 35, 39, 41, 43, 153, and 155

P. rubrum

Outstanding Features:
- ✔ Form spills up and over like a fountain
- Fine-textured leaves turn red in fall
- Maroon seed heads are showy through winter

Fountain Grass adds movement to the landscape with arching foliage that sways in the slightest breeze. Decorative seedheads are attractive, too. This plant is easy to grow in sunny spots. Also try: *P. rubrum*—reddish purple foliage.

Phlox subulata

Moss Phlox

Zones: 2-9

Light Needs:

Mature Size:
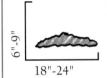
6"–9"
18"-24"

Growth Rate:
rapid

evergreen perennial

Needs: Plant in full sun in average or poor, rocky soil that's dry. Alkaline soil is preferred. Dig and divide plants in fall or let them spread naturally. Shear plants after bloom to encourage dense growth and later rebloom.

Good for: xeriscaping, slopes, ditches, erosion control, beside steps, edging planting beds, rock gardens, entries, creeping over walls

More Choices: pages 35, 39, 42, 43, 152, 153, 154, and 155

Outstanding Features:
- ✽ Becomes a carpet of flowers in spring
- Evergreen foliage forms a dense mat
- Grows in sunny, dry places

This thick, low groundcover is the answer to dry hillsides and ditches. Plants are carpeted with white, pink, or lavender blooms in spring. Lush green foliage is present the remainder of the year.

Pilea serpyllacea 'Rotundifolia'

Artillery Fern

Zones: 9-10

Light Needs:
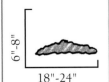

Mature Size:
6"–8"
18"-24"

Growth Rate:
medium

perennial

Needs: Plant in moist but well-drained soil, fertile is best. Plants tolerate sandy soil but will need extra fertilization. Grow in full sun or partial shade. Tolerates reflected heat from paving and walls.

Good for: narrow confined spaces, beneath eaves, filling in, edging walkways or planting beds, entries, beside steps, paving areas

More Choices: pages 35, 37, 39, 43, 153, and 155

P. microphylla

Outstanding Features:
- Chartreuse-green foliage is fine-textured
- Low, dense form with horizontal branching
- Tolerates dry soil and confined spaces

Grow this little fern in tight spaces where you need something green and low. Though fine-textured in appearance, leaflets are rounded, not feathery. Sometimes sold as *P. microphylla*. May be short-lived; use as a filler.

Primula japonica

Japanese Primrose

Zones: 5-8

Light Needs:

Mature Size:

12"-24"

12"-24"

Growth Rate:
medium

perennial

Needs: Plant in fertile soil that doesn't dry out. Soil should be acidic to neutral. Mix in composted oak leaves or peat moss at planting and add a 3-inch layer of mulch around plants each spring to keep soil rich in humus. Grow in a shady spot. Provide plants with extra water during dry periods.

Good for: wet, boggy areas, beside water features, adding color to shaded spots

More Choices: pages 37, 38, 41, and 153

Outstanding Features:
Grows in wet, soggy soil near water
Flowers from spring through midsummer
Tiers of blooms in various shades

Soggy, shaded spots aren't problem areas if you plant Japanese Primrose in them. Colorful flowers in shades of pink, crimson, and white won't grow anywhere else.

Rosa Alba Meidiland

Alba Meidiland Rose

Zones: 4-8

Light Needs:

Mature Size:

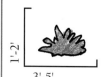

1'-2'

3'-5'

Growth Rate:
medium

deciduous shrub

Needs: Plant in moist, fertile, well-drained soil. Sun or partial shade. Add super phosphate or bonemeal to planting hole to promote root growth. Reapply every fall. No pruning needed, but plants will need plenty of room.

Good for: slopes, planting behind retaining walls, along walkways, patios, the front layer of foundation planting, around low decks, and in raised planters

More Choices: pages 35, 37, 42, 153, and 155

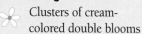
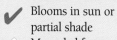
Outstanding Features:
Clusters of cream-colored double blooms
Blooms in sun or partial shade
Mounded form spreads quickly

This sounds too good to be true—a rose that cascades thickly to cover the ground with fragrant flowers and shiny green foliage. Flowers appear from summer through fall.

Rosa wichuraiana

Memorial Rose

Zones: 4-9

Light Needs:

Mature Size:

10"-12"

18'-20'

Growth Rate:
medium

deciduous shrub

Needs: Plant in fertile, well-drained soil in full sun. Feed with rose food or bonemeal at planting and when blooms begin. Minimal care is needed. Remove any dead branches in spring after buds swell. Remove faded flowers to encourage fresh blooms.

Good for: front layers of planting beds, edging walkways and patios, combining with evergreens to show off rose hips for winter interest

More Choices: pages 35, 153, and 155

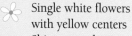
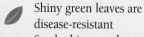
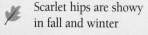
Outstanding Features:
Single white flowers with yellow centers
Shiny green leaves are disease-resistant
Scarlet hips are showy in fall and winter

This old-fashioned rose is easy to grow. Simple, single flowers cover the long spreading canes in early summer. Scarlet hips last from fall through winter. Plants can be grown upright when provided support.

Rosa 'Flower Carpet'

Flower Carpet Rose

Zones: 4-10

Light Needs:

Mature Size:

24"-30"

30"-60"

Growth Rate:
medium

deciduous shrub

Needs: Plant in full sun in fertile, well-drained soil. No spraying required. Let plants grow together to form a mass. Remove branches that grow straight up.

Good for: filling in bare sunny beds, growing as the front layer of planting areas, growing on berms

More Choices: pages 35, 43, and 153

Options: 'Flower Carpet Pink'
'Flower Carpet White'
'Flower Carpet Appleblossom'

Outstanding Features:
- Available in a wide range of flower colors
- Disease-resistant, shiny green leaves
- Easy to grow; ideal for the novice rose grower

You don't need to know a lot about roses to succeed with these. Spreading plants need sun and soil that drains. Often sold in pink plastic pots. Plants are thorny. Use two or three plants per square yard for groundcover.

Rosmarinus officinalis 'Irene'

Prostrate Rosemary

Zones: 7-10

Light Needs:

Mature Size:

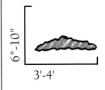

6"-10"

3'-4'

Growth Rate:
medium to rapid

evergreen herb

Needs: Plant in any soil that's well-drained and receives full sun. Poor, dry, sandy, or rocky soils are fine. Tolerates acidic or alkaline soil pH. Tolerates drought. Do not fertilize or overwater.

Good for: rock gardens, slopes, ditches, erosion control, raised planters, cascading over retaining walls, filling hot, dry planting beds, parking areas, arid areas, xeriscaping

More Choices: pages 35, 39, 41, 42, 43, 152, 153, 154, and 155

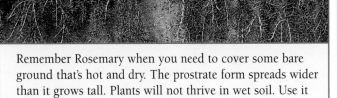

R. officinalis 'Prostatus'

Outstanding Features:
- Gray-green foliage is aromatic
- Light blue, flowers from fall to winter
- Low, mounding form cascades over walls

Remember Rosemary when you need to cover some bare ground that's hot and dry. The prostrate form spreads wider than it grows tall. Plants will not thrive in wet soil. Use it in the kitchen as well as the landscape.

Sedum acre

Goldmoss

Zones: 4-9

Light Needs:

Mature Size:

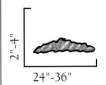

2"-4"

24"-36"

Growth Rate:
rapid

evergreen perennial

Needs: Grow in full sun in soil that's well-drained; slightly alkaline soil is best. Adapts to poor, dry locations. Tolerates drought and reflected heat.

Good for: slopes, ditches, rock gardens, tucking into crevices in paving or walls, parking areas, growing beside steps, cascading over retaining walls, filling in hot, dry areas; confined spaces, perennial gardens, containers

More Choices: pages 35, 39, 41, 42, 43, 152, 153, 154, and 155

Outstanding Features:
- Tiny, starry golden flowers in warm weather
- Forms a low, creeping mat of yellow-green
- Tolerates hot, dry conditions

Here's a fast-growing groundcover that grows well in hot, dry pockets or barren slopes. Creeping plants produce golden flowers all summer. May be sold as Stonecrop Sedum.

groundcovers **6**

Sedum spectabile

Stonecrop

Zones: 3-10

Light Needs:

Mature Size:

12"-18"
18"-24"

Growth Rate:
medium to rapid

perennial

Needs: Plant in poor, dry soils that drain well; plants won't tolerate damp conditions. Grow in full sun. Divide plants in fall when clumps grow from outer edges instead of the center. Cut plants back in June for smaller plants with additional bloom and stems that don't flop over.

Good for: rock gardens, arid landscapes, xeriscaping, slopes, entries, adding to the front layer of planting beds

More Choices: pages 35, 39, 42, 43, 153, 154, and 155

Outstanding Features:

 Blooms in late summer and fall

Grows with little water; drought-tolerant

Thick, fleshy leaves add coarse texture

Here's a plant that loves poor, dry soil—even rocky or sandy soil. Grow Stonecrop in hot spots to enjoy thick foliage and clusters of late flowers. Butterflies are an added bonus. Support elongated stems of plants growing in partial shade.

Stachys byzantina

Lamb's Ear

Zones: 4-8

Light Needs:

Mature Size:

12"-15"
12"-18"

Growth Rate:
medium to rapid

perennial

Needs: Plant in fertile soil that's moist but well-drained. Grow in full sun (with afternoon shade in hotter climates). Trim heat-damaged plants to encourage growth in fall. Dig and divide plants every 3 to 4 years.

Good for: entries, children's gardens, moonlight gardens, edging planting beds, patios, and walkways

More Choices: pages 35, 153, and 155

Outstanding Features:

Velvety leaves are silvery and touchable

Pink, white, or purplish flowers on stalks

Dependable; plants return year after year

Lamb's Ears are as soft and fuzzy as their name suggests. Grow these in patches to fill in flower beds or to edge planting areas. Water plants early in the day so leaves will dry before nightfall.

Teucrium prostratum or chamaedrys

Germander

Zones: 4-9

Light Needs:

Mature Size:

12"-20"
12"-24"

Growth Rate:
medium to rapid

evergreen shrub

Needs: Grow in full sun. Plant in well-drained, alkaline to neutral soil. Work lime into soil to increase alkalinity. For formal hedges, cut plants in early spring to within a few inches of the ground.

Good for: formal knot gardens, edging rose, herb, or flowerbeds, rock gardens, entries, edging patios or walkways

More Choices: pages 35, 41, 152, 153, 154, and 155

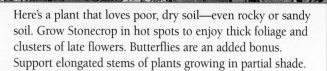
T. chamaedrys

Outstanding Features:

Tolerates pruning to form a low hedge

Grows well in alkaline soil conditions

Carmine-rose blooms in mid to late summer

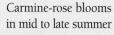

Grow Germander where you want a little row of green. Plants adapt to both a formal or informal way of life. Trim into desired forms or allow them to remain in their natural mounded form.

Thymus leucotrichus

Creeping Thyme

Zones: 5-9

Light Needs:

Mature Size:

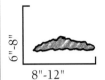

6"-8"

8"-12"

Growth Rate:
medium to rapid

evergreen herb

Needs: Plant in full sun in alkaline to neutral soil. Work lime into soil to increase alkalinity. Plants won't thrive in damp soil; select a location that's well-drained.

Good for: tucking between stepping stones, beneath benches, edging planting beds or walkways, entries, filling in between roses, growing over tops of retaining walls, tucking into rock walls

More Choices: pages 35, 39, 41, 152, 153, and 155

T. praecox articus

Outstanding Features:

- Ground-hugging, aromatic foliage
- Purplish pink flowers cover plants in spring
- Thrives in hot, dry soil with alkaline pH

Choose Creeping Thyme when you need a low-growing plant to tuck into hot, dry crevices or between stepping-stones. Aromatic leaves stay gray-green year-round and can tolerate light foot traffic. Pink flowers appear in spring.

Trachelospermum asiaticum

Asiatic Jasmine

Zones: 8-10

Light Needs:

Mature Size:

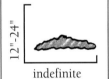

12"-24"

indefinite

Growth Rate:
rapid

evergreen

Needs: Plant in acidic or alkaline soil that's well-drained. Moist, rich soil gives best results, though plants can adapt to poor soils. Grow in full sun or partial shade. Trim regularly to keep edges and top layers neat.

Good for: hillsides, parking areas, large spaces, cover bare spots, cascading over retaining walls

More Choices: pages 35, 37, 41, 42, 43, 152, 153, and 155

Outstanding Features:

- Fine-textured glossy foliage is dark green
- Forms a thick mat of stems and leaves
- Tolerates reflected heat from paving

Asiatic Jasmine sprawls, spreads, and stays green year-round. Glossy foliage forms a thick mat that easily covers bare ground and hillsides. Leaves are a blush wine-red in cool winters. May be sold as Asian Jasmine.

Vinca minor

Littleleaf Periwinkle

Zones: 4-8

Light Needs:

Mature Size:

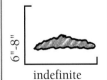

6"-8"

indefinite

Growth Rate:
rapid

evergreen

Needs: Grow in sun or partial shade north of Zone 7; southward, grow in full or partial shade. Plant in well-drained, moist, fertile soil high in organic matter. Mix in peat moss or composted leaves at planting time.

Good for: bare, shady spots, hillsides, erosion control, beneath trees, woodland gardens, underplanting with spring bulbs

More Choices: pages 35, 37, 42, 152, 153, 154, and 155

Outstanding Features:

- Trailing stems form mats of glossy foliage
- Periwinkle-blue flowers open in spring
- Little or no maintenance once established

Fill in bare, shady areas with a dense blanket of glossy green leaves. Lavender-blue flowers appear each spring. Grows slowly in poor soil. Not for coastal areas. May be sold as Creeping Myrtle.

groundcovers **6**

Chinese Wisteria (Wisteria sinensis), page 185, cloaks a wall with flowers and foliage as if from a painting.

Vines

A **dd charming finishing touches to your landscape with the addition of vines.** Observe landscapes in books and magazines, as well as eye-catching yards in your neighborhood. They usually have vines, sprawling up a post or over a wall, polishing off the composition with the lush look that makes you think an experienced gardener must live there.

Chocolate Vine
(Akebia quinata)
Page 178

Give your landscape that green-thumb look by learning about vines. Some climb by adhesive disks that will damage wood or stucco. Others climb by tendrils or twining stems, making them better choices for such supports. The selection guides make it easy to pick the right vine for your yard. See pages 39 and 41 for vines for various soil types, page 35 for vines to grow in sun, page 37 for vines to grow in shade, and pages 30-31 for vines for privacy.

Mandevilla
(Mandevilla splendens 'Red Riding Hood')
Page 212

Availability varies by area and conditions (see page 21). Check with your garden center.

Vines for low-water landscapes

Common Name	Zones	Page
American Bittersweet	3-8	179
Celastrus scandens		
Boston Ivy	4-8	183
Parthenocissus tricuspidata		
Butterfly Vine	9-1	212
Mascagnia macroptera		
Carolina Yellow Jessamine	7-9	181
Gelsemium sempervirens		
Porcelain Vine	4-8	178
Ampelopsis brevipedunculata		
Silver Lace Vine	4-9	183
Polygonum aubertii		
Sweet Autumn Clematis	4-9	181
Clematis paniculata		
Trumpet Vine	4-9	179
Campsis radicans		
Virginia Creeper	4-9	182
Parthenocissus quinquefolia		

American Bittersweet
(Celastrus scandens)
Page 179

Evergreen vines

Common Name	Zones	Page
Allamanda	10	210
Allamanda cathartica		
Armand Clematis	7-9	179
Clematis armandii		
Bougainvillea	9-10	211
Bougainvillea		
Carolina Yellow Jessamine	7-9	181
Gelsemium sempervirens		
Chocolate Vine	5-9	178
Akebia quinata		
Creeping Fig	8-10	211
Ficus pumila		
Cross-Vine	6-9	178
Bignonia capreolata		
Evergreen Wisteria	9-10	212
Millettia reticulata		
Fatshedera	8-10	181
X Fatshedera lizei		
Hall's Honeysuckle	4-10	211
Lonicera japonica 'Halliana'		
Lady Bank's Climbing Rose	8-10	183
Rosa banksiae		
Madagascar Jasmine	10	213
Stephanotis floribunda		
Mandevilla	10	212
Mandevilla splendens 'Red Riding Hood'		
Star Jasmine	8-10	213
Trachelospermum jasminoides		

Twist the canes of climbing roses or tie them to support structures to get a full-flowered effect.

Deciduous vines

Common Name	Zones	Page
American Bittersweet	3-8	179
Celastrus scandens		
Blaze Climbing Rose	5-10	184
Rosa 'Blaze'		
Boston Ivy	4-8	183
Parthenocissus tricuspidata		
Butterfly Vine	9-10	212
Mascagnia macroptera		
Chinese Wisteria	5-9	185
Wisteria sinensis		
Climbing Cecil Brunner Rose	6-10	185
Rosa 'Climbing Cecil Brunner'		
Climbing Hydrangea	4-7	182
Hydrangea petiolaris		
Climbing Iceberg Rose	4-10	184
Rosa 'Climbing Iceberg'		
Climbing Peace Rose	5-9	184
Rosa 'Climbing Peace'		
Hybrid Clematis	3-9	180
Clematis hybrid		
Joseph's Coat Climbing Rose	4-10	185
Rosa 'Joseph's Coat'		
Passion Flower	7-10	213
Passiflora incarnata		
Porcelain Vine	4-8	178
Ampelopsis brevipedunculata		
Silver Lace Vine	4-9	183
Polygonum aubertii		
Sweet Autumn Clematis	4-9	181
Clematis paniculata		
Trumpet Honeysuckle	4-9	182
Lonicera sempervirens		
Trumpet Vine	4-9	179
Campsis radicans		
Virginia Creeper	4-9	182
Parthenocissus quinquefolia		

Vines for structures

Common Name	Zones	Page
Armand Clematis	7-9	179
Clematis armandii		
Carolina Yellow Jessamine	7-9	181
Gelsemium sempervirens		
Cross-vine	6-9	178
Bignonia capreolata		
Hall's Honeysuckle	4-10	211
Lonicera japonica 'Halliana'		
Hybrid Clematis	3-9	180
Clematis hybrid		
Lady Bank's Climbing Rose	8-10	183
Rosa banksiae		
Porcelain Vine	4-8	178
Ampelopsis brevipedunculata		
Star Jasmine	8-10	213
Trachelospermum jasminoides		
Sweet Autumn Clematis	4-9	181
Clematis paniculata		
Trumpet Honeysuckle	4-9	182
Lonicera sempervirens		

Star Jasmine
(Trachelospermum jasminoides)
Page 213

groundcovers/vines

6

Groundcovers and Vines   175

Boston Ivy
(Parthenocissus tricuspidata)
Page 183

Trumpet Honeysuckle
(Lonicera sempervirens)
Page 182

Vines give garden spots a sheltered feeling,
adding leafy privacy and filtering sunlight.

Choosing Vines for Seasonal Interest

Planting vines and climbers adds color and texture to your **landscape season after season.** The selection guides that follow will help you choose vines for their flowers, colorful foliage, fragrance, and showy fruit in spring, summer, and fall. For winter interest, choose from the evergreen vines listed on page 175. Availability varies by area and condtions (see page 21). Check with your garden center.

Carolina Yellow Jessamine
(Gelsemium sempervirens)
Page 181

Chinese Wisteria
(Wisteria sinensis)
Page 185

Fragrant vines

Common Name	Zones	Page
Armand Clematis *Clematis armandii*	7-9	179
Blaze Climbing Rose *Rosa 'Blaze'*	5-10	184
Carolina Yellow Jessamine *Gelsemium sempervirens*	7-9	181
Chinese Wisteria *Wisteria sinensis*	5-9	185
Chocolate Vine *Akebia quinata*	5-9	178
Climbing Cecil Brunner Rose *Rosa 'Climbing Cecil Brunner'*	6-10	185
Climbing Peace Rose *Rosa 'Climbing Peace'*	5-9	184
Cross-Vine *Bignonia capreolata*	6-9	178
Hall's Honeysuckle *Lonicera japonica 'Halliana'*	4-10	211
Joseph's Coat Climbing Rose *Rosa 'Joseph's Coat'*	4-10	185
Madagascar Jasmine *Stephanotis floribunda*	10	213
Star Jasmine *Trachelospermum jasminoides*	8-10	213
Sweet Autumn Clematis *Clematis paniculata*	4-9	181

Spring-flowering vines

Common Name	Zones	Page
Allamanda *Allamanda cathartica*	10	210
Armand Clematis *Clematis armandii*	7-9	179
Carolina Yellow Jessamine *Gelsemium sempervirens*	7-9	181
Chinese Wisteria *Wisteria sinensis*	5-9	185
Chocolate Vine *Akebia quinata*	5-9	178
Climbing Iceberg Rose *Rosa 'Climbing Iceberg'*	4-10	184
Cross-Vine *Bignonia capreolata*	6-9	178
Hall's Honeysuckle *Lonicera japonica 'Halliana'*	4-10	211
Hybrid Clematis *Clematis hybrid*	3-9	180
Joseph's Coat Climbing Rose *Rosa 'Joseph's Coat'*	4-10	185
Lady Bank's Climbing Rose *Rosa banksiae*	8-10	183
Star Jasmine *Trachelospermum jasminoides*	8-10	213
Trumpet Vine *Campsis radicans*	4-9	179

Hybrid Clematis
(Clematis hybrid)
Page 180

Summer-flowering vines

Common Name	Zones	Page
Allamanda *Allamanda cathartica*	10	210
Blaze Climbing Rose *Rosa 'Blaze'*	5-10	184
Butterfly Vine *Mascagnia macroptera*	9-10	212
Climbing Cecil Brunner Rose *Rosa 'Climbing Cecil Brunner'*	6-10	185
Climbing Hydrangea *Hydrangea petiolaris*	4-7	182
Climbing Iceberg Rose *Rosa 'Climbing Iceberg'*	4-10	184
Climbing Peace Rose *Rosa 'Climbing Peace'*	5-9	184
Evergreen Wisteria *Millettia reticulata*	9-10	212
Hall's Honeysuckle *Lonicera japonica 'Halliana'*	4-10	211
Madagascar Jasmine *Stephanotis floribunda*	10	213
Mandevilla *Mandevilla splendens 'Red Riding Hood'*	10	212
Silver Lace Vine *Polygonum aubertii*	4-9	183
Star Jasmine *Trachelospermum jasminoides*	8-10	213
Sweet Autumn Clematis *Clematis paniculata*	4-9	181
Trumpet Honeysuckle *Lonicera sempervirens*	4-9	182

Hall's Honeysuckle
(Lonicera japonica 'Halliana')
Page 211

Vines for autumn interest

Common Name	Zones	Page
◆Showy fall fruit		
American Bittersweet *Celastrus scandens*	3-8	179
Boston Ivy *Parthenocissus tricuspidata*	4-8	183
Chocolate Vine *Akebia quinata*	5-9	178
Hybrid Clematis *Clematis hybrid*	3-9	180
Porcelain Vine *Ampelopsis brevipedunculata*	4-8	178
Sweet Autumn Clematis *Clematis paniculata*	4-9	181
Trumpet Honeysuckle *Lonicera sempervirens*	4-9	182

Common Name	Zones	Page
◆Fall flowers		
Climbing Cecil Brunner Rose *Rosa 'Climbing Cecil Brunner'*	6-10	185
Evergreen Wisteria *Millettia reticulata*	9-10	212
◆Colorful fall foliage		
Boston Ivy *Parthenocissus tricuspidata*	4-8	183
Virginia Creeper *Parthenocissus quinquefolia*	4-9	182

Pruning Chinese Wisteria

After your Chinese Wisteria has reached its desired growth, thin three times a year to promote flowering. If you make cuts during a single season, the vine will grow excessively thick foliage but yield few flowers.

Start by cutting new growth when Chinese Wisteria is dormant. You can identify new growth, even in winter, because the shoots at the end of vine tips are thinner than older branches. Locate the second bud on new growth; trim half the shoots back to this point. In spring, remove all young leafless branches. Cut side branches, leaving two or three buds and allowing all nubby spurs to remain. Follow up with summer pruning to reduce by one-half the size of side branches.

If your wisteria isn't flowering it probably just needs a little tough love. Use a shovel to sever roots about 18 inches around the base to a depth of eight to ten inches. Severing the roots will stimulate root growth and shock the plant into a flowering cycle.

Akebia quinata

Chocolate Vine

Zones: 5-9

Light Needs:

Mature Size:

20'-40'

indefinite

Growth Rate:
medium to rapid

semievergreen flowering vine

Needs: Plant in full sun or partial shade in fertile soil that's moist but well-drained. Prune Chocolate Vine after flowering to control growth. Plant two vines to produce long, purple pods.

Good for: screening for privacy or blocking poor views, covering fences, trellises, or arbors, twining up posts and rails

More Choices: page 30, 35, 37, 175, and 177

Options: 'Variegata'—leaves display patches of cream

Outstanding Features:
- Dark brown, purplish flowers in late spring
- ✔ Won't damage wooden structures
- Long, purple seedpods in fall

This vine earns its name with purplish brown blooms in spring that smell hauntingly of chocolate. Delicious and calorie-free. Delicate leaves make a fine-textured screen. Also sold as Fiveleaf Akebia.

Ampelopsis brevipedunculata

Porcelain Vine

Zones: 4-8

Light Needs:

Mature Size:

10'-25'

indefinite

Growth Rate:
rapid

deciduous vine

Needs: Vines will adapt to just about any soil except soggy. Grows best in full sun. Plant where root growth is restricted and climbing support is provided. Prune in winter to shape plants and encourage vigorous growth.

Good for: trellises, lattice, fences, arbors, entries, near patios, covering eyesores such as stumps or rock piles

More Choices: pages 35, 39, 41, 43, 175, and 177

Outstanding Features:
- Colorful fruit appearing in fall
- Fast-growing cover for all types of structures
- Adapts to a wide range of soils

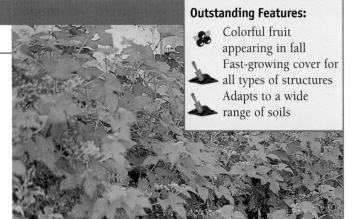

The flowers on this vine aren't noticeable, but the fruit certainly is, forming in shades of yellow, lavender, and bright blue, all on the same vine. Round, colored fruit is showiest when vines are spread out, as on a trellis.

Bignonia capreolata

Cross-Vine

Zones: 6-9

Light Needs:

Mature Size:

30'-50'

indefinite

Growth Rate:
rapid

semievergreen flowering vine
(evergreen in hotter climates)

Needs: Plant in acidic soil that's moist but well-drained. Can tolerate standing water for short periods of time. Prune in winter. Grow in sun for best flowering.

Good for: screening, trellises, arbors, fences, walls, posts, rails, natural areas, seasonal accents, walls, erosion control on slopes, covering chain-link fences

More Choices: pages 30, 35, 37, 41, 175, and 177

Outstanding Features:
- Orange-red, funnel-shaped flowers in May
- Thick, glossy foliage provides dense coverage
- Fast growth covers structures quickly

This fast-growing vine features bright orange-red blooms in mid to late spring. Thick foliage hides whatever the plant grows over. Climbing by tendrils, plants will not damage wood. Flowers have a fragrance similar to mocha.

Campsis radicans

Trumpet Vine

Zones: 4-9

Light Needs:

Mature Size:

40'+

indefinite

Growth Rate:
rapid

deciduous flowering vine

Needs: Plant in any conditions; Trumpet Vine grows in sun, shade, rich soil, or poor. It will even thrive in sidewalk cracks. Prune as needed to control. Mow over stems in lawn.

Good for: camouflaging eyesores, attracting hummingbirds, growing on tall, blank masonry walls

More Choices: page 31, 35, 37, 39, 43, 175, and 177

Options: 'Flava'—yellow flowers
'Praecox'—red flowers

Outstanding Features:
Grow in any soil type and lighting condition
Blossoms attract hummingbirds
Fast-growing for covering blank walls

This blooming beauty of a vine is as easy as a weed to grow. Shiny green leaves and orange flowers are attractive from spring until frost. Rampant growth can destroy arbors and fences or choke trees. Keep away from rooftops.

Celastrus scandens

American Bittersweet

Zones: 3-8

Light Needs:

Mature Size:

20'-60'

indefinite

Growth Rate:
rapid

deciduous vine

Needs: Plant in any kind of soil, damp or dry. Grows in sun or shade but full sun yields the most fruit. Sturdy support is needed. Prune to control size and shape. Plant both males and females for fruit production.

Good for: autumn accent, growing on fences, trellises, or arbors, natural areas, hiding scars in the landscape

More Choices: page 35, 37, 39, 43, 175, and 177

Outstanding Features:
Ornamental red-and-yellow fruit in fall
Vines cover arbors and fences quickly
Good for cutting and use in arrangements

Maturing in autumn, bright red berries are nestled inside yellow capsules. The fruit is widely used in dried arrangements in fall and winter. Plants are easy to grow and very vigorous. Vines can girdle the trunks of young trees, killing them.

Clematis armandii

Armand Clematis

Zones: 7-9

Light Needs:

Mature Size:

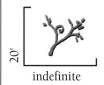

20'

indefinite

Growth Rate:
rapid

evergreen flowering vine

Needs: Plant in well-drained acidic to slightly alkaline soil that's rich in organic matter. Vines prefer to grow in the sun but roots need to be kept shaded and cool. Prune after flowering to remove tangled or dead trailers.

Good for: screening for privacy or to block poor views, trellises, arbors, rails, fence tops, climbing through trees, seasonal accents

More Choices: pages 30, 35, 41, 175, and 177

Outstanding Features:
White, scented flowers in spring
Drooping leaves stay dark green all year
Grows to great lengths and heights

Choose this fast-growing vine when you desire flowers as well as year-round foliage. Take the time to make new plants happy and you'll be rewarded with vigorous growth. May require support to get started. Initial growth may be slow.

vines

6

Clematis hybrid

Hybrid Clematis

Zones: 3-9

Light Needs:

Mature Size:

10'-20'

indefinite

Growth Rate:
slow

Deciduous flowering vine

Needs: Plant in fertile, well-drained soil that's rich in organic matter (add compost or composted manure). Set new plants about 2 inches deeper in the soil than they were in nursery pots. Keep roots cool and shaded but position vines to spread into sunny areas. After planting, cut back all stems to just above a pair of strong, healthy buds about a foot higher than soil level. Tie young plants to supports.

Good for: colorful accent, coarse texture, entries, growing up arbors, trellises, fences, posts, and poles

More Choices: page 35, 37, 175, and 177

Options: *C.* x *jackmanii*; 'Ville de Lyon'; 'Hagley Hybrid'; 'Gipsy Queen'

Outstanding Features:
- Large flowers available in many colors
- Fuzzy fall seedheads add seasonal interest
- Twining stems won't damage wood

Ville de Lyon

Hagley Hybrid

Clematis x jackmanii

When you think of flowering vines, Hybrid Clematis is probably the plant that comes to mind. Large, showy blossoms appear each spring. Numerous hybrids and a variety of colors are available.

Clematis paniculata

Sweet Autumn Clematis

Zones: 4-9

Light Needs:

Mature Size:

20'

indefinite

Growth Rate:
rapid

deciduous flowering vine

Needs: This native vine will grow in any kind of soil that isn't soggy. Slightly acidic soil pH is best. Grow in full sun or partial shade. This vigorous vine thrives on neglect.

Good for: fences, lattice, trellises, arbors, natural areas, rails, posts, growing as a groundcover in ditches and along banks, seasonal accents

More Choices: pages 35, 37, 39, 41, 43, 175, and 177

When summer flowers fade, this easy-to-grow vine bursts into bloom. Tiny pinwheel flowers cover green leaves with mounds of frothy cream. Delicate tendrils will not damage wood. Flowers are fragrant.

X Fatshedra lizei

Fatshedra

Zones: 8-10

Light Needs:

Mature Size:

10'

indefinite

Growth Rate:
rapid

evergreen vine

Needs: Plant in any soil that's moist but not soggy. Grow in partial shade or dense shade. Protect from hot, drying winds and late frosts. Pinch tips for bushier growth. Provide support.

Good for: climbing on walls, courtyards, shaded entries, adding coarse texture, providing background, beside shaded ponds or swimming pools

More Choices: pages 37 and 175

Grow this shrubby vine to add coarse texture to shady spots. It's especially useful in walled entry gardens or courtyards, where vines are protected. Vines will clamber upon the ground or grow up if provided some support.

Gelsemium sempervirens

Carolina Yellow Jessamine

Zones: 7-9

Light Needs:

Mature Size:

10'-20'

indefinite

Growth Rate:
rapid

evergreen flowering vine

Needs: Plant in any soil, including alkaline or acidic, clay or sand, wet or dry. Grow in sun or partial shade. Dense shade reduces bloom. Prune overgrown vines after flowering to regain control; stray trailers can be removed at any time.

Good for: fences, arbors, downspouts, trellises, blank walls, screening, poolside, seasonal accents, parking areas

More Choices: pages 30, 35, 37, 39, 41, 43, 175, and 177

Here's a vine anyone can grow. Stems form thick tangles of glossy foliage. Vines are naturally thin at the bottom and thick and wooly at the top. Not for formal gardens. Twining stems will not damage wood.

vines

6

Hydrangea petiolaris

Climbing Hydrangea

Zones: 4-7

Light Needs:

Mature Size:

indefinite

indefinite

Growth Rate:
slow to medium

deciduous flowering vine

Needs: Plant in fertile, well-drained, moist soil in either full sun or shade. Prune as needed in late winter or early spring to control growth. Tolerates alkaline soil.

Good for: adding texture to brick or stone walls, chimneys, courtyard walls, and tree trunks, seasonal accent, provides a coarse-textured background

More Choices: page 35, 37, 175, and 177

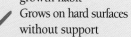

Outstanding Features:
- Lacy caps of white flowers in summer
- Coarse leaves, unusual growth habit
- Grows on hard surfaces without support

This hydrangea is an easy growing and beautiful vine. It will cover buildings or tree trunks with yards of foliage and flowers. Older stems develop exfoliating bark. The combination of flowers, foliage, and bark make this plant ideal for all seasons.

Lonicera sempervirens

Trumpet Honeysuckle

Zones: 4-9

Light Needs:

Mature Size:

10'-20'

indefinite

Growth Rate:
rapid

deciduous flowering vine (evergreen in frost-free zones)

Needs: Plant in well-drained, moist soil that's rich in organic matter. Water regularly especially during dry spells. Grow in full sun. Prune in late winter or early spring to control growth as needed.

Good for: entries, courtyards, sitting areas; covering fences, trellises, arbors, rails, and posts; attracting hummingbirds to the garden

More Choices: page 35, 175, and 177

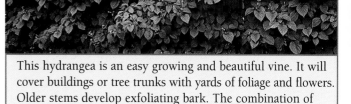

Outstanding Features:
- Red to yellow-orange summer flowers
- Bright red berries ripen in fall
- Twining stems won't damage wood

Grow this gently twisting climber to cover fences, posts, arbors, or rails with blue-green foliage and scarlet summer flowers. Easy to grow and nondamaging to garden structures.

Parthenocissus quinquefolia

Virginia Creeper

Zones: 4-9

Light Needs:

Mature Size:

20'+

indefinite

Growth Rate:
rapid

deciduous vine

Needs: Grow in any soil, from alkaline to acidic, dry to moist. Rocky soil is fine. Plant in full sun or partial shade. More sun yields brighter fall color. Tolerates heat, drought, and salt spray.

Good for: natural areas, seaside gardens, masonry or stone walls, fences, or buildings; hiding blank walls, adding coarse texture, backgrounds, seasonal accents, groundcover for erosion control

More Choices: pages 35, 37, 39, 41, 42, 43, 175, and 177

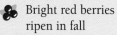

Outstanding Features:
- Leaves turn bright red in autumn
- Grows quickly; adheres to surfaces
- Tolerates a variety of soil conditions

This five-leafed native vine is easy to grow. Plant where it can climb on solid surfaces. This plant is often mistaken for poison ivy. The old saying—leaves of three let it be, leaves of five let it thrive—applies to this plant.

Parthenocissus tricuspidata
Boston Ivy

Zones: 4-8

Light Needs:

Mature Size:
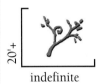

20+ / indefinite

Growth Rate:
rapid

deciduous vine

Needs: Grow in any soil, from alkaline to acidic, dry to moist. Plant in full sun or partial shade. Full sun brings out intense fall color. Plants may require more water in hotter climates.

Good for: growing on masonry walls, fences, or buildings; hiding blank walls, adding coarse texture, backgrounds, seasonal accents, giving new homes an aged look

More Choices: pages 35, 37, 39, 41, 43, 175, and 177

Outstanding Features:

- Rich, wine-red fall color
- Glossy, rich green leaves
- Adheres to solid surfaces

Grow this vine to enjoy foliage that changes with the seasons. Large leaves are green in summer turning rich red in fall. Bare winter stems lend pattern to hard surfaces for vertical interest. Adhesive disks can damage wood.

Polygonum aubertii
Silver Lace Vine

Zones: 4-9

Light Needs:

Mature Size:

25'-35' / indefinite

Growth Rate:
rapid

deciduous flowering vine

Needs: Plant in any kind of soil, including poor and dry. Grow in sun or shade. Plant vines near well-anchored supports. Prune in late winter or early spring to control growth.

Good for: coastal areas, xeriscaping, dry shade, screening, privacy, growing on fences or arbors

More Choices: page 31, 35, 37, 39, 42, 43, 175, and 177

Outstanding Features:
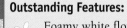
- Foamy white flowers in midsummer
- Dense foliage for quick screening
- Grows in sun or shade, in any soil

Grow this quick climber in any kind of soil to cover just about anything. Blankets of white blooms appear mid- to late summer. This vine can be hard to remove—be sure to plant it where you want it to be.

Rosa banksiae
Lady Bank's Climbing Rose

Zones: 7-9

Light Needs:

Mature Size:
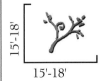

15'-18' / 15'-18'

Growth Rate:
rapid

evergreen flowering climber

Needs: Plant in any soil that isn't consistently wet. Grow in full sun or partial shade; heaviest bloom occurs in full sun. Prune after flowering. Thrives on neglect. Tie new canes to supports.

Good for: fences, arbors, hillsides, parking areas, growing through trees, entries, large planting areas, trained as a climbing vine or allowed to grow as a sprawling shrub

More Choices: pages 30, 35, 37, 39, 41, 175, and 177

Outstanding Features:
- Vigorous, arching form for informal areas
- Large clusters of white spring blooms
- Immune to nearly all diseases

Vigorous and graceful, arching canes are covered with small, fluffy creamy white flowers in spring. Give this adaptable rose room to grow. Rambling stems will not damage wood. May require protection from hard freezes.

vines

6

Rosa 'Blaze'

Blaze Climbing Rose

Zones: 5-10

Light Needs:

Mature Size:

12'-14'

12'-15'

Growth Rate: rapid

deciduous flowering climber

Needs: Plant in well-drained, slightly acidic soil. Grow in full sun. Water roots generously during the growing season. Avoid wetting the foliage. Fertilize with rose food when blooming starts. Tie new canes to strong supports. Plants are disease-resistant and carefree.

Good for: fences, trellises, arbors, walls, pillars, specimen plants, seasonal accents, entries, beside patios

More Choices: pages 35, 41, 175, and 177

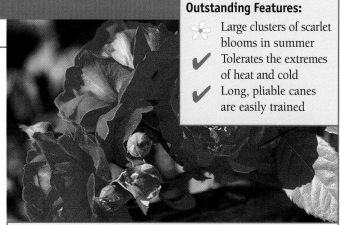

Outstanding Features:
- Large clusters of scarlet blooms in summer
- ✔ Tolerates the extremes of heat and cold
- ✔ Long, pliable canes are easily trained

Grow this rose for its abundant red blooms and tough disposition. Blaze Climbing Rose grows vigorously in cold, warm, or hot climates. Climbing hybrid of Memorial Rose. Flowers repeat throughout the hot months and have a light fragrance.

Rosa 'Climbing Peace'

Climbing Peace Rose

Zones: 5-9

Light Needs:

Mature Size:

14'-16'

12'-15'

Growth Rate: rapid

deciduous flowering climber

Needs: Plant in well-drained, slightly acidic soil. Grow in full sun. Water generously during the growing season. Avoid wetting the foliage. Fertilize with rose food when blooming starts. Tie new canes to strong supports.

Good for: arbors, fences, entries, porches, pillars, seasonal accents, specimen plants, growing near patios, decks

More Choices: pages 35, 41, 175, and 177

Outstanding Features:
- Soft yellow blossoms edged with pink
- Fragrant double flowers are long-blooming
- ✔ Tolerates both hot and cold temperatures

Famous for its large flowers, soft coloring, and end of WWII legacy, 'Climbing Peace' is a rose worth growing. For maximum flower production, train plants around supports by bending long canes into horizontal positions.

Rosa 'Climbing Iceberg'

Climbing Iceberg Rose

Zones: 4-10

Light Needs:

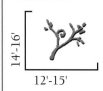

Mature Size:

14'-16'

12'-15'

Growth Rate: rapid

deciduous flowering climber

Needs: Plant in well-drained, slightly acidic soil. Grow in full sun. Water generously during the growing season. Avoid wetting the foliage. Fertilize with rose food when blooming starts. Tie new canes to supports. Provide winter protection in colder climates.

Good for: arbors, fences, posts, railings, porches, entries, courtyards, growing beside patios or decks, specimen plants

More Choices: pages 35, 41, 175, and 177

Outstanding Features:
- Clusters of pure white flowers
- Nearly continuous blooms in summer
- ✔ Vigorous canes with very few thorns

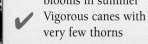

Described as one of the best climbers, this white flowering rose tolerates heat or cold. Climbing forms sometimes revert back to the shrub form. If this happens, replant elsewhere and try again with another 'Climbing Iceberg.'

Joseph's Coat Climbing Rose

Zones: 4-10

Light Needs:

Mature Size:

10'-12'
12'-15'

Growth Rate:
rapid

deciduous flowering climber

Needs: Plant in well-drained, slightly acidic soil. Grow in full sun. Water generously during the growing season. Avoid wetting the foliage. Fertilize when blooming starts. Tie new canes to sturdy supports. Provide winter protection in colder climates.

Good for: fences, walls, arbors, entries, specimen plants, seasonal accents, grow as a climber or a sprawling shrub

More Choices: pages 35, 41, 175, and 177

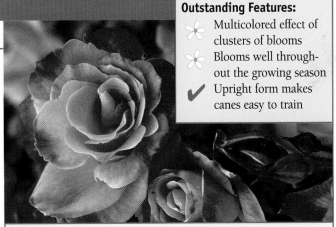

Outstanding Features:
- Multicolored effect of clusters of blooms
- Blooms well throughout the growing season
- ✔ Upright form makes canes easy to train

Appropriately named, you'll enjoy the multicolored effect of this climbing rose. Clusters of blooms change from yellow to golden orange to red. A colorful rose garden on just one plant.

Climbing Cecil Brunner Rose

Zones: 6-10

Light Needs:

Mature Size:

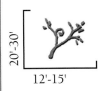

20'-30'
12'-15'

Growth Rate:
rapid

deciduous flowering climber

Needs: Plant in well-drained, slightly acidic soil. Grow in full sun. Water generously during the growing season. Avoid wetting the foliage. Fertilize when blooming first starts. Tie new canes to supports. Provide winter protection in colder climates.

Good for: screening, camouflaging eyesores, growing on fences, arbors, pillars, or trees, specimen plants

More Choices: pages 31, 35, 41, 175, and 177

Outstanding Features:
- Large sprays of small, blush pink blooms
- ✔ Vigorous climber covers a lot of ground
- Small, pointed, dark green foliage

Grow this vigorous rose where you have room to let it climb. Big sprays of small sweetheart pink roses cover stems in hot weather. Provide with a sturdy support and let it go.

Chinese Wisteria

Zones: 5-9

Light Needs:

Mature Size:

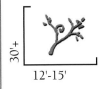

30'+
12'-15'

Growth Rate:
rapid

deciduous flowering vine

Needs: Plant in fertile, moist, well-drained soil. Grow in full sun or partial shade. Plant near well-anchored, sturdy supports. Use a bloom booster fertilizer for abundant blooms. Prune after flowering to control size or mow over vines spreading on the ground.

Good for: growing on walls, sturdy fences, or arbors, shading sitting areas, adding texture to plain backgrounds

More Choices: pages 31, 35, 37, 175, and 177

Outstanding Features:
- Purple flowers dangle like grapes in spring
- Leaves cast cooling shade in summer
- ✔ Aged stems appear muscular and strong

If you're committed to keeping this strong vine within its bounds, you'll enjoy years of drooping spring flowers, summer shade, and sculptural stems. Keep Wisteria out of trees, away from eaves, and off delicate arbors.

Vines

6

hottest climates

From the bright, tropical colors of Bougainvillea to the fine textures of palm fronds, there are many heat-loving plants with attractive characteristics. You need to consider growing conditions, mature sizes, and growth rates when selecting plants for your landscape.

Heat Seekers

I **f you live where frost is rare, this chapter is for you.** Though there is information throughout the book about plants that will live where you do, the ones selected for the following pages are particularly heat-tolerant. (See pages 26-27 for a complete list of plants in this book that will grow in Zones 9 or 10.) Selection guides group trees, shrubs, groundcovers, and vines by purpose and optimum growing conditions. For more information about specific plants, refer to the individual plant descriptions and photos in the encyclopedia.

Desert Willow (Chilopsis linearis) Page 194

A walkway leading through a lush landscape is more inviting than one cutting across a lawn.

Plants for Special Site Conditions

Availability varies by area and conditions (see page 21). Check with your garden center.

Plants for low-water landscapes

Common Name	Zones	Page
◆ **Trees**		
Arizona Cypress	7-9	194
Cupressus arizonica		
Date Palm	9-10	196
Phoenix dactylifera		
Desert Willow	8-10	194
Chilopsis linearis		
Hollywood Juniper	4-9	195
Juniperus chinensis 'Torulosa'		
Laurel Oak	7-10	197
Quercus laurifolia		
Mesquite	10	197
Prosopis glandulosa		
Olive	8-10	195
Olea europaea		
Paloverde	8-10	193
Cercidium texanum		
Pindo Palm	8-10	192
Butia capitata		
Sabal Palm	8-10	198
Sabal palmetto		
Sea Grape	10	194
Coccoloba uvifera		
Senegal Date Palm	9-10	196
Phoenix reclinata		
◆ **Shrubs**		
Bunny Ears Cactus	10	203
Opuntia microdasys		
Cape Honeysuckle	10	205
Tecomaria capensis		
Oleander	8-10	203
Nerium oleander		
Texas Silverado Sage	8-9	202
Leucophyllum frutescens 'Silverado'		
White Rock Rose	8-10	200
Cistus x hybridus		
◆ **Groundcovers**		
Barrel Cactus	9-10	208
Echinocactus spp.		
Dwarf Coyote Brush	7-10	207
Baccharis pilularis		
Freeway Daisy	10	209
Osteospermum fruticosum		
Gold Mound Lantana	9-10	208
Lantana camara 'Gold Mound'		
Hens and Chicks	4-10	209
Sempervivum tectorum		
◆ **Vines**		
Butterfly Vine	9-10	212
Mascagnia macroptera		
Flowering Vines		
Allamanda	10	210
Allamanda cathartica		
Butterfly Vine	9-10	212
Mascagnia macroptera		
Evergreen Wisteria	9-10	212
Millettia reticulata		
Hall's Honeysuckle	4-10	211
Lonicera japonica 'Halliana'		
Madagascar Jasmine	10	213
Stephanotis floribunda		
Mandevilla	10	212
Mandevilla splendens 'Red Riding Hood'		
Star Jasmine	8-10	213
Trachelospermum jasminoides		

Salt-tolerant plants

Common Name	Zones	Page
◆ **Trees**		
Hollywood Juniper	4-9	195
Juniperus chinensis 'Torulosa'		
Sabal Palm	8-10	198
Sabal palmetto		
Sea Grape	10	194
Coccoloba uvifera		
◆ **Shrubs**		
Ixora	10	202
Ixora coccinea		
Oleander	8-10	203
Nerium oleander		
Texas Silverado Sage	8-9	202
Leucophyllum frutescens 'Silverado'		
Variegated Pittosporum	8-10	204
Pittosporum tobira 'Variegata'		
White Rock Rose	8-10	200
Cistus x hybridus		
◆ **Groundcovers**		
Dwarf Coyote Brush	7-10	207
Baccharis pilularis		
Freeway Daisy	10	209
Osteospermum fruticosum		
Gold Mound Lantana	9-10	208
Lantana camara 'Gold Mound'		

Bougainvillea (Bougainvillea spp.) Page 211

Coarse-textured Sea Grape (Coccoloba uvifera) will tolerant wind, salt spray, and dry, sandy soil.

Cast-Iron Plant (Aspidistra elatior) Page 206

Plants for sandy soil

Common Name	Zones	Page
◆ **Trees**		
Crimson Bottlebrush	9-10	193
Callistemon citrinus		
Hollywood Juniper	4-9	195
Juniperus chinensis 'Torulosa'		
Mesquite	10	197
Prosopis glandulosa		
Sea Grape	10	194
Coccoloba uvifera		
◆ **Shrubs**		
Bunny Ears Cactus	10	203
Opuntia microdasys		
Chinese Hibiscus	9-10	201
Hibiscus rosa-sinensis		
King Sago	8-10	201
Cycas revoluta		
Oleander	8-10	203
Nerium oleander		
Texas Silverado Sage	8-9	202
Leucophyllum frutescens 'Silverado'		
◆ **Groundcovers**		
Cast-Iron Plant	8-10	206
Aspidistra elatior		
Freeway Daisy	10	209
Osteospermum fruticosum		
Gold Mound Lantana	9-10	208
Lantana camara 'Gold Mound'		
Hens and Chicks	4-10	209
Sempervivum tectorum		
◆ **Vines**		
Bougainvillea	9-10	211
Bougainvillea spp		

Choosing plants that are native to your area is a good way to make your house look at home in its setting.

Choosing Plants to Fit Your Needs

C **hoosing the right plant for the right place is still the rule in all climates.** For planting beside patios, choose trees that won't buckle the paving with their roots or drop messy fruit. At streetside, grow trees that tolerate car exhaust. To enhance privacy, plant trees, shrubs, and vines that grow quickly and thickly. Refer to the lists on page 189 to find plants for Zones 9 and 10 for specific uses. Availability varies by area and conditions (see page 21). Check with your garden center. Turn to the individual plant descriptions for more information.

Crimson Bottlebrush (Callistemon citrinus) Page 193

Lush, tropical foliage is a good look for hot areas with high humidity.

Queen Palms (Syagrus romanzoffianum) Page 198

Trees for specific areas

Common Name	Zones	Page
◆ Streetside Trees		
Canary Island Date Palm	9-10	196
Phoenix canariensis		
Date Palm	9-10	196
Phoenix dactylifera		
Laurel Oak	7-10	197
Quercus laurifolia		
Pindo Palm	8-10	192
Butia capitata		
Queen Palm	10	198
Syagrus romanzoffianum		
Royal Palm	10	197
Roystonea elata		
Sabal Palm	8-10	198
Sabal palmetto		
◆ Patio Trees		
Crimson Bottlebrush	9-10	193
Callistemon citrinus		
Laurel Oak	7-10	197
Quercus laurifolia		
Lilac Chaste Tree	6-10	199
Vitex agnus-castus		
Mexican Bird-of-Paradise	10	192
Caesalpinia mexicana		
Olive	8-10	195
Olea europaea		
Pindo Palm	8-10	192
Butia capitata		
Queen Palm	10	198
Syagrus romanzoffianum		
Sabal Palm	8-10	198
Sabal palmetto		

Tall Sabal Palms (Sabal palmetto), page 198, are good choices beside a multistory house.

Allamanda
(*Allamanda cathartica*)
Page 210

Shrubs for hedges

Common Name	Zones	Page
Cape Honeysuckle	10	205
Tecomaria capensis		
Chinese Hibiscus	9-10	201
Hibiscus rosa-sinensis		
Downy Jasmine	9-10	202
Jasminum multiflorum		
Indian Hawthorn	8-10	204
Rhaphiolepis indica		
Ixora	10	202
Ixora coccinea		
Oleander	8-10	203
Nerium oleander		
Sweet Viburnum	8-10	205
Viburnum odoratissimum		
Texas Silverado Sage	8-9	202
Leucophyllum frutescens 'Silverado'		
Variegated Pittosporum	8-10	204
Pittosporum tobira 'Variegata'		
White Rock Rose	8-10	200
Cistus x hybridus		

Plants for small spaces

Common Name	Zones	Page
◆ Trees		
Crimson Bottlebrush	9-10	193
Callistemon citrinus		
Lilac Chaste Tree	6-10	199
Vitex agnus-castus		
Loquat	8-10	195
Eriobotrya japonica		
Sabal Palm	8-10	198
Sabal palmetto		
White Bird-of-Paradise	9-10	198
Strelitzia nicolai		
Windmill Palm	8-10	199
Trachycarpus fortunei		
◆ Shrubs		
African Iris	9-10	203
Moraea iridioides		
Bird-of-Paradise	9-10	205
Strelitzia reginae		
Chinese Hibiscus	9-10	201
Hibiscus rosa-sinensis		
Gardenia	8-10	201
Gardenia jasminoides		
Indian Hawthorn	8-10	204
Rhaphiolepis indica		
Ixora	10	202
Ixora coccinea		
Pygmy Date Palm	9-10	204
Phoenix roebelenii		
Variegated Croton	10	200
Codiaeum variegatum var. pictum		
◆ Groundcovers		
Cast-Iron Plant	8-10	206
Aspidistra elatior		
Cuphea	9-10	207
Cuphea hyssopifola		
Dwarf Coyote Brush	7-10	207
Baccharis pilularis		
Dwarf Lily of the Nile	9-10	206
Agapanthus africanus 'Peter Pan'		
Gold Mound Lantana	9-10	208
Lantana camara 'Gold Mound'		
Hens and Chicks	4-10	209
Sempervivum tectorum		
Moss Verbena	8-10	209
Verbena pulchella		

Plants for privacy

Common Name	Zones	Page
◆ Trees		
Arizona Cypress	7-9	194
Cupressus arizonica		
Desert Willow	8-10	194
Chilopsis linearis		
Hollywood Juniper	4-9	195
Juniperus chinensis 'Torulosa'		
Laurel Oak	7-10	197
Quercus laurifolia		
Lilac Chaste Tree	6-10	199
Vitex agnus-castus		
Mesquite	10	197
Prosopis glandulosa		
◆ Shrubs		
Cape Honeysuckle	10	205
Tecomaria capensis		
Chinese Hibiscus	9-10	201
Hibiscus rosa-sinensis		
Ixora	10	202
Ixora coccinea		
Oleander	8-10	203
Nerium oleander		
Sweet Viburnum	8-10	205
Viburnum odoratissimum		
Texas Silverado Sage	8-9	202
Leucophyllum frutescens 'Silverado'		
◆ Vines		
Allamanda	10	210
Allamanda cathartica		
Bougainvillea	9-10	211
Bougainvillea spp		
Evergreen Wisteria	9-10	212
Millettia reticulata		
Madagascar Jasmine	10	213
Stephanotis floribunda		
Passion Flower	7-10	213
Passiflora incarnata		
Star Jasmine	8-10	213
Trachelospermum jasminoides		

Palm Care Basics

Give your palm the best possible start and keep it healthy.

1 **Choose a sunny spot to dig a hole twice as wide as the palm's nursery container.** The hole should be as deep as the container is tall. Because palms require drainage, add gypsum to the hole and work it into the soil. Remove the container and set the palm in place.

2 **Insert a length of PVC pipe into the hole so that it is standing upright beside the palm's root ball.** The pipe should be tall enough to extend above the ground when the hole is filled. After planting you can use this pipe to check soil conditions next to the root ball. Insert a stick. If it comes back wet, you're overwatering the palm. Fill the bottom two-thirds of the hole with native soil.

3 **Mix one-half compost with one-half native soil.** Fill the rest of the hole with this mixture. Unlike most tree roots, palm roots don't extend very far into the soil, so the amended soil mixture is added near the surface. (In extremely alkaline soils, mix one-third peat, one-third compost, and one-third native soil.)

4 **Mulch the newly planted palm.** Water it with a hose turned on to a slow trickle. Even though palms dislike standing water around their root balls, they must have moisture to thrive. Good drainage is the key.

STUFF YOU'LL NEED

✔ Round-point shovel
✔ Leather gloves
✔ Bagged compost
✔ Gypsum
✔ A length of plastic pipe, about 12 to 15 inches long, 3 to 4 inches in diameter
✔ Eye protection

What to Expect

Many palms have thorns, serrated foliage, or stiff fronds. Long sleeves, gloves, and eye protection are precautionary measures.

Design Tip

Feeding Palms

Yellow fronds may indicate that your palm needs fertilizer. Palms require minor nutrients such as magnesium and manganese. To give these plants the right nutrients, buy fertilizer labeled as palm food. Apply granular palm food to the soil around the base of the plant and water well.

Good idea!

Grooming Palms Clipping dead or damaged fronds keeps palms neat and healthy. It also prevents old fronds from falling during storms or high winds. Use pole pruners for tall palms, and loppers for plants within reach. Wear long sleeves, gloves, and eye protection; many palms have spikes or thorns.

Gardenia Care Basics

STUFF YOU'LL NEED

✔ Round-point shovel
✔ Bagged compost
✔ Peat moss
✔ Gypsum for clay soil
✔ Mulch

What to Expect

If leaves turn yellow and the root area feels wet, dig up your gardenia and plant it again with the root ball sitting higher so water will drain from roots.

Symptoms & Solutions

If your gardenia shows signs of a problem, begin treatment right away.

Symptom: New leaves are curled and stunted; foliage is shiny and sticky. Aphids and ants may be noticeable.
   Solution: Knock aphids off with a stiff spray of water. Control major infestations with insecticidal soap or a systemic insecticide for aphids.

Symptom: Clouds of tiny flying insects hover over plants.
   Solution: Control with a systemic insecticide that lists white flies on the label; repeat as directed. Coat tops and undersides of foliage.

Symptom: Leaves appear blackish.
   Solution: Sooty mold is the result of insects that secret a sticky substance. This mold will not harm your gardenia, but it is unsightly. Wipe leaves with a damp cloth to clean them if desired. Prevent sooty mold by controlling pests as described above.

Symptom: Leaves have small polka-dot bumps. Turn leaves over to see if webs are present on the undersides. Weather is usually hot and dry.
   Solution: Spray your gardenia with a stiff spray of water to knock spider mites and their webs off. Wet foliage in mornings to give leaves ample opportunity to dry. Apply an insecticide containing diazinon, wetting tops and undersides of foliage. Repeat applications as directed.

1 **Dig a hole that is not quite as deep as the nursery container.** Set the gardenia, still in its pot, into the hole to check the depth. The container's rim should protrude a couple of inches above the level of the soil. If the container sits lower, remove it and shovel some soil back into the hole, tamping firmly to prevent settling later on. Check the depth of the hole again.

2 **When the hole is the proper depth, widen it so that it's at least one-and-a-half times as wide as the nursery container.** If your soil is heavy clay, work gypsum into the bottom of the hole (see page 49). You'll also need to roughen the sides of holes dug in clay soils with a shovel to make it easier for roots to penetrate into surrounding soil. Gently remove the gardenia from its container and set the plant in the hole. Turn it so the best side is facing the most important angle of view.

3 **Fill the hole around the shrub with a soil mixture.** Mix one-third bagged compost, one-third peat, and one-third native soil. Peat moss lowers the soil pH, which is good for acid-loving gardenias. (Omit peat if planting in heavy clay that's already acidic; peat moss will retain too much water. Instead, increase the amount of organic matter.) Gently shovel the soil mixture around the plant, avoid piling it on top of the root ball. When soil is in place, the root ball should sit an inch or two higher than the soil level. This is critical to keep water draining away from sensitive roots.

4 **Mulch the newly planted gardenia well but make sure you don't pile mulch around stems.** Doing so will produce the same result—crown rot—as planting the shrub too deeply. Soak the root ball of your new plant with a slow hose.

Wisdom of the Aisles

Feeding gardenias is easy if you look for a high-iron product that's made specifically for acid-loving plants. The label should mention gardenias or camellias, azaleas, or rhododendrons. Follow package directions and water well after applying granular products.

Acacia baileyana

Bailey Acacia

Zones: 10

Light Needs:

Mature Size:

20'-30'

20'-40'

Growth Rate:
rapid

evergreen flowering tree

Needs: Plant in well-drained soil and full sun. Water when new, but don't worry about watering established plants. You can prune the main stem to encourage a more shrublike shape or develop the plant into a small tree.

Good for: single specimen and accent use; hedging and screening; growing on banks and hillsides.

More Choices: pages 34, 39, 42, 59, and 67

More Choices: pages 34, 39, 42, 59, and 67

Outstanding Features:

 Clusters of fragrant yellow flowers
 Fast growth for quick landscape accent
✔ Tolerates dry soil when established

For an attractive, fast-growing, trouble-free tree, choose Bailey Acacia. Needs little attention after planting. Covered with golden yellow flowers in January and February. Grows very quickly, but short-lived, lasting only 20 to 30 years.

Butia capitata

Pindo Palm

Zones: 8-10

Light Needs:

Mature Size:

12'-20'

12'-15'

Growth Rate:
slow

evergreen palm tree

Needs: Plant in full sun and well-drained soil. Allow plenty of room around the plant for its mature spread of 15 feet. Pindo Palm is fairly drought-tolerant; water only when soil is dry. Fertilize yearly with palm food.

Good for: single specimen or coarse-textured accent; massed in groups or planted in rows; xeriscaping; parking areas and streetside

More Choices: pages 34, 39, 42, 68, 187, and 189

More Choices: pages 34, 39, 42, 68, 187, and 189

Outstanding Features:

✔ More cold-tolerant than many palms
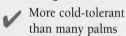 Arching, bluish fronds provide color contrast
✔ Thick, handsome trunk

This tough palm features arching, blue-green fronds and a thick trunk. Good choice for hot, semitropical locations or areas that receive short bursts of freezing temperatures. Edible fruit gives this plant its nickname of Jelly Palm.

Caesalpinia mexicana

Mexican Bird-of-Paradise

Zones: 10

Light Needs:

Mature Size:

12'-25'

12'-15'

Growth Rate:
rapid

evergreen flowering tree

Needs: Grow in well-drained soil and full sun. Water new plants frequently to get them established; after that, water only during times of drought.

Good for: small accent tree near patios or beside entries; adds shade and texture, as well as color

More Choices: pages 34, 39, 59, 67, 69, and 189

More Choices: pages 34, 39, 59, 67, 69, and 189

Options: Red Bird-of-Paradise (*C. pulcherrima*)—red-and-yellow flowered shrub to 10 feet tall. Zones 9-10.

Outstanding Features:

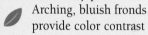 Showy flowers bloom over a long time
✔ Needs little water once established
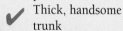 Foliage adds interesting texture

Producing bright lemon yellow flowers during all but the coolest months, this is a colorful addition to the landscape. Not frost-tolerant. Red Bird-of-Paradise is more hardy and may sprout again if damaged by frost.

Callistemon citrinus

Crimson Bottlebrush

Zones: 9-10

Light Needs:

Mature Size:

20'-25'
15'-25'

Growth Rate: medium to rapid

evergreen flowering tree

Needs: Plant in full sun and well-drained soil. Water young plants frequently to speed growth. Mature trees rarely need watering. Can be pruned to obtain a shrublike form.

Good for: Small accent tree, either a single specimen or in groups; patio plantings and around decks

More Choices: pages 34, 39, 59, 67, 69, 187, and 189

Options: Weeping Bottlebrush (*C. viminalis*)—weeping branches

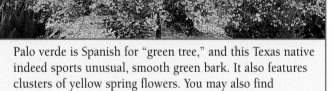

Outstanding Features:
- Tolerates heat and sandy soil
- Bright red flowers have a long bloom time
- Attracts hummingbirds to the garden

Arching to pendulous branches bear loads of brilliant red, bristle-shaped blooms in spring and summer. Foliage smells of lemons when crushed. 'Compacta'— just 4 to 5 feet tall; 'Mauve Mist'—bright pink-purple flowers, 6 to 12 feet tall

---

Cercidium texanum

Paloverde

Zones: 9-10

Light Needs:

Mature Size:

15'-25'
15'-20'

Growth Rate: medium

deciduous flowering tree

Needs: Give Texas Paloverde a place in full sun. Plant in alkaline, well-drained soil. Water frequently to get new plants started, but don't worry about watering regularly after that.

Good for: adding color and shade to hot, arid landscapes and hillsides; xeriscaping

More Choices: pages 34, 41, 42, 67, 69, and 187

 C. floridum

Outstanding Features:
- Tolerates drought and heat
- Yellow spring flowers in clusters
- Smooth green bark is ornamental

Palo verde is Spanish for "green tree," and this Texas native indeed sports unusual, smooth green bark. It also features clusters of yellow spring flowers. You may also find Paloverde sold as *Parkinsonia texana* var. *texanum*.

Chamaerops humilis

Mediterranean Fan Palm

Zones: 9-10

Light Needs:

Mature Size:

10'-20'
15'-20'

Growth Rate: slow

evergreen tree

Needs: Place this palm in full sun to light shade; you can grow it in just about any soil that's well-drained. Water frequently for the first year or two after planting, then only when dry. Keep the area around trunks free of grass and weeds.

Good for: accenting, either as a single specimen or in groups; screening and forming an impenetrable hedge

More Choices: pages 34, 36, and 39

Outstanding Features:
- Attractive fan-shaped fronds
- Hardier than many other palms
- Available in multi- or single-stemmed forms

Handsome plants flourish in hot landscapes as well as cooler, borderline areas. Plants will tolerate temperatures as low as 6 degrees F. Add tropical-looking accent to planters, patios, and decks.

Chilopsis linearis

Desert Willow

Zones: 8-9

Light Needs:

Mature Size:

20'-25' (height)
20'-25' (width)

Growth Rate:
rapid

deciduous flowering tree

Needs: Plant in full sun and soil that's alkaline and dry. You won't need to give this Southwestern desert native much water at all. Cut out extra branches to emphasize the tree's airy, arching shape.

Good for: arid landscapes; single specimens or groups of accent trees; xeriscaping use

More Choices: pages 31, 34, 39, 41, 42, 59, 67, 187, and 189

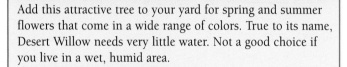

Outstanding Features:

- Dangling clusters of bright blooms
- Attract birds into the landscape
- Airy shape provides texture contrast

Add this attractive tree to your yard for spring and summer flowers that come in a wide range of colors. True to its name, Desert Willow needs very little water. Not a good choice if you live in a wet, humid area.

Coccoloba uvifera

Sea Grape

Zones: 10

Light Needs:

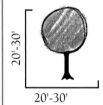

Mature Size:

20'-30' (height)
20'-30' (width)

Growth Rate:
medium

evergreen tree

Needs: Plant in well-drained, sandy soil and full sun. Sea Grape is an ideal seaside tree, standing up easily to salt spray and wind. Water new plants regularly to help establish. Plants rarely need extra water after that.

Good for: seaside landscapes, hedges, windbreaks, adding shade, coarse-textured accents, xeriscaping

More Choices: pages 34, 42, 67, 69, and 187

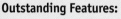
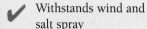
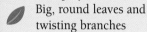
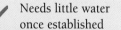

Outstanding Features:
- Withstands wind and salt spray
- Big, round leaves and twisting branches
- Needs little water once established

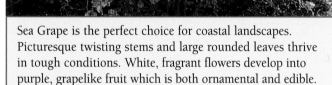

Sea Grape is the perfect choice for coastal landscapes. Picturesque twisting stems and large rounded leaves thrive in tough conditions. White, fragrant flowers develop into purple, grapelike fruit which is both ornamental and edible.

Cupressus arizonica

Arizona Cypress

Zones: 7-9

Light Needs:

Mature Size:

30'-40' (height)
15'-20' (width)

Growth Rate:
rapid

evergreen tree

Needs: Plant in well-drained soil—dry, rocky, alkaline sites are ideal. Plant in full sun. Once established, plants do not require supplemental watering.

Good for: screening to block views or add privacy, windbreaks or tall hedges, single specimen for year-round greenery; xeriscaping in dry areas

More Choices: pages 30, 34, 39, 41, 42, 59, 187, and 189

Outstanding Features:
- Likes dry conditions and poor soil
- Grows tall with attractive shape
- Keeps foliage year-round

Got an unsightly view to block? Or, perhaps you need to add some privacy. Arizona Cypress has a tall, pyramidal shape, thick evergreen foliage, and grows quickly. This is not a good choice for humid areas with plentiful rainfall.

Eriobotyra japonica

Loquat

Zones: 8-10

Light Needs:

Mature Size:

20'-30'
15'-25'

Growth Rate: medium

evergreen tree

Needs: Full sun or partial shade. Plant in any well-drained moist soil, from acidic to alkaline. Water trees regularly after planting then only when conditions are extremely dry. Mulch area around trunk. Feed with a balanced fertilizer if soils are sandy.

Good for: screening for privacy or to block views, coarse-textured background or accent tree, adding shade as a small ornamental tree

More Choices: pages 34, 36, 40, 41, and 69

Loquat works well as a background tree in hot regions providing interesting texture. Can be trained as an espalier against walls. White fragrant flowers develop into pear-shaped fruit that ripen April through June.

Juniperus chinensis 'Torulosa' or 'Kaizuka'

Hollywood Juniper

Zones: 4-9

Light Needs:

Mature Size:

15'-20'
8'-12'

Growth Rate: medium

evergreen tree

Needs: Grow in full sun or partial shade. Plant in almost any kind of soil—acidic, alkaline, clay, or sand—as long as it's well-drained. Will die in soil that stays wet. Needs water during periods of prolonged drought or when plants are new. No pruning required.

Good for: xeriscaping, single-specimen plant, entry areas, at the corner of a tall house, seaside landscapes, or along a property line for privacy

More Choices: pages 31, 34, 36, 39, 40, 41, 42, 67, 187, and 189

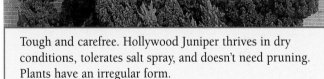

Outstanding Features:

- Tolerant of drought, heat, and salt spray
- Rich green foliage year-round
- Interesting, slightly twisting branches

Tough and carefree. Hollywood Juniper thrives in dry conditions, tolerates salt spray, and doesn't need pruning. Plants have an irregular form.

Olea europaea

Olive

Zones: 8-10

Light Needs:

Mature Size:

25'-30'
25'-30'

Growth Rate: slow

evergreen tree

Needs: Grow olives in full sun. When planting, prepare the soil by digging deeply; add gypsum if needed to improve drainage. Olives thrive in rich soil but will also grow in stony, alkaline sites. Water new plants; older plants rarely need watering.

Good for: xeriscaping, single specimen use, adding shade, planting near parking areas or patios (choose fruitless varieties for cleanliness)

More Choices: pages 34, 41, 42, 67, 69, 187, and 189

Outstanding Features:

- Likes heat and needs little water
- Soft, gray, year-round foliage adds color
- Handsome shape and edible fruit

Southern California is perfect for growing olives. These elegant, gray-leafed trees thrive in the area's hot, arid climate, which is much like their native Mediterranean setting. Olives are not good choices for humid areas with lots of rainfall.

Phoenix canariensis

Canary Island Date Palm

Zones: 9-10

Light Needs:

Mature Size:

50'-60'

30'-50'

Growth Rate: slow

evergreen palm tree

Needs: Plant in full sun. Soil must be well-drained; wet sites promote fungal problems. Select a planting location that will accommodate wide, stiff fronds without chance of human injury.

Good for: tropical effect, single-specimen accent plant; entries, parking areas, or along streets

More Choices: pages 34, 68, and 189

Outstanding Features: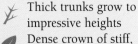
- Thick trunks grow to impressive heights
- Dense crown of stiff, wide fronds
- Drought-tolerant and easy care

Here's a big palm tree with a magnificent look. Its thick trunk grows more slowly than its wide, stiff fronds. Start off with trees that have fronds above head height. Trees may die during extended freezes.

Phoenix dactylifera

Date Palm

Zones: 9-10

Light Needs:

Mature Size:

65'-70'

40'-50'

Growth Rate: slow

evergreen palm tree

Needs: Plant in full sun with well-drained soil. Date Palms are very drought-tolerant. Discontinue supplemental watering when new plants show signs of fresh growth.

Good for: xeriscaping, street trees, large lots, arid landscapes, seaside

More Choices: pages 34, 42, 68, 69, 187, and 189

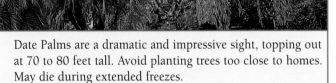

Outstanding Features: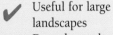
- Thin trunks grow to majestic heights
- Useful for large landscapes
- Drought- and salt-tolerant plants

Date Palms are a dramatic and impressive sight, topping out at 70 to 80 feet tall. Avoid planting trees too close to homes. May die during extended freezes.

Phoenix reclinata

Senegal Date Palm

Zones: 9-10

Light Needs:

Mature Size:

25'-35'

20'-35'

Growth Rate: medium

evergreen palm tree

Needs: Plant in any soil that's well-drained and stays sunny all day long. Senegal Date Palm is drought-tolerant after plants are established. Avoid overwatering to prevent disease.

Good for: a multitrunked accent, hiding tall walls, tropical effect, xeriscaping, coastal areas (not right on the beach)

More Choices: pages 34, 42, and 187

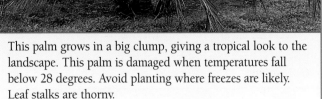

Outstanding Features:
- Attractive multitrunked form
- Arching, evergreen fronds
- Drought- and salt-tolerant

This palm grows in a big clump, giving a tropical look to the landscape. This palm is damaged when temperatures fall below 28 degrees. Avoid planting where freezes are likely. Leaf stalks are thorny.

Prosopis glandulosa

Mesquite

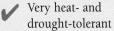

Outstanding Features:

Zones: 10

Light Needs:

Mature Size:

20'-30'
12'-15'

Growth Rate:
medium to rapid

deciduous flowering tree

Needs: Plant in dry, sandy, alkaline soil with full sun. This small tree is highly drought-tolerant. Water very little or not at all. Extra watering—even lawn irrigation or poor drainage—can cause Mesquite to sicken and die.

Good for: xeriscaping, arid landscapes, planting in lawns to cast light shade, controlling erosion on hills and slopes, screening and windbreaks

More Choices: pages 31, 34, 39, 41, 42, 59, 67, 69, 187, and 189

✓ Very heat- and drought-tolerant
◗ Gnarled trunk topped with airy foliage
✳ Yellow-green flowers in spring

Mesquite thrives even in the driest conditions of the Southwest. Adds interest to arid landscapes with its irregular, sculptural shape and spring bloom. Long tap roots make moving difficult.

Quercus laurifolia

Laurel Oak

Zones: 7-10

Light Needs:

Mature Size:

40'-60'
50'-60'

Growth Rate:
rapid

deciduous tree

Needs: Plant Laurel Oak in full sun to partial shade. You can grow this tree in most soil types, including dry, sandy soil—moist, acidic soil is optimal. Water frequently when first planted to help new trees become established. Watering is rarely needed after that.

Good for: xeriscaping, shade trees, parking areas, street trees, residential landscapes

More Choices: pages 31, 34, 36, 39, 40, 42, 59, 68, 69, 187, and 189

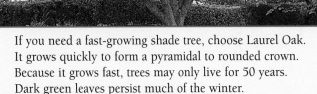

Outstanding Features:

✓ Fast growth provides quick shade
◢ Tolerates drought and sandy soil
✓ Roots won't buckle paving

If you need a fast-growing shade tree, choose Laurel Oak. It grows quickly to form a pyramidal to rounded crown. Because it grows fast, trees may only live for 50 years. Dark green leaves persist much of the winter.

Roystonea elata

Royal palm

Zones: 10

Light Needs:

Mature Size:

75'-80'
25'-30'

Growth Rate:
medium

evergreen palm tree

Needs: Plant in full sun. Rich, moist to wet soil is ideal for this swamp native. Sandy, fast-draining soils will need regular watering for best results. Fertilize once or twice a year with palm food.

Good for: street trees, parking areas, beside multistory homes and buildings, large lawns

More Choices: pages 34, 38, 43, 68, 69, and 189

Outstanding Features:

✧ Tall, smooth trunks are gray and green
✓ Tolerates extreme heat and confined spaces
✓ Car exhaust- and pollution-tolerant

Tall and stately, this Florida native gives landscapes a tropical touch. It features smooth gray and green trunks topped with graceful fronds. Trunks have a tendency to lean. Prolonged frost will kill this tree.

hottest climates 7

Sabal palmetto

Sabal Palm

Zones: 8-10

Light Needs:

Mature Size:

40'-80'
15'-25'

Growth Rate:
slow

evergreen palm tree

Needs: Plant in full sun to partial shade. Extremely adaptable—grows in most kinds of soil. Water frequently after planting until new growth appears. Once established, no extra water is needed. Prune only dead or damaged fronds to avoid ruining the rounded crown.

Good for: parking areas, patios, street trees, xeriscaping, seaside planting, entry areas, single specimens or groups

More Choices: pages 34, 36, 42, 68, 69, 187, and 189

Outstanding Features:
- Thin, skinny trunk with rounded crown
- ✔ Tolerates drought, salt, and confined spaces
- ✔ Survives heat and light frosts

Sabal Palm is easy to grow, eventually reaching heights of about 80 feet. For uniform appearance, you can plant trees with some of the trunk buried so that all are even in height. Or, plant them in stair-step fashion for added interest.

Strelitzia nicolai

White Bird-of-Paradise

Zones: 9-10

Light Needs:

Mature Size:

25'-30'
12'-15'

Growth Rate:
slow

evergreen tree

Needs: Plant in full sun or partial shade. Soil must be well-drained. Water regularly for best appearance. Feed frequently when first planted with a balanced fertilizer to help plants gain in size. Once established, taper off feeding to twice a year.

Good for: large, coarse-textured accent, tropical appearance, single specimen, entry areas, around swimming pools, hiding blank walls

More Choices: pages 34, 36, 67, and 189

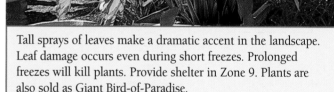

Outstanding Features:
- Big, dramatic leaves provide accent
- ✔ Upright shape and form
- White blooms resemble perching birds

Tall sprays of leaves make a dramatic accent in the landscape. Leaf damage occurs even during short freezes. Prolonged freezes will kill plants. Provide shelter in Zone 9. Plants are also sold as Giant Bird-of-Paradise.

Syagrus romanzoffianum

Queen Palm

Zones: 10

Light Needs:

Mature Size:

40'-50'
30'

Growth Rate:
medium to rapid

evergreen palm tree

Needs: Plant in moist, well-drained soil and full sun. Palms will grow in neutral to alkaline soils. Water and fertilize regularly with palm food. Grow where plants are protected from high winds. Remove dead fronds before they fall.

Good for: fine-textured accent, single specimen or in rows, cutouts in patios or decks, entry, parking, and street tree

More Choices: pages 34, 40, 68, 69, and 189

Outstanding Features:
- Gracefully arching fine-textured fronds
- Tall, straight, smooth gray trunk
- ✔ Tolerates heat and confined conditions

Large, arching fronds give Queen Palm the quintessential palm tree appearance. Trunks grow up to 40 or 50 feet tall. It is damaged or killed at temperatures of 25 degrees and below. Roots adapt well to confined conditions.

Trachycarpus fortunei

Windmill Palm

Zones: 8-10

Light Needs:

Mature Size:

20'-30'

5'-10'

Growth Rate:
slow to medium

evergreen palm tree

Needs: Plant in full sun or light, dappled shade. These palms adapt to a range of soil conditions. Place the root ball a little below soil level at planting. Water regularly. Fertilize two to three times a year with palm food. Can tolerate temperatures down to 10 degrees F.

Good for: courtyards, entries, confined spaces, containers, beside swimming pools, accent plant

More Choices: pages 34, 36, 67, and 189

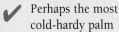

Outstanding Features:

✔ Perhaps the most cold-hardy palm

🍃 Neat fronds, fanlike in appearance

Hairy trunks provide added texture

Windmill is an unusually adaptable palm that can be used in many different landscaping situations. Grows well in the ground as well as large containers.

Vitex agnus-castus

Lilac Chaste Tree

Zones: 6-10

Light Needs:

Mature Size:

6'-25'

6'-25'

Growth Rate:
slow to rapid

deciduous tree

Needs: Plant in full sun or light, dappled shade. Any type of soil will do as long as it is well-drained. Water new plants regularly. Once established, water only in times of severe drought. To encourage treelike shape, remove lower limbs as the plant grows.

Good for: accents (single specimen or in groups), growing near patios, decks, porches, and entries; or, grow as an informal hedge

More Choices: pages 31, 34, 36, 39, 41, 59, 67, 69, and 189

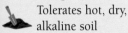

Outstanding Features:

Tolerates hot, dry, alkaline soil

❋ Fragrant blooms attract butterflies

✔ Low maintenance and adaptable

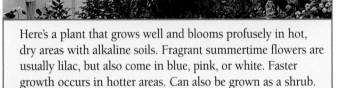

Here's a plant that grows well and blooms profusely in hot, dry areas with alkaline soils. Fragrant summertime flowers are usually lilac, but also come in blue, pink, or white. Faster growth occurs in hotter areas. Can also be grown as a shrub.

Washingtonia robusta

Mexican Washington Palm

Zones: 9-10

Light Needs:

Mature Size:

60'-100'

12'-15'

Growth Rate:
rapid

evergreen palm tree

Needs: Plant in just about any soil that's well-drained and in full sun. This desert palm tolerates dry conditions, but grows fastest when watered regularly. In humid, semitropical regions, water less frequently. Overwatering can damage or kill these plants. Remove dead fronds periodically.

Good for: single specimen, groups, parking areas, large landscapes

More Choices: pages 34, 39, 59, and 69

Outstanding Features:

✔ One of the tallest palms available

Forms an imposing specimen fast

✔ Tolerates heat and drought

Growing between 70 and 100 feet tall, this palm is best used in large, open spaces. Very tall mature size makes it incorrectly proportioned for use beside most homes. Think big when using this one. Also sold as Mexican Fan Palm.

Bouvardia longiflora 'Albatross'

Bouvardia

Zones: 9-10

Light Needs:

Mature Size:

2'-3'

2'-3'

Growth Rate: rapid

evergreen shrub

Needs: Plant in partial shade—a spot that gets morning sun followed by afternoon shade is ideal. Grow in moist, well-drained soil and water frequently. Cut flowering stems back to encourage new growth and more blooms. Make cuts just above a leaf or remove stems completely, cutting to the base.

Good for: accent plantings, entries, patios, and containers

More Choices: pages 36, 108, 109, 111, 112, and 113

B. longiflors

Grow Bouvardia—a Mexican native—for its drooping clusters of delicious-smelling flowers. It's perfect in pots placed around a terrace or patio. Does not tolerate cold; plants are damaged or killed when temperatures approach freezing.

Outstanding Features:

- Dangling clusters of fragrant white flowers
- Fine-textured foliage stays green year-round
- Well-suited to life in containers

Cistus x hybridus

White Rock Rose

Zones: 8-10

Light Needs:

Mature Size:

3'-5'

3'-5'

Growth Rate: rapid

evergreen shrub

Needs: Plant in full sun. Grows successfully in poor or dry but well-drained soil. Water regularly until the plant is established, then water little or not at all. Cut stems back occasionally to encourage thick, full growth.

Good for: low-maintenance areas, banks and slopes, along roadsides and driveways, beach plantings, informal hedges

More Choices: pages 35, 39, 42, 43, 99, 108, 112, 113, 187, and 189

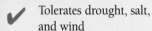
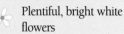
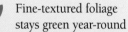

This Mediterranean native doesn't mind dry heat, wind, or drought. Sprawling stems are covered with white flowers from spring to summer.

Outstanding Features:

- Tolerates drought, salt, and wind
- Plentiful, bright white flowers
- Fine-textured foliage stays green year-round

Codiaeum variegatum var. pictum

Variegated Croton

Zones: 10

Light Needs:

Mature Size:

6'-10'

6'-10'

Growth Rate: slow

evergreen shrub

Needs: Give Croton a spot in sun or partial shade. Grow in fertile, well-drained soil. Water regularly. Prune occasionally to keep plants neat and full.

Good for: Accent plantings, entries; containers on patios, decks, terraces, or indoors; planting beds to contrast with green shrubbery

More Choices: pages 35, 37, 43, 108, 111, and 189

Options: 'Norma'—mostly red veins; some pink, orange, and yellow veins

Spice up an all-green area of your yard with Variegated Croton. Its large leaves are mottled with eye-catching patterns of red, yellow, or pink. Variegated Croton is damaged or killed by freezing temperatures.

Outstanding Features:

- Coarse-textured leaves are colorful all year
- Thrives in heat and sunny locations
- Easy-care accent for patios and decks

Cycas revoluta

King Sago

Zones: 8-10

Light Needs:

Mature Size:

6'-10' / 6'-8'

Growth Rate:
slow

evergreen shrub

Needs: Plant King Sago in any well-drained soil that receives full sun or shade. If you live in an area with occasional winter freezes, choose a spot that offers some protection, such as near a wall of your home away from the northern exposure.

Good for: accent plant, entry areas, including in a bed of groundcover, or growing in large containers

More Choices: pages 35, 36, 39, 109, 111, and 187

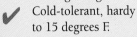

Add this slow-growing plant to your landscape for an exotic accent. Feathery-looking fronds are stiff and grow in a circle. Glossy green foliage color.

Gardenia jasminoides

Gardenia

Zones: 8-10

Light Needs:

Mature Size:

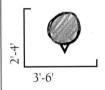

2'-4' / 3'-6'

Growth Rate:
slow

evergreen shrub

Needs: Grow in full sun or partial shade in moist, acidic soil. Improve soil by working shredded leaves, ground bark, bagged humus, or compost into the planting hole. Water frequently and feed monthly during the growing season with a fertilizer formulated for acid-loving plants. For more on gardenia care, see page 191.

Good for: low hedges or screens, containers, accents in planting beds

More Choices: pages 34, 36, 40, 101, 109, 111, 112, 113, and 189

Outstanding Features:
- White blossoms are exceptionally fragrant
- Glossy leaves stay green year-round
- Thrives in acidic soil that's moist

Gardenia will reward you with irresistible, fragrant white blossoms and attractive, glossy foliage. You'll find many different sizes and varieties to choose from. Problem insects are common. Control with insecticide at the first sign of infestations.

Hibiscus rosa-sinensis

Chinese Hibiscus

Zones: 9-10

Light Needs:

Mature Size:

8'-15' / 3'-10'

Growth Rate:
rapid

evergreen shrub

Needs: Grow in full sun or dappled shade for best flowering. Plant in well-drained, sandy, acidic soil. Water regularly to prevent wilting and stress. Feed monthly during growing season with balanced fertilizer. Prune regularly to control size and shape.

Good for: foundation planting, hedges and screens, patios and entries, accent shrubs, single specimen, containers

More Choices: pages 30, 34, 36, 40, 99, 101, 108, 109, 111, 113, 187, and 189

Outstanding Features:
- Showy flowers; wide range of color choices
- Quick-growing shrub or small tree
- Glossy, evergreen foliage; coarse texture

If you have hot sun and sandy soil, you have a spot for Chinese Hibiscus. Big flowers last just a day but are opening nearly nonstop when grown in full sun. Many colors, sizes, and forms are available.

hottest climates

7

Ixora coccinea

Ixora

Zones: 10

Light Needs:

Mature Size:

4'-6'

4'-6'

Growth Rate: medium

evergreen shrub

Needs: Plant in moist, fertile soil that's acidic and well-drained. Provide full sun or partial shade and water regularly. Feed several times a year with a balanced fertilizer. For hedges, prune as needed to keep plants neat.

Good for: foundation planting, hedges, accent, parking areas, entries, coastal locations, poolside, adding fine texture and color to landscapes

More Choices: pages 30, 35, 36, 40, 42, 43, 99, 101, 108, 111, 112, 113, 187, and 189

Outstanding Features:
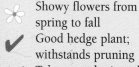
- Showy flowers from spring to fall
- Good hedge plant; withstands pruning
- Tolerates salt air and reflected heat

Grow Ixora for an accent or colorful hedge in frost-free areas. Plants are covered with clusters of red, pink, yellow, or orange blooms for several months. Regular fertilization ensures repeated blooms.

Jasminum multiflorum

Downy Jasmine

Zones: 9-10

Light Needs:

Mature Size:

3'-5'

spread to 5' (15' length as vine)

Growth Rate: rapid

evergreen shrub

Needs: Plant in well-drained soil in full sun or light shade. Water regularly. Feed two to three times during the growing season with a balanced fertilizer. Prune as needed to keep plants neat and to prevent vigorous growth from climbing into trees.

Good for: informal hedges, groundcover, parking areas, poolside, shrub beds, or growing up trellises, arbors, and fence posts

More Choices: pages 34, 36, 99, 112, 113, and 189

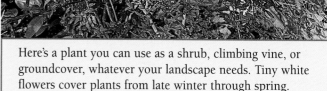

Outstanding Features:

- Profuse production of starlike white flowers
- Can be grown in various plant forms
- Foliage stays green year-round

Here's a plant you can use as a shrub, climbing vine, or groundcover, whatever your landscape needs. Tiny white flowers cover plants from late winter through spring.

Leucophyllum frutescens 'Silverado'

Texas Silverado Sage

Zones: 8-10

Light Needs:

Mature Size:

6'-8'

4'-6'

Growth Rate: slow

evergreen shrub

Needs: Plant in dry, well-drained soil—including sandy or chalky soil—in full sun. Water regularly until established; afterwards, you'll rarely need to water this Southwestern desert native.

Good for: arid areas, xeriscaping, hedges, containers, flower beds, seaside plantings, rock gardens, slopes, areas that aren't often watered

More Choices: pages 30, 35, 39, 41, 42, 43, 99, 109, 112, 187, and 189

Options: 'Compactum'—3' to 4' tall

L. frutescens

Outstanding Features:
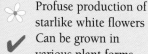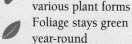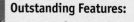
- Tolerates drought, salt, and poor soils
- Silvery foliage provides color contrast
- Purple flowers through-out growing season

Grow this silvery shrub where sun is plentiful but water isn't. Poor, alkaline soils aren't a problem either. Rose-purple flowers will be enjoyed for several months. Avoid planting in humid regions with high rainfall.

Moraea iridioides

African Iris

Zones: 9-10

Light Needs:

Mature Size:

2'-3'

3'-4'

Growth Rate:
medium

evergreen clump-forming shrub

Needs: Plant in well-drained soil in full sun or partial shade. Add organic matter to sandy soils for water retention. Plants will thrive with very little water but blooms increase with regular watering and abundant light. Plant in protected, frost-free spots. Mulch in areas with occasional cold weather.

Good for: accents, single-specimen clumps, containers, entries, patios, near pools, or low decks, parking areas

More Choices: pages 34, 36, 43, 109, 111, 112, 113, and 189

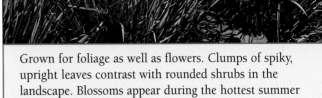

Outstanding Features:
* Butterflylike blooms of white and purple
* Spiky foliage stays green year-round
* ✔ Tolerant of heat and drought

Grown for foliage as well as flowers. Clumps of spiky, upright leaves contrast with rounded shrubs in the landscape. Blossoms appear during the hottest summer months. Formerly known as *Dietes vegeta*.

Nerium oleander

Oleander

Zones: 9-10

Light Needs:

Mature Size:

15'-20'

15'-20'

Growth Rate:
medium

evergreen shrub

Needs: Plant in well-drained soil and full sun—sandy soil is ideal. Water new plants regularly until established; rarely thereafter. Prune in early spring to keep plants neat and control size. Can plant in coastal areas of Zone 8.

Good for: parking areas, seaside and desert landscapes, xeriscaping, hedges and screens, large containers

More Choices: pages 30, 35, 42, 43, 99, 108, 109, 112, 113, 187, and 189

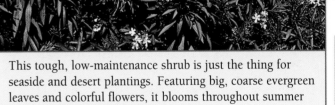

Outstanding Features:
* Bright blooms from spring until fall
* Large, coarse-textured leaves; evergreen
* ✔ Tolerates drought, salt, wind, reflected heat

This tough, low-maintenance shrub is just the thing for seaside and desert plantings. Featuring big, coarse evergreen leaves and colorful flowers, it blooms throughout summer and fall. Hand pick caterpillars to control.

Opuntia microdasys

Bunny Ears Cactus

Zones: 10

Light Needs:

Mature Size:

1'-2'

3'-5'

Growth Rate:
medium

evergreen shrub

Needs: Grow in full sun. Plant in well-drained, sandy, or gritty soil. Improve soil drainage with gravel or sand. Grow where water won't stay near the roots. Overwatering will kill this plant.

Good for: arid landscapes, xeriscaping, seaside and desert areas, containers, raised beds or berms, rock gardens, dry slopes, areas that receive little water

More Choices: pages 34, 43, 108, 109, and 187

Outstanding Features:
* ✔ Interesting shape and polka-dot bristles
* ✔ Thrives in drought and heat
* ✔ Coarse texture provides contrast

If you hate to water or can't due to watering restrictions, plant Bunny Ears Cactus. Once planted, no further care is required. Flat, oval pads give this plant its name. Bristles are sharp.

hottest climates

7

Phoenix roebelinii

Pygmy Date Palm

Zones: 9 -10

Light Needs:

Mature Size:

8'-10'

spread to 8'

Growth Rate:
rapid

miniature evergreen tree used as a shrub

Needs: Plant in any fertile, well-drained soil. Grow in full sun or partial shade. Water new plants regularly; later, water only when dry. Feed three times a year with palm fertilizer. Protect from freezing temperatures.

Good for: accent plants, single specimen, entries, courtyard, poolside, shrub beds, large containers

More Choices: pages 35, 37, 43, 108, 109, 111, and 189

Outstanding Features:

Fine-textured fronds add contrast

Smaller, more manageable size

Choose single, double, or triple specimens

Use in prominent places in your landscape for accenting with a tropical touch. Containers on patio, porch, or deck are stunning. Though it grows quickly, this one is worth spending money on for a good-sized specimen.

Pittosporum tobira 'Variegata'

Variegated Pittosporum

Zones: 8-10

Light Needs:

Mature Size:

5'-10'

spread to 10'

Growth Rate:
medium

evergreen shrub

Needs: Grow in full sun or partial shade. Plant in any fertile, well-drained soil. Slightly acidic soil is ideal but not necessary. Water regularly for best results. Feed in spring or summer with a balanced fertilizer. Clip stray stalks to maintain a natural form or shear into smooth, formal shapes.

Good for: foundations, hedges, seaside landscapes, parking areas, massed in shrub beds, barriers, background

More Choices: pages 35, 37, 41, 42, 99, 101, 109, 187, and 189

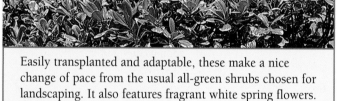

Outstanding Features:

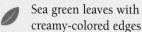
Sea green leaves with creamy-colored edges

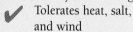
Tolerates heat, salt, and wind

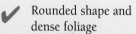
Rounded shape and dense foliage

Easily transplanted and adaptable, these make a nice change of pace from the usual all-green shrubs chosen for landscaping. It also features fragrant white spring flowers. The scent is similar to orange blossoms.

Rhaphiolepis indica

Indian Hawthorn

Zones: 8-10

Light Needs:

Mature Size:

3'-6'

3'-6'

Growth Rate:
medium

evergreen shrub

Needs: Grow in full sun or partial shade. Plant in moist, fertile, well-drained soil that's acidic or alkaline. Water regularly until established, then moderately thereafter. Fertilize two to three times a year. Pinch back branch tips after spring flowering to keep plants bushy. Let shrubs grow together to form a mass.

Good for: foundation planting, parking areas, seaside landscapes, low hedges, massing in planting beds, entries

More Choices: pages 35, 36, 40, 41, 43, 99, 101, 109, 111, 112, 113, and 189

Outstanding Features:

Glossy purplish-green leaves year-round

Clusters of fragrant white to pink flowers

Named selections need little or no pruning

You can't go wrong choosing Indian Hawthorn for your landscape. It's tough, easy to care for, and features glossy green leaves, fragrant spring flowers, and purple-black berries that ripen in the fall and persist through winter.

Strelitzia reginae

Bird-of-Paradise

Zones: 10

Light Needs:

Mature Size:

5'-6'

spread to 3'

Growth Rate: medium

evergreen shrub

Needs: Plant in fertile soil that's moist but well-drained. Grow in full sun or provide some afternoon shade. For the most spectacular blooms, feed once a month with a balanced fertilizer during hot season and water regularly.

Good for: accent plants, single specimen use, entries, courtyards, shrub beds, containers, patio plantings

More Choices: pages 34, 36, 108, 109, 111, 113, and 189

Outstanding Features:
- Brilliant, exotic flowers are orange and blue
- Clumps of big, coarse foliage
- Excellent, long-lasting cut flower

Bright birdlike blooms are showiest during cool months, but you'll enjoy the clumps of foliage year-round. Plants are not frost-tolerant; protect plants if frost is a possibility. Remove dead foliage after new leaves emerge.

Tecomaria capensis

Cape Honeysuckle

Zones: 10

Light Needs:

Mature Size:

6'-8'

spread to 4'

Growth Rate: rapid

evergreen shrub, vine, or groundcover

Needs: Plant in any soil, as long as it's well-drained. Water new plants frequently until well-established. Then moderately when soil is dry. Severe pruning will keep plants in shrub form. For climbing vine or groundcover use, no pruning is needed.

Good for: informal hedges or screens, accent shrub, groundcover, climbing vine, adding color and fine texture to the landscape

More Choices: pages 30, 31, 39, 43, 99, 108, 109, 111, 113, 187, and 189

Outstanding Features:
- Orange-red flowers fall through winter
- Fast-growing, evergreen foliage
- Versatile use from shrub to vine

Any way you grow it, Cape Honeysuckle will fill your landscaping needs. Train this plant as an upright shrub, climbing vine, or trailing groundcover. Enjoy bright red-orange blossoms all winter long.

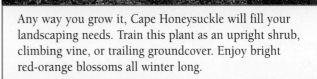

Viburnum odoratissimum

Sweet Viburnum

Zones: 8-10

Light Needs:

Mature Size:

10'-20'

spread to 20'

Growth Rate: medium

evergreen shrub

Needs: Grow in full sun or partial shade—afternoon shade in hot areas. Moist, well-drained, slightly acidic soil is preferred. Water regularly, especially in sandy areas. Prune to keep plants neat and control size.

Good for: hedges, screening, privacy, skirting raised decks, providing background in large planting beds

More Choices: pages 30, 35, 37, 40, 43, 99, 108, 109, and 189

Outstanding Features:
- Coarse-textured leaves throughout the year
- Clusters of fragrant white flowers in spring
- Plants get big and cover a lot of ground

Big plant with big evergreen leaves will take on big landscaping jobs. Grow it when you want to hide poor views, add privacy, or as a background. Fragrant white flowers appear in spring.

hottest climates **7**

Agapanthus africanus 'Peter Pan'

Dwarf Lily of the Nile

Zones: 9-10

Light Needs:

Mature Size:

12"-18"

12"-18"

Growth Rate: slow

evergreen perennial

Needs: Plant in any well-drained soil in full sun or partial shade. Water regularly during the summer months for best bloom. Established plants can get by with little or no extra water.

Good for: groundcover, containers, accent planting, flowerbeds, edging walks or shrub beds

More Choices: pages 35, 37, 152, 153, 155, and 189

Options: 'Queen Anne'—2 feet tall, blue flowers

Outstanding Features:
- Big clusters of blue flowers on erect stalks
- Clumps of flat, coarse-textured foliage
- Easy care and trouble-free plantings

Hot weather brings clusters of blue blossoms on stalks rising above straplike leaves. Plants establish easily and require minimal care. Foliage is normally yellow-green in color; if leaves turn too yellow, feed with balanced liquid fertilizer.

Ardisia japonica

Japanese Ardisia

Zones: 9-10

Light Needs:

Mature Size:

6"-18"

indefinite

Growth Rate: medium

evergreen shrub

Needs: Grow in deep to partial shade. Plant in moist, well-drained soil. Provide regular watering, especially during hot, dry periods.

Good for: groundcover in shady areas, providing texture contrast, adding color to dull, dim areas through foliage and fruit

More Choices: pages 37, 152, and 153

Options: 'Variegata'—white-veined leaves

Outstanding Features:
- Glossy, dark green leaves
- Bright red berries in winter
- Stays low with little or no pruning

Need something reliable to cover shady spots where grass won't grow? Japanese Ardisia can do the job. Hardy to 23 degrees F.

Aspidistra elatior

Cast-Iron Plant

Zones: 8-10

Light Needs:

Mature Size: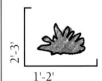

2'-3'

1'-2'

Growth Rate: slow

evergreen perennial

Needs: Plant in any soil except one that is soggy and wet. Sandy soil enriched with organic matter is ideal for helping hold moisture. Grow in filtered or dense shade. Water when dry and temperatures are high. Feed with a balanced fertilizer in spring and again in summer.

Good for: covering bare, shady areas; planting beneath eaves, decks, and overhangs; coarse-textured accent, containers, groundcover beneath trees

More Choices: pages 37, 39, 152, 153, 155, 187, and 189

Outstanding Features:
- Tolerant of poor soil conditions
- Grows in extremely shady spots
- Big leaves add coarse texture to plantings

Cast-Iron is a good choice for very shady places. It requires little attention and adapts easily to poor soil and other tough conditions. Too much sun and lack of moisture turns leaves crispy brown on the edges. Plants spread into thick clumps.

Baccharis pilularis

Dwarf Coyote Brush

Zones: 7-10

Light Needs:

Mature Size:

8"–24" / 5'-6'

Growth Rate:
medium

evergreen perennial

Needs: Full sun and any well-drained soil suits this plant, including alkaline. Water regularly until established; afterwards, plants thrive with little water. Shear old stems in early spring before new growth emerges, then feed with a high-nitrogen fertilizer to encourage new, vigorous growth.

Good for: covering hot, dry bare spots; slopes, seaside landscapes, xeriscaping, arid landscapes

More Choices: pages 35, 39, 41, 42, 43, 152, 153, 155, 187, and 189

Outstanding Features:

✓ Tolerates heat, drought, salt, and harsh wind
🌿 Spreading mats of fine-textured foliage
✓ Thrives with minimal effort and care

Here's a tough plant that doesn't mind poor dry soil, heat, wind, or salt. Individual plants spread to cover six feet of ground.

Cuphea hyssopifolia

Mexican Heather

Zones: 9-10

Light Needs:

Mature Size:

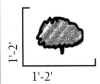

1'-2' / 1'-2'

Growth Rate:
medium

evergreen shrub

Needs: Plant in fertile soil that's moist but well-drained. Grow in full sun or light, filtered shade. Water regularly and feed frequently with a balanced fertilizer to encourage flowering. No pruning required. Protect from frost.

Good for: filling in planting beds; edging patios, walkways, shrub beds; entries and courtyards; containers on deck, patios, and porches

More Choices: pages 35, 37, 43, 152, 153, 155, and 189

Outstanding Features:

✿ Tiny flowers nearly year-round
🌿 Fine-textured foliage stays green all year
✓ Heat-tolerant, easy-care groundcover

This evergreen mini shrub covers the ground and blooms nearly year-round. Most plants have light purple flowers, but white- and pink-flowering plants are seen. Also sold as False Mexican Heather or Cuphea. These are seasonal in cooler areas.

Delosperma nubigenum

Hardy Ice Plant

Zones: 6-9

Light Needs:

Mature Size:

1"-2" / indefinite

Growth Rate:
rapid

perennial

Needs: Plant in any soil, no matter how poor, as long as it's well-drained. Grow in full sun.

Good for: rock gardens, hillsides, bare spots where there's little topsoil, beside paving

More Choices: pages 35, 39, 42, 43, 153, 154, and 155

Options: *D. cooperi*—magenta flowers; *D. velutinum*—white flowers

Outstanding Features:

✿ Numerous daisylike flowers cover plants
🌿 Small, succulent leaves add texture
✓ Plants are heat- and drought-tolerant

This ground-hugging creeper needs very little water to survive and prefers poor, dry soil. Plant it to cover bare spots and enjoy orange-red flowers in summer.

Echinocactus spp.

Barrel Cactus

Zones: 9-10

Light Needs:

Mature Size:

6"-4'

6"-3'

Growth Rate:
slow

evergreen shrub

Needs: Plant in fertile, well-drained soil in full sun. In hot desert climates, these cacti need some afternoon shade. Water about once every two weeks during summer, less often in cooler seasons. Do not overwater.

Good for: arid landscapes, xeriscaping, filling planting beds, coarse-textured accent plant

More Choices: pages 35, 43, 152, 153, and 187

Options: Golden Barrel Cactus

E. grusonii

Outstanding Features:

✔ Distinctive, barrel-shaped trunk
✔ Needs little water or attention to grow well
✲ Bright-colored flowers in summer

Barrel Cactis are available in many sizes, from small 6-inch plants to those over 4 feet tall. Contrasting spines stripe the barrel no matter what the size. In frost-prone areas, cover plants with blankets laid over a framework of branches.

Hedera canariensis 'Variegata'

Variegated Algerian Ivy

Zones: 7-10

Light Needs:

●

Mature Size:

6"

indefinite

Growth Rate:
medium

vine

Needs: Plant in fertile soil that's moist but well-drained. Grow in dense shade and water regularly. Feed in spring and fall with high-nitrogen fertilizer to encourage lush growth. Trim two or three times a year to keep beds neat.

Good for: groundcover in shady areas, growing beneath trees, erosion control on shady slopes, framing lawns with coarse texture

More Choices: pages 37, 42, 153, and 155

H. canariensis 'Gloire de Marengo'

Outstanding Features:

🍃 Vigorous growth even in dense shade
🍃 Variegated leaves brighten shady areas
✔ Tolerates heat better than English Ivy

This ivy makes a neat, dependable groundcover in shady areas. Variegated, heart-shaped leaves help lighten dark nooks and crannies in your yard. Can also be grown on buildings or in trees.

Lantana camara 'Gold Mound'

Gold Mound Lantana

Zones: 9-10

Light Needs:

Mature Size:

18"-24"

6' or more

Growth Rate:
rapid

evergreen shrub

Needs: Plant in any well-drained soil, including sand. Provide full sun. Water regularly until established, then only when dry. Prune in spring, removing dead wood. Trim during hot months to control size.

Good for: groundcover on bare, sunny spots; xeriscaping, seaside areas, arid landscapes, entries, parking areas, seasonal accent, containers

More Choices: pages 35, 42, 43, 152, 153, 155, 187, and 189

Outstanding Features:

✲ Bouquets of golden blooms cover plants
🍃 Makes a dense, thick groundcover
✔ Tolerates heat, drought, salt, wind

You can't find a more trouble-free or rewarding groundcover than Gold Mound Lantana. This tough plant produces bright yellow blooms almost nonstop during hot weather. You'll enjoy Lantana's evergreen leaves.

Osteospermum fruticosum

Freeway Daisy

Zones: 10

Light Needs:

Mature Size:

1'-2' / 10'-15'

Growth Rate: rapid

perennial for groundcover

Needs: Plant in well-drained soil, including sand. Full sun provides best bloom. Drought- and heat-resistant. Thrives with regular watering. Pinch tips to encourage bushy growth. Cut back long branches on older plants.

Good for: groundcover, seaside landscapes, xeriscaping, arid landscapes, slopes, parking areas, accent, massing in shrub beds

More Choices: pages 35, 42, 43, 153, 155, and 187

Outstanding Features:
- Grows rapidly to cover lots of ground
- White blooms with purple centers
- Tolerates drought, salt, wind

Named for its ability to grow along Southern California freeways, this tough plant likes it hot. White daisylike blooms appear throughout the year, though flowering is most profuse in spring. Hybrid varieties are compact and bloom heavily.

Sempervivum tectorum

Hens and Chicks

Zones: 4-10

Light Needs:

Mature Size:

3"-6" / indefinite

Growth Rate: rapid

evergreen perennial

Needs: Plant in gritty, sandy, well-drained soil. Grow in full sun most places but plant in partial to dense shade in hot desert climates. Water moderately during dry periods to prevent shriveling. Pinch and replant young offsets to multiply.

Good for: rock gardens, arid landscapes, xeriscaping, slopes, areas that aren't regularly watered

More Choices: pages 35, 43, 152, 153, 154, 155, 187, and 189

Outstanding Features:
- Tolerates heat, drought, and neglect
- Fleshy rosettes of gray tinged with purple
- Spreads easily with little care

This succulent plant produces plump rosettes (the "hens") which rapidly grow young offsets (the "chicks"). Plants tolerate heat, drought, and neglect. Tall, reddish flower stems occur on mature plants and reach about 2 feet in height.

Verbena pulchella

Moss Verbena

Zones: 8-10

Light Needs:

Mature Size:

8"-12" / 18"-24"

Growth Rate: rapid

perennial

Needs: Plant in well-drained soil and full sun. Avoid soggy soil. Water regularly until established. Afterwards, water moderately.

Good for: groundcover in hot, dry sites; filling in the front layer of shrub beds, slopes, courtyards, entries, edging walkways, patios, or containers

More Choices: pages 35, 39, 42, 43, 153, 155, and 189

Options: *V. goodingii*

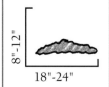

Outstanding Features:
- Bright flowers throughout summer
- Fine-textured, lacy foliage
- Tolerates heat and drought

Grow this heat-loving groundcover for its bright pink, violet, or white flowers. Fine, fernlike foliage adds textural contrast to planting beds. Sometimes sold as *V. tenera*.

Allamanda

Zones: 10	*evergreen flowering vine*
Light Needs:	**Needs:** Plant in any well-drained soil in full sun. Water regularly. Feed several times during the growing season with a balanced fertilizer. Provide support to encourage climbing. To grow Allamanda as a shrub, pinch or prune back new growth frequently to keep it bushy.
Mature Size: 4'-6' 4'-6'	**Good for:** covering walls, fences, gates, arbors, or as a freestanding shrub; colorful accent
Growth Rate: rapid	**More Choices:** page 30, 35, 175, 177, 187, and 189

Covered with blossoms for much of the year, Allamanda is an attractive vine. Fast growth and low maintenance make it a popular choice by gardeners. Allamanda is killed by freezing temperatures. Treat as an annual in frost-prone areas.

Planting Bougainvillea

Bougainvillea is an easy-to-grow sprawling vine featuring colorful papery blooms. The secret to success with this plant is handling the root ball carefully during planting. Never tug on the plant— carry it by the stems—or do anything to disturb the root ball.

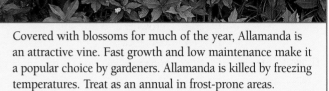

STUFF YOU'LL NEED

✔ Sharpshooter or round-point shovel
✔ Utility knife

What to Expect

Though you have to pamper Bougainvillea in the beginning, it will quickly grow to form a large, rambling plant. Give it plenty of room to grow.

1 **Dig a hole in a sunny location** that's about one-and-a-half times as wide as the nursery container. The hole should be only as deep as the container is tall; set the Bougainvillea (still in its container) into the hole to double-check depth. If the hole is too deep, add some soil to the bottom and tamp it firmly to prevent settling later.

2 **Remove the container from the hole.** Hold it firmly against the ground and slice down the sides of the pot with a utility knife. Make several cuts all around the container. Cut only the container; avoid cutting into the root ball of the plant.

3 **Peel the cut container back** to reveal the undisturbed root ball. Support the plant by holding it from below, and place it gently in the planting hole. Fill the hole with soil mix. Use one-half native soil and one-half organic matter. Gently firm the soil with your hands. Water thoroughly with a slowly trickling hose to settle the soil around the plant.

Bougainvillea 'Barbara Karst' produces brilliant crepe-paper blooms and is a rapid grower.

Bougainvillea spp.

Bougainvillea

Zones: 9-10

Light Needs:

Mature Size:

20'-40' × 20'-40'

Growth Rate: rapid

evergreen flowering vine

Needs: Plant in well-drained soil in full sun. Light afternoon shade in hottest regions. Water regularly until established, then moderately. Use balanced fertilizer throughout the growing season. Prune after flowering to encourage new growth. Will climb if tied to supporting structure.

Good for: covering walls, fences, gates, arbors; growing as a low shrub or groundcover; containers.

More Choices: page 30, 35, 187, and 189

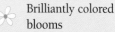

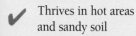
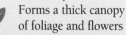
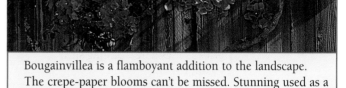
Bougainvillea is a flamboyant addition to the landscape. The crepe-paper blooms can't be missed. Stunning used as a climbing vine, groundcover, or in containers.

Ficus pumila

Creeping Fig

Zones: 8-10

Light Needs:

Mature Size:

indefinite × indefinite

Growth Rate: rapid

evergreen vine

Needs: Plant in well-drained soil in sun or shade. In hottest areas, provide some afternoon shade. Water regularly until established, then moderately or not at all. Prune or shear mature plants to keep foliage flat and neat.

Good for: covering walls and fences made of masonry, stucco, or metal; making new landscapes look older and established; providing green backgrounds for accent

More Choices: page 35, 37, and 175

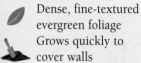
Choose Creeping Fig when you want to quickly cloak walls with greenery. Stems cling tightly to hard surfaces, covering them completely with fine-textured foliage. Avoid planting on wood structures—it traps moisture, causing rot and damage.

Lonicera japonica 'Halliana'

Hall's Honeysuckle

Zones: 4-10

Light Needs:

Mature Size:

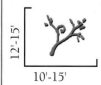

12'-15' × 10'-15'

Growth Rate: rapid

evergreen flowering vine

Needs: Plant in any soil in full sun or partial shade. Water regularly until established; after that, water moderately. Provide support—trellis, fencing, or string—to encourage plants to climb, or let them spread as groundcover.

Good for: covering chain-link and other fences (won't damage wood), arbors, trellises, erosion control on banks and slopes

More Choices: page 35, 37, 175, 177, and 187

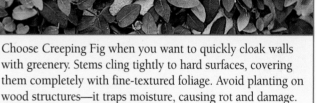

Here's just the thing for a coverup. Unsightly views are quickly removed by a covering of lush growth and white flowers. This plant is also useful as a rambling groundcover. Don't let this plant get out of hand; prune to control.

Hottest Climates 211

hottest climates

Mandevilla splendens 'Red Riding Hood'

Mandevilla

Zones: 10

Light Needs:

Mature Size:

4'-12'
4'-12'

Growth Rate:
rapid

evergreen flowering vine

Needs: Plant in moist, well-drained soil in full sun or partial shade. Water regularly. Feed monthly during the growing season with a balanced fertilizer. Provide support for it to climb up. Pinch back or prune for bushy shrub form. Roots like it cool; vines like it sunny.

Good for: covering small arbors and trellises, fences and posts; containers and hanging baskets; colorful accent

More Choices: page 35, 37, 175, 177, and 187

- Showy flowers in shades of pink
- Fast-growing cover for trellises
- Heat-tolerant vine for sunny locations

Mandevilla produces lots of big, irresistible pink blooms in hot weather. This tropical vine is not tolerant of cold temperatures but will grow just about anywhere during the summer. May also be sold as Dipladenia. Try: 'Alice du Pont'.

Mascagnia macroptera

Butterfly Vine

Zones: 9-10

Light Needs:

Mature Size:

12'-15'
12'-15'

Growth Rate:
rapid

deciduous flowering vine

Needs: Grow in any well-drained soil in full sun. Water regularly until established. Plants can tolerate drought, but weekly watering during the growing season will yield best results. Provide support for vines to climb up.

Good for: arid landscapes, xeriscaping, covering fences, gates, arbors, and other outdoor structures; colorful accent

More Choices: page 35, 43, 175, 177, and 187

Options: Lavender Butterfly Vine

- Colorful yellow flowers in summer
- Tolerates drought and sunny locations
- Once established, needs little care

This Mexican desert native sports orchidlike flowers. It requires little in the way of care and grows quickly. Butterfly Vine can tolerate cold weather and survives temperatures down to 25 degrees F. Also known as Yellow Orchid Vine.

Millettia reticulata

Evergreen Wisteria

Zones: 9-10

Light Needs:

Mature Size:

indefinite
indefinite

Growth Rate:
rapid

evergreen or semievergreen flowering vine

Needs: Plant in any well-drained soil that receives full sun. Water regularly. Provide support—trellis, fencing, or string—for vines to climb. Prune as needed to thin out excess growth and control size.

Good for: covering arbors and trellises, hiding chain-link fences, adding texture to walls, planting in cutouts in paving

More Choices: page 30, 35, 175, 177, 187, and 189

- Grows quickly to cover structures
- Clusters of purple-red flowers
- Heat-tolerant even in full sun

Here's a good choice for covering outdoor structures and chain-link fences quickly. Reddish purple flowers peep from behind lush, shiny leaves in summer and fall. Flowers are quite fragrant.

Passiflora incarnata

Passion Flower

Zones: 7-10

Light Needs:

Mature Size:

15'-20' (height)
15'-20' (width)

Growth Rate:
rapid

deciduous flowering vine

Needs: Plant in any well-drained soil in full sun or partial shade. Water regularly. Provide support—trellis, fencing, or string—for vines to climb, or let plants spread as groundcover. Prune as needed to keep this vigorous vine within bounds.

Good for: covering fences and arbors, screening for privacy, erosion control on slopes, covering sunny bare spots, colorful accent

More Choices: page 31, 35, 37, 175, and 189

P. vitifolia

Outstanding Features:
- Flowers a mix of attractive colors
- Foliage provides a dense cover
- Grows quickly and tolerates heat

Grown for its exotic blooms, Passion Flower quickly covers garden structures with plenty of lush, glossy foliage. It dies to the ground during winter in the cooler parts of its range, but returns in spring. Try *P. edulis* for a woody climber.

Stephanotis floribunda

Madagascar Jasmine

Zones: 10

Light Needs:

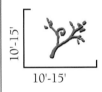

Mature Size:

10'-15' (height)
10'-15' (width)

Growth Rate:
medium

evergreen flowering vine

Needs: Plant in moist, well-drained soil enriched with humus or compost. Water regularly and feed with balanced fertilizer throughout the growing season. Place the roots in shade, and the vine in filtered sun if possible. Provide support for vines to climb.

Good for: planting near sitting areas, covering fences and arbors, training on posts, screening for privacy, containers

More Choices: page 30, 35, 37, 175, 177, 187, and 189

Outstanding Features:
- Clusters of very fragrant, white flowers
- Dark green, glossy foliage year-round
- Blooms in partial shade

Although many flowering vines need sun to bloom, this one flowers happily in a semishaded spot. White blossoms are extremely fragrant.

Trachelospermum jasminoides

Star Jasmine

Zones: 8-10

Light Needs:

Mature Size:

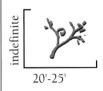

indefinite (height)
20'-25' (width)

Growth Rate:
medium

evergreen flowering vine

Needs: Plant in any well-drained soil in sun or partial shade. Water regularly. Growth may be slow at first, but will speed up when plants become established. Provide support for plants to climb, or plant in beds as groundcover. Prune for shrub form.

Good for: covering chain link and other fences, arbors, posts, screening for privacy or to block poor views, covering bare soil

More Choices: page 30, 35, 37, 175, 177, 187, and 189

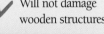

Outstanding Features:
- Clusters of white flowers spring to summer
- Dark green, glossy foliage provides quick cover
- Will not damage wooden structures

Clusters of white star-shaped flowers show off against a background of glossy leaves. Flowers are very fragrant; some people find it almost too strong. Plants are sometimes sold as Confederate Jasmine.

Plants by Common and Botanical Names

Numbers in **boldface** indicate Plant Encyclopedia entries. Numbers in *italics* indicate photographs.

Wax myrtle *(Myrica cerifera)*, 30, 34, 36, 38, 39, 42, 43, 59, 69, 86, **86**
   'Fairfax,' 86
Waxleaf ligustrum *(Ligustrum lucidum)*, 30, 35, 37, 39, 41, 43, 99, 109, 134, **134**
Weeping bottlebrush *(Callistemon viminalis)*, 193
Weeping willow *(Salix babylonica)*, 34, 38, 39, 42, 59, 69, *94*, **94**
Weeping yaupon *(Ilex vomitoria* 'Pendula'), 81
White Bird-of-Paradise *(Strelitzia nicolai)*, 34, 36, 67, 189, *198*, **198**
White oak *(Quercus alba)*, 34, 39, 40, 67, 69, *90*, **90**
White pine *(Pinus strobus)*, 30, 34, 39, 59, 87, **87**
White rock rose *(Cistus x hybridus)*, 35, 39, 42, 43, 99, 108, 112, 113, 187, 189, 200, **200**
Willow oak *(Quercus phellos)*, 31, 34, 39, 40, 41, 43, 59, 68, 69, 92, **92**
Windmill palm *(Trachycarpus fortunei)*, 34, 36, 67, 189, *199*, **199**
Wintercreeper. *See* Purple-Leaf wintercreeper
   (Euonymus fortunei 'Coloratus')
Wisteria chinensis. See Wisteria sinensis
Wisteria sinensis (Chinese wisteria), 31, *31*, 35, 37, *174*, 175, 177, 185, **185**

Y

Yaupon holly *(Ilex vomitoria)*, 30, 34, 36, 38, 39, 40, 41, 42, 59, 67, 69, *81*, **81**
   dwarf yaupon holly *(I. vomitoria* 'Nana'), 34, 36, 39, 40, 41, 42, 43, 99, 101, 108, 109, 111, 130, **130**
   weeping yaupon holly *(I. vomitoria* 'Pendula'), 130
Yellowwood *(Cladastris lutea)*, 34, 36, 39, 41, 67, 69, *75*, **75**
   'Rosea,' 75
Yoshino cherry *(Prunus x yedoensis)*, 34, 41, 43, 67, 68, 69, *88*, **88**

Z

Zelkova serrata (Japanese zelkova), 31, 40, 43, 59, 67, 68, 69, 97, **97**

Acknowledgements

Hetherington Studios
3520 SW. 9th
Des Moines, Iowa 50315
515-243-6329
dhetherington@earthlink.net

Doug Hetherington
Mara Hetherington
Sophia Hetherington
Johanna Hetherington
Steve Hetherington
John Hetherington
Matt Johnson
Matt Miller
Ella Hall
Amy Hawes

Thank you
Mary Howell Williams
Kenna Neighbors

Better Homes and Gardens® Test Garden
1716 Locust Street
Des Moines, IA 50309-3023
(515) 284-3994
www.bhg.com

Jackson & Perkins Wholesale, Inc.

P.O. box 9100
2518 South Pacific Highway
Medford, OR 97501
800-854-1766
www.jproses.com
www.surfinia.com
www.jacksonandperkins.com

City of Carlsbad
1200 Carlsbad Village Drive
Carlsbad, CA 92008-1989
760-720-9461
www.ci.carlsbad.ca.us

Missouri Botanical Garden
4344 Shaw Blvd.
P.O. Box 299
St. Louis, MO 63166-0299
314-577-5100
www.mobot.org

Minnesota Landscape Arboretum
Andersen Horticultural Library
3675 Arboretum Drive
P.O. Box 39
Chanhassen, MN 55317-0039
952-443-1400
www.arboretum.umn.edu

The Morton Arboretum
4100 Illinois Route 53
Lisle, IL 60532-1293
630-719-2400
www.mortonarb.org

Heard Gardens Ltd.
8000 Raccoon River Drive
West Des Moines, IA 50266
515-987-0800
www.heardgardens.com

The Dawes Arboretum
7770 Jacksontown Road S.E.
Newark, OH 43056-9380
800-443-2937
www.dawesarb.org

The Holden Arboretum
9500 Sperry Road
Kirtland, OH 44094-5172
216-256-1110
www.holdenarb.org

Iowa Arboretum, Inc.
1875 Peach Avenue
Madrid, IA 50516
515-795-3216
www.iowaarboretum.com

Bellevue Botanical Garden
12001 Main Street
Bellevue, WA 98005-3522
425-452-2750
www.bellevuebotanical.org

The Butchart Gardens
Box 4010
Victoria, BC V8X3X4
Canada
250-652-4422
www.butchartgardens.com

Reiman Gardens

1407 Elwood Drive
Ames, IA 50011
515-294-0028
www.ag.iastate.edu/departments/hort/rgardens/rgframe.html

The State Botanical Garden of Georgia
2450 S. Milledge Avenue
Athens, GA 30605
706-542-1244
www.uga.edu/~botgarden

Powell Gardens
1609 NW. U.S. Highway 50
Kingsville, MO 64061
816-697-2600
www.powellgardens.org

Fullerton Arboretum
P.O. Box 6850
Fullerton, CA 92834-6850
714-278-3579
www.arboretum.fullerton.edu

Des Moines Botanical Center
909 East River Drive
Des Moines, IA 50316
515-323-8900

Des Moines Waterworks
2201 Valley Drive
Des Moines, IA 50325
515-283-8755

Photo Credits

T=Top C=Center B=Bottom L=Left R=Right

Front Cover
Michael Dirr
   Cover Background
Doug Hetherington
   CoverC
Barbara Hogenson Agency
   CoverL, CoverR

Front Cover
Michael Dirr
   Cover Background

William D. Adams
   202B
Craig Allen
   178B
Cathy Wilkinson Barash
   170C, 200T, 208C
Ernest Braun
   17CR, 29TR, 49TR, 151BR
Kim Brown
   60T
Kim Brun
   186BR
David Cavagnaro
   170B, 171B
Crandall & Crandall
   184B, 212C
Chuck Crandall
   28TR, 58TR, 69TR
Stephen Cridland
   19TR, 150BL
Michael Dirr

acknowledgements

Michael Dirr
73B, 79T, 79B, 80B, 87B, 88B, 91T, 110TL,
111TL, 115T, 116T, 118T, 118B, 120T, 124T,
128B, 129T, 131T, 132T, 134T, 137T, 137B,
145B, 148B, 154TR, 157B, 170T, 192T, 195C,
196B, 205B, 206C, 207B
George DeGennaro
101BL
Harrison L. Flint
70T, 121T, 135T, 207T
Randolph Foulds
12TL, 52TL, 152TL
Susan Gilmore
30TR, 99TR, 100T, 151BR
Jay Graham
176TL
Karlis Grants
98TL, 175TR

Reddie Henderson
188T
Roy Inman
2CR, 108TR
Jackson & Perkins Wholesale, Inc.
J&P™ roses presented by Jackson & Perkins
Wholesale, Inc.
142B, 185T
Mike Jensen
52BL, 188BL
Jack Jennings
212B, 192B
Gene Johnson
66BL
Barbara Martin
44TR, 112TL

Jennie Massey McIlwain
209B
Jerry Pavia
116T, 141T, 143B, 144T, 160C, 184C, 213C
Mary Carolyn Pindar
113BR
Julie Maris Semel
4B, 66BR, 98BR, 101TR, 152BR
Bill Stites
13TR, 15TR, 59TM, 61TR , 69BL, 98TR, 107TL
Rick Taylor
7BL, 44TL, 58TL, 99BR, 189TR
Judith Watts
174T
Kent Whitmore
186TL

Take our quick survey and enter to win a $1,000 gift card from The Home Depot®

Thank you for choosing this book! To serve you better, we'd like to know a little more about your interests. Please take a minute to fill out this survey and drop it in the mail. As an extra-special "thank-you" for your help, we'll enter your name into a drawing to win a $1,000 Home Depot Gift Card!

WIN THIS CARD!
OFFICIAL SWEEPSTAKES RULES AND ENTRY DETAILS ON BACK.
No purchase necessary to enter or win.

PLEASE MARK ONE CIRCLE PER LINE IN EACH OF THE NUMBERED COLUMNS BELOW WITH DARK PEN OR PENCIL:

1 My interest in the areas below is:

Cooking	High Interest	Average Interest	No Interest
Gourmet & Fine Foods	○	○	○
Quick & Easy	○	○	○
Healthy/Natural	○	○	○

Decorating	High Interest	Average Interest	No Interest
Country	○	○	○
Traditional	○	○	○
Contemporary	○	○	○

Do-It-Yourself	High Interest	Average Interest	No Interest
Home Repair	○	○	○
Remodeling	○	○	○
Home Decor	○	○	○

(painting, wallpapering, window treatments, etc.)

Gardening	High Interest	Average Interest	No Interest
Flowers	○	○	○
Vegetables	○	○	○
Landscaping	○	○	○

2 My plans to do a project in the following areas within the next 6 months are:

	High Interest	Average Interest	No Interest
Bathroom Remodel	○	○	○
Kitchen Remodel	○	○	○
Storage Project	○	○	○
Plumbing	○	○	○
Wiring	○	○	○
Interior Painting	○	○	○
Window Treatments	○	○	○
Plant/Plan a Flower Garden	○	○	○
Plant/Plan a Vegetable Garden	○	○	○
Deck Building	○	○	○
Patio Building	○	○	○
Landscape Improvements	○	○	○

3 I estimate that I have spent this amount of money on home improvement projects in the past 6 months:
Less than $1,000 ○ $1,000-$2,500 ○ $2,500-$5,000 ○ $5,000-$10,000 ○ $10,000 or more ○

4 I purchased this book ○   This book was a gift ○

5 You *must* fill out all of the requested information below to enter to win a $1,000 Home Depot Gift Card.

Also, E-mail me with information of interest to me.

Name:

Address: Apt. or Suite #

Daytime telephone number: (   )

City:

State/Province: Country: Zip:

For D-I-Y trend research, please tell us your gender: Male ○   Female ○

E-mail address:

Thank you for completing our survey! Please mail today to have your name entered to win a $1,000 Home Depot Gift Card. But hurry—one winner will be selected soon. See rules on back for entry deadline. To find more home improvement tips, visit www.homedepot.com or www.meredithbooks.com.

A. LETTERFOLD TOWARD BOTTOM OF SURVEY FORM, ALONG ORANGE TRIANGLES AT LEFT AND RIGHT.

B. MOISTEN BOTTOM STRIP, LETTERFOLD TOWARD TOP OF FORM, ALONG ORANGE TRIANGLES AT LEFT AND RIGHT.

LH0205

Canadian customers:
See mailing details on back!

Take our quick survey and enter to win a $1,000 gift card from The Home Depot®

No postage necessary if mailed *inside* the United States.
If mailed *outside* of the United States, letterfold survey form, place in an envelope, stamp, and mail to:

Meredith Corporation
Home Depot 1-2-3 Books (LN-104)
1716 Locust Street
Des Moines, Iowa 50309-3023

▲ FOLD CAREFULLY ALONG ORANGE DASHED LINES ABOVE ▲

Plant Shapes—Quick Reference Guide

Entries for plants in this book use the icons below to indicate the shape of the mature plant.

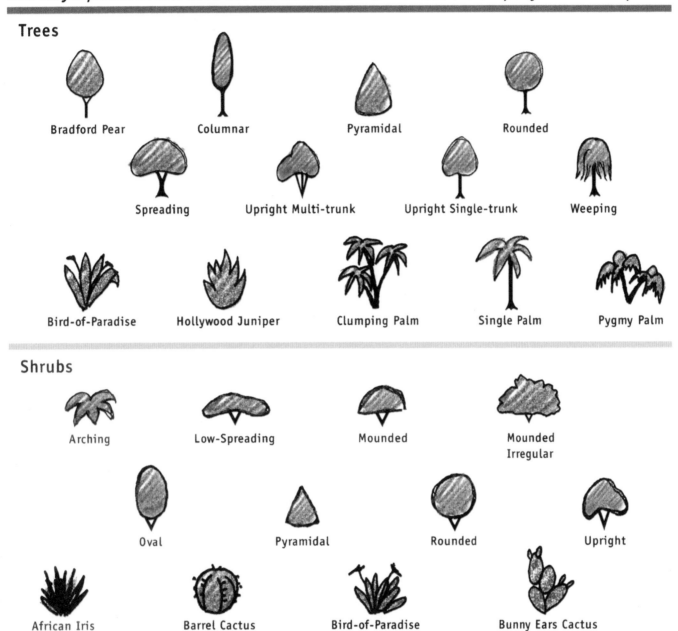

Trees

Bradford Pear **Columnar** **Pyramidal** **Rounded**

Spreading **Upright Multi-trunk** **Upright Single-trunk** **Weeping**

Bird-of-Paradise **Hollywood Juniper** **Clumping Palm** **Single Palm** **Pygmy Palm**

Shrubs

Arching **Low-Spreading** **Mounded** **Mounded Irregular**

Oval **Pyramidal** **Rounded** **Upright**

African Iris **Barrel Cactus** **Bird-of-Paradise** **Bunny Ears Cactus**

Groundcovers

Clump

Low Growing

Prostrate

Vines
Vines are indicated by the climbing icon.

Climbing

Understanding Rates of Growth

How fast a plant will grow and reach maturity depends on site conditions, how quickly it settles into its new home, and length of the growing season. With so many variables it isn't possible to predict the number of inches or feet you can expect a plant to grow per year, but they can be generally classified as rapid, medium, and slow growers. Check "Growth Rate" in the plant encyclopedia entries for more information on plants you're considering.

Nathan D. Ehrlich
Atlanta, GA

Timothy J. Cappuccio
Independence, MO

Carolyn Evans
Escondido, CA

Chris Hopkins
Orange, CA

Matt Anthony
Atlanta, GA

Shari K. Willman
Atlanta, GA

William McKenzie
Costa Mesa, CA

Troy Jackson
Olathe, KS

Bradley Phillips
Bloomington, MN

Many thanks to
the employees
of The Home Depot®
whose "wisdom of the
aisles" has made
Landscaping 1-2-3®
the most useful
book of its kind.

Rebecca M. Tainter
Atlanta, GA

James M. Ary
Duluth, GA

Kevin Altar
Cypress Park, CA

Lorn Patterson
San Marcos, CA

Steven J. Esguerra
San Diego, CA

Sherry Gugerty
Downers Grove, IL

Lissett Urso
Arlington Heights, IL

Cindy Broaddus
Gladstone, MO

Neil Hayes
Kansas City, MO

Mike Mitchell
Bothell, WA

Mike W. Moessl
Simi Valley, CA